We Flew
We Fell
We Lived

We Flew
We Fell
We Lived

The Remarkable Reminiscences
of Second World War Evaders
and Prisoners of War

Philip LaGrandeur

Grub Street • London

Published by
Grub Street
4 Rainham Close
London
SW11 6SS

Copyright © Grub Street 2007
Copyright text © Philip LaGrandeur 2006

British Library Cataloguing in Publication Data

LaGrandeur, Philip
  We flew, we fell, we lived : the remarkable reminiscences
  of Second World War evaders and prisoners of war
  1. World War, 1939-1945 - Prisoners and prisons, German
  2. Escapes - Europe - History - 20th century 3. World War,
  1939-1945 - Underground movements - Europe 4. Prisoners of
  war - Germany - Biography
  I. Title
  940.5'47243'0922

  ISBN-13: 9781904943853

Design: Carol Matsuyama

Front cover design: Lizzie B Design

Cover photographs: Top: Vickers Wellington Bomber, by Charles E. Brown; bottom, courtesy of W. Prausa

Printed by MPG Ltd, Bodmin, Cornwall

Grub Street only uses FSC (Forest Stewardship Council) paper for its books.

Table of Contents

Foreword

In the early spring of 1939 I was staying in a place called Summerland on Okanagan Lake in southern British Columbia, an idyllic spot with a lovely climate, when I received a notification from Ottawa that I had been selected for appointment to a Short Service Commission in the Royal Air Force, to commence flying training at Hamble, Southampton on 1 May 1939. It was a very welcome outcome to the application I had made a good while before, and it would make a nice change from the three and a half years of banking I had done in Vancouver and upcountry. And I had always wanted to fly.

After final interviews and medicals in Ottawa, I sailed from Halifax on the Cunarder RMS *Alaunia* with six other excited young Canadians, dreaming of flying Spitfires. Only three of us would survive the war, and little did I realize that I was on my way to five years of incarceration in prisoner of war and concentration camps in Nazi Germany. I was shot down in flames in a Wellington of 9 Squadron over Holland during an operation out of Honington, Suffolk on 5 June 1940 and captured the following day.

I am honoured to be asked to write a foreword to such a comprehensive and well-researched book by Philip LaGrandeur. At least, length of service as a POW should be one qualification for the task! The book covers a number of camps in which Canadians were incarcerated. I shall have to confine my comments to those camps to which I was assigned and, against a background of camp life as I knew it, highlight the Canadians I met there. Canadians played a prominent part in camp life, and those whom I met at this time were no exception.

The trail starts at Stalag Luft I at Barth on the Baltic in July 1940, the first camp built to house RAF POWS. The officers' compound was small, dreary, and dusty, containing two huts surrounded by two rows of 10-foot barbed wire fencing separated by a mass of coiled wire. A low warning fence ran round inside about 6 feet from the main wire: to step over it meant a bullet. At the corners guard towers replete with machine guns, guards and dogs completed the scenario.

This was the standard design for all camps, with variations. It followed that there were only three ways out of such an enclosure: over the wire, through the wire or under the wire, again with variation. The first two were not to be recommended, although some POWs succeeded in escaping this way. Through the wire included a walk-out through the gate, dressed as a German guard. This often succeeded. The favourite method was tunneling.

We soon found that food was our main concern. The daily ration consisted of one fifth of a loaf of sour black bread, a pat of margarine and a small piece of sausage, or a small portion of jam, in the evening; a bowl of sauerkraut soup and a few potatoes, often bad, for lunch; and a mug of acorn coffee for breakfast. We were always hungry until Red Cross parcels started to arrive about March 1941.

"Pappy" Plant comes to mind as the outstanding Canadian I met at this time. He had been a pilot of a Whitley and came from Alberta. A tall, spare figure with a growth of beard, he looked like an Old Testament prophet and in fact had been a lay reader; so he conducted the church services until a padre arrived. He was also a keen tunneller and ran several tunnel schemes, including one from the East Block on which I worked. However, we made the mistake of working at night when sounds are magnified, and patrolling Germans picked us up.

Another Canadian I remembered well at Barth was Dick Bartlett, a Fleet Air Arm pilot from Saskatchewan, who had had a short but very eventful career on a Swordfish and Skuas flying off the *Ark Royal*. He was shot down in a Skua at Trondheim attacking the *Scharnhorst* and the *Gneisenau*. Dickie did some very effective escaping and, I think, was unlucky not to make a home run. For the Great Escape, he was scheduled to travel with Espelid, a Norwegian, but shortly before the breakout, another Norwegian arrived, and it was thought that the two Norwegians together would have a better chance. So Dickie was pulled out. He was lucky this time. The Norwegians were both shot.

I was glad to run into Lorne Chambers at Barth, who I found came from the Okanagan not far from Kelowna where my uncle's apple orchard was situated.

There were two home runs in 1941: Harry Burton, who sawed through the bars of his cell, burrowed under the gate and took the ferry from Sassnitz on the island of Rügen to Sweden; and John Shore (nicknamed "Death"), with whom I built a short tunnel from the incinerator near the wire into the football field. Shore got out and got home, but I got caught trying to get into the tunnel.

We cannot leave Barth without a mention of Barry Davidson from Calgary who did much to organize ice hockey.

In April 1942, the whole camp was evacuated and we were transferred to Sagan in Silesia. Forty-five tunnels had been dug in the officers' compound, only two of which were used successfully. The NCOs' compound had a few tunnels, but the NCOs also had the opportunity to escape while outside on working parties.

At the new camp at Sagan, Stalag Luft III, we were put into what was called the East Compound; the North Compound where The Great Escape took place did not then exist. Here I met Wally Floody (of whom more later), John Weir and Henry Birkland. Weir, called "Scruffy," came from Toronto and had been a fighter pilot on Spitfires. He was very badly burned when he was shot down.

From September 1942 to April 1943, I was at Oflag XXIB at Schubin in Poland. My main memories are of noisy barrack rooms in which 80 of us were housed and the freezing temperatures—down to minus 20 degrees Celsius—in winter, with little heating. Nevertheless, a good deal of tunnelling went on, and there was a successful tunnel dug from an outside latrine, through which 33 escaped. All were recaptured except for Lieutenant Commander Jimmy Buckley, who had run the escape organization in the camp, and his companion Jorge Thalbitzer, a Dane who went by the name of Thompson; they were drowned trying to cross the Skagerak. The tunnel had been run by a very enthusiastic and capable Canadian called Eddie Asselin.

In April 1943 we were back at Sagan, and I found myself in the newly built North Compound, which was a mile round the perimeter, and housed 1,500 officers in 15 huts.

The Escape Committee run by Roger "Big X" Bushell was already in situ and work had started on the three big tunnels, "Tom," "Dick" and "Harry," each planned to be 30 feet in depth and up to 360 feet in length, with air pumps, electric lighting and a railway. All resources and experience focused on these tunnels, and no other tunnelling was allowed. This is not the place to go into detail about construction and planning. Suffice to say that the very soft sand required shoring every inch of the way, for which a great many wooden bed boards were used. Wally Floody, with experience of mining in Canada, was in charge of tunnelling. Lieutenant Commander Peter Fanshawe was Dispersal Chief and had devised the very effective trouser-sack ("penguin") method of dispersal; George Harsh, an American in the RCAF, was Head of Security and ran it with a rod of iron. The two main considerations in planning an escape tunnel were therefore in operation. Wing Commander "Wings" Day, the senior British officer, supported and encouraged them in every way. Wings was a colourful character and had been shot down in a Blenheim in October 1939.

During the diggings, there were a few close calls. Wally Floody, "Crump" Ker Ramsey and "Conk" Canton were working one day at the base of Tom tunnel's shaft when they noticed that sand was leaking steadily through a gap between two boards in the side of the shaft near the top. They swiftly realized the danger. Crump and Conk were up the ladder like monkeys. Wally was last up the ladder; the flood of sand covered his legs before he could be hauled to safety by the other two.

The other Canadians I remember who were active in the escape organization were Gordon King, Wilkie Wanless and Wally MacCaw. (Wally and his wife were pleased to stay with us at our house in Wales in 1995 after our POW London reunion.)

Tom tunnel was found in September 1943. All tunnelling ceased, and we pursued our various interests: music, studying and sports. The theatre was supported by a great deal of talent, and some excellent shows were produced. There was a symphony orchestra and a dance band in which Hardy de Forest was a leading member.

Harry tunnel was opened up in January 1944, after 150 feet had already been dug. With snow on the ground, the penguin method of dispersal was not feasible, but we found the theatre to be a suitable repository for the sand. A trap was made under one of the seats, and the sand that had been excavated during the day was poured down through it at night. Two dispersal teams of about 8 men each worked below every night. I led one and Squadron Leader Ian Cross (DFC for bombing the *Scharnhorst*) led the other. We packed away 90 tons while Harry was being blitzed to its full length of 360 feet; it was completed in early March.

"Escape 200" took place on the night of 24/25 March. It was freezing cold, and one of the causes of delay was the iced exit trap; the other was the distance of the exit shaft from the wood, some 25 feet, so that a man had to be placed behind a bush to signal with a rope to other escapers. I was number 39 out and was traveling with a party of 12 who had papers designating them as workers on leave from a local wood mill. At about 5 in the morning we boarded a train at a country station 15 km southeast of the camp and traveled about 100 miles south to the Czech border. However, mainly due to the brutal weather, we were all caught the next night in or around Hirschberg. A national alert of *Grossfahndung* (dragnet) was in operation.

Eight of us were taken to the local jail and wet, hungry and tired, were thrown into one cell. My companions included Jimmy Wernham, a cheery Scots Canadian from Winnipeg, who entertained us by outlining schemes for becoming a millionaire in Canada after the war. A few days later, the cell door was opened and Wernham's name together with the names of two Poles and my traveling companion, Nick Skanziklas, a Greek, were called out. We thought they were going back to Sagan; they were shot shortly afterwards, among the 50 (of the 76 escapees) whose executions were ordered by Hitler when he heard about the escape.

With Wings Day, Major Johnny Dodge (who was related to Winston Churchill) and Flight Lieutenant Sydney Dowse, I was sent to Sachsenhausen Concentration Camp where we were incarcerated in Sonderlager A, a high security compound surrounded by electrified wire, high walls and many guards. Told we could not escape, Dowse and I dug a tunnel 120 feet in length, without the "modern conveniences" we had had at Sagan. The tunnel presented us with certain difficulties. We knew that there was a Gestapo informer among the 20 inmates of the compound, so security had to be extremely tight—it entailed one of us going below, while the other kept watch. The only tool we had was a serrated kitchen knife, which served both to saw laboriously through floorboards and to loosen the soil at the tunnel face; the soil then had to be dragged back manually to the shaft, where it was dispersed under the hut. The tunnel was lonely, dark and airless, particularly at 100 feet. Five of us escaped through it on the night of 23/24 September 1944. We had been joined by Jack Churchill, a Commando, with whom I traveled. We headed north, jumped onto a freight train for 50 miles, and were recaptured near the Baltic and returned to Sachsenhausen, as were others. Again, a national alert had been in force and we heard later that about 2 million directly and indirectly were out looking for us. We did not know it then, but Himmler had ordered our execution. As I lay handcuffed in my cell, I was aware that this might be the penalty and I was wishing I had stayed in Summerland. In the event we were given 5 months' solitary confinement in the Zellenbau, a virtual death cell (not many came out alive). You never knew, when the door was opened, whether you were on your way to ablutions or the executions area. Sachsenhausen was a terrible place; 100,000 perished there between 1936 and 1945.

In April 1945 we were transported south by train and lorry through Flossenburg and Dachau to Reichenau, a camp south of Innsbruck where we joined a party of about 150 VIPs including many political prisoners: generals who had fallen foul of Hitler; von Schuschnigg, the former Austrian chancellor; Schacht, former finance minister; Leon Blum, former French prime minister, and many relatives of those involved in the 20 July plot against Hitler. It was named the Hostages Group and guarded by the SS. We never knew how long we had to live. We were liberated first by the Wehrmacht and finally by the Americans in the Tyrol.

Eight Canadians were executed after the Great Escape, probably one of the biggest percentages of any national group at Sagan. The Germans did their best to divide and rule. They told the senior Canadian officer that they had some fine accommodation arranged for the Canadians. He replied that this was fine as long as their British friends could come along, too.

Before I finish, it must be mentioned that Wally and Betty Floody took George Harsh into their home in Toronto when he was old, ill and alone, and looked after him until he died.

In conclusion, I wish Philip LaGrandeur all success with his book, which I am certain will fill a historical gap and be read with great interest by all Canadian ex-POWs and by many others.

B.A. "Jimmy" James
Ludlow, England

Preface

This book is a tribute to Royal Canadian Air Force ex-prisoners of war and evaders. It provides a Canadian perspective on life in German prisoner of war camps and the lines that helped escapees back to England. Camps evolved into sophisticated social units that reflected more than just the military institutions that brought prisoners together. The camps were full of resilient leaders— scholars, moral authorities, musicians, actors and athletes—who resumed their peacetime interests to better others and to build morale. Several factors influenced the quality and variety of programs offered. Established camps had more time to organize. It took months or years for musical instruments, sports gear, books, paper and art supplies to trickle into the different *Stalags Luft*. Logistics influenced the evolution or devolution of activities. The Red Cross coordinated the movement of equipment between philanthropic organizations, the Germans and the camps. When the tide of the war turned against Germany, supplies dried up.

The Germans exercised their authority by keeping a tight lid on activities, but consented to cultural and sporting activities because they believed busy prisoners of war (PoWs) were less inclined to escape. The Germans enjoyed music, literature, art and the competitiveness of sports as much as the PoWs because these activities provided relief from the monotony of their routines.

Prisoners of War chronicled daily activities in two ways. The Luftwaffe generously supplied cameras to photograph sports days, theatrical productions, concerts, team competitions and daily routines. The Germans obligingly produced multiple sets of the prints for PoWs to insert in their mail, and Mitluftposte (the German postal service) forwarded the letters home after censors "greprufted" the contents. Families often lent these camp pictures to Canadian newspapers, and the Germans achieved a moral victory of sorts because the publication of these pictures created a positive image of the camps. The PoWs received logbooks from the YMCA and filled pages with wonderful illustrations, stories and records. Unfortunately most PoWs abandoned or lost them during the forced marches across Germany between January and May 1945. They had to make life or death choices between a book and a few tins of food. Photographs, letters and logbooks are the only *Kriegie* primary documents that remain.

The most undesirable aspect of PoW life was the indeterminate length of one's incarceration. When PoWs became homesick, thoughts naturally turned to escape. Early escape attempts, disorganized and hazardous, were unsuccessful. Sophisticated escape organizations oversaw all aspects of planning and execution, including tunnelling, forging, scrounging, and bribing of guards. Many guards risked their lives to help PoWs because of their vehement anti-Nazi sentiments or the fact that PoWs could supply them with a few luxury items like coffee, chocolate or cigarettes in exchange for contraband.

Security remained tight. Most guards were incorruptible out of fear or loyalty to the Fatherland. Prisoners who stepped over warning wires or approached perimeter fences were liable to be shot. Luftwaffe camps maintained a prisoner to guard ratio of 4 to 1 for most of the war (Crawley 1985, 12). The Germans incorporated advanced surveillance equipment to detect tunnelling efforts. Armed guards manned towers and patrolled perimeter fences twenty-four hours a day, often with dogs. Specially trained guards, known as ferrets, roamed the compounds looking for signs of tunnelling. Of the 10,000 British and Dominion air force personnel imprisoned by the Germans, only thirty managed to escape to England or neutral territory (Crawley 1985, 3–6).

The Germans imprisoned British and Dominion personnel in ninety-five permanent or transit camps. Of these, six permanent camps called *Stalags Luft* were under direct Luftwaffe control. The Luftwaffe also operated three *Dulags Luft* or transit camps where they interrogated new captives before sending them on to one of the six permanent camps for the duration of the war. One *Dulag* was on the eastern front, another in North Africa and the third at Oberursal near Frankfurt. The Oberursal camp processed captives of Bomber Command, Fighter Command, Coastal Command, Fleet Air Arm of the Royal Navy, and Ferry Command, who were shot down over western and northern Europe.

In most instances, treatment and interrogation of PoWs followed accepted standards as defined by international law. After an initial period of discomfort and isolation, most PoWs found themselves in cattle cars bound for a permanent camp. A small percentage of the captives suffered at the hands of their interrogators. Fortunately, most of them ended up in a permanent camp where observance of the Geneva Convention resulted in better treatment.

Reichsmarschall Hermann Goering insisted that the Luftwaffe have custody of captured air force personnel. Unfortunately, one to two percent languished in prisons, concentration camps and death camps. Some stayed in camps controlled by other branches of the German military, such as *Oflags* (camps run by the Wehrmacht for officers), *Milags* (permanent camps for merchant mariners), *Ilags* (internment camps for civilians), *Feldposts* (prisons located at the fronts) and *Marlags* (camps for captured naval personnel). As the number of PoWs in German custody ballooned and German defeat was imminent, the placement of air force PoWs in Luftwaffe custody was less closely observed.

Those unable to evade capture preferred arrest by the Luftwaffe and the Wehrmacht over the SS, Gestapo, Abwehr, Field Police or local police. Flyers had a legitimate concern to fear civilian populations. Goebbels, Hitler's unscrupulous propagandist, branded flyers as *Terrorfliegers* or *Luftgangsters* and civilians reacted in kind by abusing or killing airmen before military authorities could take them into custody.

Small but dedicated groups of PoWs preoccupied themselves with escape. Escape or "X" committees kept their clandestine operations to themselves for security reasons. They usually oversaw four committees: tunnelling and sand disposal, procurement, forgery and security.

The British government gave the responsibility of coordinating the shipment of escape materials into British camps to MI9 (Military Intelligence). They set up thirty-six dummy companies to ship contraband into the camps and were careful to separate their operations from those of the Red Cross. Prisoners and guards sorted packages upon their arrival at the camps. Sorters, informed by secret radios about the impending arrival of specific packages, kept a watch for them. German mail sorters frequently found contraband and complained to the Red Cross. However, both Allies and Nazis understood that some chicanery was an accepted part of warfare.

Germany did not have the resources to provide adequately for its own citizens, let alone PoWs. Consequently, most PoWs suffered malnutrition and under-nutrition. Red Cross food parcels shipped into Germany from Allied countries staved off starvation and death. The PoWs remain eternally grateful to the Red Cross for their untiring efforts to ensure that food, mail and parcels reached the camp, as well as for their diligent efforts to monitor conditions.

Mistreatment of PoWs culminated in war crimes tribunals. War crimes prosecutors worked diligently to have courts declare all Nazi organizations as criminal. This made it easier for them to prosecute individual Germans, collaborators and co-conspirators for their offences.

Since the fiftieth anniversaries of D-Day and the end of the war, Canadians have kindled a genuine interest in learning about Canada's contribution to the Second World War. The commemoration of these historic events created the impetus for veterans to tell their personal wartime experiences. After the war most veterans had returned to Canada, got on with their lives and put all memories of conflict behind them; they married, raised families and pursued careers.

I became interested in the stories of Royal Canadian Air Force (RCAF) ex-PoWs and evaders after a visit by Australian relatives in October 1998. Andrew Gordon ("Drew") of Melbourne informed me that his father, Tony Gordon, was a pilot in the Royal Australian Air Force (RAAF) and was shot down over Europe in November 1941. He spent close to four years in Luftwaffe-administered camps, including the highly profiled Stalag Luft III, site of the Great Escape. Drew wanted to know if an organization of RCAF ex-PoWs existed in Alberta. I had no idea, but his father's story piqued my interest in the subject. After my relatives returned to Australia, a two-page story about a Canadian participant in the Great Escape, Gordon King, appeared in the 11 November 1998 edition of the *Edmonton Journal*. I thought about Drew in Australia; he had asked me to contact ex-PoWs from Stalag Luft III if the opportunity arose. He wanted me to ask if anyone remembered his father, who had been a PoW there since it opened in early 1942. After reading the Remembrance Day story about Mr. King, I hesitated because I knew the desire to learn more about PoWs would consume me. Finally I contacted him in April 1999. I told Mr. King that I was making a call on behalf of an Australian relative. I asked if he remembered a particular RAAF pilot named Tony Gordon. What a long shot—Stalag Luft III held 10,500 PoWs! Fifty-five years had also passed by. Mr. King responded, "Know him? I shared the same room with him!" Then he proceeded to give an exact physical description of Tony Gordon. We talked for some time, and I mentioned that I had led student trips to Canadian battlefields in Europe and made it a priority to teach students about Canada's involvement in the two World Wars. He invited me to make a presentation about the battlefield tours to his comrades in the RCAF Ex-PoW Association. Among the group of ex-PoWs were Canadians who had evaded capture after the loss of their aircraft over Europe.

This began a great friendship. I had the opportunity to befriend some of the finest individuals I have met in my life. These men and their wives represented a generation of Canadians who shaped Canada into the best country in the world. One of the ex-PoWs suggested that I write a book about their experiences. The thought of undertaking this project was daunting. I needed to gain the confidence of these men. Their experiences were personal, and most of them were unaccustomed to talking about them. I had to ensure that I represented their stories accurately. The process of assembling enough information to write

Flight Lieutenant Tony Gordon, 455 Squadron RCAAF, reported that his aircraft (Hampden P1201) struck a chimney in the Ruhr after a bombing operation to Cologne, 7/8 November 1941. He was transferred between several different camps before the Luftwaffe placed him in Stalag Luft III. He was slated as the 108th man out of "Harry," the tunnel in the Great Escape, but the breakout was discovered before he could escape.

a narrative for all interviewees took over two years. Their recollections were sometimes hard to follow because many of their experiences were told in streams of consciousness. The information needed placement in chronological order. The information often needed a context to make it comprehensible. This involved a multitude of research. After reviewing the information provided by each man, I would revisit or telephone him to have him fill in the details. It was important to listen well. Initially, some of these men found it difficult to reveal their inner thoughts. Over time, they spoke freely, and some revealed things they must have thought they would take to their graves. I was surprised to learn that many of their wives did not know the full details of their stories.

Many of the references used in this book were retrieved from the Canadian Department of National Defence's Directorate of History. These declassified documents are referenced with the prefix "DHist." Sources have been documented as thoroughly as possible, and all attempts have been made to give credit where it is due.

Acknowledgments

This book would have been impossible without the untiring support of several ex-PoWs and their spouses. First, Gordon King got the ball rolling. He is the inspirational leader of his group, and he encouraged his comrades to participate in the project. Behind King was June, his wife and best friend of sixty years. Second, Kenneth and Lorraine Taylor understood the nature of the project and offered excellent suggestions, which ultimately gave shape to the project. Third, enough cannot be said of H.K. "Bud" Ward, technical expert and owner of a well-stocked library known as the "War Room." If I wanted to know *any* detail of PoW life, the PoWs and their aircraft, Bud usually provided an accurate and definitive response immediately. Thanks, Bud and Muriel. I appreciated the input and guidance of Arthur Crighton. Fred Rayment became the resident expert on Stalag Luft VI at Heydekrug. Wilkie Wanless of Calgary lent his knowledge to the project; his lifelong dedication to the preservation of RCAF ex-PoW history is extraordinary and provided additional insights for the book.

I would be remiss if I did not mention how much I appreciated the gracious support and encouragement of the remaining PoWs, evaders and their families: Wm. and M. Poohkay; R. and R. Dutka; H. and M. Bertrand; D. and I. High; R. and E. Thompson; L.L. and D. Geddes; J.G. and M. Middlemass; R. and P. Wiens; J. Flick; W.D.J. MacCaw and family; H. and E. Newby; C. and M. Loughlin; D. and M. Hall; M. MacNeill and family; W. and M. Prausa; Wm. Studnik; J. Patterson; B. Chaster; Wm. and C. Dunwoodie; G.W. and H. Findlay; F. Dunn family; R.E. Nelson; and H. Bastable. I also received kind assistance from the following: M. Williams, President, RCAF Ex-PoW Association, Calgary; B. Davidson Jr.; D. Bates; C. English and Raydan Trucking, Nisku; Daniel and Kevin Hunt, England; J.A. MacDonald; D.A. Budd; N. Bodnaresk; M. Shepley; Lt. Col. L. Dent (ret); from several Royal Canadian Legion Branches in Leduc (No. 108), Sundre (No. 223), McGrane (No. 28), Blairmore (No. 7), Hines Creek (No. 174), Coalhurst (No. 273), Big Valley (No. 70); and from A.W. Lyons, Alberta Aviation Museum, Edmonton; A.E. Sutherland, Wartime Aircrew Association, Edmonton; and S. Harris, Chief Historian, Directorate of History and Heritage, Ottawa.

I am also indebted to Squadron Leader B.A. "Jimmy" James for writing the foreword, and to my family for their support and patience throughout this project.

Glossary of PoW Terminology and German Vocabulary

Abort—Washroom (English bog)

Abwehr—German counterintelligence branch under the control of Admiral Carnaris

ACM—Air Chief Marshal, Head of Bomber Command. For most of the war, Sir Arthur "Bomber" Harris controlled the operations of Bomber Command

aircrew—May include all flying ranks; otherwise they are "Air Force personnel"

airmen—In the Air Force, all non-commissioned ranks

Aktion Kugel—Hitler's order to liquidate PoWs recaptured after any mass escape

Appel—Roll call: "*Austreten zum Appel*" (All out for roll call)

Appelplatz—Parade square

Bankau—Stalag Luft VIIB, an NCO camp established in spring of 1944 east of Stalag Luft III.

Bash—To be busy

beat up—Flying low

Belaria—A satellite camp of Stalag Luft III, opened in 1944 to alleviate overcrowding

Big S—Head of security for the X Escape Committee, F/L George Harsh, RCAF

Big X—Code name for leader of the X Escape Committee, S/L Roger Bushell, RAF

block—Barracks or hut

blockhead—Senior officer in the barrack block

bought it—(was) killed

brew up—Tea, coffee, or other

Brot—bread

Bürgermeister—Mayor

caterpillar pin—A pin, consisting of a gold caterpillar with red eyes, awarded to an airman who had survived the destruction of his aircraft by parachuting from his aircraft. (Silk used in parachutes had been spun by caterpillars.) The Caterpillar Club was started in 1922 by the Irving Parachute Company, with membership open to anyone who bailed from a damaged aircraft with an Irving parachute

chop—Getting the "chop": killed or executed

chow—Grub, food

Churchill man—Anyone who believed the war would end in 1945

circuit—Walk round the perimeter of the compound

commandant—Commander or officer in charge of a PoW camp

Commando order—1942 directive from Hitler ordering the execution of all captured Allied commandos

compound—Area enclosed by barbed wire and guarded by sentries

cooler—Prison cell in the Vorlager. PoWs who broke rules or who attempted escapes were sentenced to a few weeks of detention to "cool off"

crate, kite, ship—Aircraft

Dakota—Twin-engine transport of the Allied air forces. Also referred to as a DC-3.

Ditched—Crash landed in water

dobby—Washing of one's kit

dobby stick—Stick used to agitate clothing in a washtub

duff gen—misinformation

Dulag—*Durchgangslager*, a transit camp

Dulag Luft—*Durchgangsluftwaffenlager*, an interrogation camp for members of enemy air forces

Duppel—Germans' form of Window. See Window

Durchgangslager—Transit camp. The camp at Frankfurt to where captured Air Force prisoners were first sent for interrogation, identification and classification before being assigned, generally according to rank to appropriate *Stammlagers*.

Duty pilot—Lookout in the PoW camp who monitored the movement of guards and ferrets

ersatz—Substitute, artificial; e.g., ersatz coffee or jam

essen—"food" (a noun; also a verb, "to eat")

feint—Diversionary stream of bombers used to draw German defenders away from the main bomber force

Feldwebel—German sergeant

ferret—German guard who received special training in tunnel detection

Fishpond—Device used by a wireless operator to detect the approach of an enemy fighter from below. Fishpond was added to the H2S navigational system

FLAK—*Flieger Abwehr Kanonen*, German anti-aircraft fire

Flieger—Flyer

foodacco—Food and tobacco exchange system within a PoW camp

Führer—Leader

gardening—Laying mines in bodies of water

gash—Extra, surplus

Gee—Early navigation system used to direct RAF bombers to a target. Radio towers transmitted simultaneous signals across the continent in a grid pattern that bombers picked up and used to locate their intended target. This technology had limited use because signals directed bombers to within roughly ten kilometers of their target. Named for the "g" in grid

Gefreiter—German private

Geneva Convention (1929)—International agreement signed by 47 nations, outlining the general principles for the humane treatment of PoWs. The USSR and Japan were the major nations who had not signed the accord at the outbreak of the Second World War

Gestapo—German secret police, feared for their brutality; they worked outside of any legal constraints

glop—German food; porridge

Goering, Hermann—Chief of the Luftwaffe (German Air Force)

Goldfish—One who survived the ditching of his aircraft in a body of water; a survivor qualified for membership in the Goldfish Club

gone for a burton—missing or killed

goons—German guard (an English word derived from a comic book character)

goon boxes—German sentry towers built on the perimeter fences of PoW camps

geprüft—Proofread. All mail entering or leaving a PoW camp was censored

griff—information

H2S—Navigation device that reflected an image of the topography back up to the aircraft, allowing the navigator to make a visual identification of targets

Happy Valley—The Ruhr, industrial heartland of Germany, heavily defended by flak

Hauptman—German captain

Heavies—Four-engine heavy bombers, including the Lancaster, Halifax and Stirling

Heydekrug—Stalag Luft VI, an NCO camp located in East Prussia on the border with Lithuania

hooch—Homebrew made in camp with dried fruit from food parcels

humdinger—Very good

Hundführer—German dog handlers

Ilag—*Internierungslager*, a civilian internment camp

Jahowl—"Yes Sir!"

Jerry—German

Ju88—German fighter aircraft

Kamerad—Friend

kaput—Finished or broken

Kartoffeln—Potatoes

kill—Credit for the destruction of an enemy aircraft

Kiwi—New Zealander

Krankenlager—Sick room

Kraut—A German

Kriegie—Slang for prisoner of war

Kriegsgefangenen—Prisoners of war; abbreviated to Kriegies or PoWs.

Kriegsmarine—German navy

Kühler—"Cooler," or punishment cell found in the Vorlager

Lager—Camp

Limey—Englishman

Little S—Codename for the security head in each barrack block of Stalag Luft III

Little X—Second in command in the X Escape Committee, S/L Abraham, RAF

Lübeck—City in north Germany; the area where the PoWs of North Compound, Stalag Luft III, were liberated in May 1945

Luckenwalde—Stalag 3A, which held 25,000 PoWs at war's end

Luftwaffe—German Air Force

Luftwaffelager—PoW camp specifically for aircrew; also referred to as *Luftlager*

Man of Confidence—The elected leader in a PoW camp for British NCOs, he was not always the most senior man in the camp, but often the most capable.

Maquis—The French resistance in occupied France: a loose network of cells, divided by political persuasions but united by the common hatred of Nazi Germany

Maquisard—Member of the Maquis

Marlag—German-administered prison camp for sailors and marines, home for Stalag Luft III PoWs between the winter and spring marches

Me109—German fighter aircraft

Me110—German night fighter equipped with an upward-firing 20mm cannon

mess pot—Jilted by letter. A PoW might receive a letter from a girlfriend, fiancée or wife announcing that their relationship was over because she had met someone else

MiD—Mentioned in dispatches, an honour bestowed upon an officer or enlisted man for a conspicuous act in the line of duty

Milag—Camp for merchant marines

milk run—Flight over the continent used to activate German radar defences or ground defence units, often with the purpose of drawing attention away from the main bombing force

Mitluftposte—German mail service provided for PoWs

MUG—Mid upper gunner

Mühlberg—Stalag IVB, a Wehrmacht-administered NCO camp for many nationalities. Two RAF compounds were added for captured air force personnel

muster—to organize or bring men on strength to a unit, detachment or squadron

nickel run—Bomber flight from England over Nazi-occupied Europe to drop information leaflets giving the Allied version of the war

Nix—Slang word for "nothing" (*nichts*)

North Compound—Added to Stalag Luft III in early 1943 to accommodate air force officer PoWs. The Great Escape originated from this compound on 24/25 March 1944

nutty—Chocolate

Obergefreiter—German master corporal

Oberst—German colonel

Oboe—Primitive radar system that used two radio impulses to help guide a pilot to his target. When the two transmissions overlapped the bomber crew knew they were over their target and could commence dropping bombs. Oboe's effective range was limited to 300 miles due to the curvature of the earth

Observer—Bomber crewman who performed dual roles as navigator and bomb aimer

Oflag—*Offizierlager*, PoW camp for officers

ops—operations

OTU—Operational Training Unit, the final phase of training before a posting to an operational squadron

palliasse—Mattress, commonly a gunney sack filled with shavings or paper

parole—Promise by a PoW to not flee if given "temporary" freedom. Breaking terms of parole brought *severe* repercussions

Pathfinders—Bombers leading a force of bombers to a designated target by locating the targets and marking them with flares or target indicators (TIs)

PFF—see Pathfinders

pit—Kriegie bed

Postern—German private, lowest non-commissioned rank

prang—to crash an aircraft

pranger—Anything acting as a hammer

purge—Relocation of PoWs from one camp to another

rackets—Monopolies

RAG—Rear air gunner

Raus (ruse)—"Get up, get moving quickly!"; also, *herauf*

Repatriate—One who is sent home from captivity usually due to physical disability or mental impairment

Reserve Lazart—Hospital unit

round the bend—Mentally deficient, mad or insane

Sagan—Town nearest to Stalag Luft III in Lower Silesia; renamed Zagan when the territory was returned to Polish control

SBO—Senior British Officer

scarecrows—German flares that illuminated the night sky by exploding in a chandelier effect; they clearly exposed bombers for fighter interceptors

schnell—Quickly, fast

Schweinhund—Pig-dog (insult)

Second Dickie—Co-pilot, usually a recent graduate of OTU riding along to gain experience

SHAEF—Supreme Headquarters Allied Expeditionary Force

shocker—Aggravating person

skipper—Pilot in charge of an aircraft

Sonderkommando—punishment camp where prisoners were sent for hard labour

Sonderlager—"Special camp" for PoWs who were considered to be discipline or escape problems. (Colditz was a *Sonderlager*)

South Compound—Originally an NCO compound in Stalag Luft III, it became the USAAF officer compound in mid-1943. The Commonwealth NCOs originally in the Centre Compound were removed to a new NCO camp at Heydekrug

sprog—New air force recruit (RCAF)

SS—*Schutzstaffel*, elite police under the direct control of the Nazi party, who acted with impunity and used force and terror to achieve their end. They assumed control of PoW and concentration camps in the last years of the war

Stalag—Permanent camp administered by the Wehrmacht

Stalag Luft—Permanent camp for air force officers and men, administered by the Luftwaffe

Stammlager—Abbreviation "*Stalag*"; permanent camp, a *Stalag* from a basic administrative area within which labour detachments may be designated

stooge—Person doing odd jobs

stooging—(1) Watching German movements (2) Circling over a target in a bomber

strafe—Machine gunning of targets by aircraft

Strafelager—Punishment camp

stube—Room in which a PoW lived

Stufe Rohme III—Upgrade to the *Aktion Kugel* order, it ordered the execution of all escapees.

Target Indicators (TIs)—Flares dropped from Pathfinders or Mosquitoes that marked where success waves of bombers were to drop their ordinance

Terrorflieger—Flying terrorist, term applied to a member of a bomber crew

TI—Target Indicators

tin bashing—Making things from the metal food cans of Red Cross parcels

Unteroffizier—German rank equivalent to corporal

V1, V2 rockets—*Vergeltungsfeuer* (vengeance of fire)

verboten—forbidden

Village Inn—Device that activated the machine guns mounted in the rear turret of a bomber when the IFF determined that the approaching aircraft was an enemy. The technology was referred to as AGLT (Automatic Gun Laying Turret)

Vorlager—Administration block. Each PoW camp had a Vorlager, which contained the camp headquarters, medical room, storage and a cooler

WAG—Wireless air gunner

Wanganui—Codename given to a targeting procedure in honour of a New Zealander killed in bomber operations. The system involved the dropping of bombs on to a target marked by the dropping of target indicators or flares

Wehrmacht—German army

whizzo—good

Wimpy—Nickname given to the Wellington bomber

Window—Strips of aluminum foil dropped by bombers to jam German radars. Hundreds of thousands of strips floating through the air deflected radar signals in every direction and gave German radar technicians the impression that the skies were filled with bombers

wire job—Cutting through the fence

WOG—Wireless operator/gunner

X Committee—Escape Committee, organized under Squadron Leader Roger Bushell in Stalag Luft III

Rank Structure

Rank Structure in the British Commonwealth during the Second World War and the Canadian Equivalent in 2004

Second World War	2004
Commissioned Officers	
Air Chief Marshal	Chief of Air Staff (Lieutenant General)
Air Vice Marshal	Deputy Chief of Air Staff (Major General)
Air Commodore	Brigadier General
Group Captain (G/C)	Colonel
Wing Commander (W/C)	Lieutenant Colonel
Squadron Leader (S/L)	Major
Flight Lieutenant (F/L)	Captain
Flying Officer (F/O)	First Lieutenant
Pilot Officer (P/O)	Second Lieutenant

Non-Commissioned Officers (NCOs)	
Warrant Officer I	Chief Warrant Officer
Warrant Officer II	Warrant Officer II
Flight Sergeant (F/Sgt)	Sergeant
Sergeant (Sgt)	Master Corporal
Leading Air Craftsman (LAC)	Corporal
Aircraftsman 1	Private
Aircraftsman 2 (AC2)	Mechanic, recruit

Introduction

Prisoner of War Camps

The German military incarcerated captured Allied air force personnel in ninety-five permanent or temporary camps.† Excluding prisons, concentration camps, and death camps, seven categories of PoW camps were established:

1. Oflag	Camp operated by Wehrmacht, for captured officers
2. Stalag	Permanent camp
3. Dulag	Temporary or transit camp
4. Ilag	Internment camp
5. Feldpost	Camp administered by the German Field Police
6. Stalag Luft	Luftwaffe administered camp for captured air force PoWs
7. Marlag and Milag	Kriegsmarine administered camp for captured naval PoWs

By 1942, Reichsmarschall Hermann Goering established five Stalag Lufts for captured Allied air force PoWs under Luftwaffe control at the following locations:

Stalag Luft I	Barth Vogelsang
Stalag Luft III	Sagan and Belaria
Stalag Luft IV	Sagan and Belaria
Stalag Luft VI	Heydekrug
Stalag Luft VII	Bankau, near Kreulberg, Upper Silesia

Separate Royal Air Force compounds were established within larger camps:

Stalag IVB	Mühlberg am Elbe
Stalag VIIIB (344)	Lamsdorf, Teschen

The Luftwaffe established an interrogation centre for air force PoWs captured in northwestern Europe, near Frankfurt am Main:

Dulag Luft	Wetzlar, Oberursal

---

†There are only thirty documented escapes of Allied PoWs to England and neutral countries from German administered camps in the Second World War (Crawley 1985, 3–6).

"R.C.A.F. Prisoners of War" (Courtesy of S. Gordon King)

Organization of Stalag Luft PoW Camps

Prisoner of war camps during the Second World War were microcosms of the outside world. While in captivity, PoWs developed a culture best understood by those who lived it. RCAF PoWs who were captured from 1939 to 1942 entered into the general populations of a select few camps, where the highest percentage of PoWs were British. Most RCAF NCOs were dispersed to Stalag IXC at Bad Sulza, Stalag IIIE at Kirchhain, and Stalag VIIIB at Lamsdorf; RCAF officers ended up in Stalag Luft I at Barth. In April of 1942 the Luftwaffe opened a new camp, Stalag Luft III at Sagan, which started with a centre compound for air force NCOs and an east compound for air force officer PoWs.

In the first three years of the war, few RCAF personnel actually became German PoWs, although several Canadians serving in the RAF became captives. Nonetheless, the Germans recognized them as British. Nine Canadians shot down over Europe arrived in Stalag IXC in mid-1941. Nineteen others went to Stalag IIIE between July and September 1941, and forty-five others ended up at Stalag VIIIB between September and November 1941. These seventy-three Canadians formed the nucleus of the Canadians who were later sent to the NCO compound at Stalag Luft III in April 1942. There they found some sort of normalcy for the first time; the camp provided four essentials—proper food, sports, entertainment, and various other activities to occupy the mind.

Germany could not build PoW camps quickly enough, especially after the Americans entered the war. A new compound adjacent to the Centre Compound housed the overflow of British and Commonwealth air force personnel. Later, the Germans moved all RAF NCOs out of Centre Compound and replaced them with officers of the United States Army Air Forces.

PoWs busied themselves with a variety of activities that fit into six broad categories: camp administration; education; escape-related activities; circulation of news; recreational activities; and music and theatre.

Camp Administration

The discipline and routines in a PoW camp followed the usual patterns established on air bases throughout Canada and England. The Germans permitted senior officers and non-commissioned officers to run the camp their own way but monitored activities on an ongoing basis.

The Canadians in the NCO compound of Stalag Luft III immediately organized an executive committee of five Canadians: Sergeant I.B. Quinn, President; Sergeant J.R. Gordon, Vice-President; Sergeant J.C. Bredin, Secretary; and Sergeants W. Menzies and W.L. Jacobsen, Counsellors. The committee immediately contacted various organizations in Canada as a means to secure badly needed goods for Canadian PoWs. The Red Cross received PoW lists and names of missing personnel, and based on the camp rosters submitted by the committee, sent food parcels. The Canadian Prisoners of War Relative Association organized themselves to serve the individual needs of PoWs. The committee organized a variety of sports and educational and artistic endeavours in the camp. They requested the Royal Canadian Legion to send sporting goods, educational materials, books and general information on Canada. The Canadian and International YMCA supplied sports equipment, musical instruments and writing materials, including logbooks bound with art paper and pages for daily entries. The committee sent letters to the RCAF to facilitate the promotion, and commissioning of personnel in the camp. The RCAF commissioned many NCO captives because the Germans would treat officers with more respect than they did the NCOs. Many other organizations worked to improve the quality of life of PoWs.

The executive met at least once a month and oversaw most aspects of PoW life. Meticulous records of each PoW were maintained on a separate index card, complete with two photographs, a frontal shot and a side profile. Each card listed all pertinent personal information, pre-war occupation, level of education, service and PoW number, and the date each prisoner was posted to and removed from camp.

The committee formed the Canadian Communal Fund to help new arrivals adjust to camp life. Older Kriegies pooled extra razors, soap, socks, clothing and blankets that they had received from home and made them available for the newcomers. These acts of generosity often provided PoWs with enough of the essentials until their first parcels from the Red Cross or packages from home arrived. Most PoWs put items back in to the pool, and exchanges of goods between the compounds facilitated a minimum level of comfort. Cigarettes arrived from Canadian sources in such large quantities that the committee dispersed lots of fifty to Poles and Americans in adjacent compounds.

Canadians involved in the camp's administration could assist in the distribution of Red Cross parcels, or prepare and distribute items from the cook houses, such as turnips, potatoes, bread, sugar and jam.

German guards conducted roll calls once or twice each day on the *Appelplatz* (parade square), and the speed at which these roll calls commenced often depended on the cooperation of the senior officers or NCOs.

A mini-economy flourished in most PoW camps. Enterprising PoWs established their own stores, which later earned the moniker "Foodacco." Prisoners traded in cans of food they did not like, surplus cigarettes, or woollens sent from home, for something else. They also turned in unwanted items to accumulate points, which were later cashed in for food or other products. Under the terms of the Geneva Convention Relative to the Treatment of Prisoners of War, Allied authorities forwarded up to twenty percent of an officer's pay to a PoW through the Red Cross. The principled Germans converted the hard currency to a camp currency called *Lager Geld*. Useless outside of the camp, it facilitated transactions at a dismally stocked canteen where a PoW might acquire tooth powder, laundry soap, water softener (wash fix), sheet music or the odd musical instrument. An enterprising owner of a Berlin music store sold sheet music to the PoWs in exchange for their *Lager Geld* and converted it to German marks. Arthur Crighton purchased the complete works of Franz Liszt from the camp canteen. Strict rationing within Germany created acute shortages of

(Drawing by R.M. Woychuk, courtesy of H.K. Ward)

Lagergeld. (Courtesy of A. Crighton)

everything, which ultimately meant that goods did not reach PoW camps. Many prisoners purchased the white tooth powder for smearing over and brightening the dark ceiling and walls of a poorly lit barrack block. In Italian camps the guards were more compliant and eagerly ran errands for PoWs in exchange for hard currency; they even acquired fruit and vegetables for PoWs, when these came available.

Education

Though PoWs received encouragement to continue learning, programs in the camps lagged because materials requested from the Canadian Legion Educational Body failed to arrive—probably as a result of the intermittent mail service.

Ambitious PoWs attempted to prepare themselves for the post-war period by studying mathematics, psychology, law, economics, and the arts and sciences. The two most popular courses were agriculture and navigational studies. Qualified PoW instructors from universities, technical schools and secondary schools offered courses. An added incentive for the ambitious student was the chance to earn a "degree" from the "University of Sagan," providing content followed outlines from affiliated universities in Britain. In reality, little recognition accompanied the holder of a degree from Sagan in the post-war era, but the knowledge and skills accumulated were useful to some men when they returned to civilian life. Practical application for trainees was limited because Germans refused to provide equipment for fear it might be utilized in escape-related activities. Nevertheless, some PoWs received accreditation for a trade under the auspices of the Royal Navy.

Crowded living quarters were not conducive to learning as illustrated in the cartoon drawn by a PoW in Stalag Luft VI at Heydekrug, East Prussia. Many men started out with the intention to use the time to improve themselves, but the effects of hunger, cold, homesickness and inadequate facilities extinguished their ambitions before long.

Families and philanthropic organizations sent books and phonographs to the camps. These provided a link to the world that PoWs had known before captivity. Good books became worn and pages became dog-eared as they circulated from block to block. The less popular editions were seconded for use in privies. The senior Allied officer in Stalag Luft III reported that PoWs abandoned 300,000 titles in January 1945 at the onset of the winter march. Some suggest this number is outlandishly high; however, it made the point that Luft III was well stocked with reading material.

Escape-Related Activities

A PoW usually turned his thoughts to escaping at some point during his incarceration. Prisoners attempted escape by excavating blitz tunnels, burying themselves in refuse trucks, dressing in replica uniforms and walking through the front gate, or cutting through the wire. For the few who succeeded freedom was invariably temporary. Planning escapes filled the days and helped one manage the desire to be free. Outwitting guards and attempting breakouts evolved into a sport of sorts. Escape committees, under the auspices of the senior British officer, or a Man of Confidence in NCO camps, coordinated all plans of escape, evaluated their merits, organized resources and prevented separate groups from interfering with each other. Over time, escape organizations became more sophisticated, and all plans required the approval of a committee. Escape groups flourished in Stalag Luft I at Barth from the early stages of the war. At Stalag Luft III originally the NCO compound (Centre Compound) was the hotbed of escape activity; and then enthusiasm spread into adjacent compounds.

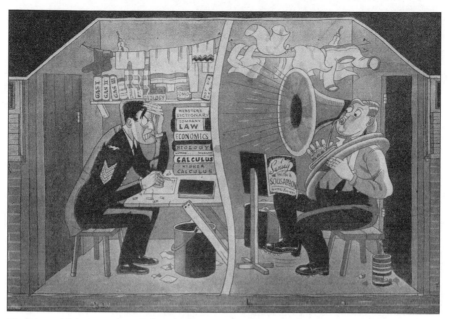

Novice musicians perfected their musical (in)abilities, to the chagrin of their comrades who shared the same barrack block. Although most PoWs studied little, the incessant noise drove them to the brink of madness. (Courtesy of Fred Rayment)

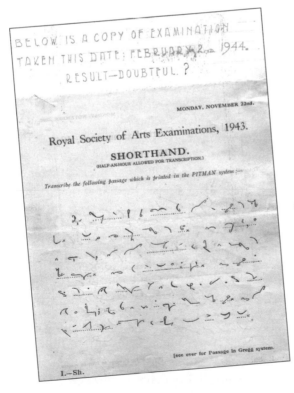

Gordon King studied shorthand, a skill he could use with the City of Winnipeg after the war. (Courtesy of S.G. King)

Squadron Leader Roger Bushell brought his experience as a master escape artist to Sagan and transformed the "X," or Escape Committee into a finely tuned organization in control of all escape-related activities. The Germans unwittingly sent escape know-how to other camps when dispersing the PoW populations. When they relocated RAF NCOs from Centre Compound to Heydekrug, Poland, they sent PoWs who already possessed the vast array of skills and know-how to establish a sophisticated X committee there. The Germans believed that they had thwarted escapes by having the Heydekrug compound built over sand beds, but the Heydekrug NCOs used bed boards to shore up the sand tunnels.

The X-types proved annoying to some PoWs, but most everyone tolerated the inconveniences while fully understanding that PoWs had the duty to escape. Several tunnellers even questioned their sanity when they went below ground. Digging in dark, poorly ventilated shafts that were prone to cave-ins was miserable. No known deaths were attributed to suffocation, but diggers remembered many close calls.

Every conceivable scrap, can, piece of wire, wood and broken glass was scrounged and stored in tunnels in case a need arose for it during the operation. PoWs acquired contraband from German guards, work parties, or civilians working in the camp.

The Germans conducted regular searches for contraband. They tore apart bedding and mattresses, kit bags and clothing. False walls hid many items, and guards often found radio parts, film, developing chemicals, maps, parts of uniforms, and electrical wire. Items were usually replenished by bribing guards with scarce chocolate and cigarettes. British intelligence, under the guise of philanthropic organizations, smuggled contraband into PoW camps through the mail system but minimized the quantities sent because they did not want to jeopardize the delivery of future shipments, and they did not have the financial resources for such undertakings. British PoWs had to rely more on their own resourcefulness than on items sent from the outside. American intelligence devised ingenious methods to get complete radios into the camps; for example, they concealed radios in crib boards and shipped them into the camps with the regular mail.

Circulation of News

Secret radios in each camp kept PoWs abreast of the progress of the war and in direct communication with London. Senior officers in the camps and officials in England kept in regular contact. German guards knew of the radios and often asked PoWs for the BBC version of the war. Both PoWs and Germans knew that a mixture of both versions created a relatively accurate account of the war. Messengers circulated from barracks to barracks with news of Allied advances. They scrawled news on scrap paper which was tied to a rock and tossed over the wire.

The Canadians in Centre Compound began one of two newspapers in Stalag

(Drawing by R.M. Woychuk, courtesy of H.K. Ward)

The confusion in this picture illustrates the extent of support for escape-related activities. In the foreground a map-maker, a carpenter and forgers are busy at work. On the left is a PoW tucking away forged documents. In the middle of the picture, to the right, is a "goon" who has stumbled into the room during a flurry of activity. (Courtesy of Fred Rayment)

Luft III. Named *Canada Calling*, the newspaper pieced together tidbits of information that came in private letters from home and in reports from new arrivals to the camp. After the dispersal of the NCOs from Stalag Luft III in 1943 to Heydekrug and Lamsdorf, the tradition of *Canada Calling* was maintained until the delivery of mail all but dried up in the last eight to ten months of the war.

Recreational Activities

Recreational activities played a pivotal role in the maintenance of morale and the release of energies and frustration. Gamblers and card players had their regular poker, whist and bridge nights. Betting became a big part of camp culture, with cigarettes and chocolate as the currencies of choice. Men who were short on cigarettes and *Lager Geld* borrowed from their friends and wrote promissory notes to repay their debts after the war. After PoW repatriation to England, British banks were inundated with notes scrawled on scraps of paper brought back by ex-PoWs. Most banks honoured the IOUs as long as a repatriated Kriegie had not already closed out the account.

Usually sent through the Red Cross and the YMCA, the earliest shipments of sports equipment reflected British influence, and rugger and soccer emerged as predominate sports in most camps. Some PoWs received softballs and basketballs from home, and pickup games evolved into full-fledged leagues. The Canadians secured hockey equipment from home, and the Germans permitted them to flood ice surfaces in several camps.

Many accomplished sketch artists populated the camp. The YMCA provided logbooks, or diaries, and those illustrated histories of camp life that survived are wonderful testaments to Kriegie culture.

Occasionally, the Escape Committee called upon the sports and entertainment committees to provide diversions that would distract guards from escape activities happening at the other end of the compound. The PoWs accepted the challenges enthusiastically, which, to be successful involved the cooperation of everyone. The PoWs received briefings ahead of time to make sure that they did not stare towards an escape in progress or point at anything unusual. Hank Bertrand remembers that the only man to go over three perimeter fences at Lamsdorf did so in broad daylight when the guards were caught up in the excitement of a baseball game.

Many activities served as diversion when loud noises related to chiselling, cutting or digging might have alerted guards. Harry Newby, raised in Wetaskiwin, Alberta, participated in the famed "wooden horse" breakout from East Compound of Stalag Luft III in 1943. While the vaulting horse served to distract guards during the course of tunnel construction, its hollow interior also concealed the entrance and held sand to be carried off the exercise yard. Its placement near the perimeter wire shortened the overall length of the tunnel. The pounding feet and shouting provided cover as men excavated below. At the end of a session, exhausted vaulters moved the horse, with the diggers inside, and sandbags from the grounds to a storage room off the kitchen. Musicians often practised in the compound, and most were unaware that their sounds minimized the chances of guards hearing any surreptitious activities.

Music and Theatre

Music and theatre demanded the undivided attention of its participants. As early as 1941, most camps had organized stage bands and choral groups, which performed the popular music of the day. The first PoW orchestra at Stalag Luft I performed four concerts before the camp was closed down and the officers were relocated further inland to East Compound of Stalag Luft III in April of 1942. Arthur Crighton recalled that the quality of the music increased in Stalag Luft III as the PoW population grew. Prisoners in its North Compound erected a theatre with a capacity of 350 in late 1942. Those who had previous acting experience presented high quality performances of many London plays that were running concurrently in London. Theaters troupes in Heydekrug and Bankau also produced magnificent plays for the enjoyment of fellow PoWs. Organizers needed to draw up a complex schedule for the different performances and rehearsals. Set builders, make up artists and tradesmen made elaborate sets with rudimentary materials. Stage hands, carpenters, electricians, painters, directors and producers all contributed to the efficient operation of the theatre.

Stalag Luft III's music program received direction from several dedicated individuals including Roy Wilkins of South Africa; Arthur Loveland, a choral conductor; Melville Carson, a violinist; Les Lucas, a professional trombonist; and Arthur Crighton, a music teacher and conductor. The orchestras and ensembles performed a variety of classics. Orchestral and jam music could be bought easily; what could not be bought could be replicated by talented musicians who laboriously copied music onto sheets while listening to phonographs—an amazing feat. Most contemporary dance music was taken off phonographs in this way, and the reproductions could not be distinguished from the original scores. The orchestra at Stalag Luft III provided the incidental music, as the "pit orchestra," during the drama productions—a job rarely enjoyed by the musicians as these performances demanded more attention than did symphonies.

German Treatment of Allied Prisoners of War

A June 1945 summary by RCAF officials on the treatment of RCAF prisoners of war in German custody concluded that German authorities in charge of *Oflags* and *Stalags* abided by the terms outlined in the Geneva Convention in most situations, and that the percentage of PoWs receiving treatment that violated terms of the Geneva Convention was low. German authorities treated

Jimmy Wernham at bat in East Compound, Stalag Luft III, 1942. (Courtesy of Barry Davidson family)

An early game of scrimmage. (Courtesy of W. MacCaw)

A boxing match at Sagan. (Courtesy of W. MacCaw)

Swimming in the reservoir. (Courtesy of Barry Davidson family)

Anyone who believes a Stalag looked like this has a lot to learn. (Courtesy of W. Prausa)

Part of a collection from Walter Prausa's logbook, which he received on arrival at Stalag IVB in 1943, this illustration lists the members of his crew, all PoWs in the Stalag. PoWs usually received a logbook as a gift from the YMCA. (Courtesy of W. Prausa)

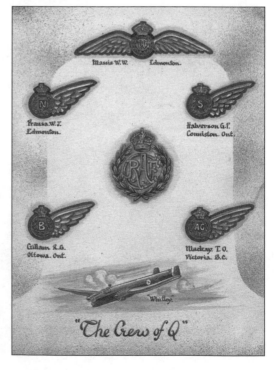

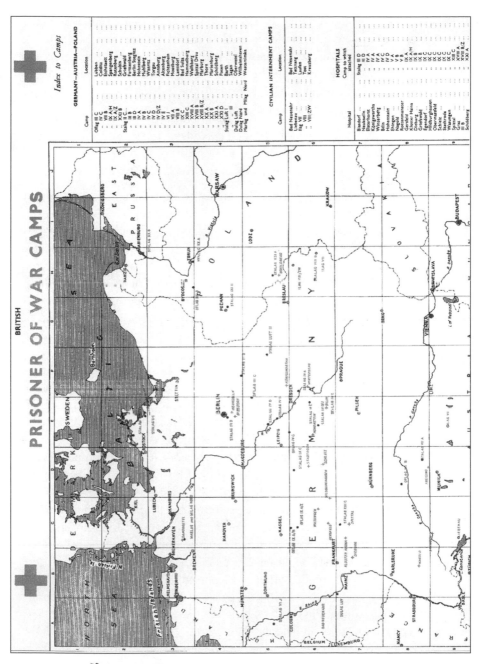

This map illustrates all German-administered camps housing Canadian PoWs during the Second World War. (Courtesy of H.K. Ward)

PoWs as best they could under the circumstances. However, standards of care and general treatment deteriorated in the last year of the war, especially during the mass evacuations of camps and the winter marches. Most documented occurrences of brutality were attributed to the SS, Gestapo, Kriminal Polizei, Abwehr and Sicherheitsdienst (SD), but not to the Luftwaffe.

Treatment of PoWs was usually influenced by three factors.

The military or civilian agency that took custody of the PoW.
The stage of the war during which the PoW became a captive.
The administration of the camp in which the PoW was interned.

Air force personnel taken prisoner by the Luftwaffe (Air Force), Wehrmacht (Army) or Kriegsmarine (Navy) usually received the proper standard of care. However, the processing and treatment of captured air force personnel changed in 1943 when the Nazi High Command issued the following order to deter PoWs from escaping in civilian apparel from Dulag Luft (the Luftwaffe interrogation centre): "Each PoW has to be informed that escaping in civilian clothing or German uniform, he is not only liable to disciplinary punishment but runs the risk of being court martialled and committed for trial on the suspicion of espionage and partisanship; in the affirmative he may even be sentenced to death." (James 1983, 96)

The acceptance of punishment, torture and murder as tools of control originated at the highest levels of German government. Heinrich Himmler, head of the RSHA, or Central Security Headquarters, implemented Stufe Romisch III, authorizing the use of deadly force against PoW escapees in early 1944. The directive ordered that all recaptured PoWs be turned over to the Gestapo and not returned to Luftwaffe custody. In March 1944, Himmler implemented Aktion Kugel, a directive ordering all recaptured PoWs, other than Americans and Britons, to be shipped to Mauthausen and executed. (James 1983, 104–6). In post-war interrogations of Luftwaffe personnel the British learned that in fact recaptured PoWs whose arrests were known to the public, local government officials or military units were returned to their camps. All other recaptured PoWs went to the nearest police unit. The police then contacted security officers at No. 17 Air Force Inspection Station, who passed the information on to OKW Abt Kriegsgefangenerenwesen in Torgau. This department ordered the "disposal" of recaptured personnel. Files on the condemned were stamped with *Geheimhaltung* (Secret) or *Keine Geheimhaltung* (Not Secret). (DHist Ref:181.009 [D624]).

The Gestapo, SS, SD or civilian police often withheld arrest information from the Luftwaffe or Red Cross. Upon learning of the unreported detention of an air force PoW, the Luftwaffe had the authority to demand his handover. Reichsmarschall Hermann Goering used his authority to "rescue" 167 air force PoWs from the grips of the SS at the Buchenwald concentration camp in December 1944. Red Cross officials from neutral Switzerland and Sweden, under the terms of the Geneva Convention, inspected camps and holding facilities to monitor PoW treatment and ensure their names were added to nominal rolls. Intervention by the Red Cross minimized the potential for PoW abuse.

Prisoners of war whose arrests remained secret were kept in other facilities, away from the prying eyes of the Red Cross. They endured solitary confinement and deprivation as well as other psychological and physical abuse. The Gestapo, SS, SD or civilian police could then pursue their line of interrogation, often outside the parameters of international law. They accused new captives of spying or sabotage in order to pressure them into revealing Allied secrets—or the names of those who had helped them to evade so they could lure them to their deaths. Fortunately most PoWs survived these ordeals and finished the war in regular PoW camps. A low percentage went to concentration and death camps, where their status as PoWs had no bearing. Some PoWs were executed, usually by the SS or Gestapo.

Availability of Food, Shelter and Medical Care

One of the most important points of the 1929 Geneva Convention Relating to the Treatment of PoWs established the standard of care for PoWs. They were entitled to the same rations, shelter and medical attention as local garrison troops. However, the German military ranked its personnel by their relative value to the Nazi war machine. The Nazis in turn divided their military personnel into five categories and provided for them according to their relative value to the *German* war machine; for example, front line troops received the most food; camp guards, usually unfit for other duty, gravitated to the bottom of the military hierarchy and subsisted on minimal rations. Major Hans Thiede, the German officer in charge of the security of all German armed forces prisoner of war camps, described guard personnel as "rabble of the halt, maimed and blind with a sprinkling of mentally deranged whose only interest was the obtaining of cigarettes from the prisoners (Addendum 6 to the Summary of Information on German Personalities). The Nazis skirted their moral and legal responsibility to provide adequately for PoWs by tying their rations to those issued to the lowest ranking German soldiers.

Most German guards treated PoWs as well as they could under the circumstances. Problems did arise regularly, more likely from neglect than from malice. Nonetheless, abuse of Canadians occurred constantly in every corner of the Third Reich, and the RCAF has numerous accounts on record. The tying and chaining of Lamsdorf PoWs for a year and a half, as well as the reprisals against the Fallingbostel PoWs in the last months of the war, were exceptional examples of mass punishment imposed by officials in Berlin. German authorities mistreated RCAF personnel in Kriegswehrmachtsgefangnis Brussels/St. Gilles between 3 June and 2 September 1944. A document filed with the Supreme Headquarters Allied Expeditionary Force (SHAEF) reveals that the Geheime

Feldpolizei sent 25 to 30 RCAF personnel in civilian clothing to the prison at St. Gilles even thought their PoW status had been confirmed. An interrogation of one Canadian lasted thirteen hours; another spent close to three months in solitary confinement; two others spent four to five weeks in solitary. Food consisted of 75 percent of the lowest issue of German rations. The PoWs slept on bare floors without mattresses or blankets (DHist Ref. 181.009 [D618] 85223 4 Oct 1944).

Local constabularies, not affiliated with military units, were notorious for mistreatment of PoWs. Often unsophisticated, poorly educated and drunk with their own self-importance, these low-level functionaries abused their power by ignoring any modicum of decency when dealing with downed airmen. It was reported that one Hans Schwarz, Gendarmeriewachtmeister of Wallmerod, Germany, brutally kicked, shook and shouted at RCAF serviceman John Kenney, the sole survivor of a crashed bomber on 20 December 1943, when he failed to stand up as ordered. Schwarz relocated Kenney to a barn and told the local farmer that he would be shot if he provided the gravely injured flyer with food, water or medical attention. In a post war inquiry physicians provided medical records of Kenney's injuries, stating that the Canadian was brought to them with crushed feet and compound fractures in both legs. Doctors amputated his lower left leg because of infection (SHAEF Court of Inquiry, 7 April 1945. DHist Ref.181.009[D618]).

A particularly disturbing example of prolonged abuse of an RCAF officer came to the attention of war crimes investigators by way of testimony from Knut Siem Knudsen of Trondheim, Norway in October 1945. Knudsen retold what he learned from fellow inmate RCAF Squadron Leader Ronald Nickoll Seddon de Saint Clair, MC, DSO, at No. 77 Punishment Kommando. Saint Clair had evaded capture for seven months before the Gestapo caught him in 1940. At no time in the following five years did the Germans grant him PoW status. He spent much of the war in Compiègne and Sachsenhausen/Oranienburg concentration camps. Knudsen believed that Saint Clair perished in Bergen-Belsen (DHist Ref. 181.002[D68] K9449/NOR/11).

The Royal Canadian Air Force assembled a report on 25 RCAF prisoners of war repatriated from Germany in January 1945. These PoWs underwent amputations in PoW hospitals and were classified as non-combatants, but they attributed their care to PoW medical staff, not to the Germans. The repatriates praised the staff for their untiring dedication to the wounded despite serious shortages of sulfa drugs, anesthetics, bandages and other necessities. Prisoners in the Hermann Goering Luftwaffe Hospital in Berlin stated that they received very good medical care from the attending French physicians (Interrogation of RCAF Prisoners of War Repatriated from Germany, Jan 1945).

The SS sent 27 Canadians, including Flying Officer David High, to Buchenwald Concentration Camp for extermination in August 1944. High had been one of 168 air force personnel held in Paris' Fresnes Prison before the Gestapo shipped them to Germany in a cattle car. A quirk of fate led to his transfer out of Buchenwald to Stalag Luft III in December 1944.

Pilot Officer Lyle C Smart RCAF J96703 of Leduc, Alberta, filed a lengthy report about his mistreatment at the hands of various agencies. His problems began after he swapped identities with a British Army private named Joslin at Stalag IVB and escaped from Work Kommando No. 1155 on 16 June 1944. Recaptured after nineteen days, Smart underwent observation at a German hospital. He reported that he weighed 93 pounds. He escaped a second time and the Gestapo beat him into signing a false confession. They moved Smart to Altergrabau, Stalag XIB near Berlin, amidst rocket test facilities and a tank testing range. Interrogators beat him over a two-week period and locked him in a filthy cell with over 160 other prisoners, whose food was dispensed in a single barrel. He witnessed guards savagely beat a Russian and shoot another prisoner. The Gestapo returned Smart to Stalag IVB and authorities placed him in solitary for five weeks. Smart escaped again with three other men, with the assistance of the Escape Committee. The committee provided a passport complete with his picture and a set of travel papers that stated he worked as an electrical engineer. A search party recaptured Smart and one other escapee (DHist Ref. 181.002[D68] File No. S50-1-2 Stewart, HR G/C).

Warrant Officer Henry Dufour, RCAF R79166, escaped from Cosol, an annex of Stalag 344 on 20 June 1944 and was recaptured at Metz, France on 22 June by two Luftwaffe officers. They turned him over to Wehrmacht police, who in turn put him into the custody of the Railroad police. Despite confirmation of Dufour's PoW identity, civilian police confiscated his papers and his RCAF and PoW identity discs and then placed him with British Army PoW Sergeant James Kemp, 2871872, in an eight-by-ten-foot cell for nine weeks at Wappy Concentration Camp. They subsisted on black bread and water for seven of the nine weeks and went without exercise. Guards beat the pair with fists, boots and truncheons before moving them to Sachsenhausen Concentration Camp, where the Germans denied everyone PoW status. There Dufour met seven British Army personnel captured in Norway and several Royal Navy personnel. The Germans quarantined Dufour's cell from 9 September to 9 October 1944 because of a typhus outbreak. Later the Germans transferred Dufour and Kemp to Stalag 383 (DHist Ref. 181.002[D68] Cas.5/2/112).

Ten SS soldiers broke into a camp run by German Field Police in Normandy, then beat and shot Warrant Officer First Class Griffin James Young, RCAF R85855, P/O J88753 (Posthumous), as well as a British Army Captain, two British gunners and one American infantryman on 25 August 1944 (Ref: 181.002 (D68) DHist S56-66 Holt, W. S. 15 Sept 1944)

Flying Officer William Dunwoodie suffered catastrophic wounds when a shell exploded in the cockpit of his Halifax bomber on Christmas Eve, 1944. After he parachuted into Germany he was fortunate to be arrested by soldiers; five of his crew were murdered by a lynch mob. While he was recovering in an SS hospital in Krefeldt, a vengeful nurse doused one eye with a caustic liquid, blinding him permanently.

Treatment of Pows at Dulag Luft

Treatment of PoWs at Dulag Luft usually followed the guidelines of the Geneva Conventions. However, post-war tribunals convicted interrogators of mistreatment. German Colonel Erich Killenger, Commandant of Dulag Luft, received a five-year jail term for torture. He, Major Heinz Junge (Chief Interrogation Officer) and Leutnant Heinrich Eberhardt served jail terms for locking PoWs in asbestos-lined "hotboxes" to make them disclose secrets. A member of the SS shot a British flyer in the face for no reason (James 1983, 96). Pilot Officer Myron Williams of Calgary, Alberta, evaded capture for seven days at the onset of the Battle of the Bulge in December 1944. His captors at Dulag Luft refused to believe that he had evaded without the assistance of Germans and they wanted to know who had helped him. Interrogators brutalized him, breaking his feet and jaw, before subjecting him to a mock firing squad. After six weeks, they transferred Williams to Stalag Luft VII at Bankau. He barely survived the forced marches at the end of the war.

Segregation of PoWs According to Branch of Service

The Germans segregated Army, Navy and Air Force PoWs into separate camps by early 1942. They also separated officers from non-commissioned ranks. The personality of camp commandants influenced how civilly camp staff treated PoWs. Prisoners of Stalag Luft III were fortunate to have Oberst von Leindiner-Waldau as their camp commandant. Von Leindiner-Waldau, a principled career military officer of Prussian extraction and former aide-de-camp to Kaiser Wilhelm of the German Empire (1885–1918), treated his charges with respect. Prisoners of Oflag XXIB at Schubin, Poland, and Stalag Luft VI at Heydekrug, East Prussia, described their German commandants as intellectuals inconvenienced by the duties of their office.

Prisoners exploited the situations to undermine camp operations. Memories of the mass escape of over forty PoWs from Schubin are forgotten, but the breakout had profound effects for PoWs in every other camp. The SS assumed control of Oflag XXIB and eventually returned all its PoWs to Stalag Luft III where better security was presumed to exist. Stung by a continual rash of escape attempts in various camps, a frustrated Nazi High Command issued several secret orders that examples were to be made of large groups of escapees in order to deter breakouts. The mass breakout of seventy-six men from Stalag Luft III in March 1944 resulted in the murder of fifty officers, and the SS, under Heinrich Himmler, took control of all PoW camps. From the point of the SS, the takeover of camps occurred out of necessity because many of the regular guards had become complacent. The SS enforced strict routines, and PoWs trod cautiously. Even the regular camp guards exhibited a genuine fear of the SS. Stalag Luft VII's one and only commandant had assumed his command after serving at Sagan during the Great Escape; he lived through the wrath of the SS after they assumed control of the camp and the commandant implemented extreme measures to control PoWs during his tenure at Bankau. Wehrmacht guards despised the RAF PoWs locked at Stalag IVB Mühlberg, which was an army PoW and labour camp. Many of the Wehrmacht guards were swept up by Goebbels' propaganda campaign to discredit Bomber Command crews as terror bombers or air gangsters, and they needed little reason to plant their boots into the heads of air force prisoners.

Forced Marches, January to April 1945

The advance of the Russian armies from the east in late 1944 precipitated the evacuation of camps in Poland, Czechoslovakia and eastern Germany. Guards escorting columns of PoWs had instructions to shoot stragglers or escapees. Few documented shootings exist. However, one guard shot three Sagan PoWs during the forced marches: Unteroffizier Max Kreutzen shot Flight Lieutenant C.K.L. Bryson on 19 February 1945 at Marlag-Milag; he died on 9 April 1945. On 11 April Kreutzen shot and wounded Flight Lieutenants D. Matheson, RCAF, and Bowker near Zeven (DHist Ref. 181.002[D68] S566-1-6 Johnson, GKM Capt, 12 July 1945). Prisoners remembered several guards who pummelled PoWs with rifle butts for moving too slowly.

In the latter stage of the war, most guards were elderly and weak and relied on the good will of prisoners to survive the trek; prisoners even carried their guns and rucksacks. Guards openly mused about what their fates would be once the Russians caught them; PoWs worried more about being killed by friendly fire than by the guards in the final weeks of the war. With Germany about to collapse, everyone suffered equally—PoWs, guards and civilians. Long time Kriegies noticed the guards' change of attitude; when Germany was winning, the guards had been arrogant; when they knew the war was lost, they thought twice before they made life more miserable than it had to be.

The Germans could do little for the PoWs, even if they wanted to. Hitler succeeded in making the final days as bloody as possible and in destroying as much of the country as possible before it fell into enemy hands.

Germany Strictly Observes Geneva Convention

The Nazis dropped a propaganda leaflet on Canadian soldiers during the ferocious Battle of Falaise Gap in Normandy, France, in August 1944. The outcome of this pivotal battle sealed the fate of German forces in occupied

France and forced their withdrawal soon after. Below is the text of the leaflet:

For every soldier, even the best, the moment may arrive when fighting on would mean senseless self-destruction and no benefit for his country. It is recognized by all nations at war that under such circumstances the soldiers are justified in surrendering. If you should face a like situation, keep the following points well in mind.

FIRST

You will be taken for a few days to a Dulag (transit camp) right beyond the front. The Dulags are no [sic] hotels. They are fitted out simply as conditions of the front permits, but you will be safe and well-treated. You may send home a message at once via radio << Invasion Calling >> telling your wife and family you are alive. If you are wounded or sick, you will immediately receive the best of medical care exactly like a German soldier.

SECOND

You will be transferred to a (Stalag) permanent camp. The Stalags are up-to-date camps with all the conveniences. The food is prepared in modern kitchens.

It is ample and of the same high quality as the food of the German soldier. Besides, you are allowed to receive a package every week through the International Red Cross.

You will be housed in clean airy rooms, which you may decorate according to your own taste.

Lavatories and toilets are of high sanitary standard.

If you wish to work, your qualifications will be taken into consideration.

You will be given the opportunity to learn a trade, to improve yourself in your profession, and you can even acquire a university degree.

All Stalags have athletic fields and modern sporting equipment. There are motion pictures and plays for your entertainment.

If you are artistically inclined, you may carry on your study of the fine arts.

You may receive any amount of mail. The forwarding of letters is administered by the International Red Cross . . . You . . . are permitted to write 8 postcards and 6 letters per month.

THIRD

The fighting will be over soon. Nothing more can happen to you and above all you'll be safe.

YOU WILL RETURN HOME SAFE AND SOUND AFTER THE WAR

. . .

Royal Canadian Air Force ex-prisoners of war scoffed at the wildly exaggerated claims made in this propaganda leaflet. The Geneva Convention Relative to the Treatment of Prisoners of War compelled Germany to permit representatives of neutral nations into the camps to monitor conditions, and thousands of POWs would have perished without the efforts of the International Red Cross. The Red Cross forwarded millions of food parcels to POWs from Allied nations. Unfortunately, there were continual food shortages, and the withholding of food was a commonly used tool of control. Shortages of food and other basics for POWs were a consequence of war but many POWs remain adamant that the Germans could have done more to relieve suffering, such as releasing emaciated POWs to Western powers months before the May 1945 capitulation. Long-serving POWs coped better with the hardships than did their recently captured counterparts, who had little time to adapt to their circumstances. In the last year of the war, conditions deteriorated rapidly, in part because the Germans did not have the means to transport goods supplied by the Red Cross. Americans captured in the Ardennes offensive of December 1944 faced "near-starvation" before liberation (Churchill 1959, 550).

Nazi propagandists heralded the quality of their Stalags in this leaflet. However, a prison was still a prison. Camp compounds consisted of low, uninsulated barracks encircled by barbed-wire fences and patrolled by armed guards and their dogs. Chronic fuel shortages prevented the proper heating of the barracks in winter and the provision of hot meals for much of the year. Next to food shortages, boredom was probably the most significant problem encountered by POWs. Resourceful organizers within each camp, assisted by the Red Cross, wrote to organizations back home with requests to send anything that could relieve the ennui associated with the weeks, months and years of incarceration in the same ten- or twenty-acre compounds. Dedicated Western philanthropic organizations, Allied governments, universities, technical institutions and families of POWs shipped goods to camps for the self-improvement and entertainment of prisoners. The fact that German-administered camps had activities was a testament to the intelligence, fortitude and leadership abilities of the men contained within, not of their captors. It was the POWs who developed their own social organizations and cultural activities.

Incidents of extreme mistreatment and murder of POWs are well documented, though they were not the norm. The Germans manacled 1000 Canadian and British POWs for over a year at Lamsdorf in retaliation for the Dieppe raid of 1942. Rations were reduced, and food packages were opened and allowed to spoil in some camps. It was common, though not widespread, for prisoners to languish in Gestapo or police jails. Escapees sometimes faced execution when recaptured, a direct violation of the Geneva Convention. The mass murder of 50 Western air force officers after the Great Escape reflected the low value placed on life by the Nazis. German units murdered POWs at Dunkirk, and elsewhere in France, Norway, and Belgium. An SS Panzer division captured, then executed over 130 Canadians, mostly from the Royal Winnipeg Rifles, a few miles inland from Juno Beach two days after D-Day. In December 1944, German tank crews used small arms fire to kill 129 American captives during the Battle of the Bulge (Churchill 1959, 542). Though these anecdotes are not intended to paint all Germans with the same brush, readers must be cognizant of the perilous conditions faced by POWs and the ludicrous nature of the claims outlined in the Nazi propaganda leaflet.

In contrast, German POWs incarcerated in camps in Canada were so well treated that many of them applied to emigrate to Canada after their repatriation. They said that Canada was a great place because the government treated them as prisoners of war better than their own government treated them as soldiers.

Part A

Prisoners of War (Kriegsgefangenen)

Stalag Luft VII, Bankau

Stalag Luft VII opened at Bankau on 6 June 1944. The Germans built the new compound in a hayfield and enclosed it with a six-foot-high perimeter fence of shiny new barbed wire. Tiny structures, each intended as living quarters for six men, earned the title of "dog houses" because of their small size and over-crowded conditions. Permanent barracks did not come available until October.

RCAF Warrant Officer Richard A. Greene, RCAF R66340, Bankau's Man of Confidence from 21 June to 21 December 1944, provided detailed insight into the camp's operations. He assumed the role of Man of Confidence at the request of the German authorities because he had performed similar duties at Italian Campo 66 at Capau.

Major Peschel, an ardent Nazi and member of the dreaded Abwehr became Bankau's first and only camp commandant. Peschel's previous experience at Stalag Luft III tainted his relations with PoWs, and his demeanour caused the relations between the PoWs and guards to be strained from the onset. To complicate matters, the German staff lacked experience in dealing with PoWs. Repeated interventions by Red Cross and Swiss delegations made no apparent difference, according to Greene. Peschel ordered guards to shoot any PoW who attempted escape, but under pressure, he modified the order to "fire upon any PoW attempting an escape." Greene contended that Peschel went out of his way to antagonize PoWs by delaying delivery for two to eight weeks of Red Cross parcels, mail, and YMCA materials including paints, paper, ink, drawing instruments, wire, string and cardboard cartons. "Red" Hayes, a rear gunner aboard the same Lancaster as David High, recalled that the delivery of mail was non-existent by December 1944.

Visits by Red Cross and YMCA representatives failed to rectify issues, and PoWs eventually resorted to bribery to acquire goods and curry favour with the guards. Greene's request for a British medical officer and a Church of England padre were denied by Peschel. Harold "Red" Hayes of 419 Squadron described Bankau's guards as unmotivated. Most were past the age of forty and easily controlled with the occasional cups of tea and coffee from Red Cross parcels. They wore belts with the inscription *Gott mit uns*, roughly translated to "God is with us." Bankau PoWs used to give these guards a rough time by telling them that the inscription really meant, "God is going to get you, especially when the Red Army comes!" Instead of retaliating against the prisoners or locking them in the cooler for insubordination, guards just shrugged their shoulders and walked away.

The prisoners lived in the doghouses for four months without water or electricity. Only one pipe supplied water for 800 PoWs before a new adjacent compound opened. The Germans threatened to keep the PoWs in the dog-houses indefinitely if PoW labour (instead of German workers) did not complete the construction of the camp. When the PoWs refused, German workers responded with a work slowdown to delay completion of the barracks. Supplies and equipment lay outside the wire despite German claims of supply shortages. Fortunately, the new compound opened before winter, on 13 October 1944. Its primitive facilities were luxurious in comparison to those of the original com-pound; they were outfitted with a kitchen, better water supplies, and facilities for the occasional warm shower. Prisoners converted a section of the cookhouse into a theatre. The Germans continued to frustrate PoWs by withholding tools, wood and supplies for minor modifications to the structures. The PoWs enjoyed the use of the larger facility for only three months before the Germans ordered the camp evacuated in early 1945.

Kenneth G. Taylor, Myron Williams and R. "Ernie" Nelson were three of 1500 Bankau PoWs. They set forth from Bankau on 18 January 1945 in an arduous forced march that ended at Stalag IIIA (Luckenwalde). The Cossacks liberated Stalag Luft VII on 22 April 1945.

Luckenwalde PoWs were fortunate to receive U.S. Army tents through the Red Cross. (Courtesy of Wilkie Wanless)

Pilot Officer Kenneth G. Taylor

Whether to join the Royal Canadian Air Force before completing high school was a daunting decision for any eighteen-year-old to make. Ken Taylor of Halkirk, Alberta found himself attracted by the allure of flying and by the air war in Europe. His father wanted him to finish high school and recommended that he confer with the town's lawyer, a reserve officer in the Calgary Tank Regiment, before making a decision. Volunteering seemed the appropriate thing to do. Towns emptied as their young men enlisted, and pressure mounted for friends to follow. The news created a romantic notion that war was an adventure, albeit a dangerous one. Patriotism might have played a role in Ken's decision; he was proud to follow in the footsteps of his two brothers, who were already in the RCAF.

Casualty lists from Bomber Command, published regularly in Canadian newspapers, did not deter him from enlisting. Post-war casualty figures revealed that for every 100 operational aircrew:

> 9 died in crashes during training in England,
> 51 were killed on operations,
> 3 suffered serious wounds,
> 12 became prisoners,
> 1 evaded capture after being shot down over enemy or enemy-occupied territory, and
> 24 emerged from the war physically unscathed.

Enlistment and Training

Ken Taylor submitted his enlistment papers to the RCAF in Edmonton in December 1941. He joined a squadron of new recruits at No. 3 Manning Depot, now called Northlands. New recruits, called "sprogs," plodded through basic marching and rifle drills for two months. Basic training was followed by a tour of guard duty. He also qualified for the elite 99-member drill team, a group who silently executed a series of 99 consecutive precision movements without commands. Members of this crack drill team received an exemption from guard duty.

No. 3 Manning Depot (Courtesy of William Poohkay)

Initial Training School in Saskatoon was the last course Taylor took before a selection board decided the specialization for which he was best suited: navigation and bomb aiming, air gunnery, wireless operation, flying or engineering. He trained with a class of bomb aimers before receiving a posting to the Bombing and Gunnery School at Dafoe, Saskatchewan. Leading Air Craftsman Kenneth Taylor returned to the Municipal Airport in Edmonton for a six-week course in navigation and aerial photography. On 18 December 1942 he graduated with the rank of sergeant.

Transatlantic Crossing

Following a short embarkation leave at Christmas, Ken boarded the *Louis Pasteur* at Halifax for the transatlantic voyage to Glasgow, Scotland. A friend from McLennan, Alberta summed up both men's destiny in a brief statement: "If anyone, a year ago, had said that I would be bouncing around like a cork in the middle of the Atlantic in the cold of January, I would have said they were crazy." (With sadness Taylor reminisced that this young man never returned home to Canada.) The vessel cut a zigzag pattern to avoid detection by prowling U-boat wolf packs. To further minimize the chances of interception, convoys would travel in different sea lanes each voyage and dock in different ports.

The Royal Canadian Air Force reception centre at Bournemouth was a pleasant starting place for Taylor's wartime experience. Minimal bomb damage in the immediate area and the mild British winter proved preferable to the cold prairie winters of Alberta. The landscape was green and the air was warm. Bournemouth seemed too idyllic for a nation at war. Ken thought to himself, "If this is war, I don't mind it."

Training and Operations

The shortage of aircraft delayed Sergeant Taylor's assignment to an operational training unit. To maintain his physical strength he joined the Royal Air Force Regiment in the Midlands, where he learned to march all over again and crawl through bogs and over hills. (In retrospect, Taylor appreciated the value of that training when the Germans force-marched him through snow banks in 1945, with little food and minimal shelter.) He resumed aircrew training with the Advanced Flying Unit at Westfreugh, near Dumfries, Scotland where he refined his air bombing skills. He practised bomb aiming in the antiquated Whitley bomber with 19 Operational Training Unit at Forres, Scotland. Trainees crewed up at Forres, and Ken was the only Canadian among seven. He finished his formal training on a Halifax bomber at 1663 Conversion Unit at Rufforth, Yorkshire. The RAF posted Taylor to 102 (Ceylon) Squadron in 4 Group, RAF on 22 October 1943. He joined 78 Squadron at Brighton in February 1944.

Inclement weather forced Bomber Command to cancel forty-four operations between October 1943 and May 1944. Taylor remembers stress levels were just as high for cancelled operations because for an entire day crews had prepared themselves psychologically before commanders told them to stand down. The mess frequently served Canadian bacon and eggs as a ritualistic "last supper" before operations—a treat, considering rationing was in effect. Nerves occasionally gave out en route to a target. Some crew broke under the strain of battle, and a pilot might return to base before the completion of a raid if he deemed someone's behaviour a threat to a bomber's safe return. Pilots made difficult decisions, because a man suffering emotional distress faced a charge of "lack of moral fibre," a euphemism for cowardice. Shirkers were dogged with that label for life. In the Second World War, a breakdown was still considered a weakness of character, not a psychological disorder. Affected airman often went untreated and suffered posttraumatic stress. A logbook entry for a cancelled operation might be "WOG US," indicating a wireless operator/gunner was unserviceable. Crewmen thought the best of their comrades and hoped a legitimate reason would be acceptable to the authorities. Taylor wondered how it would be construed if a genuine bout of appendicitis occurred. Four of Ken's fifteen operations between October 1943 and February 1944 were raids on the German capital during the Battle of Berlin. These were extremely hazardous because of the heavy defences that ringed the city.

"Death by Moonlight"

The blackest day in Bomber Command history occurred during the Nuremberg raid of 30 March 1944. German fighters and flak downed nearly one hundred bombers in the light of a full moon. Crews dubbed raids conducted in the shimmering moonlight "death by moonlight" for obvious reasons. In Martin Middlebrook's book, *The Nuremberg Raid,* historian Alfred Price describes the operation as the "greatest air battle of all time." Of the 1009 bombers dispatched, 108 aircraft did not return, as listed below (Middlebrook 1974, 275).

Crashed on take-off	1
Shot down by night fighter	79
Shot down by flak	13
Hit by night fighter and flak	2
Collided	2
Shot down by a "friendly bomber"	1
Crashed or crash-landed in England	9
Written off after battle damage	1

The losses were staggering in terms of manpower: 723 officers and men were killed, wounded or taken prisoner. Of the 545 killed, 109 were Canadian (Middlebrook 1974, 278–9). Empty messes and barracks spoke volumes the following morning.

Taylor's Halifax H was airborne for over seven and a half hours and came close to ditching in the English Channel because of critically low fuel levels. Distress calls from pilots on the verge of ditching or crash-landing filled the airwaves. Air traffic controllers redirected many bombers to training stations along the British coast; still, some crash-landed into hillsides and stands of trees because crews were unable to locate runways in the dark. Taylor's Halifax glided to a smooth landing on an unlighted runway, just as the giant engines sputtered on the last drops of fuel.

After de-briefing, Taylor's crew was met by a member of the Women's Auxiliary Air Force and eagerly offered drinks. She said, "I know that you chaps are entitled to a rum ration after an operation, but I'm not sure how many of these shots you are allowed to have." The aircrew consumed several before the mess opened for breakfast, and everyone was in high spirits until the grim news of the night's losses was reported. Levity surrendered to sobering silence. For the remainder of the war, Bomber Command suspended operations during phases of the full moon.

Pathfinder Losses Mount

Taylor had flown just twelve operations before rumours circulated about Bomber Command's need of replacement personnel for Pathfinder squadrons. Usually only experienced crews volunteered for Pathfinder duty. Taylor had moved to the top of the "experienced" list by default. He flew his first Pathfinder operation in a Lancaster III to Mantes, France on 6 May 1944 with the newly created

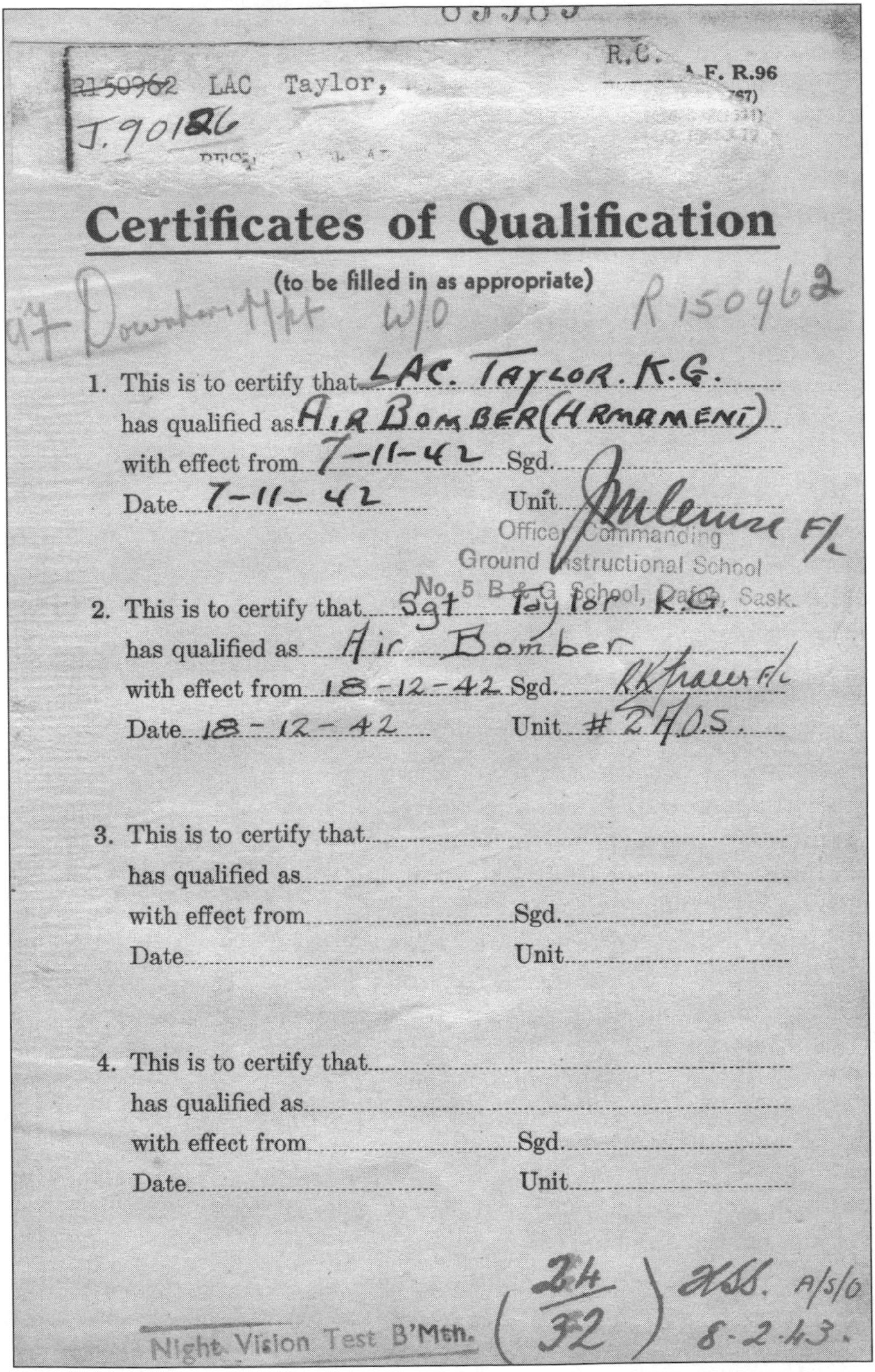

2150962 LAC Taylor,

J.90186

R.C. A.F. R.96

Certificates of Qualification

(to be filled in as appropriate)

R 150962

1. This is to certify that LAC. TAYLOR. K.G.
has qualified as AIR BOMBER (ARMAMENT)
with effect from 7-11-42 Sgd.
Date 7-11-42 Unit

Officer Commanding
Ground Instructional School
No. 5 B & G School, Dafoe, Sask.

2. This is to certify that Sgt Taylor, K.G.
has qualified as Air Bomber
with effect from 18-12-42 Sgd.
Date 18-12-42 Unit # 2 H.O.S.

3. This is to certify that
has qualified as
with effect from Sgd.
Date Unit

4. This is to certify that
has qualified as
with effect from Sgd.
Date Unit

Night Vision Test B'Mth. (24 / 32) 8-2-43.

This Certificate of Qualification entitled the airman to fly in the nose of a bomber over
enemy territory, in the cover of darkness. (Courtesy of K.G. Taylor)

635 Pathfinder Squadron in 8 Group. Transfer to a Pathfinder squadron carried some prestige, but new members accepted the assignment with trepidation.

Thirty operations constituted a tour for bomber crews. Crews who completed ten operations considered themselves lucky. They also considered ten flights to be payback for the government's investment in their training. Most declined the offer of a second tour and opted for demobilization, training new recruits, or administrative duties. Ken found that the Pathfinders required a man to complete forty-five operations (counted as two tours) before he could qualify for other duties. As the war progressed, Bomber Command continued to increase the minimum number of operations required to complete a tour. Taylor's rear air gunner, Warrant Officer First Class Robin Stuart, DFM, a Scotsman, completed fifty-seven operations by age twenty and refused to fly for the remainder of his life.

Target Areas Were Hot

When the navigator indicated that their Lancaster was approaching the target, Taylor crawled into the glass nose cone and aligned the bombsight over the target. If the crosshairs of the bombsight did not line up with the intended target, the pilot made another pass. Ken guided his pilot by directing him with the commands, "Left, left, ri-i—ght," or "Steady." Some bomb aimers occasionally ordered pilots to "Back up a bit!" just to bring comic relief. When Ken pressed the button on the "tit" to release the bomb load, the nose of the aircraft rose sharply as the weight of the bombs disappeared.

Shot down

Taylor was on his third Pathfinder operation, and fifteenth overall, when flak tore into his aircraft near Duisburg on 21 May 1944. The aircraft shook with a violence he had not experienced before. When a second shell scored a direct hit and sent the Lancaster into a steep dive, the pilot issued the order to bail out. The damaged escape hatch was immovable. Prospects of an early death and contemplation of his mother's receipt of a telegram gave Taylor the energy to kick the door free.

He now faced another grim hurdle. He had neglected to replace his damaged parachute even though he had known about it for several weeks. Before the crew had departed England, Ken's British wireless operator had blurted, "If you have to go out in that thing tonight, you've bloody had it." That was history. Taylor sat at the escape hatch and let his legs dangle in the slipstream. He hoped he could manage to keep the parachute on his back by clamping on to the left side of the pack with an iron grip. The lack of oxygen was disorienting but he continued to focus his thoughts on pulling the ripcord's D-ring. The chute failed to deploy! Taylor recalled stories of horribly mangled bodies found on the ground because of defective parachutes; some men were found dead with fingernails

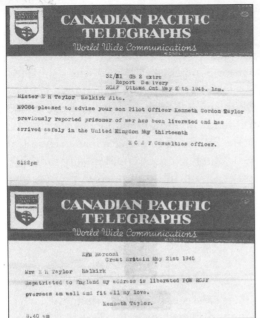

Ken Taylor's mother in Halkirk received notification of her son's fate. The first telegram stated he was missing in action, and the second stated he was a prisoner of the Germans. (Courtesy of K.G. Taylor)

ripped loose after attempts to release their chutes. Ken was lucky. He managed to tear open the casing and unfurl the parachute while keeping both sides of the harness from sliding off his shoulders.

Captured in Holland

Water in dykes and inland water systems can drown a parachutist. Taylor could see the water from the sky and he succeeded in sufficiently manipulating the tethers on his harness so that he drifted away from the water and came down on a high point of land. Weariness overpowered the adrenalin rush, and Taylor fell into a deep sleep in a barn until two German sergeants roused him. He remembers feelings of intimidation brought on by these enemy soldiers, not because of their machine pistols but primarily because they were ten years his senior. Numbness consumed him during his ride to Amsterdam. A few hours before, he had been flying home, and now he faced an indeterminate time in captivity.

Local police locked Taylor in the basement cell of their barracks for five days with guards who were unable to converse in English. Loneliness and depression swept over him. A window in the wall above his head afforded Taylor a view of rooflines, nothing more. He clutched the bars of his window and pulled himself up the wall to peer outside. The colours of the daffodils outside his window were more vibrant than he could remember. He missed the May sunshine and the colours emerging in spring. He could hear other Allied airmen but contact was limited to a chance meeting in the corridor on the way to the lavatory. To deter thoughts of escape, at the end of the hall sat a German guard behind a machine gun mounted on a tripod.

Taylor and fifteen other airmen went to a large holding facility in Venlo, Holland before moving to the main Luftwaffe interrogation centre at Frankfurt am Main. He suffered no emotional or physical abuse. He felt no shame eating blades of grass that grew along the perimeter fence. For the first time in his life he realized how little food he could survive on.

Stalag Luft VIIA at Bankau

After two weeks of confinement in Dulag Luft, Taylor and one hundred other non-commissioned officers boarded a train for Bankau, a small town in south-western Poland. Taylor became Stalag Luft VIIA's sixty-second prisoner of war. Statistics provided by Bomber Command show that for every twelve airmen who became prisoners of war, fifty-one perished in action. The 1500 Bankau prisoners represented the 6400 comrades who died in operations.

The Germans had opened Bankau just days before Taylor's arrival. Hay stood high within the compound. Prisoners lived in 180 temporary "dog huts" until the completion of the new full-sized barracks in October. At 5 feet 7 inches tall, Taylor had to duck to get through the door of his shelter. He shared the space with five others in a space suited for two. He slept on the floor with a shavings-filled gunny sack. A drinking pump and a washing pump in the centre of the camp provided water for all inhabitants. One building housed the kitchen, chapel and theatre. PoWs constructed a volleyball court, two ball diamonds and a football pitch.

Taylor's thoughts turned to escape. He knew that the Germans walked PoWs with dental problems to a nearby village for treatment. He feigned a toothache. He hoped he could escape from the group somewhere along the way. Apparently a Spitfire pilot had the same idea that day. The presence of four guards with small arms deterred both of them from making a break.

Taylor remembers that medical care at Bankau was inadequate at best. He suspected that he suffered from jaundice during the winter. After waiting for hours to see a doctor in a line that did not seem to move, he collapsed in a snowbank. Taylor returned to his hut, lay on the floor and suffered it out.

The Winter March

On 19 January 1945, PoWs of Stalag Luft VIIA set out on one of the most gruelling forced marches of the war. Their first destination was Sagan, 70 miles to the west. Guards did not distribute Red Cross parcels as they walked out the gate; each man received the equivalent of two loaves of heavy, dark bread to last for two weeks of walking. To survive, many resorted to scrounging oats and barley from farms. Medical supplies were limited to what one doctor and three orderlies could carry. Taylor's column spent the first night in dreadfully overcrowded conditions in an unheated barn. Wet socks and boots froze overnight, and it was nearly impossible to pull them on to blistered, cold feet the next

This illustration appears on the first page of Ken Taylor's logbook. He was PoW No. 62 at Stalag Luft VII at Bankau from June 1944 to January 1945. (Courtesy of K.G. Taylor)

This drawing from Ken Taylor's logbook shows the layout of the original Bankau compound occupied by PoWs from 6 June to 13 October 1943. (Courtesy of K.G. Taylor)

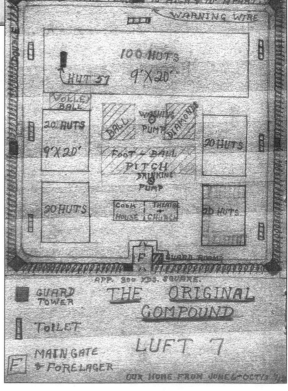

morning. Against the advice of the medical officer, prisoners ate beets and potatoes. Within hours, intestines were wracked with dysentery. The PoWs arrived in Sagan to find the compounds of Stalag Luft III abandoned except for the weak and sick. The Germans had evacuated the camp just four days before. Many Bankau PoWs remained at Sagan when the march resumed to the next camp, near Goldberg. The Soviets followed quickly and liberated Stalag Luft III within days. Russian authorities went to great lengths to ease the suffering of those PoWs left behind. They provided the best medical assistance and food available under the circumstances, and moved 500 sick prisoners to the warm-water port of Odessa on the Black Sea and repatriated them to England.

The Bankau PoWs bound for Goldberg were about to enter the most gruelling phase of their forced march. When they arrived at the rail hub of Spremberg, the Germans divided them into two groups: American prisoners moved towards Patton's armies in the south of Germany; airmen of the Commonwealth were directed towards British and Canadian forces in the northwest. The next four days were the worst of their lives: from 5 to 8 February, Taylor and the 1500 other prisoners remained crammed so tightly inside boxcars that they were unable to move around or sit down. Taylor stood in the corner of a boxcar near two small openings cut into the sidewall. Prisoners passed him the can filled with effluent, and he flung it out, on a guard if possible. On the verge of its collapse, Germany could not provide adequate care for PoWs.

Luckenwalde

The Bankau PoWs arrived in Stalag IIIA where the prisoner population of 17,000 swelled to 25,000. Taylor and several hundred prisoners were fortunate to find shelter in a low-roofed barn. Each prisoner received his own two-by-six-foot spot on the hard floor covered with dirty straw. Taylor and his friend crunched vermin beneath their boots. To their credit, the Germans felt responsible for the plight of their prisoners, but their own conditions were equally appalling and they could do nothing to relieve the misery.

Two officials, whom Taylor assumed were from the Swiss legation, assessed the health of the Bankau PoWs. They stopped in front of Taylor and his friend and requested the two to stand and lift their shirts. The doctor took only a few seconds to declare that they were slowly starving to death. Dr. Howatson, Captain of the Royal Army Medical Corps, also a prisoner, issued a report to the Swiss Commission. On 17 February 1945 he summarized the bleak conditions of his charges in his Report of a Forced March Made by Occupants of Stalag Luft 7, Germany, from 19 January to 8 February:

> There were numerous cases of dysentery, and facilities for men to attend
> to personal hygiene were inadequate . . . As a result of this march and the
> deplorable conditions, the morale of the men is extremely low. They are

suffering from an extreme degree of malnutrition, and at present, an outbreak of dysentery. There are numerous cases of frostbite and other minor ailments. They are quite unfit for any movement. Food and better conditions are urgently required. We left Bankau with no Red Cross supplies and throughout the march all rations were short issued, the most outstanding being bread, which amounts to 2,924 loaves [for 1500 men for a 240 kilometer march].

The Last Days

Compiled in the early 1990s, the following is an abridgement of Ken Taylor's recollections about his last days in Germany:

On the morning of May 7, 1945, I awoke in a very comfortable bed in a beautiful country home, a few miles south of Berlin. I was with two friends, one from North Bay, Ontario, and the other from somewhere in Saskatchewan. We presumed that the German occupants of the home had fled shortly before we had arrived, as the beds were unmade and dirty dishes were in the sink. The Russian Army had recently captured the area before its final assault on Berlin.

Why were three young (all aged 21) Canadians roaming around in a war zone, close to where the last shots of the war were being fired? About two weeks prior, the Russian Army had overrun the German prisoner of war camp where we were anxiously awaiting freedom from the barbed wire, little food and bare boards for a bed.

The Russian tanks had smashed down the barbed wire and continued on to Berlin, but the administrators who followed would not permit us to leave until we provided certain information (the Cold War was on even before the real one was finished).

After several days of the frustration of being freed but still confined, five of us tried to get out but were caught and sent back with some pretty rough treatment from the Russian officer and sergeant. We walked back toward camp but when the coast was clear three of us went over the ditch and into the bush and moved as fast as we could for a couple of hours. It was at the end of the day that we came upon the deserted beautiful home, where we stayed for the night.

In the morning (May 7) we found some rhubarb in the garden, which provided us with a good breakfast. (As best as I can remember, we had no food with us.) I had all my possessions in a cardboard box measuring 10 inches by 10 inches and five inches deep (I still have it!) We left the house as tidy as we found it and we were on our way.

We soon came to a highway and after walking for an hour or so a Russian Army convoy of about 20 trucks came along. By sign language, we got the message across that we would like a ride. They put each of us on separate trucks. We sat on top of whatever it was that they were carrying, along with a Russian soldier carrying a machine gun. Conversation was impossible. It was a nice sunny, warm spring day and we seemed to be going west. After a while, my travelling companion hauled out what appeared to be a slab of pork fat, and with his pocketknife cut a slice and offered it to me, which I was pleased to accept. He had a couple of slices and I was hoping for seconds but they were not forthcoming.

In the middle of the afternoon, the convoy stopped for a break and my two friends and I were able to get together for a conference with the truck drivers. The best we could make of it was that we were heading for the Elbe River. That is where we wanted to go because the Americans were on the west bank.

We mounted up again on our individual trucks and were on our way heading west.

It was evening when we arrived at some spot supposedly close to the Elbe River. It was getting toward dusk and a bit misty, and it took some time to find my buddies. In the approaching darkness, with shots ringing in the distance and seeing the body of a German soldier by the side of the road, the thought entered my mind that if I were older and smarter I would have stayed in the PoW camp.

On the way to the river we met a small group of displaced workers who said they had been turned back and could not cross. Shortly after, an American Army truck came along towing another truck (they, along with many others, had been to our PoW camp to pick us up, but the Russians wouldn't release us).

We asked the driver if we could catch a ride. No words, just a nod of his head toward the truck box and we were on in a flash. We were a few hundred yards from the pontoon bridge crossing the Elbe River.

The driver slowed for the Russian guards but they waved him on. Our heart rates had peaked! Four minutes later we were out of the truck talking to American soldiers. Upon asking about the progress of the war the response was, "She's all over—ended today" (May 7, 1945, 9:30 p.m.).

Return to Civilian Life

In June 1945, Ken was back in Halkirk. The RCAF put him on an extended leave, with regular pay still supplemented by aircrew danger pay. He received a lump sum of back pay, bought himself a surplus military Harley-Davidson motorcycle and spent the summer cruising around Calgary and Banff. On 20 September, the air force discharged him because the war with Japan had ended a few weeks before. In mid-October Ken enrolled in courses to finish Grade 12. The government thought his wartime experience had been worth something and credited him with Grade 12 Social Studies. Veterans were allowed to write their final exams every two weeks, and Ken earned his diploma after his exams in July 1946. From the time of his arrival in Calgary he lived in a boarding house with a group of young people. He said it gave him the opportunity to catch up on part of his youth. Adjustment to civilian life was stressful, and it took a few months before he was able to reacquaint himself with the joys of life denied to him as a prisoner. He now lives every day to the fullest and feels that the past sixty years have been a bonus.

Taylor learned the fate of his flight crew after the war. The pilot had managed to limp the Lancaster back to England with five of the seven crew still aboard. Taylor and the wireless operator, Doug Scopes, had bailed out before the captain rescinded his order to abandon the aircraft. Scopes had exited from the side door at the rear of the Lancaster; the force of the wind drove him into the starboard tail plane, and his right arm became jammed in the mechanisms before he fell to earth. The Germans interned in Stalag Luft VIIA at Bankau. Three of Taylor's crew died in subsequent operations. Ironically, bailing out over Holland had probably meant the difference between life and death.

All three Taylor brothers were alive at the end of the war. Jack beat the odds and completed thirty-seven operations as a navigator. Stan originally enlisted in the Royal Canadian Army in 1941, but transferred to the RCAF in England and became a pilot. He trained bomb aimers and navigators flying out of Malton (later renamed Lester B. Pearson Airport) in Canada. He was not sent back overseas because the Canadian forces would not risk the lives of all the brothers.

In the fall of 1946 Ken was accepted into the Faculty of Agriculture at the University of Alberta. He is a member of the Agriculture Class of 1950, who initiated the "Bar None" mixer, which has been ongoing for over fifty years, and founded the Bar None Endowment Fund, which dispersed its first scholarship in 1999. Ken married Lorraine McDonald in 1949, and he fondly remembers taking their six-week-old daughter to the inaugural Bar None function.

In the mid-1950s Ken joined the Army Reserves. He was captain in the 19th Alberta Dragoons, an armoured regiment based in the Connaught Armouries (a building now used by Club Malibu). During the height of the Cold War Ken attended the Federal Emergency Measures College in Arnprior, Ontario. As an agricultural specialist he received instruction on how to protect food products from radioactive contamination in the event of a nuclear attack.

Ken started his first job as an appraiser for the Canadian Farms Loans Board, now the Farm Credit Corporation. In 1960 he moved to the Alberta Farm Purchase Board and eventually was promoted to chairman of the board. The Edmonton branch of the Alberta Institute of Agrologists elected him president in 1969, and in 1971 he became president of the provincial association which has a membership of about 750 professionals. When the Agricultural Development Corporation was incorporated in 1972 he became its first general manager.

In 1973 Ken started working with the Agricultural Service Board and from 1976 to 1978, with the Farm Law branch. After retiring in 1978 he worked in real estate for ten years. In 1981 Ken and Lorraine ventured into property develop-ment and management.

Ken was a member of the Southside Optimists' Club and served as the organi-zation's president in 1965. He and Lorraine purchased a farm near Beaumont that same year. The farm was a haven for relaxation, and up to a few years ago Ken farmed it himself. He has also been active in the Edmonton RCAF Ex-Prisoners of War Association, and the Meals on Wheels program since 1989. He and Lorraine have two daughters and a son, and four grandchildren.

Pilot Officer Robert E. "Ernie" Nelson

Ernie Nelson received his commission as a pilot officer on the morning of his sixteenth and final operation. Because Ernie did not have the time to replace his chevrons with the appropriate stripes, he claimed to be "the only officer in the RCAF never saluted!" Pilot Officer Nelson, a mem-ber of RCAF 429 "City of Lethbridge" Squadron, received credit for destroy-ing a Ju88 as his own damaged Halifax plunged to earth. Nelson spent a rela-tively short time in captivity but his incarceration occurred when the Third Reich was collapsing and con-ditions in the camps were deteriorat-ing rapidly.

Happy Valley

Nelson's squadron received orders to bomb targets at Castrop-Rauxel in the Ruhr during the night of 16/17 October 1944. Flights into the heavily fortified "Happy Valley" were risky because the Nachtjagd (German night-fighter force) had mastered the "wild boar" defence formation used over German cities. A combination of radar-guided searchlights, flak and interceptors contributed to Bomber Command's heavy losses. Just minutes away from the target, bullets and cannon fire from a Ju88 shook Nelson's Halifax and ignited its fuel tanks.

The German pilot had used the cloak of darkness to get within a few hundred yards of the bomber before the rear gunner spotted him. Pilot Sid Mitchell plunged his bomber into an evasive corkscrew maneuver. From his rear turret Nelson raked the tip of the Ju88's port wing and then moved along the leading edge of the wing towards the cockpit. He made eye contact with the pilot, and to this day Nelson is unsure why he could see the German pilot's face so clearly. The flames consuming the Halifax might have illuminated his adversary's face, or the German could have had his cockpit light on during the attack. He watched the pilot crumple over in his seat as the Ju88 spun off into the night. Flight Lieutenant Mitchell confirmed the kill.

Modifications to the Rear Turret Saved Nelson's Life

Halifax MZ 377 continued to the target. Mitchell found it difficult to maintain control of his aircraft and ordered his crew to bail out after the bombs were dropped. Fatality rates for rear gunners were high because the cramped rear turret prevented the wearing of a chest or a seat parachute and in the turmoil of an attack gunners could not locate their parachutes. Nelson had prepared for this moment by having his ground crew remove the seat from his turret so he could wear a seat parachute at all times. This seat modification probably saved his life because when the bail out order came, Nelson just rotated his turret 180 degrees, leaned back and fell into the night sky.

The Halifax's port wing burned and fell off, causing the aircraft to spiral. The crew tumbled around the inside of the fiery fuselage, making it impossible to extricate themselves. A parachute pack had opened inside the fuselage and closed off the front exit in the Halifax. Mitchell attempted to force himself through the escape hatch in the top of his cockpit, but the opening proved too small. Miraculously, a violent pitch threw him clear of the burning aircraft at an altitude of less than one thousand feet and he managed to open his chute at less than 100 feet and survive his fall to earth. He suffered serious burns from the oil and petrol spread about the crash site.

The bomber crashed through the roof of a house in Langenburg before ploughing into the yard. No one on the ground was wounded or killed. Five of the crew perished: Wireless Operator Russ Almas of Ancaster, Ontario; Mid Upper Gunner Clarence "Barney" Wert of Maidstone, Saskatchewan; Navigator "Johnny" Johnson of Toronto, Ontario; Bomb Aimer Robert McEachern of Edmonton, Alberta; and Flight Engineer Walter "Pop" Harris, RAF. Four of MZ 377's crew were burned beyond recognition and the twisted remains of one airman were recovered outside the wreckage. After the war, the Commonwealth War Graves Commission exhumed the bodies of these five crewmen and reburied them in the Reichswald Military Cemetery in Cleves, Germany. Nelson suffered a broken ankle on landing and was taken to a hospital, where he saw his pilot, Sid Mitchell, wrapped from head to feet with gauze. Nelson passed through Dulag Luft quickly and was forwarded to Stalag Luft VII, where he faced the prospect of waiting out the war.

Internment in Stalag Luft VII, Bankau

The combination of an inexperienced camp administration, shortages of rations and fuel, and unfinished facilities made camp life difficult at Stalag Luft VII. The guards were an undisciplined lot. Nelson remembered one American-born guard who had answered Hitler's call for people of German heritage (*Volksdeutsch*) and had returned to the Fatherland in 1938. This pathetic guard lamented about the beautiful home and backyard swimming pool that he had left behind in Florida for the misery of the Third Reich. A frequent visitor to the huts, "Fritz" fraternized with the PoWs and became intoxicated on several occasions with the "hooch" that was brewed up from the dried fruit enclosed in Red Cross parcels. The American expatriate often drank himself into a stupor and fell asleep on one of the bunks with his rifle cradled across his chest. On one occasion, Nelson took the rifle from the man's arms, removed the bullets along with the bolt and hid them under his mattress. The guard cried like a baby when he awoke. He ran about the compound pleading with PoWs to return everything. The guard had not been a bad sort, and after the initial excitement had died down Nelson returned the bullets and rifle mechanism. The same guard came into Nelson's hut in tears a few months later because he had just received orders to ship out to the Russian front.

Evacuation

Before the evacuation of Bankau PoWs in January 1945, Nelson wisely collected bars of soap from the huts and then bartered them for pieces of bread during the march. Nelson contended that he and his friends secured at least twice as much food because of it. Unfortunately thirty-nine men died during the forced march—some froze to death, others gave up or succumbed to disease. The Bankau PoWs spent the last three months of the war in Luckenwalde. Its compounds overflowed with canvas US Army tents brought in by the Red Cross after the capture of thousands of Americans in the Battle of the Bulge. The food crisis was so severe that many more lives would have been lost if the war had lasted longer.

Liberation by the Russians

Luckenwalde's guards abandoned their posts just hours before the arrival of the Red Army. Euphoric PoWs watched Russian tanks roll along the barbed-wire enclosures. Cases of vodka appeared, and the Russians insisted that the PoWs gulp it down with them. The prisoners were not sure how to react to the aggressive and uncultured Russian conscripts. Those who hesitated or drank too slowly became more enthusiastic when Russian soldiers held pistols to their heads.

Ernie Nelson's crew in 1944. Rear (l-r): Johnny Johnson, Navigator; "Barney" Wert, Mid Upper Gunner; Sid Mitchell, Pilot; unknown. Front (l-r): Bob McEachern, Bomb Aimer; Walter "Pop" Harris, RAF, Flight Engineer; Ernie Nelson, Rear Gunner. Wireless Operator Russ Almas is not present in this photo.

The Russian liberators of Luckenwalde were a rough bunch whose determination routed the Nazis. The female soldiers were as rugged as their male counterparts. (Courtesy of W.A. Wanless)

The number of female soldiers in the Soviet ranks astonished Nelson. They wore equipment stripped off German dead and displayed a viciousness found in battle-hardened veterans. When a PoW from Spirit River, Alberta, who was fluent in Russian hollered "Kill him!" to one female soldier holding a German prisoner on the front fender of a tank, she responded by planting her boot in the small of his back, pushing him off and machine-gunning him as he lay on the ground, before the track rolled over him. Nelson did not witness any further shootings but assumed that most German soldiers in the area could have met a similar fate.

Relations between the Russian liberators and senior officers deteriorated rapidly. The Soviets wanted all liberated PoWs to take up arms, but the senior Allied officer refused to allow his men to join the Russian advance. Consequently, Allied PoWs found themselves back in the compound under martial law. In contrast, the 600 able-bodied Russian PoWs within Luckenwalde received weapons and went into action. The Soviets also attempted to force the Polish soldiers into battle. They treated all Norwegian PoWs with contempt and removed their senior officer, General Ruge, from camp. His fate remains unknown.

Prisoners of war received permits to leave the camp during daylight hours to scrounge for food and other necessities on the condition they returned by nightfall. In retrospect, the controls imposed upon the PoWs were probably for their own good as pockets of German resisters continued to operate behind the Russian lines, and throngs of hostile German civilians, many of them armed, hounded PoWs. Ongoing skirmishes between Axis and Russian forces limited the PoWs' opportunities to forage, thereby worsening already dire conditions within the camp. Determined German and Italian conscripts looted the countryside. Thousands of hungry Dutch, Belgian, French, German, and Italian refugees attempted to break down the front gates of Luckenwalde. The possibility of disease threatened the general health and discipline of PoWs in the camp. Soviet authorities reproved the senior and American officers in Luckenwalde for failing to stop the exodus of British and American PoWs to the west, even though it was obvious that the Soviets were deliberately delaying repatriation of Allied PoWs. The Russians threatened to use force against anyone leaving the camp without authorization. They even turned back a convoy of American trucks that were sent to retrieve the sickest PoWs after VE Day!

The marriage of convenience between communist east and democratic west quickly dissolved with the defeat of their common enemy, fascist Germany. Recently liberated Western PoWs had to remain behind Russian lines until Stalin received assurances from Western powers that all Russians in their zones of occupation had been repatriated. The ex-PoWs became the first pawns in the Cold War. Eventually the Soviets permitted American trucks to enter Luckenwalde and move them to Brussels, where squadrons of Dakotas ferried them to

England. Western military leaders prioritized their repatriation, even if it meant compromising safety. Nelson recalled, like so many of his comrades, that the aircraft in which he flew experienced temporary engine failure; all on board believed they were about to die. It was an ironic way to go after all they had endured as PoWs.

Epilogue

Though Ernie Nelson's seven months in captivity were difficult, he returned to Canada in good health. He contends that two small decisions made the difference between life and death. The first involved his choice to have the seat in his rear turret modified so that he could wear his parachute at all times. His second lifesaving decision involved the last-minute collection of pieces of soap before leaving Stalag Luft VII, and bartering them for food during the arduous march to Luckenwalde. Robert Ernest Nelson passed away on 15 October 2004 at the age of 79 in Edmonton, Alberta.

Pilot Officer Myron A. Williams

During the Second World War the Luftwaffe established a reputation for fair but firm treatment of prisoners of war. Myron Williams' treatment was an exception: the Germans captured him in a high security corridor just before the launching of the Battle of the Bulge, and his interrogators would not accept his assertion that he had evaded capture for a week without the help of the underground; they tortured him for information. In a personal interview in the summer of 2002, Williams clearly stated that he would never allow himself to become a prisoner of war again!

Battle of the Bulge: the Last Stand of a Collapsing Regime

The Nazi High Command devised plans for a final stand in the west in September 1944, but weather delayed implementation until December. The success of the German strategy hinged on overcast conditions to conceal infantry and armoured movements from the eyes of Allied air force reconnaissance units. The Germans played the waiting game for three months, all the while fearing the Allies would learn of the offensive before it started. When the Germans discovered Williams behind the line, paranoia took over and they had to find out, at any cost, if their captive had received help from sympathetic Germans linked to a spy network. Myron Williams had no connection with the German underground; he had parachuted into the wrong place at the wrong time.

Early Training

Williams enlisted in the RCAF on 9 July 1941 and completed Air Gunnery School at Mount Pleasant, Prince Edward Island, before the air force deployed him to England on 6 June 1943. He trained on Wellington bombers at Finningly, then underwent conversion training on the Halifax and Lancaster in September. Williams received secret training at Hemswell on the Q Box. Sworn to secrecy about this technology, he heard reference made to the device just three or four times in his lifetime. The Q Box coordinated the firing of four machine guns in the rear turret at incoming enemy aircraft. Its screen and transceiver, mounted beneath the seat of the rear gunner, monitored airwaves for the Morse code letter of the day which was transmitted by incoming friendly aircraft. German fighters, instead, created a buzz in the Q Box, and this alerted the rear gunner to activate a switch that would cause the machine guns to fire automatically when the enemy aircraft came within range. The RCAF referred to this technology as AGLT (Automatic Gun Laying Turret).

On Operations

Williams' preference for night operations stemmed from the havoc he witnessed during two daylight operations. Congestion caused mid-air collisions. Gaggles of bombers that rained their bombs on aircraft below made him wonder how long before a "friendly" bomb would blow up his aircraft. He witnessed small arms fire shoot down the lead bomber during a run through a valley near Dresden. In the same raid, a solitary bomb lifted a brick church from its foundation in one piece before the explosive power sent bricks flying in every direction. Williams breathed a sigh of relief when he returned to night operations. He contended that anyone who experienced combat knew fear; what separated men, during battle, was whether they continued to think coherently while under fire. Williams contended that those who claimed they were unafraid did not fly enough. Flak struck his Lancaster twenty-six times during his inaugural operation to Bochum on 4 November 1944, and the aircraft was written off. In all the operations that he flew, continuous bursts of flak called scarecrows illuminated the night sky to make it easier for anti-aircraft batteries to spot bombers. Phosphorous bursts of flak, referred to as chandeliers because of the iridescent arches they created, made bombers sitting ducks for roving fighters. The novelty of the flashes spurred Williams' navigator to come forward into the cockpit for a full view of the fireworks—just once. "Je-sus Chr-r-rist!" he exclaimed and remained huddled over his equipment in the fuselage on subsequent flights! Williams fired his machine guns just once in ten operations. He warded off an attack of a German fighter with a volley of tracers over the canopy. The German rocked his wings up and down in acknowledgment as he turned away.

Damaged Beyond Hope

On the night of 12 December, an Me110 equipped with an upward firing 20mm gun fired a shell into the port wing of Williams' Lancaster. Flames spread across the wings and into the fuselage so quickly the rear gunner could not locate his parachute pack. Williams insisted they jump in tandem. In the face of death, the rear gunner refused and ordered Myron, the mid upper gunner, to jump before it was too late for both of them. The rear gunner and the pilot died in the crash.

On the Run

Williams drifted down into German territory and sought shelter beneath dead-fall in a ditch. He spread his silk parachute over the branches to keep out wind and sleet. A chance encounter with an old woman gathering kindling should have cost him his freedom. Her yappy terrier drew her attention to where he lay under the parachute and the brush. She pretended not to notice him, took her dog and scurried off. Evidently she told no one. Williams made the decision to walk north to Denmark. He estimated the Rhine River to be just fifteen or twenty miles to the west but the chances of crossing its swift waters into Belgium were nil. Aided by a small compass hidden within a button on his tunic, Williams navigated fields by night until he witnessed a landmine blow apart a dog. After that episode he travelled along roads in daylight hours.

Williams wore a brown insulated flying suit, unfamiliar to German ground units, and passed himself off as a migrant German labourer. He removed the insignia from his blue air force uniform, pulled his forage cap around his face and slung a rake over his shoulder. He avoided speaking to passersby by feigning the mannerisms of a deaf mute. He ate well enough; stockpiles of vegetables in root cellars or in clutches along the roads supplied ample rations. The coolness of December began to wear on him after a week. He sought refuge in an old barn. Only afterward did he realize that he had walked into a stable with living quarters attached. Williams interrupted a German family eating breakfast, and the wife ran off to fetch the police. He thought about running but he knew his period of evasion had ended. The father and young lad spoke passable English, and they offered him real coffee, a surprise in a nation subjected to rationing. They exchanged small talk until the police arrived and removed Williams to the local guardhouse. Kindly guards fed him crackers, liverwurst and coffee before sending him to Luftwaffe authorities at Frankfurt. Guards escorted him through Cologne, where the destruction inflicted by the Allied air forces astounded him. He could not comprehend how people survived years of bombardment; the only evidence of life was the scattering of potato peelings amid the rubble. Williams had no idea that the next six weeks would be the worst period of his life.

Barbarity at Dulag Luft

Myron Williams' prolonged period of evasion in a high security area raised serious questions among the German military and his captors even contemplated the possibility that the Special Operations Executive had parachuted him in. Interrogators attempted to break him mentally through isolation, deprivation and intimidation. Guards denied Williams access to bathroom facilities for prolonged periods. When he defecated on the floor of his cell, they punished him. When he defecated in his bowl they flew into a violent tirade. One forced him to wash it repeatedly before the guard smashed it on the wall of the *abort*. Then guards refused to feed him for two or three days because he did not have a bowl. Sleep deprivation and lights kept on in his cell for twenty-four hours a day turned Williams' schedule upside down; days meant nothing to him anymore. He remained in Dulag Luft from 19 December to mid January. In contrast, most PoWs were processed through Dulag Luft in a week.

German interrogators shocked him with the accuracy and the extent of the personal information they had about him. They knew about his five brothers and two sisters, and when he had joined the RCAF, as well as details about a brother, who was also in the RCAF. They knew he had grown up in Cessford, Alberta and they even told Williams the legal description of his parents' farm. He wondered how they knew so much about him. Then it dawned on Myron that he had revealed all these details to a German immigrant who had laboured on the same farm at Milo before the war. This German had shown so much interest in Williams; he even possessed a township map and wrote the names of the Williams family on their home quarter of land. Myron knew that the man had returned to Germany before the war started. The fact that this same information had made its way to Dulag Luft, years later, haunted Myron.

Interrogations followed the same pattern for several days. Guards usually took him for questioning in the morning and sometimes for a second session in late afternoon. Myron remembered his instructors in basic training saying that there was no use lying to an interrogator because he would know it was a lie. Consequently he responded to all questions with the same answer: "No. R-11-32-36 . . . Williams, M. A." They made him homesick by asking him what he thought his mother and father were doing at Christmas and New Year's. Then they would slip in a question like "What were you doing on the 14th of December, the day after you were shot down? Where did you go from there? And what did you do? What were you doing with that rake, the one that you left outside of that barn?" Then they became pushy. Williams was sure that they would beat him if he reacted to anything so he shut right down. The interrogator became more impatient and the sessions became rougher. Frustrated, Williams' interrogators changed their tactics. They stood him at attention, and if he moved the slightest bit, they hit him. They circled him and struck without provocation. They sat him in a chair with a guard on either side of him and landed solid blows to his mouth. The first time Myron instinctively flew out of the chair and punched his interrogator as hard as he could; the guards held him down and beat him senseless. In all subsequent interrogations Williams never hit back again and said nothing. Later he stated that he must have had a "glass jaw"—he believed it had been broken in the early stage of his captivity, and the interrogator knew it. The senior interrogator enjoyed inflicting pain; he liked to punch Williams in the jaw during each session because it made him pass out. Before the interrogator finished each session he made a point of knocking Williams senseless, one more time. He karate-chopped him repeatedly on his lips, to the point they swelled into a blue-purplish mass that crowded his nose. Williams trembled uncontrollably each time they took him for questioning, especially when the sadistic interrogator entered the room. At the end of one session, an English-speaking German guard, escorting Williams back to his cell said, "You better tell them what they want, they're going to kill you, you know!"

The brutality intensified. Guards slammed their rifle butts on to his bare feet and broke bones. When that failed to break William's silence, the Germans resorted to the unthinkable. Guards dragged him to the courtyard, tied him to a post and marched a squad of six men to firing positions fifteen feet in front of him. Williams trembled as the soldiers went through the motions of aiming their rifles at him. He awaited the order to shoot. On the verge of death, he still did not utter a word. He was not sure if they fired blanks or whizzed bullets into the wall behind him, because he collapsed.

Williams remembered nothing from the time of his mock execution at Dulag Luft until his arrival at Stalag Luft VII at Bankau, some days later. His arrival at Bankau marked his first interaction with other PoWs since he had parachuted from his aircraft two months earlier. Emotionally fragile, he trusted no one, not even the Stalag's Man of Confidence.

Stalag Luft VII, Bankau

Conditions at Bankau deteriorated considerably in the last weeks of the war. Williams shared an unheated, dirty room with eighteen men in a space meant for six. The stench of unwashed bodies overpowered him. Someone wrapped Williams' broken feet but they could do little else for him. He lay in the shadow of his bunk, unable to interact with others. The Canadian Man of Confidence, Warrant Officer II W.P. "Bill" Chandler, RCAF 106751, PoW 10, introduced himself to Williams and was shocked at how he cowered. Chandler learned that

Whether this picture is staged or not is a point of contention among PoWs. It was
printed from a roll of film found in a camera that was seized by PoWs at Lucken-
walde after German guards had abandoned the camp. Myron Williams, an RCAF
PoW from Calgary who was marched before a firing squad by his tormentors at
Dulag Luft, scoffs at the contrived nature of the shooting as depicted in the photo.
(Courtesy of W.A. Wanless)

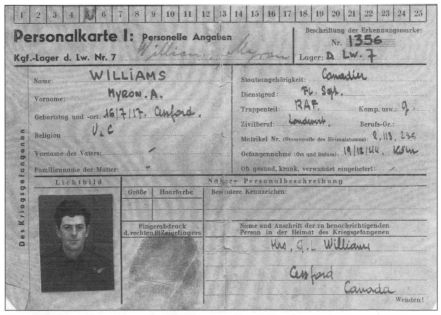

"Personalkarte" of Myron Williams. (Courtesy of M. Williams)

Williams had grown up outside Calgary, and tried to make conversation. When he mentioned that he grew up near a small village called Milo, it triggered an uncontrollable rage in Williams because Milo was where he had made the acquaintance of the German spy before the war. He wondered how interrogators in Dulag Luft and a man in Bankau could come up with the name of the same town in far-off Alberta. Instinctively Williams barked, "F___ off . . . now!" and fellow PoWs left him alone.

The Winter March

The Germans evacuated Bankau days after Williams' arrival. Unable to walk, he was transported on a homemade sled by fellow PoWs until they were too weak to pull him. Then he struggled along under his own power, pulling himself along on his hands and knees. Williams attempted to stay ahead of the column by starting out early in the morning; however, it was not long before the group passed him. Other PoWs fell by the side of the road from exhaustion; the lucky ones found room on a wagon hauled by fellow PoWs. Williams remembered a padre leaning over one corpse and muttering "Thank God, he's not one of ours" when he discovered it was a German. At one point, Williams told his navigator he did not think he was going to make it. The navigator said, "Come on Willy, do it for Vi; come on Willy, get going, do it for Vi! I'll get you on that wagon; you can't walk anymore." During the 250-kilometer march, the Bankau PoWs were locked inside cold, unventilated train cars for days until a locomotive hooked up and moved them to Luckenwalde.

Luckenwalde—The Last Stop

The Russians liberated the Luckenwalde camp in late April, but close to 3700 British army and air force prisoners and 4900 American army prisoners remained in Soviet custody until the Allies agreed to return all Soviet prisoners within their zones of occupation. American trucks eventually gained access to Luckenwalde and removed the PoWs to an American base at Haley, where the abundance of food, especially white bread and pineapple, overwhelmed them. A pick-up squadron repatriated Williams to England on 4 June 1945, nearly a month after the unconditional surrender had been signed and nearly seven weeks since his "liberation" by the Soviet allies. After a layover of ten days at Bournemouth, he set sail for Canada.

Legacy

Myron Williams was not bitter about his experiences. Instead, he wanted to turn them into something useful. Discipline has been the main influence on his life and the military taught him the importance of listening well and following instructions. Williams refused to tell his wife, family or PoW friends about the torture he endured while at Dulag Luft, because he could not prove it happened.

He disclosed dark details of his mistreatment at Dulag Luft for the first time during an interview at his home in Calgary in the summer of 2002. His revelation was so overwhelming that he collapsed before he could finish his account. Williams stated that he had never lifted a rifle because he knew exactly how a deer felt during a hunt. His greatest joy was to watch his children grow up in peace. He felt that schools have a responsibility to teach the history of conflict in order to give people a realistic understanding of the suffering endured by belligerents and innocent civilians. He hoped that with this knowledge, people would be less inclined to support aggression.

Williams believed the devastation of war taught the German people enough to know that they did not want a repeat performance. The Allied forces brought the war to their doorsteps, and the horrors the German people experienced moderated their militarist and expansionist foreign policies. Williams takes pride in the fact that he played a role in this. If there was any consolation for the anguish and pain inflicted on Myron Williams, it was in knowing, as Hitler's Armament Minister Albert Speer revealed in a post-war interrogation in the London "cage," that the damage inflicted by the 540 RAF bombers in that raid, Williams' last, was considered one of the most devastating in the six years of war (Middlebrook 1974, 630). Only six Lancasters failed to return that night. Flight Sergeant Myron Williams was among the crews brought down.

Commissioning a Memorial to the Martyrs of Stalag Luft III

Myron Williams commissioned a painting to commemorate the memory of the fifty Allied air force officers murdered after the Great Escape from Sagan. The work is titled *Stalag Luft III, Tunnel Martyrs* and is bordered by photographs of the fifty men, six of whom were Canadians: Henry Birkland, G. Wiley, George McGill, G. Kidder, Pat Langford and James Wernham. The painting is a composite of six scenes: a scale drawing of the tunnel; a scene in the hut beside the entrance to the tunnel; a scene depicting the excavations below ground; a scene illustrating the breakout from the camp; and last a picture of the memorial cairn built to contain the urns of ashes—which is still in existence at Sagan on the former grounds of Stalag Luft III. The concept was inspired by Iga Tobolska, widow of one of the victims, Polish airman Paul Tobolski. Myron Williams researched every detail surrounding the Great Escape to ensure that the artist's work accurately depicted events as they happened. Bill Holder of Okotoks, Alberta created the artwork.

Myron Williams served as president of the Calgary branch of the RCAF Ex-PoW Association for many years. He passed away in May 2004 after a long struggle with cancer.

Stalag Luft III Tunnel Martyrs, by Bill Holder, commissioned by Myron Williams of Calgary, 1997. On 24 March 1944 the single largest escape of prisoners during the Second World War took place from the North Compound of Stalag Luft III, at Sagan. Under cover of a moonless night, 76 Allied air force prisoners of war broke out from a tunnel 348 feet long, 30 feet underground, in a determined bid for freedom. The heroic attempts of the escapees ended in tragedy when 50 of them were murdered on orders from Hitler, in direct contravention of the Geneva Convention. Three escapees made it to Britain and freedom, defying an exhaustive manhunt by German military and civilian forces. The rest were returned to various prisons and concentration camps.

The above painting depicts the sequence of events of their escape attempt. We see a Lancaster bomber caught in searchlights being raked with flak, the capture of the airmen, and the layout of the wire-enclosed prison camp. Then during the tunnel construction we see the men stationed as lookouts (one at the window, another ready to move the stove which covered the entrance) for the dangerous, tedious and difficult excavation work in the confined space of the tunnel, dubbed "Harry." The gold-coloured sand on the snow emphasizes the difficulty of dispersing the excavated sand, undetected by the guards.

Finally we see the daring departure by night. The mouth of the tunnel unfortunately came up short of the woods, and required a hastily rearranged system to guide the escapees out to the woods. Then we see the appalling murders of the officers by the Gestapo, and the monument constructed to honour them. Surrounding the painting are the German PoW identity photographs of the murdered airmen. (Courtesy of M. Williams)

Stalag IVB Mühlberg

Stalag IVB's complex consisted of ten PoW compounds. Its first occupants were French and Dutch soldiers captured in 1940. The Germans filled other compounds with Belgian, Czech, Polish and Russian soldiers. When Mussolini's government collapsed in 1943, a compound was added for Italian soldiers. Mühlberg also served as a transit camp for prisoners designated for other camps. With greater numbers of aircrew in custody, the Germans moved RAF prisoners into "D" compound and into four huts in "C" Compound, also known as the French Compound. In the last year of the war, air force PoWs comprised three-quarters of Mühlberg's population. Edmonton residents Walter Prausa and H.K. "Bud" Ward were prisoners in the RAF compound.

Conditions at Mühlberg were austere. The sheer number of RAF prisoners in "C" Compound eventually forced the relocation of French PoWs elsewhere. The 1500 RAF PoWs shared one communal latrine facility, a windowless, doorless brick building outfitted with forty seats arranged in two rows of twenty. No one had access to the *aborts* in the communal latrine after curfew, and if a PoW ventured out after hours to use it, a guard shot him. Instead, 250 to 300 PoWs used a night facility in their barracks outfitted with just two seats. "C" Compound's

Main Gate at Stalag IVB, a drawing by Raymond Navell. (Courtesy of Walter Prausa)

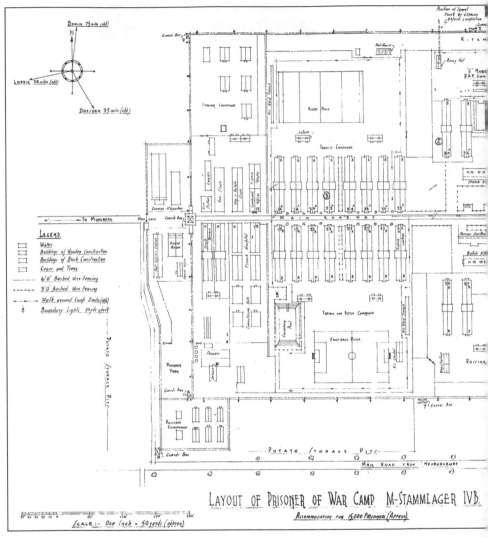

LAYOUT OF PRISONER OF WAR CAMP M-STAMMLAGER IVB.

ACCOMMODATION FOR 15,000 PRISONERS (APPROX.)

SCALE:- ONE INCH = 50 YARDS (APPROX.)

(Courtesy of H.K. Ward)

single water source was in the latrine. Water dripped from a single pipe, it never flowed. Water trickled along a cement trough that had holes drilled in the bottom. A PoW would place his mug beneath a hole and wait several minutes for it to fill; excess water collected in a tank at the end of the trough. Wash basins did not exist. PoWs were marched, in an orderly fashion, to a communal shower facility outside the main gate once every six weeks. They shivered in uninsulated, unheated huts in the winter and often ate cold rations, as briquettes of coal were in short supply. Ill air force PoWs were still required to report for roll call. Two men carried Bud Ward to the *appel* square twice a day

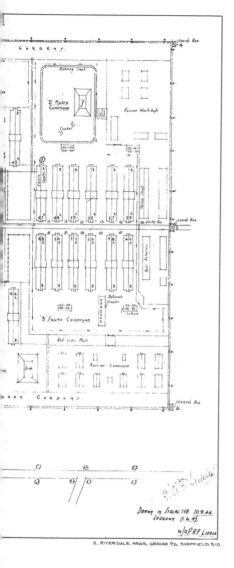

Drawn in Stalag IVB 10.9.44.
Redrawn 11.6.45.

W/o/P R.F. Liddle

2. RIVERDALE NEWS, GRAHAM RD. SHEFFIELD S10

after he succumbed to pleurisy. Short of bunks, the Germans made Ward sleep on the cold cement floor of his hut for the first few months. With the inadequate rations and cold weather, he wished he could die.

Mühlberg was under the control of the Wehrmacht. The German guards absolutely despised having air force PoWs in the camp. They regarded them as *Luftgangsters*, or criminals who bombed them from the air. The quality of guards was suspect; they were soldiers unfit for active duty. Many had lost limbs or fingers and hobbled about on legs of different length or with half a foot; others had frozen lungs during winter campaigns. Most guards had an axe to grind and could not be trusted. Trigger-happy guards did not hesitate to shoot RAF PoWs. Ward recalled that a few PoWs died when they slipped out of their barracks after curfew to scrounge coal from the storage shed. Normally, PoWs acted cautiously to avoid giving a guard a reason to shoot. Ward said that the commandant never interacted with PoWs but had earned the reputation as a "rank and file" Wehrmacht officer; he disappeared after the failed assassination attempt on Adolf Hitler in July 1944.

Russian PoWs received worse treatment than the RAF prisoners did. Denied regular allotments of food, hungry Russians stood the bodies of their deceased comrades between them during roll calls in order to collect extra allotments of food. In April 1945, the camp's liberators found eight such cadavers in one Russian PoW hut. During the summer of 1944, Bud Ward recalled a despicable killing of a Russian soldier. Several Russians were hauling a wagon of turnips into the RAF compound, and a starving Russian tucked one into his jacket. The German guard walking behind raised his rifle and shot him point-blank in the back. The bullet passed through the Russian's body and wounded an Englishman standing six feet from Ward. The Germans left the corpse to rot in the compound and no one dared to move the body.

Mühlberg's occupants avoided a forced march in the last months of the war because of the camp's northerly location. Instead, it served as a collection area for tens of thousands of other PoWs. The guard contingent knew the Russians were coming and most fled the night before the assault. A few hardcore Nazis remained behind and fought to the death. They positioned themselves in "saw-toothed" trenches, no more than three feet wide, that zigzagged outside the perimeter fence. A Cossack regiment under the command of Major Kraikov overran the camp in one of the bravest charges witnessed in modern times. When he issued the order to charge, the horses took off at a full gallop, ears tucked back, their riders leaning over to one side, holding on to the reins with one hand, and brandishing a machine gun in the other. As the horses leapt over the trenches, the Cossacks sprayed bullets down into the trench at the Germans. The battle ended very quickly, and the Russians entered the camp.

The Russian soldiers were merciless, hunting down the remaining Germans in the camp. Some Western PoWs surrounded a few of the decent Germans and saved them from a sure death. The Cossacks exacted swift revenge against those Ukrainians and Russians bearing arms for the Germans. They rounded up two of these traitors, beheaded them and had their headless corpses dragged behind horses that were whipped to make them run wildly.

The Russians exacted revenge after the war. Civilians of Mühlberg whose homes were too badly damaged moved into Stalag IVB, where there was light, stoves and a water supply. When the Red Army returned to the area after the cessation of hostilities and found German civilians living in the camp, they were incensed. They forcibly removed them, blew up every single building in the PoW compound, and destroyed the only water supply for miles around. The Russians hanged Mühlberg's Bürgermeister (mayor) for selling the land used for the camp.

Flight Sergeant H. K. "Bud" Ward

Harry Knight "Bud" Ward volunteered for service in the RCAF at the age of sixteen and trained as a rear gunner. He flew six operations in Wellingtons and thirteen in Lancaster bombers. He was taken prisoner just after his eighteenth birthday and spent nearly two years in Stalag IVB at Mühlberg in southeastern Germany. Shortages of good quality food, warmth and proper medical care during Ward's captivity have had a pronounced impact on his quality of life.

"The Biggie: to Berlin"

On 3/4 September 1943, 316 bombers assembled from all parts of England for a raid on Berlin in an operation recognized as the first "all Lancaster" raid of the Second World War. Flight Sergeant "Bud" Ward flew with the Royal Australian Air Force's 460 Squadron, in Lancaster Mk III bomber W4988, AR-Q, dubbed "Queenie." Cloud cover protected the aircraft from ack-ack and roving bands of enemy fighters for most of the journey. Just before Berlin the cloud broke. Approximately forty searchlights illuminated the sky immediately in front of Queenie and blinded the aircraft's pilot, Pilot Officer A.F. Randall. Randall initiated evasive maneuvers and ordered the bomb aimer to jettison the load to increase the bomber's maneuverability; however, the Lancaster could not break from the blue glare of the searchlights.

Two weeks before Ward's last operation, the Germans had initiated a new defensive strategy over Berlin called the "Wild Boar" formation. Instead of German fighters staying in fixed boxes, they roamed freely in search of bombers. Searchlights scanned the skies for incoming aircraft, and if they "coned" one (trained several searchlights on it), flak batteries discontinued their fire to allow the night fighters to move in and finish off the aircraft. German fighter pilots had an advantage because bomber crews experienced temporary blindness from the lights.

To reduce the intensity of the lights Flight Sergeant Ward crouched behind the armoured plating affixed to the front of his guns. He saw a Ju88 night fighter sweep in from the rear port upper with its "guns fully ablaze," rocking the

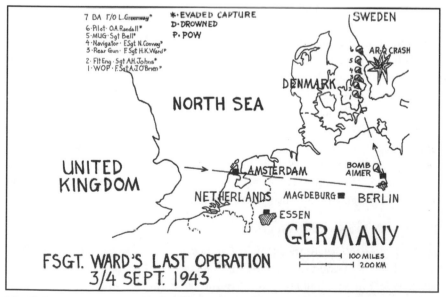

The flight plan of Bud Ward's last operation on 3/4 September 1943. His Lancaster crashed in Sweden. Each dot represents where a crew member parachuted out of his aircraft. (Reproduced from *Berlin Raids*, Martin Middlebrook, courtesy of H.K. Ward)

Lancaster with bullets and setting the outer port and starboard engines afire. The flight engineer feathered the engine propellers and managed to extinguish the fires in the engine compartments. The encounter with the Ju88 was the closest Ward came to using his guns. Like most air gunners, he never had an opportunity to fire his weapons in anger.

When Pilot Officer Randall issued the order to bail out over Berlin, the bomb aimer, Flight Lieutenant Lindsay G. Greenaway of Sydney, New South Wales, made a hasty exit through the escape hatch. Ward learned of Greenaway's fate in 1945: apparently, he hung from a tree in complete darkness, just inches above the ground, until morning. The remainder of the crew stayed in the Lancaster because the pilot of the German aircraft broke off his attack, presumably after he spotted the first crewman drop from the belly of the bomber, and Randall rescinded the order to bail out. In essence, Greenaway sacrificed himself for the crew. Ward believes that the Ju88 pilot was an "old timer" because he broke off when the bomber appeared to be damaged enough to have it confirmed as a kill.

Remarkably, instead of disintegrating in mid-air or burning up the Lancaster held together, and Randall flew it north toward Sweden. The flight engineer kept the aircraft aloft by harmonizing the flow of the remaining six hundred gallons of fuel to the two remaining engines and monitoring the speed of the engines to ensure they did not overheat. The navigator's true abilities shone when he guided the aircraft to the north end of the Danish island of Zealand (Sjaelland) without navigational aids. He correctly estimated that the Lancaster required an hour to reach neutral territory.

Ward's navigator maintained a bearing to Sweden, and after one hour he informed Randall that they were flying over Zealand and were about to enter Swedish air space. Randall issued a new order to bail out. Without visual verification, no one could be sure if they were about to bail out over land or water. They abandoned the aircraft moments too soon. The wireless operator and Ward jumped inland over Zealand, several miles short of Sweden. The flight engineer landed in a secluded region along the coast of Denmark, and the underground succeeded in smuggling him over to Sweden after seven or eight days. The navigator was presumed drowned in the Baltic because his body was never found. The mid upper gunner and the pilot parachuted into the ocean and were rescued by a Swedish patrol vessel and repatriated to England.

Bud Ward's Leap over Denmark

Flight Sergeant Ward jumped from the belly of the Lancaster into10/10ths cloud during blackout conditions. Though the misty sky reduced visibility to zero, he saw a wide "crimson" halo spread across the sky to the northeast several minutes later, followed by an explosion. Ward assumed he had witnessed the crash of his bomber and he learned after the war that it had crashed on the Swedish coast near Larod among several farm homes, without causing death or injury.

Remnants of Flight Sergeant Bud Ward's Lancaster, which crashed on Swedish soil after he parachuted onto the Danish island of Zealand on 4 September 1943. (Courtesy of H.K. Ward and the Swedish Air Ministry)

A Swedish official looks into the impact crater of "Q" for Queenie. (Courtesy of H.K. Ward)

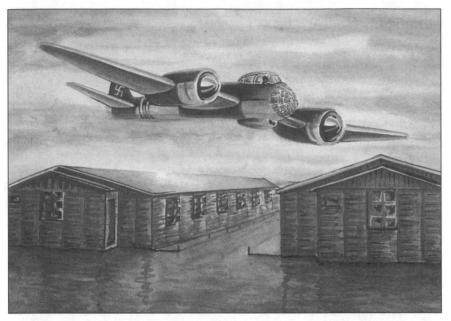

A Ju88 flying over Stalag IVB hit a downdraft and nearly crashed. The event was recorded in pen and ink in Walter Prausa's logbook. (Courtesy of W. Prausa)

A Rough Landing

Ward received no warning that he was about to land. He smashed hard into the earth, his body crumpled and his head came down hard on the iron rail of a train track. He awoke with a pounding headache that he equates with what a hockey player would feel who had suffered a debilitating concussion. Bud lifted himself up from the gravel bed and stumbled down the tracks towards a dim light. He straddled a fence, and only when his parachute became entangled in strands of barbed wire did he realize he was dragging it behind him. His blurred vision and poor balance made it difficult for him to separate the material from the wire. He eventually pulled it free and moved into the dew-soaked grass of the pasture. Ward had the presence of mind to bury the light-coloured parachute in the loose dirt of a molehill before plodding on to a barn. He towered in the doorway and stared down at a couple who were milking cows. His appearance at four in the morning, with his bruised and bloodied face, a bleeding ear and glazed eyes, petrified the couple.

Bud's spirits plunged when he learned that he had bailed out just a few miles from the Danish coast instead of in Sweden. He had landed near Hillerod on the island of Zealand. He sensed that the Danish woman wanted to assist him but she hesitated—the Germans shot anyone who assisted evaders. She had the decency to allow him to lie on a cot beside the stove in her kitchen. Ward remembers that he staggered over to the stove and burned the contents of his escape kit to prevent it from falling into German hands. He slipped back and forth into unconsciousness several times before the woman's brother-in-law, a known collaborator, returned to the house with German soldiers. A Wehrmacht sergeant roused the unconscious aviator by jabbing his Luger into his ribs. Bud barely managed to focus his eyes on the eight German soldiers standing over him. They demanded some identification but Ward had just burned everything in the stove and he had forgotten his dog tags back at his barracks in Binbrook, Lincolnshire. Unfortunately for him, a saboteur had blown up a nearby bridge the night before, and these soldiers wondered if they were staring at the perpetrator. The only remaining proof of his identity lay with his parachute, buried under one of a thousand molehills in the pasture; it had his regimental service number inscribed on the harness. Ward stumbled out to the field with his captors and watched helplessly as the soldiers moved from mound to mound, probing for the parachute with their bayonets. It looked grim for Ward until a German shouted and pulled up a bundle on the tip of his bayonet. The soldiers went wild and tore off pieces of fabric. The Wehrmacht sergeant discharged his pistol in the air to get them to stop. That worked, but the crack of the pistol fired inches from Ward's ear nearly caused his heart to stop.

Two German pilots escorted Flight Sergeant Ward to Verlossa, a cavalry base originally built for the Danish army in 1910 and converted to a Luftwaffe aerodrome in 1940. A German doctor confirmed that Ward suffered severe concussion. The commandant, Senior Hauptmann Sonntag, spoke to Ward in English and attempted to put his prisoner at ease. He explained that he had been a PoW in Britain from 1916 to 1919 after bailing out from his aircraft over France, and he respected the British for the civil treatment he had received in captivity. Sonntag indicated that he would respond in kind. He gave Ward a bed in a small room attached to his office.

The Germans moved Ward to the Danish coast and put him aboard a ferry that moved him across the Baltic Sea to the German city of Rostock. Then they would escort him by train to the Luftwaffe interrogation center in southwestern Germany. The guards placed him in an inner hold of the ferry, presumably because they did not want him to see a damaged German convoy headed for the Leningrad front. A Danish deckhand informed Ward that the RAF had pummelled the convoy the night before as it lay at anchor. The Dane smuggled him a bottle of beer and took him to a porthole to see the damage before the ship set sail for Rostock.

Ward traveled to Frankfurt on a train crowded with civilians and soldiers. His guards abandoned him temporarily at Hanover while they secured passes. An elderly German woman noticed "Canada" on Bud's shoulder flash and in her halting English told him that her son was a prisoner of war in Ontario and she was thankful that his Canadian captors treated him so well. When the woman discovered that Ward had not eaten for thirty-six hours, she fetched a bowl of asparagus soup from a military soup kitchen in the railway station. The woman spoke solemnly, "I hope my countrymen treat you as well as your countrymen have treated my son."

Dulag Luft Interrogation Center

The Germans held Ward in solitary confinement for most of his eight days at Dulag Luft, alternating the temperature in his "hotbox" between stifling hot and freezing cold. They painted the glass window in his cell to make his surroundings bleaker. His interrogators attempted to confuse Ward, using well-constructed questions, and to make him homesick. Guards outside the interrogations conversed with him in English and treated him fairly. They provided him with a towel, toothbrush, razor, and a change of underwear and made sure that he had several good meals, made from the contents of Red Cross boxes, before he left.

Shipment off to a Permanent Camp

Ward's treatment deteriorated from this point forward. He and ninety other prisoners found themselves squeezed so tightly together in a French train carriage that it was impossible to sit or move around. A small square window approximately thirty centimeters square and crisscrossed with barbed wire provided the only ventilation. Prisoners used a single pail and a small hole cut in the floor for ablutions.

The train halted once when bombs dropped by American aircraft exploded alongside the cars containing the PoWs. Humanitarian aid originated with a German conscientious objector who circulated from car to car, monitoring the general condition of the prisoners. A Jehovah's Witness, he had escaped military service by joining the Swiss Red Cross to act as their representative in this area. He still feared retribution from the Nazis if they discovered his religious persuasion.

Stalag IVB, Mühlberg

Internment at Mühlberg began miserably for Bud Ward because the arrogant Germans could not conceive losing the war in 1943. He filled in the long days by walking circuits around the soccer pitch. Continuous foot traffic wore the grass track down to the dirt; not a blade of grass could be spotted anywhere in the compound. During the evening of 30 April 1944 Bud Ward witnessed a horrific death and the injury of several of his friends as they shuffled along the circuit near him. A Ju88 aircraft swept in from the south end of the compound just above the ground with the intention of scaring the airmen walking below. A downdraft forced the aircraft to drop suddenly and the propellers on the left wing decapitated Warrant Officer Herbert Mallory of Woodstock, New Brunswick. The slipstream of the Ju88 threw Canadian Walley Massie onto the ground and the force shattered his legs. The German pilot failed to pull back quickly enough and the barbed wire on the perimeter fence caught on the belly of the aircraft. The wires sang as the aircraft stretched them skyward. Remarkably, the aircraft did not crash, it veered towards a guard tower on the right, forcing the guard to jump twenty feet to the ground below. The starboard wing sliced through the glass of the "goon box" and severed a corner post supporting the roof. The Luftwaffe pilot received a reprimand, nothing more, after an investigation was held by a court of inquiry. Ward speculates that the pilot was let off because the Luftwaffe was so short of pilots at this stage of the war. However, low-level flights over the camp were strictly prohibited after this incident. Warrant Officer Herbert Mallory's remains are interred in the Berlin War Cemetery at Charlottenburg, Germany.

PoWs Dependent on Red Cross for Survival

Rations provided the equivalent of 800 calories per day. The Germans distributed a "disgusting" two-kilogram loaf of dark German rye bread, supplemented with wood shavings, for six to eight men every three or four days. Every crumb counted. Each PoW ensured that he received his entitlement by using rulers to divide loaves into equal pieces. The PoWs received five or six *kartoffeln*, or potatoes, each day, many of which were rotten because they had been stored in huge underground pits. Prisoners kept the potato skins and spoiled food for the starving Russian soldiers who risked their lives by crawling into the RAF compound at night to retrieve any leftovers. Guards took no mercy and shot anyone who was outside of his barracks after curfew. The PoWs ate a soup disparagingly referred to as "swill," a tasteless turnip or cabbage soup prepared in a communal cookhouse. Occasionally an ox or horse head was added for flavour. Ward said that nothing was more unnerving than to have an eye stare up from the bottom of the pot!

With Red Cross parcel supplements, prisoners raised their caloric intake to 1800 calories a day, but this figure was still short of their minimum needs, especially in the colder months. Canada and the United States were the main suppliers of parcels. The Red Cross stated that the purchase, packaging and shipment of each ten pound parcel to a prisoner in Germany cost $2.50. Each Red Cross package was intended to provide enough nourishment for one man for a week. Unfortunately, in the last year of the war it was common for one parcel to be shared among five to sixteen men in a week.

The PoWs considered the Canadian Red Cross parcel superior to those produced in the United States, Britain and the rest of the Dominions. A typical Canadian Red Cross parcel included:

16 ounces of whole milk powder	8 ounces of dried prunes
16 ounces of butter	8 ounces of sugar
4 ounces of cheese	16 ounces of jam/marmalade
12 ounces of corned beef	16 ounces of Pilot biscuits

10 ounces of pork luncheon meat	1 ounce of salt and pepper
8 ounces of salmon	4 ounces of tea
4 ounces of sardines or kippers	2 ounces of soap
8 ounces of raisins	

The Germans punctured every can before handing it over and PoWs had to gorge themselves before the food spoiled. After that, they endured subsistence levels of rations until the next shipment arrived. As a consequence of these chronic shortages, PoWs' digestive tracts could not handle so much rich food in such a short period and many prisoners brought up the food they so desperately needed.

Mühlberg was located close to the Swiss frontier, and for this reason its PoWs received a steadier supply of Red Cross parcels than did prisoners in other camps. During times of desperation, especially in the last year of the war, the Germans entrusted several Canadian army personnel who had been captured at Dieppe to drive German trucks, painted white and emblazoned with red crosses, and pick up Red Cross parcels from a central depot. Armed escorts accompanied the Canadians, but Ward recalled that they were unnecessary as Red Cross supplies were so appreciated by the PoWs that nothing would be done to jeopardize the delivery of food to the camp.

Bare Essentials

The Germans issued new PoWs with a spoon, nothing more. PoWs, referred to as tin bashers, fabricated Klim and Spam cans into cups, plates, kettles and dishes. Knives were prohibited under the terms of the 1929 Geneva Convention but steel bands were ripped off rain barrels and sharpened into knives, wooden handles were cut from wood scrounged in the camp. The ingenuity of the prisoners was evident with their homemade electric kettles. A food can from a Red Cross parcel had its lid cut off and was filled with water. The water was brought to a boil by an electric filament wound from a piece of wire and laid in the bottom of the can; the filament was attached to two wires strung to light sockets. The electricity generated the heat that boiled the water. Sometimes the power draw for kettles flipped breakers or caused brownouts in the camp. Camp leaders issued directives telling the men to reduce energy consumption or the Germans would confiscate all homemade appliances. The prisoners also constructed miniature blowers, or smokeless burners, that increased the efficiency of wood- or coal-fired units. The fans were made by cutting fins into the three-inch metal bottoms of cans. They were rotated with a little wheel cranked by hand. The wheel and the fan were aligned on a frame and joined by a belt of tied-together shoelaces.

Ablutions

The only soap in the camps came in the form of two-ounce bars included in Red

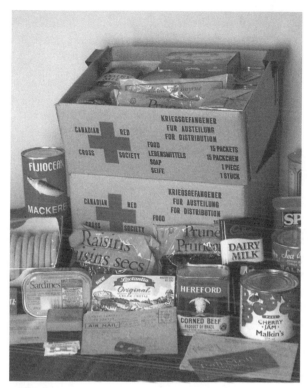

Availability of Red Cross parcels meant the difference between life and death for PoWs. (P. LaGrandeur collection)

This photograph, taken in secret, shows the drabness of Mühlberg camp. The walkway along the perimeter fence between the two compounds was referred to as "Main Street." (Courtesy of H.K. Ward)

1. Coffee/tea mug made from empty Red Cross No.1 butter can.
2. Eating/cooking plate made from empty powdered milk can.
3. Dhobie stick, a plunger apparatus to maintain suds in laundry, done in a pail if available.
4. A "blower" for boiling water; worked on blacksmith's forge principle.
5. Italian billy can for boiling water on blower.
6. First Nazi daily newspaper; strictly party line.
7. Homemade butcher knife. Vital for apportioning loaves of bread (5 or 6 portions to loaf). Usually made from steel bands on rain barrels. Illegal.
8. Army-issue black bread, chaff and all. Disgusting.
9. *Kartoffeln*, or spuds, about 6 per man per day, usually some rotten.
10. Cheese from British Red Cross parcel.
11. Swill (soup), usually nearly tasteless turnip; from communal cookhouse. Heads of cows/oxen sometimes added for flavour.
12. Electric kettle, crude but worked like a charm.
13. *Schiessen pumpen*. There being no running water or plumbing facilities, Russian prisoners regularly had to pump out large cesspools of human waste.
14. Powdered milk from Canadian Red Cross parcel. From this metal most tinsmithing originated.
15. Airmail (*Mit LuftPost*) from home. All Allied air forces mail was censored at Stalag Luft III, Sagan, by female Luftwaffe personnel.
16. Canadian Red Cross parcel, the preferred parcel of most PoWs. Contained

Cross parcels. Prisoners heated wash water in the same cauldron in which they cooked their food. Dirty clothes were agitated in the cauldron with a can nailed to a short stick. Limited supplies of wood and charcoal as well as water made it difficult to give any uniform a good soaking and rinse. Two hundred and fifty men relied on a single water source in the barrack block, and men lined up with pails to catch water dripping into a trough.

A secret photograph of Russian PoWs emptying the latrines in the Allied compound. (Courtesy of H.K. Ward)

15 major food items plus face soap (also used for laundry). Fifty cigarettes were also the norm. This was a researched, scientifically balanced food regimen, to last one week.

17. English kippers.
18. English meat & veg, from British Red Cross parcels.
19. Sentry box (goon tower) with searchlight on top; can be equipped with mounted machine guns. Sliding glass panel windows. Guards constantly patrolled the exterior perimeter as well as internal compounds. Dogs were not used within Stalag IVB proper.

If it were not for the protecting power (Switzerland) and the International Red Cross, particularly in Canada and the United States, death by starvation would have been the lot of PoWs. The conditions were worsened by dreaded disease and epidemics such as typhus. Russia had refused to sign the Geneva Convention for the Protection of Prisoners of War; hence, millions of Russian prisoners were starved to death by the Germans. Signatory nations to the Geneva Convention (Canada, Australia, New Zealand) were afforded assistance from the International Red Cross.

The Germans did not issue drinking utensils, plates or cooking cutlery, other than a spoon, to the PoWs in the camps. There were no toilet facilities, no running water, basins or sinks. Prisoners might be allowed a shower on an average of once every six weeks in the communal shower house, which had a capacity of up to 250 prisoners. Everything for comfort or survival was basically manufactured by prisoners from Red Cross food containers. Being a prisoner of the Germans was a daily ongoing battle against deprivation. (Courtesy of H.K. Ward)

Six brick buildings, called *aborts* (washrooms), served all Mühlberg PoWs. Cold winds whipped through them because the Germans refused to close in windows and doors. Toilet paper was not issued, and PoWs used the German propaganda news sheets, *Völkischer Beobachter*. Each week six or seven emaciated Russians came into the compound and pumped the effluent from the holding tanks into a tank on a wagon that was hauled around by strands of barbed wire tied to the front axle. The Germans had the Russians PoWs haul the effluent out of the camp and spread it on asparagus crops grown in commercial fields surrounding the camp. Prisoners were sickened by the brutal treatment of Russian PoWs by the German guards.

Regular fumigation of the barracks failed to control infestations of vermin. The PoWs grew shaggy beards because they could not receive razor blades in a Red Cross parcel for fear they would be used as weapons. Occasionally the Germans provided flimsy blades that broke before they dulled.

The Russians Are Coming!

Liberation day came on 23 April 1945 when Russian Cossacks broke down the front gate of the camp with a tank. The Russians apologized that they had nothing to feed the PoWs because their rapid advance had left the soup kitchens in the rear echelons. The Russian cooks needed a week to catch up. The Russians permitted hungry ex-PoWs to go outside the confines of their camp each day to search for food with a stern warning to return before sundown. The Russians despised the Germans and made no attempt to differentiate between a good one and a bad one. They tried to kill one well-liked German driver on several occasions; he was shot through his wrist as he walked through the compound, and he would have been finished off if airmen PoWs had not offered themselves as human shields.

Post-war Germany

The world had changed greatly in the eighteen months since Bud Ward was shot down. Everyone wondered if the Russians really were their friends because they delayed the repatriation of ex-PoWs, even when the Americans drove trucks to Mühlberg's gate to repatriate them. Finally Ward and a dozen others defied orders to remain in the camp and headed south a week after liberation. The Red Cross had replaced their tattered air force blues with new American uniforms, and they felt confident they would not be mistaken for German soldiers. A squad of American PoWs jumped from a stand of trees and ordered them to halt. The ex-PoWs pulled their German PoW dog tags from beneath their shirts to allay the concerns of the edgy Americans. The ex-PoWs had just spotted an ominous black plume of smoke billowing in the distance and inquired about it. The Americans warned them to stay away because it was the remnants of a concentration camp named Buchenwald. American forces had torched it to contain a typhus epidemic that started in boxcars of decaying Jewish corpses, parked on the tracks outside the camp.

With the cessation of hostilities, not a single German claimed to have supported Hitler's rise to power. Many sidestepped the issue of German ethnicity by claiming they were Swiss nationals. Bud stresses that German youth were not to be judged by the deeds of their fathers and grandfathers; however, the German nation was still culpable for the crimes committed. He remains steadfast that Nazis were a disgrace to any who wore a uniform.

Lingering Effects of Malnutrition and Privations

The RAF repatriated Ward to England on 29 May 1945 after twenty months of captivity. Ward continues to suffer from the effects of deprivation and malnutrition brought on during his incarceration. Impetigo scarred him. He has Whitlow's disease, a rotting of the fingernail buds brought on by poor diet. He also suffers from Raynaud's disease, a condition where blood flow to the hands and feet is restricted because of prolonged exposure to cold and damp conditions. Pleurisy permanently scarred his lungs. Ward believes that he would have died if British army medical staff, captured in Crete, had not kept vigil over him for four weeks. The staff had the authority to dispense special Red Cross hospital parcels fortified with additional vitamins and minerals, to assist in his recovery. Pleurisy almost barred Bud Ward's entry to the RCMP in 1946. An X-ray revealed extensive scarring on the bottom of his right lung. He signed a waiver, or "Acquaintance of Claim," agreeing that he would not hold the police force accountable for any lingering effects of the lung disease.

Epilogue

In 1987 Bud and Muriel Ward were the guests of honour of the Swedish air force and the Swedish press corps. They visited the air base near the beet field where Bud's bomber had crashed and burned. They met Sten Persson who was nineteen years old when "Queenie" crashed on his farm. Persson had rummaged through the Lancaster wreckage before it was removed, and had some fun firing a machine gun that survived the crash. He kept seven rounds of .303 ball ammunition from Bud's turret because he knew "someday someone from the Lancaster crew would show up." In addition, Persson had salvaged the Lancaster's identification plate from the port fin rudder and presented them all to Bud and Muriel forty-four years later.

Bud and Muriel Ward crossed the narrow straits of the Baltic and toured the Danish farm where he had been taken prisoner, as well as the Verlossa air base where he was interrogated in 1943. Bud met the woman who had taken him into her house. Apparently, her brother-in-law disappeared at the end of the war, fate unknown; the man's twins, a son and daughter, committed suicide. War exacted a revenge even after the cessation of hostilities.

Pilot Officer Walter Prausa

Walter Prausa and his crew were still in training when they became PoWs in September 1943. Their Operational Training Unit had sent them to France on a "nickel run" to drop propaganda leaflets, when their Whitley bomber took flak and ditched in the English Channel. The five members of Prausa's crew spent eighteen months as captives in Nazi Germany, without flying a single combat operation.

Faint Hope

Initially Pilot Wally Massie of Edmonton hoped his damaged bomber would limp back to England. Instead, the engines quit after clearing the Normandy coast and the Whitley ditched in the English Channel. Mercifully, the crew survived a night on the water. A flight of British Spitfires, on their way to attack targets in France, spotted them in the life raft and rocked their wings to let them know they had radioed in to have a rescue boat dispatched. A German aircraft on its way to England also spotted the castaways and dropped marking flares around the life raft before continuing across the Channel. It became a race to see which navy would rescue the crew first. A German E-boat arrived and transported them back to France. The PoWs spent their first two days of captivity in a medieval chateau that commanded a magnificent view of the Channel. A motorcar transported the five PoWs across France and Belgium to the Luftwaffe interrogation centre at Oberursel, Germany.

Interrogation at Frankfurt

Guards at Dulag Luft put Flight Sergeant Prausa on minimum rations during his solitary confinement. Jailers used sarcasm, cynicism and intimidation to bully him. He found their veiled threats childish. The Germans determined that they knew more about the RAF than Prausa and the other trainees, and sent them to a permanent camp in Saxony, Stalag IVB, for the duration of the war.

Stalag IVB—Last Stop!

New arrivals at Mühlberg underwent delousing, had identification pictures taken, and received a single blanket, a paper mattress filled with shredded paper, and a dozen boards to hold the mattress on the bunk.

The immensity of the Mühlberg complex left Prausa awestruck. A "main street" ran down the middle of fourteen separate enclosures, including the Vorlager, guard residences, at least ten separate PoW compounds, sports facilities, convalescence huts, a French-administered hospital, and an intake centre used to process new arrivals. The camp included a tailor shop, a workshop, a mail-sorting shed, a hothouse, chapels, the "Empire" theatre, two separate coolers (prisons), and underground vegetable storage pits. As expected, the perishables rotted quickly. Russian labourers worked garden plots situated between warning wires and perimeter fences. Six-foot barbed wire fences separated each compound. For exercise, the PoWs walked the two-mile route around the camp under the watchful eye of "goons" perched in their guard boxes at two-hundred-yard intervals along the perimeter fence. Boundary lights illuminated the perimeter every fifty yards. The entire camp covered an area approximately 700 yards by 800 yards and had a capacity of up to 15,000 men. Poorly worded signs still transmitted the message that if they violated a rule, "Prisoners of War will be fired on without warning."

German rations failed to meet the basic nutritional and energy needs of PoWs. Prisoners received spoiled potatoes, turnips and cabbages and might have had a difficult time surviving without Red Cross food parcels to supplement the rations. Westerners were well off in comparison to the Russians, who received nothing from home and subsisted by rooting through refuse piles or begging for food through the barbed wire fences.

Prausa remains eternally gratefully to the Red Cross and the YMCA organizations for food shipments, as well as books, sports equipment, musical instruments and items for the camp theatre. German *Luftpost* delivered parcels from home. Strict rules prohibited families from mailing anything that crumbled or spoiled. Most bundles contained cigarettes, chocolate, sweets and hand-knitted clothing—items that were easily bartered for vegetables, bread, radio parts and items not available to PoWs.

Many PoWs believed that the Germans only bothered to observe the basic rules of the Geneva Convention Relative to the Treatment of Prisoners of War because they were afraid of retaliations against their own PoWs.

Mühlberg Camp was Highly Organized

Royal Air Force PoWs organized theatrical works, published a weekly news sheet and ran academic and technical classes. The camp included a rugby pitch, soccer field, running track, cricket ground and access to a water reservoir that doubled as a swimming hole in the summer. Fastball games and volleyball matches were popular. The British set up a Foodacco along Main Street where they could exchange cigarettes, contents of their Red Cross parcels, and items received from home for other items.

Prisoners attempted to dig out through tunnels originating beneath their huts. The Germans built PoW huts just inches above the ground, which made it easier

Crews fortunate enough to survive the ditching of their aircraft still faced insurmountable odds. They had to pull themselves out of frigid waters within minutes to avoid hypothermia. The chances of rescue were still slim because it was difficult to spot a liferaft in thousands of square miles of rough water. (Courtesy of W. Prausa)

(Courtesy of W. Prausa)

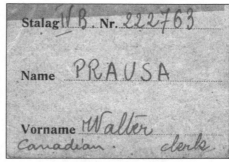

Stalag IV B . Nr. 222763

Name PRAUSA

Vorname Walter
Canadian . clerk.

Walter Prausa received this photograph and identification card on his arrival at Stalag IVB at Mühlberg. (Courtesy of W. Prausa)

THIS BOOK BELONGS TO

W. J. Prausa

Stalag IV.b

Mühlberg - on - Elbe, Saxony,

Germany.

Y.M.C.A.

This illustration is the opening page of Walter Prausa's logbook, given to him by the YMCA on his arrival at Stalag IVB. (Courtesy of W. Prausa)

The winged Goldfish is the symbol of those who survived the ditching of their aircraft. The recognition was bestowed on Walter Prausa and his crew. Survivors of a ditching applied for membership in the Goldfish Club, headquartered in England. (Courtesy of W. Prausa)

(Courtesy of W. Prausa)

Poorly worded warning signs dotted the landscape of Stalag IVB. (Courtesy of W. Prausa)

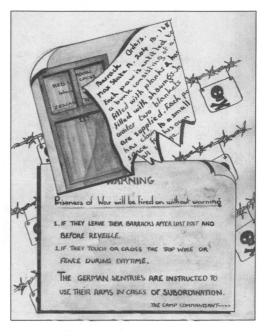

This drawing from Walter Prausa's logbook illustrates the ethnic diversity within Stalag IVB. (Courtesy of W. Prausa)

Unpainted huts, rusty barbed wire fences, the absence of grass, and deeply rutted pathways were indicative of the drabness of PoW complexes. Camps could create an immediate sense of despondency in PoWs, if they let it. (Courtesy of W. Prausa)

ITEM	Gr per Man	MONDAY	TUESDAY	WEDNESDAY	THURSDAY	FRIDAY	SATURDAY	SUNDAY
Meat Fresh or Tinned		25	30		30	35	30	40
Fish Paste	250							100/3
Brawn				60/30				
Cooking Fat	68	10	10	10	10	8	10	10
Potatoes	2750	450	450		450	450	450	500
Sauerkraut	225							225
Turnips	2400		800		800		800	
Dried Veg	50	50						
Oats	75			75				
Peas Pea Flour	150					150		
Rye Flour	76	76						
Margarine	150	30	20	20	20	20	20	20
Coffee-Sub	17.5		6		5.5		6	
Cheese	46.8	46.8						
Bread	2125	325	300	300	300	300	300	300
Sugar	175	25	25	25	25	25	25	25
Tea-Sub	7	1.75		1.75		1.75		1.75
Jam	175							
Salt	105	15	15	15	15	15	15	15

RATION SCHEDULE For Week Ending Feb. 18, 1945.

This chart represents Walter Prausa's food allotment for one week in February 1945. The types of food given are listed in grams. (Courtesy of W. Prausa)

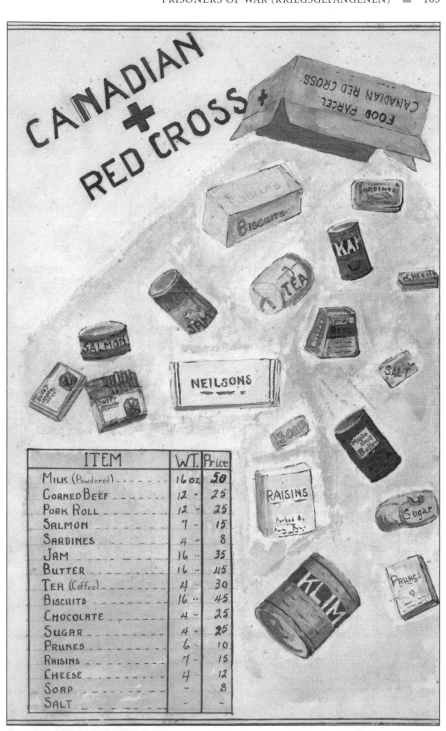

(Courtesy of W. Prausa)

for diggers to tunnel without detection. Later the Germans raised new barracks two feet above ground level to make tunnelling activities easy to monitor. They had built the Mühlberg compound over a bed of sand to discourage tunnelling. Innovative diggers shored tunnels with bed boards. One excavation eclipsed all others. In the northwest corner of "C" Compound, it originated in a building that doubled as the library and barbershop. The tunnel exceeded one hundred and fifty feet, running underneath Guard Tower No.3 on the perimeter fence, alongside the rifle range, and into a farmer's field. The Germans discovered the operation by accident when an ox's hoof broke through a section of the tunnel, in the farmer's field outside. The Germans used effluent from the aborts to backfill the tunnel.

Mock "Shoot Up" over RAF Compound Causes Death and Injury

German pilots from a nearby Luftwaffe base regularly "shot up" the camp. One hotshot German pilot made a low-level pass over the RAF compound and claimed the life of one Canadian and injuring three others. The Ju88's propeller injured Walley Massie, Walter Prausa's pilot, who spent months convalescing in a Berlin hospital.

The placement of two or three hundred Polish women in the compound of Stalag IVB's transit camp created quite a stir among the men of Mühlberg. Subdued during the Polish Revolt of 1 August to 2 October 1944, these women were sent to Mühlberg to await deportation to concentration and death camps. They arrived at Stalag IVB with furs and fashionable clothing; some appeared stunning. The men could smell their perfume everywhere. By the time the Germans shipped them off, these women were shells of their former selves.

This June 1945 news account gives a detailed description of the flyover that resulted in the death of one Canadian and injuries to three other PoWs. (Courtesy of W. Prausa)

War Prisoners Hurt by Plane

BOURNEMOUTH Eng., June 7 (CP)—A bomber command crew who were shot down in their first trip over enemy territory—a leaflet dropping mission over France —in September, 1943, have arrived safely at this R.C.A.F. returned prisoner-of-war centre after being liberated from a German prison camp.

And the crew including WO1's W. W. Massie of Edmonton, pilot; Walter Prausa of Edmonton, navigator; Thomas Mackay, Victoria, rear gunner, had stories to tell.

LANDED IN CHANNEL

Their big Whitley was so badly damaged by flak on their first mission they had to ditch in the Channel just off the French coast. German planes found them next day and formed an umbrella above until Nazi launches came out to pick them up.

The Canadian crew remained together through their interrogation and through prison camp. They were at Muhlberg together when the camp was overrun by the Russians. After their liberation they quickly made their way through the American lines and were flown back to England.

STILL HAS LIMP

Massie still has a limp as the result of an incident near Muhlberg. The cocksure Nazi pilots training near the camp took pleasure in "beating up" the prisoner-of-war cages by flying just a few feet off the ground.

Massie, walking with another unidentified Canadian airman across the camp, dived as a German plane zoomed down at them. Massie's friend was killed by the spinning prop and Massie has his leg broken in five places when struck by the tail of the low-flying German plane as he fell flat.

Massie and the rest of the crew have only one regret—they never met that German pilot.

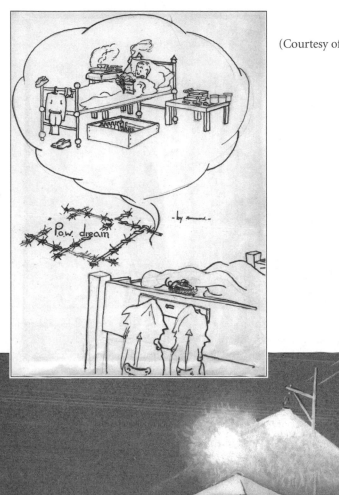

(Courtesy of W. Prausa)

Stille Nacht, Germany. The light over the guard tower illuminates the ice crystals in the air and highlights the hoarfrost of a cold night in Germany, a rare glimpse of nature's beauty in a prison camp. For Canadians, the frigid temperatures, ice and snow reminded them of home. (Courtesy W. Prausa)

The day the Russians rolled in. Liberation Day at Stalag IVB, 23 April 1945. Left to right: Regimental Sergeant-Major J. Smith, senior British Army NCO; Cossack Army Major Kriakov; and RCAF Warrant Officer I J.W. "Snowshoes" Meyers, R59567, Man of Confidence. (Courtesy of H.K. Ward)

End of the War

After the camp's liberation in April 1945, disgruntled PoWs, including Prausa, broke camp, headed west and found American ground troops at Leipzig. After a year and a half in captivity, Walter Prausa returned to England.

Stalag VIIIB Lamsdorf
(Renamed Stalag 344)

Lamsdorf served as a PoW camp for three conflicts: the Franco-Prussian War of 1870–71, and the First and Second World Wars. At the outbreak of the Second World War the Germans designated Lamsdorf for Polish soldiers and then added British and Dominion PoWs in 1940. They constructed an annex in 1941, Stalag VIIIF, for Red Army PoWs captured on the eastern front. Lamsdorf contained separate compounds for British Army, Canadian Army, Royal Air Force, Royal Australian Air Force, and Indian, Palestinian and British Army service personnel, as well as separate compounds for various Eastern European conscript labourers. The Germans changed Stalag Luft VIIIB's name to Stalag 344 when Stalags 318, VIIIF and VIIID (Teschen) were united under one administration after June 1943. The Central Prisoner of War Museum erected at Lamsdorf, renamed Lambinowice after the war, claims that 300,000 PoWs were interned there over the course of the war, comprising 200,000 Red Army soldiers and about 100,000 service personnel from western nations, including members of the RAF and RCAF. Their records suggest that 40,000 Soviet prisoners died during that period and were buried in mass graves.

Lamsdorf sat between Breslau and Krakow in what is now Poland. Because the Yugoslav and Czech borders were in close proximity, Lamsdorf escapees generally attempted to move south to join partisans in Yugoslavia or Czech resistance forces. The Luftwaffe segregated the RAF in a high security compound, and the hands of 1000 airmen were bound for eighteen months in retaliation for the Dieppe raid. These airmen would swap identities with British Army soldiers just to get outside of the RAF compound, and the army PoWs agreed to exchanges to get a break from the grind of the labour battalions.

Cecil Loughlin, Donald Hall, Hank Bertrand, Jack Patterson and Robert Thompson were Lamsdorf prisoners of war. Hall, Bertrand and Patterson swapped identities with British Tommies so they could volunteer in work battalions and escape, and they worked in different regions under assumed identities for periods of up to two years. Hall and Bertrand returned to Lamsdorf in late 1944. Patterson worked at an Auschwitz annex for over two years and never returned; he joined the exodus of Allied PoWs who were force-marched away from the Russians in January 1945. A chance encounter with a German doctor probably saved his life when a serious foot infection set in. The doctor pulled Patterson from the line and placed him in a Czech hospital for a month's convalescence. Bertrand broke off from the Lamsdorf column at Görlitz and assumed the identity of a deceased Italian. The Germans "repatriated" him to

Italy with 500 Italian conscripts. Robert Thompson spent two months at an *Oflag* near Eichstätt, before the Germans evacuated officers to the Munich area. Cecil Loughlin and Donald Hall survived the full 500-mile march from Lamsdorf to Cologne, where Americans forces liberated them in mid-April 1945.

The binding and shackling of their hands for a year and a half added a dimension of misery for these prisoners that was not experienced by PoWs in other Stalags. It prevented the Lamsdorf PoWs from engaging in recreation activities, writing letters home or even performing the most basic activities, such as adding extra layers of clothing when it was cold or using the latrine. To add to their misery, the Germans prohibited PoWs from lying on their bunks during the day. Anyone caught breaking rules faced menial but degrading punishments.

Flight Sergeant Donald Hall

Flight Sergeant Donald Hall's Christmas Day arrival in Liverpool coincided with some of the darkest days in Bomber Command history. Bomber Command's value as a strategic force was repeatedly challenged by the Royal Navy and the British Army because they wanted bombers to support their operations instead of flying operations to Germany and the continent. Sir Dudley Pound, Chief of Naval Staff, argued that England might fall without aerial patrols for German U-boats and surface vessels; the Army needed more bombers in North Africa and India. Fortunately for Bomber Command, Sir Arthur Harris became its new Air Marshall on 22 February 1942. He believed that Bomber Command best served England's interests by bombing the industrial centres of Germany because these operations would deprive all branches of the German war machine of resources. He believed that an aerial war would lead to the defeat of the Third Reich and he refused to cave in to the demands of the Admiralty and General Staff (Barker 1965, 25–30) Horrendous losses forced "Bomber" Harris to alter his tactics; he halted daylight operations in favour of night bombing. The RAF incorporated "Gee" technology and experimented with bombing by moonlight and saturation bombing to improve their accuracy during night operations. Losses remained high and, in reality, had little effect on the course of the war. However, the strikes into the German heartland boosted

British morale when the war still could have gone either way. Donald Hall served in Bomber Command during the early months of Harris' tenure, before the Allied victories in North Africa, Stalingrad and the North Atlantic. The RAF did not accrue the effects of the air war until August 1944, after the Stettin raid. From that point of the war onward, the RAF stopped tracking the number of bomber losses incurred during each operation (Middlebrook 1974, 569).

Despite changes in tactics, the odds were against crews completing a tour of operations. Less than half of the air crew who entered the service survived. Don Hall represented the 12 percent of air crew who became PoWs. An intruder downed his aircraft during a saturation raid on Duisburg. He attributes his survival of the three exceptionally difficult years in captivity to the skills imparted by a friend named Menacham Slor, a Palestinian Jew, who demonstrated the propensity to survive desperate situations.

Hall Trains for Operations

Flight Sergeant Hall underwent initial training as a Wireless Operator/Gunner (WOG) at Dauphin, Manitoba, before transferring to England for additional wireless training and aircraft recognition courses at Cranwell. The RAF requested interested WOGs to apply for training as a bomb aimer or navigator, two new positions created by splitting the duties of the observer. Hall volunteered; he thought these courses might prove useful if a crew member was injured or killed in flight. Experienced crews sought out "spares" with additional training because these men could perform a variety of tasks aboard the aircraft.

From "Death by Moonlight" to Saturation Bombing

A new navigational technology, Gee (for "grid"), involved simultaneous transmissions of radio signals in parallel grids, from towers located every ten miles along the British Isles, across the English Channel to the continent. The observer used the signals to guide his aircraft to the general vicinity of the target. However, crews quickly realized Gee's limitations; precision bombing was impossible because the ten-mile intervals between signals contributed to a wide margin of error over the targets. To compensate, pilots descended into murderous flak to make visual confirmation of a target. Consequently the risks associated with bombing at lower altitudes offset the benefits of flying at night. In addition, the curvature of the earth limited Gee's effective range, which proved useless for targets deep in the Reich; the signal reached targets in the Ruhr, but not much further east. In its final estimation, Gee proved a marvelous navigational aid for shorter flights but did little to assist in precision bombing or to reduce aircraft losses.

The decision to send bombers out during phases of the full moon made it much easier to identify targets, but the moonlight also illuminated Allied bombers for German night fighters and flak batteries. Disastrous losses were incurred during moonlit nights and forced the British to abandon their strategy of "bombing by moonlight" in favour of saturation bombing. Don Hall's inaugural operation coincided with the RAF's first saturation bombing raid on 31 May 1942. The logic behind this new tactic involved carpeting a German city (in this case Cologne) with the bombs of 1000 aircraft. Strategists expected most bombs to fall clear of the intended targets, but they hoped that enough bombs would find their marks and inflict serious damage to property and the enemy's morale.

No amount of training or experience prepared Hall for the deafening explosions and concussions of flak bursts during that initial operation. Flak tore big holes in the fabric skin of his Wellington and knocked out one of the bomber's two engines. A raid of this magnitude caught the Germans napping, and flames consumed Cologne. Buoyed by the success of this raid, the RAF dispatched bombers on a second saturation raid to Essen the following night. Overcast conditions resulted in perilously high losses. No one foresaw the dangers associated with bombers flying through layers of fog at 11,000 feet. Moonlight that shimmered off the clouds silhouetted the bombers perfectly for German flak batteries and fighters. The same fog obscured the ground, forcing Hall's pilot to drop his bomber to 8000 feet to locate the intended target. Ultimately Hall released the bomb load on the railway marshalling yards, an equally important target.

Conversion Training to a Heavy Bomber

Donald Hall underwent conversion training to the four-engine Halifax bomber in June 1942. Trainees, like himself, flew over the North Sea to search for bomber crews who had "ditched" in the ocean on the way back from raids over Europe. These trainees rarely expected to find anyone alive because most men froze to death before search operations commenced. Sadly, chances of spotting a small yellow dinghy in heavy waves were nil.

Re-assigned to 158 Squadron RAF

Hall was re-assigned to 158 Squadron RAF, which was deployed to targets near Duisburg on 25 July 1942. A Messerschmitt 110 opened up on his Halifax after searchlights coned it. The attack killed the mid-upper gunner, George Collins. The pilot jettisoned the bombs and feathered the damaged propellers of the two starboard engines. The extra burden placed on the two port engines cause them to overheat and seize. The crew bailed out over Holland and became prisoners. Don Hall had seen just seven weeks of service in Bomber Command.

Life as a PoW

Hall began his incarceration at the stage of the war when the Germans believed they would win. He assumes that most Germans did not intentionally abuse PoWs, but they did nothing to change harsh treatment and conditions. His

Nineteen-year-old Don Hall standing beside the Wellington bomber in which he flew during the 1000-aircraft raid on Cologne in May 1942. (Courtesy of D. Hall)

At Pershore Aerodrome before take-off on the RAF's first 1000-bomber raid to Cologne. L to r: Jack Patterson, Observer, RCAF; Geoff Porter, Pilot, RAF; Frank Linklater, Wireless Operator, RCAF; Don Hall, Bomb Aimer, RCAF. (Courtesy of D. Hall)

relocation from the interrogation centre at Oberursal, in the west to Lamsdorf in southeast of Germany indicated he would be in for a difficult incarceration. The Germans crowded Hall and fifty other captives into an unventilated train carriage, stenciled on the exterior wall with "40 hommes ou 8 chevaux" (40 men or 8 horses). Prisoners drank from a communal water pail and received a link of sausage and a bread ration once a day. Trains stopped twice daily for prisoners to relieve themselves along the track bed.

The trainload of PoWs arrived in Lamsdorf, the largest prison camp in the Reich. At its peak, its population crested 25,000 men. Camp administrators segregated prisoners of many nationalities, including conscript labour and PoWs, into different compounds. British soldiers rounded up at Dunkirk in 1940, Australian and New Zealand troops captured in Greece and Crete in 1941, and Canadians from Dieppe comprised most of Lamsdorf's army prisoners. The Germans squeezed roughly 1000 RAF PoWs into an airmen's compound where overcrowding, chronic shortages and uncleanliness affected everyone's health and morale. Wind whistled through the forty-hole communal toilets, diseased rats ran amok and effluent remained untreated in tanks for a week at a time. Guards extinguished all lights from a central panel each night at 9:00 p.m. and locked down all shutters over the barracks windows. Any man who ventured from his hut after curfew risked being shot on the spot. The PoWs wasted tedious hours in darkness and shivered the winters away in their uninsulated and unheated clapboard huts. Cement floors chilled the huts' occupants to the bone, and PoWs could not keep ahead of the mud and dirt tracked in by boots. The rustling of two hundred men in one barrack made a restful sleep nearly impossible. Hall welcomed a pair of pajamas sent from home because they protected him from the itch of woolen blankets; they also allowed him to trap fleas next to his skin and crack them between his fingernails. Despite periodic fumigation of the barracks, pestilence controlled the camp.

Every day, guards escorted two men from each hut to scrounge for deadfall or chop out stumps outside the wire but they were limited to what they could carry back. As the war dragged on, wood parties hiked further and further from the Lamsdorf compound to recover wood, a daunting task considering the camp needed fuel for 25,000 men.

If the men were not on starvation rations, they were close to it. Few drank the mint tea served at breakfast as it made many men nauseous on their empty stomachs. At noon each man received an allotment of six ounces of soup. In winter the soup was invariably turnip thickened with an occasional bit of horsemeat; some suspected that the cooks threw in the odd rat as well. In summer the soup tasted more palatable because PoWs could grow vegetables. An occasional serving of bland oatmeal porridge proved a welcome change. The British said they preferred the turnip soup to the fish-head soup or the unpalatable "fish cheese" served up in the winter of 1941–42. Rye bread supplemented with sawdust, a medium-sized potato, a dab of margarine and a bit of sausage rounded out the afternoon meal. Red Cross parcels arrived regularly in summer but less frequently in winter, especially after the German military prioritized the use of trains for moving troops to the Russian front instead of delivering food to unimportant PoWs. Over time, some hungry prisoners lacked the stamina to walk around the perimeter and exhibited the classic symptoms of malnutrition. Men attempted to ease the discomfort of inflammation and open sores (chilblains) on their feet by standing barefoot in the snow; several succumbed to pneumonia. In the spring of 1943, Red Cross parcels and mail from home resumed to former levels.

Enterprising British PoWs set up small exchanges and kept a percentage of the goods in exchange for their services. Germans supported the racket because they wanted cigarettes, coffee and chocolate from the Red Cross parcels, as well as the woolen items sent to PoWs from Canada and England. In exchange they surreptitiously provided razor blades, army forks, spoons, the occasional good butcher knife, some articles of clothing, books, radio parts and other contraband.

Hardships

Don Hall's arrival in Lamsdorf coincided with the arrival of the first Dieppe PoWs. This period is remembered as one of the darker times for Allied PoWs in the Second World War. As punishment for the Dieppe raid of August 1942, guards tied the wrists of 1000 RAF PoWs from seven in the morning to seven at night, every day for over a year. Prisoners, including Hall, had the twine removed at noon to eat and relieve themselves, and then were re-bound until evening. Twine frequently cut into the skin and limited circulation when tied too tightly. Fortunately the German officers empathized with the plight of the PoWs and loosened the twine, as necessary. However, the intent of the treatment was to punish, and the Germans made life intolerable in other ways. They refused the men permission to sit or lie on their bunks during the day. The days passed slowly because the binding of wrists prohibited them from engaging in most activities—cards, ball or writing. Hall thought that the guards would fail to notice if he removed the twine. He was caught on a few occasions and they retaliated by leaning him face first into a wall, with hands bound behind his back, for a couple of hours at a time. A few of these episodes achieved the desired effect. Prisoners had little to do; walking was out of the question as they could not put on their coats. Winter winds, rain, snow and mud forced most prisoners to remain in their freezing barracks.

Hall remembered Christmas Day 1942 because the Germans left everyone's hands untied for the day. An RAF chorus thought they could lift PoWs' spirits by walking through the barracks, singing carols. The carollers were well intentioned but they created the exact opposite effect: the men became even more homesick and despondent as they thought of families, food and warm homes. In preparation for the Yuletide, Kriegies put aside precious portions of their meagre rations in the preceding weeks, just to enjoy a larger than usual meal. The Germans supplemented regular rations with a thicker soup, a few extra potatoes and a single link of sausage per man on Christmas. They returned to the usual routine the following morning, including the binding of the hands.

New Year's Day 1943 brought a major change to the camp when the Germans replaced the twine with handcuffs. The shackling seems as bad as tying the wrists, but the change actually improved the conditions under which PoWs lived. Prisoners fashioned homemade keys and removed their shackles when the guards left their barracks.

Hall grew accustomed to most of the hardships of camp life except the constant hunger that gnawed in his belly. Making the effort to spread the contents of a Red Cross food parcel over an entire week took willpower, and no one was above gorging himself on an entire box in one sitting. After downing the box of food, one subsisted on German rations until the next disbursement of food parcels.

Swap Over and Escape

Air Force PoWs were confined to the RAF compound. The Germans had a twisted sense of reality because they believed an airman was more inclined to escape than his army counterpart. Hall wanted a break from the monotony of shackling and inactivity and chose to swap his identity with a British soldier who was permitted to work outside of the camp. It was easy to find someone with whom to switch because most soldiers looked forward to doing nothing, even if it meant having their hands tied or chained. Don Hall and two buddies found three British privates willing to swap identities. Hall assumed the identity of a Scotsman who bore little resemblance to him. Luckily, overworked guards paid little attention to anyone. The three swap-overs melded in with a work party of fifty to sixty prisoners assigned to a mine near Gogolin. One of Hall's friends returned to the RAF compound almost immediately because of a bout of appendicitis. Hall and another Canadian, Johnny Kormylo, waited for an opportunity to escape the labour gang. Kormylo dyed pajama tops and threadbare army pants to pass them off as civilian clothing. The pair hid chocolate and biscuits in the quarry and planned to take them when an opportunity to escape came to fruition.

The heavy labour in the mines made the men desperately hungry. One older Yorkshire PoW risked his life by killing a goose grazing in a nearby field. He intended to smuggle the carcass into the camp under his shirt and cook it up. After he killed the bird, he sized up the pitifully thin carcass and decided his prize did not warrant the risk of having it found in his possession. Kormylo and Hall picked it up, concealed it in a pail and carried it to their barracks at the end of the shift. After plucking it, they threw it into an abort when they discovered that the bird was more starved than they were!

In spite of the hardships, Hall and Kormylo found the work in the mine preferable to confinement in the RAF compound. Information provided by British PoWs who had laboured in the pit over the previous winter warned the Canadians about the upcoming difficulties. Hall and Kormylo left the quarry by scaling a rock face of the quarry, out of the view of the young guard, who was almost immobilized because his lungs had frozen on the Russian front. They covered their uniforms with their other clothes, ascended the perilously steep wall and set out in a southeastern direction toward Krakow where Kormylo believed he had contacts. After a few days of relatively uneventful walking to the east, they found the Polish-German border. It was marked with a simple concrete marker emblazoned with a "D" for Deutschland on one side and a "P" for Poland on the opposite. The Germans had trimmed back their underbrush, while the Polish countryside remained in a natural state.

After several days on the run, a chance encounter with two forest wardens, a German and a Pole, ended their bid for freedom. Kormylo, fluent in Polish, claimed that Don was in need of a doctor, but eventually he acknowledged they were British escapees when they could not produce travel documents. Hall stood by as the three men argued with each other. Later that evening Kormylo revealed that the Pole had wanted to shoot them and throw their bodies into the woods. The Pole had told the German that no one would ever know who murdered the two escapees. Fortunately, the German asserted his authority and turned the PoWs over to the Gestapo. After their return to Lamsdorf, the officer presiding over their court-martial sentenced them to a two-week stint in the cooler. Guards purged Kormylo to a more secure camp, far from the Polish frontier. His captors could not find his handcuffs when they transferred him out— Johnny Kormylo's family has them to this day.

Untold Hardship and Cruelty

Accounts of cruelty and hardship remain burned in Hall's mind. One heart-wrenching episode unfolded at a railroad siding. Wailing and crying emanated from several cattle cars filled with Ukrainian women separated from their families. Hall witnessed the flogging of old men, women and children who were marked with the Star of David. Conscript Poles marked with a "P," emaciated Ukrainians and Russians marked with "OST" and Russian PoWs toiled as forced labourers under guards who waited for the slightest provocation to kill one of them.

Don Hall, still in the British Army compound, befriended a Palestinian Jew named Menachem (Mem) Slor, after Kormylo's transfer from Lamsdorf. Slor, a volunteer in the British Army, was captured in Greece in 1941 and managed to live better than many PoWs because he bartered with everyone. Hall marveled at how Slor eked out an existence with nothing. The Palestinian conducted business in Hebrew, Arabic, and German and managed with two or three other languages. He spent hours bartering for goods, and although each deal might take a few days to complete, Slor secured enough to survive. He did not have the benefit of Red Cross parcels, or packages from home, unlike his Canadian, British and American counterparts. Slor exchanged his labour for commodities. He scrounged two scrubbing brushes and washed laundry for food and cigarettes. Slor invited Hall into his little enterprise because Don had the potential to draw in business: he had access to potential customers in the RAF and Canadian compounds. When shortages during the winter of 1943–44 caused a general deterioration of conditions among the PoW population, Slor devised another plan to ensure their survival. He and Hall raffled the contents of a Red Cross food parcel to Canadian soldiers; the currency was cigarettes. To avoid accusations of a set-up, they conducted each draw in full view of all participants in the Dieppe compound. Slor and Hall collected enough cigarettes to trade for the equivalent value of two or three parcels. No one seemed to mind the pair's activities, as gambling added a welcome escape from the humdrum routines.

The brisk laundry business elevated the pair to a position where they could refuse undesirable articles of clothing and dirty handkerchiefs. The work was not easy, especially in the winter, as the water from the tap was cold enough to freeze to the faucet. Slor heated some water with charcoal he had acquired in exchange for cigarettes. The dampness of the laundry service added a chill to the already cold rooms. The communal cooking vat served as an excellent washtub, but it retained a residue from the washing which appeared in the food. Circumstances made the pair somewhat unpopular with other hut mates.

In spring of 1944, Slor arranged for him and Don Hall to join a Jewish work party mustered from British Army prisoners. The group ended up at a mine site near Katowitz, where accommodations and food surpassed those in Lamsdorf. With some astute trading of coffee and cigarettes, Hall experienced better standards there than during any other period as a prisoner. Hall and Slor secured work above ground. Many of the PoWs worked too hard and suffered hernias, serious back strain and joint problems from carrying heavy timbers and rails. Hall avoided complaining of illness because the German midwife, who acted as the medical orderly, showed little sympathy. She made a judgment on the spot, and if she deemed the complainant well enough to work, the shirker ended up underground as punishment. The Germans treated the Jewish prisoners as well as any British PoW—unless they escaped. That was excuse enough to shoot them. The Jewish inmates orchestrated arguments amongst themselves to get out of work. If four men carried something, they would argue over who would go to what end; once underway, someone would stop to complain about shouldering too much of the load. Obviously unaccustomed to manual labour, some attempted to effect a transfer back to Lamsdorf by drinking benzene, a trick that sent their hearts racing. Others clubbed themselves with sand-filled rubber hoses in attempts to break their arms. The German midwife usually fell for the racing heart problem, but denied a PoW a reprieve for a broken arm unless it actually appeared broken.

Turned In

Don Hall and Mem Slor continued with their escape plans even after the news of the fifty murders at Sagan had reached Lamsdorf. A British officer at Katowitz feared that the Germans would shoot Hall and Slor if they escaped and, consequently, revealed Hall and Slor's identities to the Germans in a genuine belief that he was looking out for them. The Germans moved the pair to a transit camp in Czechoslovakia filled with Russians, French Foreign Legion Spaniards, some British and Italians. The Germans attempted to force Italian PoWs to fight Bolsheviks on the Russian front. Many Spaniards in the camp were Communists and threatened to slit the throat of anyone who agreed to go. Hall presumed the Germans concluded that the Italians would be a liability and sent them out to work, instead.

Hall returned to Lamsdorf after seven months to find the camp being operated differently. He found rules less rigidly enforced, and the contingent of guards, many of whom were Slavic, reduced to a skeleton crew. Russian and Ukrainian volunteers in the German army feared reprisals from the Soviets for switching allegiances. Many PoWs slipped away from Lamsdorf, but the majority stayed because they feared that they would be murdered by vengeful German civilians or Soviet troops. Negative perceptions about the Soviets gathered momentum when the camp heard that they had abandoned Polish resistance fighters during the general uprising in Warsaw. A small number of the fighters ended up in a concentration camp a few kilometers from Lamsdorf. Hall always believed that the Poles' ordeal exemplified Russian duplicity. Churchill had implored the Russians to allow the RAF to drop supplies to the beleaguered fighters of the Polish underground in Warsaw, but his plan required RAF aircraft take on fuel in Russia in order to make the return trip to England. Stalin refused to cooperate and history reveals that the Soviet forces waited for the Germans to subjugate the Polish people. The Cold War had begun, even before the war against fascism was over.

Forced March

In early 1945, PoWs evacuated Lamsdorf for destinations unknown. Despite frozen footwear, hypothermia and food shortages, they empathized with German civilians and refugees who shared the same crowded roads and privations. Hall's column arrived at Görlitz where thousands of demoralized Americans lamented after their capture at the Battle of the Bulge. An American sergeant told Hall that his unit had surrendered without firing a shot. Hall and

Slor told some Americans that the Germans did not like PoWs, especially Americans. To help them, the pair traded their short unlined British battle dress for US Army-issued parkas so the guards would treat the Americans better.

The Germans' savage contempt for Slavic and Jewish people continued to the last days of the war. Hall's column met one group of Jews lugging a wagon piled with guards, gear and supplies. The German guards whipped them mercilessly. Russian prisoners clogged the roads, and guards shot any who foraged for sugar beets in piles alongside roads. Hall recalled passing a column of Jewish women who were freezing and starving. When a PoW tossed his scarf to one woman, a guard clubbed her over the head with his rifle. Hall recalled that the SS terrorized everyone. The column passed a group of fifty immaculately dressed SS on beautiful black horses, looking for deserters to hang.

Hall and Slor wandered on to a farm and found a dozen French PoWs living comfortably without guards. They had signed a "parole" agreement with German authorities. The Frenchmen attempted to run the pair off but Slor, in his German, warned they would suffer punishment for collaboration. These French labourers softened their stance knowing the war's end was near. They provided a good meal, hot showers and a warm bed. Hall and Slor rejoined another column the following day.

The marchers fended for themselves as supplies from the Germans were not forthcoming. Men devoured potatoes roasted into charcoal to fight dysentery. Hall had access to just one sixteenth of a Red Cross parcel during the march from Lamsdorf to Cologne. He traded packets of instant coffee for morsels of bread. German civilians were more than willing to fork over food because they had not tasted coffee since the start of the war. Hall and Slor would eat half of what they gained, then barter the remainder to PoWs for their watches, rings or packets of coffee. They acquired more bread and repeated the process. They tended to a frail comrade who, like many others, did not have the skills to survive on his own.

Liberation and Repatriation

The German guards disappeared during the night of 12/13 April when they heard the rumbling of American tanks. The liberators overwhelmed the marchers with endless supplies of hot food, warm clothing, a thorough cleaning and proper accommodations. Slor mistook white bread for cake. Repatriation happened quickly. Pick-up squadrons ferried ex-PoWs to England, and Hall met his brother Bill, a veteran of thirty operations, at the Canadian reception centre at Bournemouth. Flying Officer Hall received his discharge papers from the RCAF in September 1945.

Hall's operational career spanned less than two months; he was fortunate to survive active duty and three years of captivity. The war had a lasting effect on Hall. Senseless acts of cruelty still bother him after six decades. He learned how little people needed to survive. He got on with his life after his repatriation to Canada. He received a letter from Mem Slor in the mid-1950s but he could not pen a reply at that stage of his life because he wanted to forget the war. Years later he did try to make contact with Slor, but distance and translation of letters were major obstacles to rekindling the friendship. Donald Hall passed away in May 2005 at the age of 84 and is survived by his wife, Margaret and family.

Flying Officer Robert L. Thompson

Robert Thompson bailed out over the German capital on 29 December 1943 during the phase of the air war referred to as the Battle for Berlin. Incarcerated in Lamsdorf and Eichstätt for thirteen months, he survived friendly fire from American pilots who mistook his PoW column for German infantry during the infamous forced march and, after his liberation, the fiery crash of a Dakota transport sent to repatriate ex-PoWs. Thompson's account provided a riveting description of the dangers faced by bomber crews as well as the tactics used by Bomber Command up to the end of 1943.

TACTICS

Flying "Feints" Alleviated Horrific Losses

Bomber Command implemented diversionary tactics to reduce losses in September 1943. Bombers flew "feints," that is, they changed course en route to targets and smaller bomber streams drew German defenders away from the main force. On 29 December 1943 Flight Sergeant Robert Thompson, a twenty-year-old pilot of a Canadian-built Lancaster, flew at the vanguard of a stream of 700 bombers, ten miles wide and twenty miles long, to Leipzig before diverting to Berlin. German defenders believed the primary force intended to bomb Düsseldorf, Leipzig and Magdeburg, not the capital. The diversion worked because RAF losses on that operation amounted to an impressively low 2.8 percent; only 20 of 712 bombers failed to return—11 Lancasters and 9 Halifaxes (Middlebrook 1974, 462).

Congestion over the target created numerous perils. Aircraft frequently crashed into one another or accidentally released their bombs on friendly bombers beneath them. Thompson knew when he flew close to other bombers because their slipstreams rattled his bomber. Pilots could not take evasive actions to avoid flak and tracers because of the possibility of accidentally flying into another aircraft. Sweeps by searchlights revealed how congested the target areas were. Once coned, the lights made it nearly impossible for the aircraft to escape. The beam of a searchlight, five to six feet across at its source, spread to a width of a half-mile at 20,000 feet. Crews called the searchlights "silent death." The blinding glare of the blue lights illuminated the inside of Thompson's bomber enough to read a newspaper, if he'd had the time. When searchlights lit the sky over a target, bombers circled until the beams converged on one of them and drew fire. The unlucky bomber was passed from one bank of lights to another until flak or fighters finished it off.

Crews Bombed Through Clouds to Avoid Detection

Crews trained to precision-bomb targets through 10/10ths cloud with guidance from target indicators (flares) dropped by Pathfinders. They referred to the technique of blind precision bombing as a "musical Wanganui," named after the hometown of the New Zealander who was killed while performing this tactic. Thompson marveled at the bravery of Pathfinder crews who flew as low as 6000 feet and returned several times to mark targets for successive waves of bombers.

Four-minute Bombing Windows

Execution of an operation depended on successive waves of aircraft arriving at prescribed times. Bombers usually received a twenty-minute window to complete a raid. If bombing commenced at 2300 hours, the first wave would drop its load and leave the target area within four minutes to prevent congestion. The second wave would begin its drop at 2320 and be cleared in the next four minutes. Any aircraft arriving early had to "stooge," or circle, over the area until the appointed time, a nerve-wracking ordeal.

HURDLES

A Casualty of War

The port inner engine of Thompson's Lancaster took flak near Leipzig, moments before the aircraft was due to change its bearing and head for Berlin. The Lancaster dropped 2000 feet, then stabilized on the three remaining engines. Thompson could have aborted the operation and returned to England, but instead he chose to fly on to Berlin. Just after they released their bombs over the city, flak tore through the fuselage, sliced off the bomber's rudder and knocked out the starboard outer engine.

Bail-Out Over Berlin

Thompson always tracked his bomber's progress in case his navigator was incapacitated or killed. When his bomber was hit, he devised the fastest overland route to the Baltic Sea and relayed the information over the intercom before ordering the crew out. No amount of training or experience prepared him for his last lonely moments in the cockpit. The acrid smoke that filled the aircraft necessitated him to feel his way along the fuselage to the escape hatch. He dropped out of his Lancaster from 14,000 feet. The slipstream ripped off his boots and socks when he deployed his parachute. His mind raced through a myriad places he might descend: water was probably the worst; next was an area populated with hostile civilians. He made out the horizon after several minutes and was petrified to see that he was descending into an urban area.

An all-Canadian Lancaster crew. Back row, l to r: Bob Thompson, Pilot, Windsor; Sandy Carroll, Air Gunner, Windsor; Herb Webb, Navigator, Regina; George Cooper, Flight Engineer, London, Ont. Front row, l to r: Bill Barry, Air Gunner, Toronto; Joe Maloney, Bomb Aimer, Sudbury; Bob Bilyard, Wireless Operator, London, Ont. (Courtesy of R.L. Thompson)

He crashed onto the roof of a small shed behind a house and thought civilians would be on him in seconds, but none appeared. Thompson cut pieces of silk from his parachute and bound them around his feet. He scooped the remainder into a tight bundle and buried it in the unfrozen ground of the garden along with his wings, insignia, and money, before scrambling over a fence. He chuckled as he contemplated the look on a German's face when he worked up the garden in the spring!

Evasion!

Moving undetected through enemy territory would be difficult. Thompson had landed approximately one hundred miles south of the Baltic. He wanted to make his way to a seaport because he had heard that sympathetic sea captains risked transporting evaders to neutral Sweden. They signaled their inclinations by hanging shirts and pants in a particular order on their masts. Thompson traveled by night and slept in barns or stands of trees. On one occasion he awoke to find frost outlining where he had slept. An elderly German man and a young child nearly discovered Thompson when he sought refuge in a barn. Fortunately their eyes had not yet adjusted to the low light conditions and Thompson used the moment to slip up a ladder into the hayloft and hide beneath loose straw before they spotted him. After they left, Thompson cut canvas strips from the take-up reel of a binder and tied them to his feet with his suspenders.

Captured!

Evading capture was very stressful. Thompson lost count of the days he spent on the run. He fell down a steep embankment on his third or fourth night and lay in agony on a heap of boulders. He failed to see an overhead bridge and he walked back and forth along the river for over an hour before he spotted it—right where he had taken his tumble! Instead of being angry with himself, he realized he was succumbing to the effects of exposure and exhaustion. His decision to travel by night cost him his freedom. A soldier who challenged him for being out after curfew was elated when he saw the trademark white turtleneck of a flyer. He herded Thompson to a nearby farmstead. The soldier pushed the farmer from his own house and ordered him to summon the local police after he lunged at the prisoner. After a night in a Wehrmacht cell, Thompson was taken into custody by two immaculately dressed Luftwaffe officers. Their integrity was apparent immediately. They saluted the PoW, offered him a cigarette and expressed their dismay when they learned that the guards had stolen Thompson's personal possessions. Thompson chuckled when the Luftwaffe officers chastised the army commandant for allowing the theft to occur. Soldiers scrambled to the Vorlager to retrieve his items.

The Luftwaffe officers talked cordially with Thompson during the trip to the

Templehof aerodrome, Berlin's major airfield. They even left him alone on the railway platform when they went to retrieve a ticket for the train. They laughed when Thompson remarked how casually they guarded him. "Oh no," they replied, "The civilians would have torn you apart if you had attempted to flee!" A nurse treated Thompson's bloodied and frostbitten feet before issuing thick socks and new leather boots from Luftwaffe stores. Thompson's rear gunner was locked in the adjacent cell. The only guard was a forlorn lad of sixteen whose family had died during a recent Berlin air raid. Thompson thought the four Luftwaffe guards escorting him and the rear gunner to Frankfurt were overkill until he realized the guards were not there to deter their escape but to protect them from angry civilians. Hostile citizens glared from the rubble where their houses once stood.

Interrogators Took Custody of Thompson at Dulag Luft

At Dulag Luft Thompson began solitary confinement in a stuffy, windowless, four-by-six-foot cell sealed with a steel door. Temperatures alternated between extreme heat and cold. Interrogators wanted to know about bombers, types of bombs used, strength of his bomber group, names of squadron cohorts, even the serial number of his aircraft. They interspersed serious questions with trivial questions in attempts to get him talking. Thompson pleaded ignorance to everything. In one session an exasperated interrogator retorted, "You're one dumb pilot!" and locked him up for three more days. German thoroughness amazed Thompson. They had a thick dossier on him and his squadron. They knew his home, the schools he had attended, courses he had completed, his postings and names of associates in England. They even asked him about the squadron's favourite watering hole, The Olde Oak Tree, and the nice-looking waitress who served drinks. The Germans ended the sessions abruptly when it was apparent that Thompson would not talk.

Thompson harboured no ill will towards the Germans who guarded him. He did not have a quarrel with the ordinary soldier because they experienced as much discomfort as he did. Dogged by constant hunger, the guards ate the same dark rye bread and watered down turnip soup as the PoWs. If their food allotment indicated anything, these guards were of little value to the Third Reich. One young guard wheezed with each step, his lungs having frozen on the Russian front. Others, too old or weak for duties, or invalided out, worked alongside him. Thompson assumed PoWs ate better than the guards did because their rations were supplemented with food from Red Cross parcels. He did not begrudge his captors for any of the conditions under which he existed, nor did he believe any one of them denied him a proper share. If Thompson had allowed any of this treatment to bother him, it would have destroyed him mentally. He rejoiced when guards reunited him with every member of his crew on the way to Stalag VIIIB at Lamsdorf.

INTERNMENT

Stalag XIIIB, Lamsdorf

The number of PoWs in Lamsdorf precluded any chance of decent care. The Germans failed miserably at controlling infestations, rats and the overpowering stench of ablutions. Nauseating odours permeated the barracks. Straw-filled mattresses, or palliasses, hosted millions of sand fleas that attached themselves to the inside of belts, shirts or pants—anything close to a man's skin. The parasites drove their hosts to the brink of insanity. Prisoners rose each night to turn pajamas inside out and then waited for the bugs to work their way back to resume the feeding frenzy. Barrack block walls lacked insulation and stoves stood unused, even in cold months, due to fuel shortages. The Germans ignored requests to replace broken window glass. As far as they were concerned they were adhering to the terms of the Geneva Convention since none of the subsections of the protocol stipulated anything about replacing broken windows. The PoWs eagerly awaited receipt of packages from home as the few extra items, particularly chocolate, soap or woolens, made the difference between life and death—especially when Red Cross packages arrived less frequently as the tide of the war turned.

Gestapo Treated Airmen Poorly

Thompson realized that his difficult circumstances paled beside those of a haggard and thin Canadian, named Ross Mingay, who arrived in Lamsdorf after spending ten months in Gestapo custody. Mingay was living proof of the ill treatment one could suffer if arrested by authorities other than the Luftwaffe. The Gestapo denied Mingay the rights outlined in international protocols. They withheld information of his arrest from the Red Cross, and therefore he did not receive Red Cross food parcels, medical attention and other amenities while in their custody. The RCAF had assumed that Mingay had died in action, and they paid out his life insurance to his estate. After Mingay's arrival at Lamsdorf, another five months passed before the Red Cross registrations went through. He might have starved to death if Bob Thompson had not shared his rations with him.

Escapes

Authorities at Lamsdorf punished escapees by locking them in the "cooler" for a week or two. Some PoWs wanted to be caught escaping because a few days in the cooler meant time away from the overcrowded conditions in the barracks. A PoW in solitary could just curl up on the heated, wooden floor of his punishment cell and enjoy a good novel without interruption. The guards occasionally permitted PoWs to stretch their legs and mingle with other prisoners in the cellblock as long as German officers were not present. Thompson served a stint in the cooler next to an impetuous Belgian who claimed to have escaped at least twenty-nine times. While he seemed to know everything—the German language, customs, money, train schedules and the direction home— the hapless Belgian always ended back in custody. Another PoW broke out, then turned himself in after a few days away from the camp. He said he had needed a break from the monotony of camp life.

Intentionally Spoiled Food

The Germans spoiled the contents of Red Cross food parcels by opening every can, package and container of liquid before handing them over to the PoWs. To add insult to injury the guards at Lamsdorf dumped all the food into a Red Cross box, forcing recipients to run back to their barracks at full tilt before the mixture of peanut butter, fish, corned beef, jam, butter and preserves soaked through the cardboard and fell into the dirt. After complaints about the food reached the Red Cross, the Germans stopped dumping the food into a glutinous mass but continued to puncture all cans and tear open packages. The food might have been more palatable, but it spoiled just as quickly.

Secret Radios

PoWs received news of the war's progress via hidden radios. Thompson remembered the elation when they received news of the D-Day landings in June 1944, and conversely, the terrible letdown during the Battle of the Bulge in December 1944. He recalled one particular event that boosted morale for weeks. Some PoWs played a prank on guards during a search for radio sets. They strung a long antenna between the eaves of buildings and made sure that the guards noticed the wire glistening in the sunlight. Guards in one of the goon boxes alerted the ferrets on the ground, who immediately embarked on a mission to find a radio attached to the end of the wire. They traced the wire into the abort. The Germans were impressed by how cleverly the PoWs had hidden the radio from them. One crawled down into the effluent and found the wire affixed to an empty Klim can with a simple message scrawled on a piece of paper: "Nix radio!" A chorus of hoots and catcalls greeted the German as he crawled out of the toilet!

Transfer to Eichstätt

Robert Thompson received a promotion to the rank of Flying Officer in June 1944, but the Germans delayed his transfer to an officers' camp because Allied air power had exerted itself so successfully and made it too risky to transport prisoners. Six months passed before the Germans transferred him to Oflag VIIB at Eichstätt, a camp initially established for Canadian Army officers captured during the Dieppe raid of August 1942. Thompson made the acquaintance of Lieutenant Marcel Lambert, future Member of Parliament and Speaker of the

House of Commons during the Diefenbaker years. To his chagrin, Thompson found Eichstätt's camp administration corrupted by PoW racketeers who bribed them with gifts of chocolate and cigarettes. The Germans tolerated the PoW ringleaders, who controlled the flow of goods in and out of the camp. The administrators refused to add Thompson's name to their nominal roll, a requirement for anyone wanting food. Unscrupulous racketeers stole food, sold it to the highest bidders and shared the booty with the Germans. Thompson needed to eat and circumvented the rackets by trading his allotment of cigarettes and personal possessions for food, despite death threats.

Racketeers ran Eichstätt. These petty criminals controlled the food supplies. Fortunately, most camps were too well organized to allow this practice to develop. The racketeers were invariably the only overweight men in the camp. (From *Handle with Care*, courtesy of A.F. Rayment)

The Winter March

Lamsdorf officials instructed PoWs to prepare themselves for evacuation to the west in January 1945. Guards relaxed their rules and permitted PoWs to help themselves to the stockpile of Red Cross boxes. Some weighed themselves down with several boxes of food before they left. Bob's friend tied a blanket to the end of a pole and filled it with food, but the load slid off before he walked out of the front gates of Eichstätt. Thompson chose to travel light. He sewed two battle jackets together, closed off the sleeves and filled the cavity with cartons of cigarettes, and planned to barter them away for eggs, milk or vegetables along the route. Thompson knew that his comrades, weakened by months of confinement, short rations and the cold weather, would unload much of their food in a day or two, and he would pick up their discards from the side of the road.

Disaster courted the PoW column from the moment it walked through the gates of the camp. From the air, the ragtag column of PoWs resembled a formation of German soldiers. Two United States Army Air Force Mustangs and eight Thunderbolts mistook them for German soldiers and strafed the PoWs with their fifty-calibre machine guns just outside of the camp. Thompson never forgot the sound of the half-inch bullets slicing through the air, the tinkling of the empty brass shell casings as they fell from the skies, and how much they hurt after falling several hundred feet. Thompson and one German soldier huddled behind a tree as a line of bullets snapped through the snow towards them. Thompson pulled his head back in time, but the German kept looking and his head exploded. Each of the eight Thunderbolts took its turn dropping five-hundred-pound bombs on the marchers. The survivors broke for the relative safety of the camp compound, and contemplated their next move. The guards agreed to the PoWs' suggestions to travel by night. The PoWs cut the letters P-O-W from white bedsheets and planned to wave them at aircraft to ward off further attacks.

Witness to the Awesome Firepower of the American Army

Munich became the staging area for over 165,000 PoWs, including more than 30 Russian generals. Rumours circulated among the PoWs that the Germans also had British Prime Minister Winston Churchill's son-in-law there. Senior PoW officers worked closely with German commanders to avert needless casualties. General George Patton's Third Army moved into the area, and "Old Blood and Guts" demanded the unconditional surrender of all German troops in the region by 0900 hours the following day. With the war winding down, Patton too wanted to avoid casualties. German commanders declined to surrender, and a battle unfolded just outside the PoW holding area. Contrary to orders, Thompson and hundreds of other PoWs climbed on top of buildings and walls to view the fight on the plains in front of them. At the appointed hour American tanks crested hills, followed by infantry and reinforced by howitzers. Aircraft pummelled Wehrmacht defences. Thompson thought, "If a ship comes down the river, I've seen the whole war!" Tanks from Patton's army broke away from the main attack force and rolled over the fences encircling PoW encampments. General Patton took a few moments to address the men. Even though he had liberated many concentration camps in the preceding few weeks, he expressed his shock and exhibited an uncharacteristic fury over the deplorable conditions endured by these PoWs, who were supposedly protected by the Geneva Convention.

Liberation Did Not Bring Relief

Their needs exceeded Patton's capacity to care for the PoWs. Officials from Supreme Headquarters Allied Expeditionary Force assembled 100 C-47 aircraft of an American pick-up squadron to begin their repatriation to England within three days. The mass evacuation of thousands of PoWs relegated safety to the back seat. During heavy rains aircraft continued to fly from fields already deeply rutted by overuse. Accidents began to happen. Thompson's overloaded C-47 crashed on take-off. It veered to the left and slammed into six other aircraft. The transport burst into flames, killing two of the twenty-eight men on board. Thompson testified at the crash inquiry. Officials determined that the crash occurred because the C-47 was overloaded by at least a thousand pounds and its liftoff was further impeded by the poor conditions. The catastrophe grounded the fleet, and the remaining PoWs traveled by truck to the French city of Reims. Thompson and his friends arrived in time to witness the signing of Germany's unconditional surrender, between Supreme Allied Commander General Dwight D. Eisenhower and the German delegation. Within a few days the RAF repatriated Robert Thompson to England.

Return to Canada

Bob and Evelyn Thompson were married upon his return to Canada. In 1946, he joined the parts department of Studebaker Corporation in Windsor, Ontario, and in 1947 began to work as a sales representative out of the Hamilton office. He received a promotion to district sales manager in 1951 and worked out of Moncton, New Brunswick until 1955, accepting orders for Studebaker cars from dealers in Nova Scotia, New Brunswick, Prince Edward Island and Newfoundland. The Thompson family then moved to St. Lambert, Quebec, where Bob became Studebaker's district manager for the province of Quebec. Studebaker merged with Packard in the mid 1950s and Bob worked out of corporate headquarters in Hamilton until 1959. He left the car company and moved to Winnipeg to direct the distribution of Mack Trucks in Western Canada. Two years later he moved to Calgary to head the local Mack Truck dealership. In 1964, Bob and his family decided Edmonton would be their home. He and Evelyn bought three stores and entered the retail sales market in marine products under the names of Garneau, Scona and Holiday Marine. Bob had been an avid golfer all his life and served on the board of directors for the Mayfair Golf and Country Club. In the 1970s he also served on the board of directors for the Edmonton Eskimos Football Club. Bob and Evelyn have three daughters, Janice, Pamela and Sharon; eight grandchildren, and two great-granddaughters. Robert Thompson passed away in February 2002.

Flying Officer Henry "Hank" Bertrand

High unemployment and limited job prospects influenced Hank Bertrand's decision to volunteer for duty in the Royal Air Force in 1938. The RAF offered Bertrand a conditional short service commission with pilot training if he could arrange his own transport to the British Isles. Though he knew war loomed on the horizon, Hank's long-term plan involved returning to the Canadian north to establish his own commercial flight service. He signed on with a British-bound Greek freighter in Vancouver that was set to depart on 5 September 1939, but the German invasion of Poland on 1 September resulted in the cancellation of all arrangements. Undeterred, Bertrand walked into the RAF recruiting centre in Vancouver, and their response to him was, "You're exactly what we need nine months from now—a rear gunner!" Bertrand hung around the docks for nearly a year before he found a vessel willing to exchange his labour for passage to England. A merchant ship, desperate for replacements when two deckhands went AWOL, agreed to take Bertrand on strength if he could ship out immediately. Within twenty-four hours he was bound for the Panama Canal, followed by stops at Jamaica and Bermuda before arriving in Halifax to join a convoy bound for Britain. The convoy followed a North Atlantic sealane to avoid U-boat wolf packs that congregated mid-ocean.

Bertrand, a prairie boy, thought that the inhospitable weather and the swells were a high price to pay to avoid the German submarines. The shores of northern Scotland were a welcome sight! The ship then followed the east coast of the British Isles and lay anchor at the port of West Hartlepool in late July 1940. Bertrand anticipated immediate release from his onboard duties but the captain had other plans for Hank—the ship had to be refitted. Following his discharge, Bertrand twice asked the captain if his obligations were over. Confident there could be no repercussions, Bertrand promptly told the overbearing sea dog to go to hell, and left the vessel.

Part I: Recruitment and Training

Bertrand arrived in England at a most opportune time. The RAF could not replace pilots quickly enough during the Battle of Britain, and recruiters displayed a genuine interest in him. Hank commenced his pilot training at Woking in December 1940. Desperately short of aircraft, the RAF rigged Tiger Moth trainers to drop eleven-pound training bombs on German troops if they stormed British beaches. The training staff took immediate notice of Bertrand's natural flying abilities and his exceptional eyesight. His training began on the Oxford, an impressive twin-engine aircraft with retractable landing gear and engine cowlings. Hank flew Avro Ansons, then converted to the Hampden bomber at the Operational Training Unit (OTU) in Upper Heyford. Trainees dubbed the base "Happy Heyford" because a day did not pass without multiple funerals for men killed in training accidents.

The entrenchment of the British class system irritated Bertrand as the Royal Air Force commissioned sons of well-connected families ahead of the best pilots because of birthright, not merit. Bertrand believes he was a casualty of the antiquated British hierarchy. After graduation parade, they left him standing on the tarmac after his blue-blooded classmates received their commissions despite inferior flying skills. Bertrand assumed that his mother's Polish origins and his father's employment with the Teamsters limited his chances for promotion. Undaunted, Bertrand looked forward to a posting with an operational squadron, and rumours had his class destined for 144 Squadron.

Service with Coastal Command

These OTU graduates went to Coastal Command at Leuchars, Scotland, to train on Hampdens that had been converted to carry a single one-ton torpedo, eighteen feet in length and twenty inches in diameter. The torpedo extended beyond the original dimensions of the bomb compartment into the rear turret, requiring the gunner to lie on his belly during operations. A formidable weapon, the torpedo could inflict serious damage on any vessel.

Flights of ten or twelve aircraft practice-dropped inert torpedoes on American lend-lease destroyers at Scapa Flow, the Royal Navy's primary base in northern Scotland. Pilots "attacked" targets from just fifty feet above the waterline. Bertrand recalled how tall the destroyers stood above the horizon as he guided his bomber toward them. After the observer released the torpedo toward the target, Bertrand dropped his Hampden another twenty or thirty feet to get below the field of fire unleashed from the ship's gun batteries. In one exercise, he flew his Hampden beside the conning tower of a British destroyer, then narrowly avoided the two 12-inch guns over the bow of the grand battleship HMS *Prince of Wales* by banking his aircraft and dropping his port wing between them. Bertrand's abilities earned him the reputation as one of the finest pilots in the squadron.

Bertrand remembered that the temperamental Hampden aircraft was incredibly difficult to fly, and many crews died before Bomber Command figured out what made the Hampdens yaw, or pitch, unexpectedly. The tail plane slid sideways and the Hampden could fall into a steep dive if the pilot kicked the rudder

Hank Bertrand's Hampden bomber, equipped with a camera in its nose, took this picture of another Hampden bomber simulating an attack on a lend-lease destroyer in the North Sea off Scapa Flow. (Courtesy H. Bertrand)

Air and ground crews of 144 Squadron. This Hampden, as well as Bertrand's, was lost over Finland to an Me109 on 11 September 1942. Note the most impressive size of the bull terrier mascot—definitely intended for a Hampden. (Courtesy of H. Bertrand)

even slightly. When the pilot depressed the pedal to the floor, the opposite wing would dip, often further than expected. The aircraft was awkward to maneuver because the centre of gravity was so far ahead. The disproportionately large side surface of the tadpole-shaped fuselage prevented sideslipping, a necessity for a pilot needing to undertake evasive action. Flying in close formation proved deadly on many occasions as unskilled pilots could not hold the twenty-foot spacing between aircraft.

Off to Murmansk

Engine trouble forced Bertrand to sit out his squadron's only patrol of the Norwegian coastline. The RAF re-assigned twenty-eight Hampdens of 144 and 455 Squadron to Arctic submarine patrol between Murmansk and Archangel because German aircraft and vessels, including the *Tirpitz,* had decimated convoy PQ17 off Norway. The convoy lost 22 of its 33 vessels, including 200 aircraft, 430 tanks, 3,350 vehicles and 100,000 tons of supplies. The Germans lost only five aircraft. A desperate bid to supply the Russians before the onset of winter forced the dispatch of a second convoy, PQ18, in early September (Moyle 1989, 44). Air and ground crews departed the Shetland Islands for a Russian air base at Vaenga to provide cover for the convoy. In the early hours of 11 September 1942, 32 Hampdens (Moyle 1989, 48) flew north, parallel to the coast of Norway, just 500 feet above the North Sea to minimize the chances of detection by German radar. Arrival in the Murmansk area was contingent on the navigators' ability to keep the aircraft on the most direct course to avoid wasting fuel. Limited to 4000 gallons of fuel and a cruising speed of 140 knots per hour, the Hampdens could reach their destination but could go no further. Bertrand recalled that James Catanach, Squadron Leader of the RAAF's 455 Squadron, dropped his bomber onto a beach along the Arctic coast because of dwindling fuel reserves. The Hampden landed relatively intact and the Germans were upon the crew before they could destroy the contents of the aircraft, including the radios and the identification friend or foe device. Catanach was later among the 50 officers murdered after the Great Escape.

Repeated malfunctions in the navigational equipment forced Bertrand to follow flame floats dropped by lead aircraft. His magnetic compass spun wildly each time he accidentally knocked the heater hose under his seat with the heel of his boot. At the Norwegian city of Trondheim, the squadron went east and climbed to a ceiling of 11,000 feet to clear mountains. Without the benefit of oxygen masks, anoxia was an ever-present danger. Icing caused the crash of one Hampden. The Hampden's thin aluminum skin and uninsulated cockpit made flying uncomfortable, to say the least. Bertrand worried that an ice build-up on the leading edges of his wings could crash his aircraft, too. Despite the dangers, the beauty of the nature could not be lost. Seventy or eighty miles off his port wing, he marveled at the array of colours dazzling across the waters of the Arctic Ocean during sunrise.

"Attack, Attack!"

Bursts of anti-aircraft fire signaled entry into Finnish airspace. The Finns, caught between two warring empires, allowed Nazi troops on their soil to help repel the Soviets. While darkness and cloud had protected the waves of bombers, the sun dissipated the cloud cover at daybreak and glistened off the Hampdens, making them easy prey for German pilots. An Me109 came at them from out of the sun. Hank's observer barked, "Enemy plane coming up quick on the port quarter!" Hank dropped his port wing after tracers sliced up the sky in front of his cockpit, but the German fighter stuck with the slower, less maneuverable Hampden. When tracers lit up the floor of the cockpit he knew he would have been dead were it not for the half-inch thick armour plate on the back of his seat. Bertrand glanced back to see a crew member crouching just behind him on the d-spar, ahead of the flames that were filling the fusclage. A 20 mm round had creased his forehead and the wound was bleeding profusely. Hank lifted his aircraft to 800 feet, then ordered the crew out. He assumed the two men in the back of the aircraft, as well as the ground crew in the belly of the aircraft, were dead already. With flames licking at his back and one hand on the control arm, Bertrand crawled through the side window of the cockpit on to the wing as the aircraft flew along the treetops, just above stalling speed. The force of the wind knocked his feet from beneath him. Hank dangled from the wiring harness attached to his leather headset, which had caught in the levers beside his seat and would not tear free! He deployed his parachute and prayed that the drag would pull him clear of the tail plane. It did, and he rolled into the tops of tall coniferous trees where he suffered his first, and only, wound of the war, a superficial scratch on his leg as he slid through the branches. Hank cut himself free from his harness and fell to the ground. As he started to run, he felt a searing pain run up his leg from his shin. The harder he ran, the more it hurt! He glanced down and saw the hammer of his revolver bouncing off his shin every time he made a stride. The revolver had fallen out of the holster and hung by its lanyard. What a relief—no serious wounds. The aircraft crashed a short distance away; its ammunition magazines, tires and pneumatic canisters of compressed air exploded in rapid succession.

Bertrand later heard that nine Hampdens had failed to reach Murmansk. Pilot Officer Dave Evans of 144 Squadron, piloting a bomber of 455 Squadron, crashed into a mountain over Sweden because of engine failure. His gunners and navigator died. Evans and the ground crew survived and walked down the peak. Swedes repatriated them to England in less than ten days. Mountain climbers discovered the wreckage of the bomber in the 1970s, with three skeletons inside (Moyle 1989, 46). Two Me109s shot down another crew near

Petsamo, Finland's northern port. Australian pilot John Bray had his Hampden shot down forty miles south of Bertrand's crash. Another flew too far north and a Hurricane, piloted by a Russian, shot it down after the Hampden's rear gunner mistakenly opened up on the fighter.

Evasion Begins

The rattle of small arms fire to the east made Bertrand realize how closely he had flown to the Russian lines. The sounds of fighters resonated from a nearby German base. He assumed that a search party had already been dispatched to search for the wreckage and survivors. Bertrand heard the shrill blast of a whistle and he rendezvoused with Wireless Operator/Gunner Ken Baker and Observer Kenneth C. Smith of Toronto. Another man refused to run; he discovered a German communications line, cut it, sat down and waited for a German repair crew to arrive and arrest him. Bertrand, Baker and Smith headed west for neutral Sweden without the benefit of maps. They trudged across tundra for five days and encountered no signs of civilization until they intersected the only north-south road in Finland. Without shelter, food or warmth they decided to approach a woodcutter working alongside the road. Startled by their sudden appearance, the logger reached for his machine gun and unleashed a salvo of bullets in their direction. A squad of German soldiers rushed from the trees and surrounded the trio. It was over—they had just become prisoners of war.

Their captors put them aboard a truck bound for a Russian PoW camp near Roumini-Rovanimi, a Finnish settlement north of the Arctic Circle. Russian officers and soldiers on the verge of death were the only prisoners in the camp. These starving souls received nothing from the outside world except tattered, brightly coloured clothing sent in by a Western philanthropic group. When Wehrmacht guards gave Bertrand, Baker and Smith the choice of staying put or moving south to a Luftwaffe-controlled camp, they jumped at the chance to leave. The PoWs traveled in the baggage compartment of a Helsinki-bound train that made several stops before reaching the Finnish capital. Curious onlookers, wanting to practise their English, received permission from guards to speak with the three prisoners. Bertrand told someone that he was originally from Rocky Mountain House, Alberta, and a local newspaper duly reported the capture of the three airmen. A Finnish family named Jackson, who had emigrated to Bertrand's hometown, maintained its subscription with the same paper. They read about Hank's fate and informed his parents of his PoW status—two months before the RCAF sent a telegram telling them the same news!

Part II: Internment at Lamsdorf

Bertrand's arrival in Lamsdorf coincided with a notorious footnote in Canadian military history: the tying of 1000 air force PoWs' hands for twelve hours a day for over a year and a half. Boredom and inactivity influenced Hank to swap his identity with a private named Dick Law, a Tommy captured at Dunkirk in 1940. Law was ten years his senior and bore no resemblance. They memorized the minutest details of each other's personal histories and felt confident that the overworked guards would fail to notice their features. Guards rarely conducted photo identifications and if they noted a discrepancy, they usually attributed differences to the growth of a beard, weight loss or aging. Bertrand attempted to inform his mother of his "swap-over" in coded letters under his assumed identity of Dick Law, because German censors read everything. Ambiguous messages confused his mother and she could not understand why a British soldier sent her mail. On the other hand, Bertrand wrote to Dick Law's parents in England and they caught on immediately.

Bertrand welcomed the change of comrades. He found the British soldiers refreshing; they maintained a positive outlook because they knew repatriation would occur in time. Career soldiers, they viewed captivity as an expected consequence of enlistment and took their loss of freedom in stride. Many had served in isolated locales during the inter-war era, and had seen action in North Africa or Crete during the war. Their resilience inspired Bertrand to accept his captivity in the same spirit. Unfortunately many were troublemakers before the war and they picked up where they left off once they fell into German hands. A group called the Glasgow Razor Gang instilled terror among fellow PoWs by slashing them with razors to get them to kowtow. A group of Canadian softball players, irritated by these hoodlums, paid homage with their baseball bats. Other cliques engaged in racketeering to the detriment of the general population.

The PoWs tried every conceivable way to escape: tunneling, hiding in garbage trucks, or disguising themselves and walking though the main gates. The Germans made an example of anyone standing too close to the wire by shooting him. Going over the perimeter fence or breaking through the wires with homemade cutters was suicide. Bertrand recalled an exception: a brazen Canadian scaled the perimeter fences in broad daylight during a baseball game. He placed a plank on the top of the fences, scrambled across it and ran for cover as guards watched the game. Though his liberty was brief, it boosted morale for weeks.

Bertrand joined a labour battalion at a synthetic oil plant where PoWs and slave labourers worked side by side. The PoWs antagonized guards by moving slowly, hiding in buildings or smoking instead of working. A few walked off the work site repeatedly without fears of repercussion, because the Germans respected the British uniform. In contrast, Jews, eastern European, and Russian slave labourers risked death if they broke rules. Hank recalled one sadistic Nazi guard who tied a Jewish inmate beneath a shower of cold water in the winter and left him there to freeze to death. Bertrand worked alongside a Rothschild whose Jewish pedigree resulted in his deportation from France. He expected to perish in the camp and asked Hank to relay word of his impending fate to English relatives. Hank memorized the man's personal details and mailed a card to an address in London on his behalf. Numerous labourers succumbed to disease and exhaustion. Bertrand assisted a British Army PoW doctor in carrying out an autopsy on a Russian cadaver whose green lungs indicated he had succumbed to a respiratory ailment. The doctor opened the chest and sliced off pieces of lung, in the same manner one cuts slices of cheese, then analyzed the tissue samples to assess the potential of an epidemic.

Every PoW experienced a roller coaster of emotions during captivity. Exhilaration and despondency wracked Bertrand each time American B-17s bombed targets in the Lamsdorf region. He looked up at those bombers and thought to himself, "You lucky guys, you'll be home in three hours and we've been stuck here for two years." Conditions deteriorated quickly and Red Cross food parcels and delivery of mail dwindled as the Allied forces tightened the juggernaut around the Reich. The PoWs realized that their situation would deteriorate even more before liberation. They kept low profiles after sadistic SS and Gestapo thugs took control of Lamsdorf in early 1944, a direct result of the mass breakout at Stalag Luft III.

Part III: Escapes

Bertrand's first escape opportunity unfolded at a paper recycling plant near Casel Hafen. Work parties walked unescorted back to their barracks after a shift, and Hank simply broke away from the group and headed for a German airfield to steal an aircraft and fly it to neutral Switzerland. After narrowly averting capture by a guard dog and handler, Bertrand stuck to roads and traveled by day in khaki coveralls, issued to him at the plant, with his army uniform underneath. He even barked "Heil Hitler," and gave the Nazi salute to passersby who, like him, seemed to salute out of necessity rather than loyalty. Hank found the base easily, but getting to an aircraft parked on the tarmac was impossible. A series of misadventures led to his being discovered in an ashbin outside one of the hangars.

The base commandant appeared unruffled by the intruder and wanted Bertrand's court-martial over quickly. Bertrand answered a few cursory questions and received seven days' solitary confinement for escaping the labour battalion. He did his time in a vacant hospital room and was to subsist on bread and water. In reality, Bertrand's confinement was anything but punitive. His guards stood outside and stomped their frozen boots on the snow while Bertrand read books, smoked cigarettes and curled up on a bed with as many blankets as he wanted. Each day a cook met Hank at the latrine with a bowl of hot food. Not all Germans were bad. On completion of his week of confinement, Bertrand underwent a physical by a British PoW doctor. Instead of giving him the green light for Lamsdorf, he diagnosed Hank with an imaginary ailment and arranged three extra weeks of clean bedding and warm food in the hospital.

Bertrand returned to the British Army compound at Lamsdorf as Dick Law and immediately volunteered to work at an aluminum smelting plant near the Yugoslav border, where he teamed up with a London gangster, named Eddie, who had been captured at Dunkirk. The pair prided themselves on their lack of productivity. Instead of shoveling ore on to a conveyor belt, they pressed the mouths of their shovels into the rubber belt until it split in half. Guards ignored Bertrand as he pushed an empty wheelbarrow about the work site. Lax security allowed him and Eddie to slip away. The Cockney's working knowledge of German made it easy for them to reach the Yugoslav border but an alert German corporal on the frontier arrested them and turned them over to the Gestapo.

Back to Lamsdorf

Guards in Lamsdorf suspected Bertrand of swapping identities and returned him to the RAF compound after a year's absence. Owing to the chronic labour shortage, the Germans finally permitted RAF personnel to work outside the camp. Bertrand immediately volunteered for work and became a one-man wrecking machine. His first duties involved collecting and cutting used timbers from railroad track beds for mineshaft shoring. Bertrand cut each timber shorter than specified, and PoWs were permitted to take the substandard timbers and use them for firewood. He poured sand into the wheel bearings of diesel locomotives parked on railway sidings. The Germans would have shot him if they had known.

Part IV: the Forced March and Repatriation Through Italy

Bertrand joined thousands of Lamsdorf PoWs for a thirteen-day forced march to Görlitz in January 1945. When the march resumed after a layover, Hank and his British swap-over, Dick Law, hid in the rafters of a hut for five days. They came down when they ran out of water, to find several hundred Russian invalids and five or six hundred tubercular Italians guarded by a handful of Germans. Bertrand and Law assumed the identities of two deceased Italian soldiers. Bertrand learned a few phrases in Italian and became the late Marco Milack, a Yugoslav conscript who had succumbed to tuberculosis a year earlier. The Germans attempted their repatriation several times but Allied bombers bottled up all rail traffic by destroying the lines between Germany and Italy. Hank was a virtual prisoner aboard the train for twenty-two days as it wound through Prague and Innsbruck. The USAAF destroyed the Inn River Bridge, the last crossing from German-held territory into Italy, which forced PoWs to row across the swift waters of the Inn River. A train was waiting on the other side to move them south through the Brenner Pass. Control of the rail system alternated between the Germans and Italians at each station. At one stop the Germans had their rifles slung over their shoulders and the Italians worked; Italian partisans guarded the German soldiers at the next. The PoWs negotiated passage from one train to another. Allied aircraft bombed every railroad yard regardless of who held it. At Bolzano Bertrand realized his days as a PoW had ended, because the only German left on the train was a hospital orderly with orders to report to the Russian front, wherever it was, after the Italians reached their destination.

When a comrade woke him early one morning with news of American patrols in the area, Bertrand ran to a nearby road and waited. He boldly blocked a jeep manned by three American soldiers and informed them he was a lone Canadian mixed among hundreds of Italians staying at the marshalling yard. As they were hardly convinced, Bertrand pulled his RAF dog tags from beneath his shirt and showed them his identification papers. The Americans waved him on to Bolzano where the Allied Armistice Commission, set up in the former German headquarters, could begin his repatriation. In the true irony of war, German troops patrolled one side of Bolzano's streets while the Allies watched them from the other. German military policemen directed traffic through main intersections. Convoys of German trucks were followed by columns of Italian partisans and Allied soldiers. Bertrand could only shake his head. He found the Armistice Commission with little difficulty, but a German sentry was guarding the entrance and he refused Bertrand entry. Bertrand circled the block and returned to discover the German sentry replaced by a British guard. An RAF group captain arranged to have Bertrand picked up at the marshalling yard and taken to an airfield the next morning. Pushed into a waiting DC3, he was startled to see German generals inside, guarded by a lone British soldier who was brandishing a Tommy gun; they were on their way to sign an armistice with the Allies. A convoy met the delegation at Florence and left Bertrand alone on the tarmac. An American correspondent emerged from a building and took him over to the base canteen. There two stone-faced military policemen took Bertrand into custody until MI9 verified his identity.

Back Home

Bertrand received his commission shortly after his repatriation to Canada. He enrolled in the Faculty of Engineering at the University of Alberta in 1946 but withdrew from studies for one term after his first year to recoup from the effects of post traumatic stress. He graduated with a degree in petroleum engineering in 1950. Hank married a childhood friend, Margaret Kony. Their careers took them to British Columbia, Alberta and the Northwest Territories. Hank regularly flew his private plane to various places in the Arctic as part of his job. They retired to their hometown of Rocky Mountain House in 1984 to the house owned by Margaret's parents. Hank is eighty-nine years young. He and Margaret remain active, enjoying home computers and visiting about the community.

Wreckage Recovered Six Decades Later

An amazing closure to the Bertrand story unfolded in April 2001. Brothers Daniel and Kevin Hunt, of England, traveled to Russia to arrange the recovery and return of Hampden P1273, fifty-eight years after it crashed. Crews recovered a flying helmet that belonged to Corporal Desforges, a member of the ground crew. Gunfire had inflicted heavy damage to the tail section and fuselage. Fire failed to destroy the identification markings, and researchers used them to locate Hank Bertrand. Their intent is to have the wreckage assembled into a permanent memorial dedicated to those who did not return.

Hank Bertrand had the honour of belonging to a squadron with an outstanding history. Hampden crews from 144 Squadron participated in 276 bombing raids, 42 mine laying operations and 6 "nickel runs" (leaflet drops) over enemy occupied Europe during the Second World War, flying a grand total of 2045 sorties with a total of 62 lost aircraft (Middlebrook and Everitt 1985, 746). The Hampdens played a crucial role in protecting Convoy PQ18. Though the Hampdens participated in just one sweep of the Arctic coastal waters, the Germans kept surface vessels, including the *Tirpitz*, away from the convoy

The wreckage of P1273, recovered in the Russian tundra in 2001. It was returned to England to be used for a memorial to those air force personnel who did not return. (Courtesy of D. and K. Hunt)

The engine recovered from P1273, Hank Bertrand's Hampden torpedo bomber. (Courtesy of D. and K. Hunt)

because they did not want to risk attacks from the torpedo squadron. While the convoy lost 13 vessels, including a tanker, a destroyer, and a minesweeper, the Germans lost 4 U-boats and 41 aircraft (Moyle 1989, 48).

Pilot Officer Cecil Loughlin

Cecil Loughlin volunteered for duty on 6 January 1941 at the age of nineteen and received his discharge from the RCAF on 30 August 1945 after four and a half years of service. Within two weeks of enlistment Loughlin, along with 2000 other "sprogs," boarded the Dutch passenger liner *Volendam*, a vessel converted to a troop transport for use between England and its dominions. He enlisted before the British Commonwealth Air Training Plan took to the skies of Canada, and received his aircrew training in the British Isles.

Transatlantic Crossing

The effects of wartime rationing created untenable conditions aboard the troop ship. The *Volendam* had completed a circuitous journey to Canada, sailing first from England to South Africa where it took on fuel, food and troops, then back to England to pick up German PoWs destined for camps throughout Canada. Loughlin and the other recruits walked off the vessel twice in protest after finding the vessel filthy and much of the food inedible. Promises to requisition fresh supplies of food persuaded men to return each time but went unfilled. To avert further disruptions the navy ordered the ship to lay anchor in the middle of Bedford Basin and remain there until departure. Disgruntled protesters received encouragement to jump overboard and swim the mile to shore to report their complaints!

The *Volendam* joined three ships and departed Halifax on 10 February 1941. A German U-boat lay in wait just off the Nova Scotia shore and sunk one escort, a Tribal class destroyer. Anxiety wracked the two thousand men aboard the *Volendam* as they watched the destroyer slip below the water. A former United States Navy destroyer, brought out of retirement under the Lend-Lease Program, served as the convoy's only protection for the transatlantic passage to the British Isles. Sprogs, assigned bunks deep in the hold, slept in the halls of the upper deck in case they needed to jump overboard. It would not have made much difference as strict rules prohibited other ships from stopping to rescue survivors of a torpedoed ship since they would be easy targets for other submarines still lurking in the area.

The Germans attempted to demoralize the British public through the voice of an English ex-patriot disparagingly referred to as Lord Haw-Haw. Over the airwaves of Europe Lord Haw-Haw broadcast the German version of the truth from Berlin in English. The German propaganda machine heralded the sinking of the Tribal class destroyer off Halifax as a "major naval victory." Lord Haw-Haw claimed that the German submarine had sunk several ships in Loughlin's convoy. The British caught up with Lord Haw-Haw after the war, convicted him of treason and hanged him for his treachery.

Early Training

Severe shortages of training aircraft deferred Cec Loughlin's aircrew training. Alternatively, the RAF sent him to train with the Royal Canadian Army, specifically the 49th (Loyal Edmonton) Regiment, to keep him physically fit and mentally alert. He commenced training in January 1942 on obsolete two-engine Hampden bombers at Cottesmore Operational Training Unit. In September Loughlin transferred to 149 Squadron for conversion training on Stirling bombers, the RAF's first heavy bomber. His training as an observer, wireless operator, gunner and aerial photographer made him a welcome addition to any crew because he could perform the duties of other men killed or injured during operations.

Loughlin's first operation, in January 1943, involved an attack on U-boat pens at Lorient, a French port on the north side of the Bay of Biscay. Radar-guided anti-aircraft batteries, assisted by searchlights, blasted away at the bomber as it approached its target. Loughlin's pilot took violent evasive actions to break from the blinding glare of the searchlights by dropping below the searchlight beam to 8000 feet. Loughlin's stomach rose up into his throat several times, and all the while he pondered how much punishment an airframe could withstand before the aircraft disintegrated. He just hung on as the pilot took his aircraft back for a second pass.

Loughlin flew in just four more flights: one to Turin, two more to the Lorient submarine pens and one to Cologne. On this last flight, flak bursts crippled the Stirling and killed the rear gunner. The pilot nursed the slow-moving bomber into French airspace where a German intruder intercepted and finished it off. Loughlin, the front and mid-upper gunners and the wireless operator safely evacuated; the pilot and the flight engineer went down in the flaming wreck.

Despite a year of service to the RAF, Cecil Loughlin did not qualify for the Air Crew Europe medal because he had lasted only six weeks in combat, well short of the mandatory ninety-day qualification period. The Luftwaffe interned Loughlin at Lamsdorf on 1 March 1943, and the Germans earmarked him as one of the 1000 RAF PoWs to be shackled, a punishment that contravened the Geneva Convention.

Escape Plans

Cec Loughlin and a friend planned an escape in early 1944 by swapping identities with two British soldiers from the army compound. They hoped to get out of the main compound in a labour battalion. The pair anticipated a rigorous evasion so they walked circuits around the soccer pitch to build up their stamina. They stockpiled non-perishable food and sewed scraps of cloth into knapsacks. All escape-related activities halted when the information of fifty murdered officers from Sagan camp reached Lamsdorf. Via radio communiqués the British High Command sent messages into the camp to discourage further breakouts. New PoWs delivered the same message. The risks associated with a breakout were too high, especially with an Allied victory in the works.

The Last Months of the War

The final chapter of Loughlin's war was written during the forced march of Lamsdorf PoWs to Görlitz, beginning 22 January 1945. Poorly conditioned men set out in knee-deep snow. Loughlin recalled that his leather shoes absorbed water and froze solid. The march became a blur after two days. Prisoners discarded blankets and possessions not essential for survival and devoured anything along the way; they would have starved to death if they had not scrounged. Men snatched cans of fresh milk from roadside stands; each man scooped out a cupful and passed the vessels through the column. Those PoWs who stopped to help a German family butcher a horse in the middle of an icy stretch of road

A Short Stirling bomber of 149 Squadron RAF. (Courtesy of MacNeill family)

received its head; the men lugged it to the next stop where they boiled up—complete with hair, teeth and eyes! Prisoners found sacks of wheat and boiled it into gruel. They should have known better than to eat cereal grains, because everyone suffered agonizing bouts of diarrhea as their digestive tracts were unaccustomed to that kind of diet. Starving men devoured remnants of frozen sugar beets disposed of by farmers who had extracted their sugar by-products. Those PoWs who were lucky enough to leave Lamsdorf free of dysentery succumbed to its effects soon enough.

They rested at Stalag VIIIA (Görlitz) after two weeks on the march. It already overflowed with PoWs. Among the incarcerated were several thousand bewildered and disoriented American soldiers taken prisoner at the Battle of the Bulge just weeks earlier. Loughlin empathized with the despondent men; in their few weeks of captivity they had not overcome their sense of helplessness because they had not been PoWs long enough to learn survival skills. Loughlin did not judge them; he assumed he acted no differently when he was first taken prisoner.

Disease, exposure and short rations took their toll. The Germans abandoned hundreds of sick and exhausted men at Görlitz when the march resumed on 8 February. Loughlin knows he would have perished alongside the road if his comrades had not put him aboard a wagon already overloaded with other weakened marchers. The presence of a British medical aid station administering typhus shots to prisoners behind German lines came as a shock. Loughlin believed the harsh conditions under which he existed were about as tough as they could get, until the Lamsdorf PoWs were locked in an abandoned brick factory with Russian soldiers at Dobeln. Initially, the air force PoWs felt revulsion as they mingled with the dirty, lousy Russians. Loathe turned to respect because they realized these Russians had no control of their sad conditions. The Russians survived without the luxury of Red Cross parcels and without the protection of the Geneva Conventions. The PoWs learned how the Russians did it: they stole anything they could get their hands on. Consequently, PoWs sat on everything they owned.

Guards pressed on with no apparent destination. The RAF PoWs joined a column of 800 British Army and 200 French prisoners bound for Zeitz. They found that the German civilians had grown weary of the exodus of PoWs through their towns because everything was in short supply. Cecil remembered the days after 9 March 1945 as the most desperate period since leaving Lamsdorf. He and several other PoWs broke from the column to search for food and if guards noticed them leaving, they did not seem to care. German field police arrested them at Eisenberg, and every prison in the area refused to take them in because they could not care for those already in their custody. The last days before capitulation were mayhem. Loughlin was among a trainload of prisoners moved to Stalag IXC at Mälhausen, Thuringia. Allied air forces bombed everything. At least PoWs had the protection of cement air raid shelters. The constant wailing of the sirens on the roof drove everyone to the brink of insanity. American P-38 Lightnings unleashed rockets and cannon fire into PoW barracks at Göttingen two weeks later. Loughlin decided that Allied aircraft posed a greater threat to his survival than the enemy did, and he risked heading out on his own for Allied troops further west. German soldiers paid no attention to him as he walked past them. A lad of nine or ten took exception and wanted to kill him, but a German police officer interceded at the last moment and returned Loughlin to Göttingen for his own protection.

The End of the War

The end of hostilities arrived quickly. German civilians accepted defeat and hung white flags from their windows before American tanks could bombard the town. Tanks lobbed two shells over the town to warn the remaining defenders to lay down their weapons. Guards abandoned the camp, but freedom did not come as the PoWs had anticipated. War-weary prisoners, eager to show their gratitude to the Americans, found their liberators indifferent—they had already freed thousands. GIs tossed boxes of K-rations and cigarettes to PoWs without stopping. Loughlin remembers his liberation date, for it coincided with the death of President Franklin D. Roosevelt, 12 April 1945.

Last Days in Germany

For the first time in over two years, no one told PoWs what to do. Cec and a few friends took the liberty of commandeering a house from its occupants. Then an American officer backed by a squad of soldiers, with rifles at the ready, attempted to force the PoWs out. Loughlin stood fast, and the Americans grudgingly moved on.

Russian soldiers exacted a terrible revenge on the German people. Loughlin witnessed Red Army soldiers remove wounded German soldiers from their hospital beds at Salzgitter and string them from trees. The Russians would not stop the killings even when American soldiers attempted to intervene.

Repatriation began three days later. Loughlin flew to Brussels then on to Manston Airbase in England where he underwent a medical and received dental care and unlimited quantities of quality food. The most obvious effect of the war on Loughlin was the reduction of his body weight from 165 to 110 pounds. The *Ile de France*, a French luxury liner, took aboard 10,000 American combat troops and just 20 RCAF ex-PoWs at Glasgow for the transatlantic voyage to New York. The ex-PoWs enjoyed three "five-course" meals per day; everyone else received two! Loughlin thought it peculiar that the US Army kept him and the other ex-PoWs under armed guard from the time they docked in New York until their arrival in Montreal, despite verification of their identities by British MI9. The RCAF commissioned Cecil with the rank of Pilot Officer and then discharged him in August 1945.

Reflection

Cec Loughlin feels no bitterness or animosity toward the German people. They treated him as well as they could; most suffered as much as PoWs in the latter stages of the war. The war created hardships for everyone, and the German people generously shared food and shelter during the forced march, when possible. Loughlin approved of the arrest and convictions of those members of the Gestapo, SS and Hitler Youth who had committed horrific crimes against civilians and service personnel. Time and time again, Loughlin witnessed senseless acts of brutality. The despicable treatment of 200 Jewish women from Romania continues to haunt him. SS guards beat them mercilessly when airmen gave them scarves and bits of food. He doubts any of them survived to see the end of the war, because they were making their way to the Buchenwald concentration camp for liquidation. The airmen passed hundreds of Jewish men on the verge of death.

Cec Loughlin traveled to Lincoln, England, in 1990 and 1992 for reunions with his surviving crewmates: a Rhodesian, a South African and three Englishmen. In his own words, Loughlin summed up his ordeal: "To come out alive was our main objective. Mission accomplished."

Flying Officer John Patterson

Flying Officer John "Jack" Patterson, RCAF No. J966166, is thought to be the only Canadian airman sent to Auschwitz. From November 1943 to 10 January

1945, Patterson laboured alongside three hundred British Army PoWs in a satellite of the extermination camp. Surprisingly, the standard of care received at Auschwitz exceeded the standard of care he experienced at Lamsdorf. Nonetheless, three years of captivity exacted a toll on Patterson's health, and he has endured a lifetime of debilitating effects resulting from poor diet, exposure and disease. Patterson realized he was fortunate to have survived captivity and he has cherished every day of his life since the war.

Six Operations in Bomber Command

Jack Patterson participated in the RAF's first two 1000-aircraft raids in mid-1942, and became a PoW as a result of his sixth operation on 16/17 July1942. He parachuted out of his damaged Halifax over Holland, underwent interrogation in Frankfurt, and began internment in the RAF compound at Stalag VIIIB. Patterson arranged a swap-over with a British Army private named Sammy Crichton. He thought he might be able to escape from a work party that went outside the wire, but sixteen months passed without a single escape opportunity materializing. When the Germans called for volunteers to work elsewhere in the Reich, he jumped at the opportunity.

Auschwitz

Patterson would have refused the change if he had known his destination would be the notorious Auschwitz-Birkenau extermination camp, a collection of compounds dispersed through an area of approximately thirty square kilometers. His labour battalion comprised a mixture of workers of many nationalities. Patterson quickly found that his German guards demonstrated a certain respect for labourers wearing British uniform, and they left him alone if he did as he was told. The guards warned all labour conscripts to remain in their compound, except while working, to avoid being shot. From German civilians employed at the camp Patterson learned of mass exterminations conducted in other Auschwitz compounds. They told him of Nazi plans to cleanse Europe of the Jews, Slavs and Gypsies. One worker told Patterson of the barbarous execution of a trainload of Hungarian Jews who had recently arrived in the death camp; members of the *Einsatzgruppen*, or SS killing squads, had stood the condemned along the top edge of a ditch that had been excavated by a bulldozer, and then systemically machine-gunned them. Apparently, four crematoria worked overtime to extinguish evidence of the "Final Solution."

A clearly defined social order existed in Patterson's satellite camp of 7000 prisoners. The English reigned and generally avoided trouble with the guards. French prisoners, most captured during the fall of France, enjoyed a status above other nationalities in the camp but were of lower status than their British counterparts. These Frenchmen toiled in nearby factories. In exchange for their compliance, the Germans granted many of them, most of whom were still in uniform, short periods of unescorted leave to visit families in France if they worked hard. They invariably returned from their sojourns for fear of reprisals against their families. Thousands of Ukrainian peasant women performed the backbreaking labour. German political prisoners, criminals, Dutch citizens, Czechs and ethnic Poles gravitated at the bottom of the pecking order.

SS guards tormented and abused thousands of Jewish teenagers and feeble men before sending them to the gas chambers. Sympathetic British soldiers who offered Jews bowls of their watery turnip soup received stern warnings: "Leave them alone if you want us to leave you alone!" Patterson witnessed SS guards beat Jews without provocation. Wehrmacht guards treated prisoners with less contempt than did their SS counterparts, but they remained a constant threat. Interactions with Wehrmacht guards led Patterson to conclude that most were ordinary people and shared many of the same interests as he but some had well-entrenched prejudices. Many admitted to succumbing to the allure of Nazism in the interwar years, but few expressed remorse over the ill treatment of Jews. A few guards even wondered how Allied nations tolerated Jews.

Patterson preferred Auschwitz to Lamsdorf for several reasons. He ate better in the death camp. Guards in Lamsdorf viewed RAF PoWs as *Luftgangsters* and treated them with contempt, whereas at Auschwitz, guards left Patterson and the other British soldiers alone. On top of that, Patterson avoided the extra punishment inflicted on him and 1000 RAF PoWs—the binding of their wrists. Patterson hated Lamsdorf because time passed slowly; and PoWs did little except walk circuits or think about when the next Red Cross food parcels would arrive. The Germans placed the same 1000 men on short rations and withheld Red Cross food parcels during one three-month stretch. In contrast, the Germans fed the British PoWs at Auschwitz better because they needed well-fed labourers. At Auschwitz Patterson received half a Red Cross parcel per week (about five pounds of food) on top of the daily allotment of Swede (turnip) soup, a potato, a slab of dark bread and mint tea. In fact, Patterson believed he might have been one of the few PoWs to return to England heavier than when he left.

Despite constant bombardment of Auschwitz's factories by RAF and USAAF bombers from bases near Turin, Italy, Patterson still preferred Auschwitz over the hellhole of Lamsdorf. He learned how imprecise precision bombing really was. Bombs rarely hit their targets and it seemed safer to remain in factories during an attack than seek cover in the concrete shelters outside the factories. Allied air raids inadvertently claimed hundreds, if not thousands, of lives of Auschwitz inmates. Near the end of the war, a bomb missed its intended target and killed eight British PoWs in the same bunker as Patterson. He normally sat in that spot where the shell exploded but for an unknown reason he sat in another section of the shelter that night, a decision that spared his life. Included in the dead was a British Spitfire pilot who had swapped identities and gone to

Auschwitz in the same labour battalion as Patterson.

Memories of a Jewish man named Franz Irving, a teacher originally from Berlin, have haunted Patterson all of his life. He and Irving met regularly for over a year, usually over meal breaks and Patterson would slip him some of his food. Irving recounted his life history after Hitler's rise to power. The Nazis had stripped Irving of his citizenship after implementation of the Nurenberg Decrees, laws that empowered the Nazis to arrest Jews and deport them to labour camps. They separated Irving from his family before the war started, and he assumed his family had perished in a death camp long before he met Patterson. Irving shocked Patterson with his firsthand knowledge of the Holocaust. He knew that the Nazis exterminated Jewish workers too weak to work, as well as women and children upon their arrival to camps. Patterson never forgot their last meeting. With the Russian army advancing upon them from the east, Irving exhibited an uncharacteristic despondency because he knew the Germans would not let him live to see the war's end. He bitterly denounced Patterson for not doing more to save him. Patterson did his best to secure parts of a uniform and smuggle them over to Irving so he could slip back into the British Army compound with him. Unfortunately most soldiers had little kit left except the rags they wore on their backs and could spare nothing. Irving's indignation and Patterson's feeling of helplessness remain vivid in his mind.

Evacuation

The Germans force-marched British PoWs out of Auschwitz to Czechoslovakia in January 1945. Patterson fell ill with tuberculosis, pleurisy and a serious foot infection. A German doctor pulled him from the line and placed him in a hospital thirty miles from Prague, before the Wehrmacht imprisoned him in a local jail. Sympathetic Czech civilians passed food through the barred window of his cell.

Return to Canada

Jack Patterson returned to Canada suffering from the effects of three years of deprivation, malnutrition and exposure. Two years of treatment helped him beat tuberculosis. He aspired to earn a university degree, but the responsibilities of marriage and a young child prevented him from continuing his education. Jack's wife contracted tuberculosis and became very ill during her second pregnancy. He left school and returned to his pre-war job in a bank.

Patterson does not think he is a hero. He wants Canada to remember those 18,000 Canadian air force officers and NCOs who gave their lives for freedom and for Canada. One of the twelve percent of aircrew who became PoWs, Jack attributes his survival to fate. Captivity removed him from battle. Despite three years as a PoW and a lifetime of poor health, he is grateful for a second chance at life. He took the debilitating effects of tuberculosis and pleurisy in stride. He remains haunted by recurring memories of Franz Irving. The Nazis annihilated as many Jews as possible before the Reich collapsed. Thoughts of "what if" remain. Patterson did his best to help Irving but the opportunity to escape never arose. He did what he could—he shared bread with him and gave him hope.

Stalag Luft I, Barth

Stalag Luft I was located on the Baltic Sea near the German town of Barth. It opened in July 1940 to hold air force prisoners of war from the United Kingdom, the British Commonwealth, and Europeans from nations occupied by the Axis powers. The Germans closed the camp in early 1942 and moved its RAF officers and men to the newly opened camp further inland at Sagan, Stalag Luft III. Overcrowding in existing PoW camps forced the re-opening of Stalag Luft I in July 1943. The Red Cross recorded 3463 PoWs imprisoned in three compounds, North, West and South, in April 1944. At the time of the camp's liberation a year later, the PoW population totaled 7717 Americans and 1427 officers and men of Bomber Command.

North Camp was divided into three smaller compounds. North One, superior to the five remaining compounds because it was originally a site for training Hitler Youth, was outfitted with running water as well as an inside kitchen and latrine system; the others were poorly outfitted. The PoWs moved between the five compounds to take advantage of the two small sports fields. Two orchestras existed in the last year of the war, and a theatre group produced several plays. The YMCA provided PoWs with musical instruments, sports gear, art supplies and books. Education programs offered courses in the arts, humanities, sciences and mathematics.

A harsh climate, inadequate cooking and washing facilities, overcrowding and poorly heated barracks made life difficult. American intelligence reports suggested that conditions deteriorated dramatically in April 1944, shortly after the mass breakout of 76 officers from Stalag Luft III. German guards reportedly shot five PoWs inside the wire between May 1944 and March 1945 for not scrambling fast enough after the sounding of air raid sirens. Apparently, the guards had the authority to shoot PoWs who "insulted the German honour." The Americans blamed inadequate supplies of food and clothing on uncooperative camp administrators and supply problems. However, the general welfare of PoWs deteriorated rapidly as the Allies advanced from the west and the Russians advanced from the east.

Barth PoWs remained in the camp to the end, despite efforts by the German commandant to evacuate them in the forefront of the Russian advance. The Germans abandoned the camp on 30 April, and the Russians arrived at Barth on 6 May 1945.

Flying Officer William Studnik

Flying Officer William Studnik, RCAF No. J87618, became a PoW on 22 March 1944 following two attacks by an enemy aircraft. Cannon fire and bullets ripping through the fuselage of his Halifax sounded like trip hammers on a tin roof. His rear gunner, though struck by shrapnel, indicated he could continue with his duties. The five other crew members escaped the first attack unscathed. The starboard wing took the brunt of the damage: much of the landing flap was missing and fuel poured from a wing tank. The flight engineer rerouted fuel through crossover lines to prevent fuel starvation to the four engines and Studnik continued to pilot his bomber to Frankfurt. In a second attack, most likely originating from the same fighter, Studnik attempted to lose him by dropping the aircraft's starboard wing in a tight corkscrew maneuver, an evasion pattern taught to him in training. The enemy pilot must have possessed considerable combat experience because he clung to the bomber and finished it off with ease. Flying Officer Studnik watched his bomb aimer, navigator and wireless operator drop through the escape hatch. He hoped to meet the crew after the war, if not within days.

The International Red Cross reported Bill's capture a few weeks later but the fate of his six crew members remains a mystery to this day. At least three of them should have turned up in some PoW camp because they got out of the aircraft alive. Based on his experience, Studnik contends that it was entirely possible his comrades died while in military custody or at the hands of German civilians. (After sixty years, Studnik continues to harbour feelings of guilt because he survived the war and his comrades did not.)

His mistreatment began when a guard found a photograph of him in civilian clothes, which was sewn into the lining of his uniform. It was common practice for aircrew to carry passport-type pictures in the event enemy fire downed their aircraft and they evaded. Members of the underground could provide false documentation with ease, but wartime rationing and inventory controls on photographic paper and processing chemicals made the acquisition of pictures nearly impossible. Studnik's interrogators considered the possibility that he was a Special Operations Executive saboteur parachuted behind enemy lines, so they turned him over to the Gestapo. Studnik had not helped his case by removing all identifying RCAF insignia from his uniform before his capture. Interrogation sessions under the Gestapo became rough.

Parachuting Created Anxiety

Parachute training consisted of learning to snug up the harness. Practice jumps were unheard of and simulated jumps were thought to undermine morale. Studnik recalled stories of Americans who suffered broken limbs because they tensed up when they saw the ground coming. When he jumped that night, he was at an advantage because he could not see the ground. Fortunately a thick stand of lilacs cushioned his fall and he landed intact. Studnik bundled his parachute, Mae West lifejacket, cap and insignia into a ball and stuffed them beneath deadfall in a ditch. The light skiff of snow soaked his feet because his boots had slid off during his descent. The outline of his white parachute must have stood out against the night sky because a shotgun-wielding farmer appeared within minutes to arrest him. Studnik sensed the man was unaccustomed to handling a weapon, and he feared he stood a greater chance of death by an accidental shooting than out of anger. The farmer's kindly wife sensed Studnik's anxiety and put him at ease by drying his socks over the hot stove, giving him a pair of wooden clogs and feeding him before her husband took him into town.

The farmer took him before the Bürgermeister and council. They appeared as uncomfortable with Studnik as he was with them. Preconceived notions about ruthless *terrorfliegers* evaporated quickly. They searched the Canadian several times for a weapon and were incredulous that this "ferocious" man did not carry a sidearm. The awkwardness of the situation dissipated when someone pulled a bottle of schnapps from a drawer. Studnik shared his cigarettes and the group drank until the arrival of a Luftwaffe sergeant and a pair of riflemen.

Passage to Dulag Luft

Studnik feared for his life every inch of his journey to the interrogation centre at Dulag Luft, because German civilians wore their contempt on their sleeves. Hostile throngs who had lost everything in air raids could have easily overpowered his escorts and lynched him. Fear consumed him when his protectors left him unattended on a rail platform while they secured tickets. Hitler Youth surrounded him and stared him down with deathly cold eyes. Studnik's skin crawled as they placed their hands on their daggers. He truly felt relief to have his guards back!

Frequent Allied air raids forced the train to make unscheduled stops. Three Luftwaffe escorts took turns guarding him during the trip to Frankfurt. One guard, a veteran of the Eastern front, barely noticed the explosions outside the train car. This was nothing compared to the death and the destruction he had witnessed in Russia; a few random explosions along the railway lines paled in comparison to days and weeks of constant barrages. Outwardly he appeared calm, but Studnik knew that the stress had taken its toll because the guard, in his early twenties, looked like an old man. The guard produced several photographs from his breast pocket, one of which portrayed him at the entrance of a snow shelter made from rough-cut logs. He told Studnik of soldiers who shot themselves to escape cold, food shortages and relentless attacks by Soviet troops. He expressed contempt for the Nazi party and admitted that the war was lost. The German was grateful for a cigarette and inhaled it deeply. Studnik knew he would be treated fairly as long as he behaved himself. He developed an entirely new perspective about war as explosions rocked his train car in the marshalling yards at Giessen. A sense of helplessness swept over him; running was useless. Though Studnik empathized with German civilians, he felt no responsibility for their situation. The German nation had started the war and changed the nature of warfare by terror bombing civilian populations. Goering directed his Luftwaffe to destroy non-military targets to demoralize civilian populations.

Dulag Luft

The interrogation process intended to take advantage of Studnik's demoralized state and break his will to resist. Studnik assumed the guards were chosen for their demeanour as well as their rough, exaggerated appearances. These guards were less intimidating after a few days. Unsophisticated conscripts, they performed their jobs without malice and endured much of the same hardship as the average PoW. Most of the garrison troops did not speak English but they respected their prisoner and fed him the same food as they ate. In contrast, Studnik remained wary of the officers and interrogators after the first session started poorly. The interrogator had intimidated him by saying that the three recent raids on Frankfurt "bothered" him, knowing Studnik had participated in one of them. The German's voice hardened when he talked of how the latest raid had inflicted enough damage on industrial sectors to deprive half the city of water, electricity and gas; casualties were high—948 people died and over 120,000 people were bombed out of their homes. Two nights earlier the RAF had pummeled Frankfurt and leveled 5495 houses, 99 factories, 412 businesses and 56 public buildings. Officials listed 421 civilians killed and another 55,500 made homeless. On 24/25 March, Studnik experienced the destructive power of 162 American B-17s firsthand as he sat in his cell. According to archives in Frankfurt, these three raids obliterated Frankfurt from the map (Middlebrook and Everitt 1985, 482–3). Another interrogator revealed his racist attitude toward Jewish people when he spoke of the economic benefits brought to the German people by Hitler. The *Volksdeutsche* had houses, jobs and their beloved Volkswagen—all benefits of Nazi economics. The interrogator berated Western democracy. Studnik simply responded that democracy provided its citizens with many benefits without the shadows of Nazism. The German snorted that democracy never existed, because it involved Jews!

The Germans demonstrated masterful interrogation techniques. They veiled threats with cordial conversation, and unimportant questions with inquiries about the latest British technology. These Germans wanted information on Oboe, a radar system installed in bombers. Studnik told them to contact Winston Churchill for more information, as he "only flew for the outfit." A bemused German responded, "Ya, ya, we would like to ask him." Interrogation took a nasty turn when one of the guards found the photograph sewn into the lining of his uniform. The Gestapo used force on Studnik but he stuck to the facts: he was downed during a bombing operation, nothing more. He demanded protection under the Geneva Convention and insisted on an immediate transfer to a PoW camp. They told Studnik they had plans to shoot him. His perseverance paid off because they shipped him to Stalag Luft I.

Transport to Stalag Luft I at Barth

Before their departure for Barth, a Luftwaffe officer assembled the captives in the compound. He stood on a mound and issued an ominous pronouncement in English, "The number of guards in this escort detail equals your number. We are not afraid that you will escape. Rather, German civilians will kill you if they get the chance to do so. Therefore, stay together for your own good." The officer had not exaggerated. Civilians waited along the road, amidst the rubble, and hurled insults and horse turds at the passing PoWs. One particular woman screamed, "Bandits, *Schweinhunde!*" The situation deteriorated quickly, and the guards hustled the PoWs into waiting boxcars without counting them. Obviously, the train crew had gone through this routine enough times to know to stop once they cleared the city limits. Guards counted the PoWs and distributed one Red Cross parcel to each man, before pushing forty prisoners into small, thirty-by-eight-foot boxcars, small by North American standards. Barbed wire divided each car into three sections. The centre third was cordoned off for six guards who enjoyed the comforts of a small stove and an abundance of vegetables and sausages. Miserable PoWs tore into their Red Cross parcels and finished them off. Someone forgot to mention that the parcels were intended to last for up to a week, or longer, depending on the number of times the train needed rerouting on the account of constant harassment by Allied aircraft. The PoWs sliced holes into the enclosed cans with a knife passed through the wire by a guard and dug out the contents with their fingers.

Stalag Luft I, Barth

New PoWs to Barth received a shower, a cursory examination for lice, and a quick dusting with DDT. Studnik found the barracks well used but clean. Guards issued six boards to support his sawdust mattress. He tied twine between the rungs of the bed frame to keep from falling through onto the man in the lower bunk after the Escape Committee requisitioned three of the six bunk boards for tunnellers. Surprise searches, lice, fleas, inadequate rations, the cool Baltic air and boredom eroded morale.

Russian Pows Denied Protection of Geneva Convention

Studnik's austere circumstances paled beside those endured by Russian officers in the adjoining compound. The Nazi attitude of racial supremacy played a major role in their treatment but Stalin's refusal to ratify the Geneva Convention Relative to the Treatment of Prisoners of War guaranteed abuse. The barbarity sickened the air force PoWs. They received terse warnings from the guards that they faced severe punishment or death if they attempted to assist the Soviets. While RAF PoWs ate Red Cross food parcels, the Soviets subsisted on swill, a few pieces of bread, moldy potatoes and peelings tossed over the fence. Some philanthropic organizations managed to get clothing to the Soviets but not enough to make a difference. The Germans further dehumanized and humiliated them by assigning them latrine duty in the other compounds.

Morale in Studnik's block remained high due to the unflagging efforts of a career British Air Force officer, Wing Commander Hilton, a stickler for discipline and cleanliness. He conducted room inspections on a weekly basis. The officers turned out smartly for their regular weekly inspection, and Studnik recalled Hilton insisting that the minutest threads be cut from threadbare uniforms. Barrack block rooms were spotless, and he had his adjutants conduct cursory examinations for dust with white gloves. Studnik felt this was the right thing to do since the lethargic were prone to depression. Compared to the American prisoners, Commonwealth service personnel were a smart-looking group. Studnik admired how the senior British officers humiliated the German commandant at weekly inspections. As a final act of defiance, the senior British officer would always wait for his German counterpart to salute first!

Ravensbrück

Prisoners in Barth bore witness to events that gave rise to war crimes tribunals after the war. The Germans contravened the Geneva Convention by situating Stalag Luft I next to an active military base and a radar training station in order to deter Allied bombing raids. The Germans regularly parked military vehicles in the PoW camp and conducted military exercises nearby. They also situated a compound of the Ravensbrück concentration camp next to Stalag Luft I. Conscript labour at Ravensbrück served as slave labour in nearby factories. These workers hauled wings and tail sections of damaged Heinkel aircraft to storage areas in nearby forests. When they had scavenged enough parts, they dragged them out and constructed another aircraft. The Germans even salvaged Lancaster parts. They flew a black Lancaster over the camp, complete with German markings. After liberation, wretched souls from Ravensbrück attempted to break down the gates of Stalag Luft I in search of food. It was the first time Studnik saw these people close up. The pasty greenish pallor of their skin sickened him and he guessed some of the men were down to eighty pounds. They were turned away for fear they would introduce diseases to the PoWs. Studnik investigated the Ravensbrück concentration camp after his liberation and was shocked by the vast array of drill presses and lathes used by slave labour to manufacture aircraft parts.

No Winter Marches at Barth

Barth's northern location precluded the need for evacuation in the final months of the war. Female soldiers in the Soviet army assisted in the camp's liberation, and Studnik required some time to overcome the initial shock of their presence. They contributed to their lack of femininity with the number of weapons tucked under their arms and in their belts. They brandished leather belts taken from the bodies of the German soldiers they had killed, and wore them as badges of honour. At night the Russians sang, danced and played instruments. The women, heavy on their feet, danced gleefully with machine guns draped across their shoulders. They were as tough as the male soldiers. None of the PoWs dared to refuse a dance.

The Russian military imposed martial law over the sectors they liberated. A strict internal passport system was instituted to curb the movement of German soldiers attempting to flee to the West or meld among PoWs. Studnik knew of one German who had slipped through the system and had made his way to England before Allied authorities discovered his identity. The Russians detained PoWs for two weeks and justified this delay by telling the British and American authorities that each man needed a passport to prove he was not German. This was a Catch-22 situation: prisoners needed passports to leave, but they had to be in the custody of their own militaries to get passports.

Repatriation

The Russians eventually permitted the USAAF to send Flying Fortresses into the airfield near Barth to evacuate Allied PoWs. The process of repatriation began with those in captivity the longest. Studnik happened to be in Barrack Block 8, alongside the longest serving prisoners, and he flew out with the first wave, a week after VE Day, 15 May 1945. He landed at the Ford Aerodrome in southern England, and as soon as he stepped from the aircraft, a corpsman sprayed him with DDT to kill any unwanted German "tourists." All repatriated servicemen received new uniforms and underwent debriefing at Bournemouth.

Concerns that these men might not be able to integrate into civilian society created some anxiety for British authorities. To help them make the adjustment, or at least give the men a chance to work out their frustrations, the base administrators organized a dance. Studnik made the acquaintance of two sisters who invited him to their home where their mother operated a small teashop. She graciously provided chocolates and cookies, something he had not seen for over a year, and a real pleasure for someone who had lost twenty-five to thirty pounds in captivity.

The Aftermath

Bill Studnik wrote to the families of his six missing crew out of compassion. All families had hoped he could provide some information about the demise of their loved ones. After six decades, he looks back to his days in the RCAF almost as if they existed in another lifetime. Time faded his memories to the extent that they are more like scenes from a movie. He finds it hard to believe he piloted a heavy bomber on eight operations, was shot down, taken prisoner, and lost six good friends. Although he has no sad feelings about his experience now, it took some time to get over the stress and trauma of the war. The experiences have tempered with time. He remains sad about the loss of his crew; they were like brothers. Because of his own experiences with the Gestapo and mobs of civilians, he suspects foul play . Studnik recalled a Welshman who suffered grievous treatment at the hands of a lynch mob and narrowly averted death before his arrival at Barth. "Taffy's" bruises provided ample evidence of a severe beating inflicted by civilians who would have finished the job if soldiers had not intervened.

Bill Studnik felt fortunate to have returned home alive, but he felt alienated from fellow Canadians who had not experienced war. It did not help to return to his former job and work beside someone who continually taunted Studnik by saying he was the German fighter pilot who had shot him down and he was pleased Studnik had spent time in a PoW camp. His employer told him to let it go or it would affect his career. Bill did let it go and rose in the ranks of his company. He finished his apprenticeship as a machinist and rose to a position of general superintendent in an internationally known Canadian company, where he worked for forty years in Montreal, New Westminster, Winnipeg, and Edmonton. Bill Studnik passed away in June 2004 in Edmonton.

Stalag Luft VI, Heydekrug, East Prussia

Prisoner of War Camp for NCOs

June 1943–September 1944

The influx of thousands of new Bomber Command and USAAF prisoners of war created a logistical nightmare for the Luftwaffe. It necessitated the construction of additions to existing camps and the construction of new Stalag Lufts elsewhere in the Reich. The Nazis constructed PoW camps as far east as they could to minimize the chances of escapees reaching freedom. In June 1943 the Luftwaffe relocated British and Dominion air force non-commissioned officers (NCOs) of Stalag Luft III's Centre Compound to a new camp at Heydekrug in East Prussia. They had decided to place as many USAAF officer PoWs as possible in a centralized location—Centre Compound, Stalag Luft III. The newly constructed Heydekrug camp was austere, even rustic. It required PoWs to build prisoner organizations from scratch, and they enthusiastically transformed the camp by replicating the Centre Compound organizations they had left behind at Sagan. Heydekrug consisted of four compounds, two that held two thousand men each and a third built for one thousand men. A fourth compound remained unoccupied because the Luftwaffe abandoned the camp before pressing it into service. The compounds covered an area of eight acres. Eight wooden structures stood in each compound: two were designated as washhouses and latrines; four as living quarters; one as cooking facilities and storage areas, one section of which the PoWs converted into a small theatre and library over time; and one as the administrative block (*Vorlager*). The Germans divided each barrack block into nine rooms, with up to sixty men to a room. Tents for new arrivals checkered one compound. Each compound included a playing field that doubled as the *Appel* square.

Richard Dutka, Fred Rayment, Doug McNeill and Frank Dunn arrived at Stalag Luft VI between June and September 1943. They remained for a year before the Germans evacuated PoWs of Stalag VIA and Stalag VIK to Stalag XXIA in Thorn, Poland, starting in July 1944. Relocation signaled the onset of misery. In the first purge of PoWs to Thorn, the Germans transported 1200 through Poland by rail, and a few weeks later moved 1500 NCOs to Thorn in the hold of a ship via the Baltic Sea. In November 1944, the last columns of PoWs left Heydekrug for Stalag XIB at Follingbostel, a camp north of Hanover. Follingbostel earned the reputation as "Belt-Tightening Camp" because of chronic ration shortages. The relocation of the Heydekrug PoWs

Cooking facility at Heydekrug, Stalag Luft VI. (Courtesy of the J.D. McNeill family)

represented the longest forced march of Allied prisoners in the Second World War, from the summer of 1944 to April 1945.

Canadian Influence in Heydekrug

The NCOs of Stalag Luft III's Centre Compound were recognized for establishing the premiere PoW organization of all Luftwaffe-administered camps, and they reinvented the camp at Heydekrug, using the Canadian model of governance. The "Canada Council" created a communal fund by pooling all pay received by PoWs through the Red Cross, and making group purchases as items became available from the local area. The camp took on a distinct Canadian flavour. Within a few months the Canadians staged the "Flieger Jockey Club Day" and set up a pavilion featuring various aspects of Canadian culture, complete with music, landscape scenes, costumes, cowboys, Indians and impersonators of the female persuasion.

The Canadians produced two plays with all-Canadian casts: "Front Page" and "Boy Meets Girl." They organized an intercompound sports day on Dominion Day, 1 July 1944, that culminated in an outdoor extravaganza in the evening. The Canadians earned the respect of other nationalities in the camp for their selflessness and solidarity. In December 1943, Canadian PoWs generously divided their Christmas allotment with those PoWs who had received nothing from their families or their home governments. The Germans attempted to

(Courtesy of S.G. King)

drive a wedge between the different national groups by offering the Canadians preferential treatment, but the Canucks steadfastly refused any semblance of segregation because everyone in the camp had taken up arms to defeat the Nazis and would stand together until the end of the war!

Escape Activities

The Germans had chosen the Heydekrug site for the compound because of its bed of sand, which they believed would impede tunnelling activities. Unknown to the Germans, the recent transferees from Sagan had already mastered the art of tunnelling in sand by shoring excavations with bed boards. The escape organization, headed by Flight Sergeant Alexander, RAF, began a tunnel from the boiler room of a washroom. Dispersal crews disposed of sand in the aborts. Fifty men, outfitted with maps, compasses, food, cigarettes, and matches planned an escape in March 1944. An alert guard spotted the movement of some of the first escapees outside the wire, and trapped forty would-be escapees in the tunnel and washhouse. Each man served time in the cooler as punishment before authorities purged suspected ringleaders to other camps. Ironically, most of them returned to Stalag Luft III because they had received commissions and were due for a transfer to an officers' Stalag.

Evidence gathered in postwar statements gave insight into the sophistication of the Heydekrug escape network and the outside support network that was made possible through the assistance of sympathetic German guards. Warrant Officer First Class M. F. Sikal, RCAF No. R61024 provided the Director of

Prisoners excavated tunnels under the very noses of the guards. (From *Handle with Care*, courtesy of A.F. Rayment)

Intelligence, Group Captain H.R. Stewart, RCAF with testimony that Warrant Officer G. Grimson (also known as Grimstead), RAF, had escaped from Heydekrug compound in November 1943 and remained in the area to assist other PoWs in escape attempts. Grimson/Grimstead spoke German and used his skills as a make-up artist to gain entry to Heydekrug in the guise of a German soldier on several occasions. (DHist Ref. 181.009[D618] File No. TS45-19-15 D of I). Unfortunately Grimson's fate was unknown at war's end and officials assumed the Germans eventually discovered and executed him for his covert activities.

The Tide of the War Turns

The Red Army's advance into the Baltic states in July 1944 resulted in the dispersal of 175 Canadians to Stalag Luft IVB at Mühlberg and 425 other Canadians to Stalag 357 at Thorn, Poland. Many of the PoWs had spent up to four years in captivity and had accumulated a fair number of possessions over that time. The Germans permitted them to carry out as much as they could on their backs but the strain of the load forced most of the PoWs to abandon coveted possessions, including precious clothing and blankets, along the way. The process of evacuation continued while the Russians fought their way into the German heartland. Instead of permitting liberation of the Heydekrug PoWs, the Germans moved them again, from Thorn to Follingbostel. As the Reich collapsed under the onslaught, the Nazis remained vengeful to the end, and in late December 1944 declared Follingbostel a "reprisal camp." Guards cut the already scant ration allotment to starvation levels, confiscated all straw mattresses, removed furniture and cut off meagre supplies of charcoal briquettes. The PoWs combined the boards of two bunks into one, shared their thin blankets and huddled together at night to preserve body heat. The Germans stripped them of their educational and recreational privileges and denied requests to supply building materials. The food situation became critical. The PoWs had thought life was difficult when they subsisted on a half parcel of food per man per week at Thorn, but Follingbostel guards cut rations to nothing. The PoWs would wait outside the guards' kitchen for turnip peelings and spoiled vegetables.

Finally, Liberation

As the British Fourth Armored Division closed in from the west, the Germans marched the PoWs eastward from Follingbostel. The column trudged about aimlessly for two days before returning to the camp. In those last days British fighters mistook the column of PoWs for German soldiers, killing thirty-seven Allied personnel. Most of the German guards deserted the PoWs before Montgomery's British Second Army liberated them on 16 April.

The Germans could have abandoned the PoWs to the Russians in late 1944, but instead put them through horrific marches and stressful conditions in various camps for an additional eight months. They could have been more humane by topping up starvation rations in the final months at Follingbostel. The Heydekrug PoWs possibly endured more deprivation and hardship than most PoWs in other camps because their initial evacuation started in September 1944, four to five months before the commencement of the other infamous winter marches.

Flight Sergeant James A.G. "Dixie" Deans, Man of Confidence

The PoWs spoke highly of their Man of Confidence, Flight Sergeant Dixie Deans, who provided the leadership that guided the prisoners through crucial periods. He maintained discipline in the ranks, which was most noteworthy when the camps received news of the mass murder of fifty officers after the Great Escape. His presence averted the unnecessary killing of PoWs by guards in the last months of the war. The prisoners recognized Deans' leadership qualities by electing him Man of Confidence at Stalags Luft I, III, VI and Stalag 357. His integrity inspired Kriegies and commanded the respect of the German commandants because he had the ability to maintain control of his men and gain the trust of the guards. He refused to allow the Germans to segregate Jewish PoWs from the general population.

Deans also involved himself in the camp's covert activities. He oversaw the work of an elaborate escape organization and used his influence to gain the cooperation of several German guards. He coordinated the flow of intelligence from PoW camps by encoding messages in letters sent from PoWs to loved ones. Calton Younger, British journalist and editor of *The Kriegie* newsletter for ex-RAF PoWs, praised Dixie Deans in his 1989 eulogy for the risks he had taken in sending embedded messages. Discovery of his involvement in these activities would have meant death. Commandant Oberst Hermann Ostmann recognized the volatile situations at Thorn and Follingbostel and worked closely with Dixie Deans to control problems that neither of them could rectify. In the last week of the war, the commandant permitted Deans to take a truck through the front line to a Red Cross depot at Lubeck and bring back some food for the hundreds of men in his charge. When British Typhoons mistook a column of PoWs for German soldiers Deans pedalled his bicycle through both the German and British lines to secure medical attention for the survivors; he returned in time to accept the surrender of Oberst Ostmann the following day. Deans' presence ensured a smooth transfer of power from the Germans to the British. His heroic efforts enabled the repatriation of many who might otherwise have perished in the tumultuous last months of the war (RCAF Ex-PoW Association).

Flight Sergeant A. Fred Rayment

Before completing Grade 12 Fred Rayment aspired to enlist in the RCAF and train as a pilot or navigator. He excelled in mathematics, physics and geometry even without the benefit of formal instruction. Fred originated from families who placed the highest importance on education. His mother was educated at Oxford University in England. His father, a Vimy Ridge veteran, was an architect by profession, and he instilled in Fred a sense of the moral obligation to defend Europe against the aggressive Third Reich.

Initial Training

Sergeant Fred Rayment, No. R121901, served as a navigator in the Royal Canadian Air Force's 408 Squadron, "City of Edmonton." He trained on the two-engine Anson trainers at Regina, Saskatchewan. At the Operational Training Unit in Wellesbourne, Rayment was instructed on the Wellington bomber before converting to the heavy four-engine Halifax at Topcliffe. His operational career spanned just two deployments. On 13 June 1943, the cannon fire of a German fighter rattled his Halifax so intensely that he knew it was lost. Fred removed his oxygen mask prematurely and collapsed into unconsciousness. He later assumed that the wireless operator had pushed him into the night sky with his hand wrapped around the D-ring of the parachute release mechanism. Fred is unsure how the parachute opened, and he remembers nothing of his landing or subsequent capture.

Fred Rayment flew with 408 City of Edmonton Squadron, RCAF, which chose the Canada goose as its symbol. (Courtesy of A.F. Rayment)

" *For you the war is over.*"

Not every airman shot down in enemy-occupied Europe received a cordial reception. The Germans denied Rayment medical attention for his broken neck. (Courtesy of A.F. Rayment, *Handle with Care*. Note: Illustrations supplied by A.F. Rayment are from a compendium of drawings published in 1946 by two Heydekrug PoWs, R. Anderson and D. Westmacott, in a small book they called "Handle With Care." The collection, started in 1943, survived the trials of PoW life and three arduous relocations between 1944 and mid-1945. The sketches serve as a tribute to PoWs and provide some insight into Kriegie life.)

In Captivity

A bewildered Rayment awoke in a room without knowing how he had arrived there. He cared less about one officious, garlic-breathed Nazi who was leaning into his face, barking down at him. His thoughts focused on the painful throbbing emanating from his neck, an invisible wound as a result of his evacuation from the bomber. Rayment believes the Germans ignored his pleas for medical attention because he showed no outward sign of injuries and managed to walk unassisted. In fact, the Nazis declined him access to a doctor during the entire time of his two years in captivity. Post-war X-rays revealed that Fred suffered two broken vertebrae.

Dulag Luft

During Rayment's transfer to Dulag Luft, the perpetual rocking motion of the train car drove him to the brink of madness. He attempted to minimize his misery by cradling his head in his hands, but every position failed to alleviate the neck pain. Officials at Dulag Luft allowed a cursory examination of Rayment by a medical orderly, but the absence of an X-ray machine precluded any opportunity to make a conclusive diagnosis, and Fred went without treatment. The prospect of paralysis frightened him, especially when his hands went numb.

Non-existent Medical Resources

As Stalag Luft VI had opened just days before Rayment's arrival, it came as no surprise that the camp lacked hospital equipment and physicians. Medical technicians captured in North Africa and Italy treated the PoWs. Rayment marveled at their level of expertise despite their lack of formal training and equipment. These corpsmen correctly diagnosed his fractured vertebrae and used first aid, battlefield experience and practical experience gained from treating sports-related neck injuries to stabilize his condition through a regimen of massages and heat lamp therapy over a six-month period.

Man of Confidence in Heydekrug

New PoW camps experienced growing pains, and Fred Rayment believed the plight of Heydekrug's PoWs might have been worse without the leadership of Flight Sergeant Dixie Deans. Deans' natural leadership abilities and integrity earned the respect of his peers. They elected him A Lager's Man of Confidence over PoWs senior to him. (As a matter of note, NCO camps operated differently than officer camps. Non-commissioned officers elected their camp leaders; the senior man did not automatically become the camp leader as was the custom in the officer camps.) Deans acted as spokesman for PoWs and oversaw the operation of all facets of camp operations including the administration of the cookhouse, distribution of Red Cross parcels, planning of sports days, education, the library, sick parade, presentation of grievances to German officials, and resolution of disputes between PoWs. Deans gained the cooperation of the German staff when it became apparent the collapse of the German war machine was a matter of time.

Heydekrug's Commandant

Rayment recalled that Heydekrug's commandant, ineffective as a military leader, avoided all interaction with PoWs and exiled himself to his office. Stories circulated that he was an unwilling participant in the war, pried away from Berlin's intellectual community. Fully recognizing this limitation, the Luftwaffe had placed him in a position where he could do himself and others no harm. As a result, Heydekrug operated without typical German efficiency. Rayment remembers every roll call had the potential to degenerate into chaos because PoWs knew they could push the boundaries of decorum without much fear of reprisal. American PoWs openly flaunted their contempt for authority by demonstrating a disregard for rules.

Escape Activities

Rayment offered his services to the Escape Committee, an organization fash-ioned after the one that existed in Centre Compound of Stalag Luft. He served as "duty pilot," or lookout, for those who went underground or participated in prohibited escape-related activities. He mastered basic German, thinking that a working knowledge would be helpful if he ever escaped. In one escapade, the PoWs had filled a blank file with a dummy for five days before the Germans discovered that one of the PoWs had escaped. After weeks of digging, fifty Heydekrug PoWs tried to escape through a 145-foot long tunnel on 29 August 1943, but a guard spotted the first group of escapees slipping to the cover of trees during the breakout. This threw the Germans into a panic. From the *Vorlager* the guards retrieved PoW records, complete with individual photographs, to iden-tify each man remaining in the camp. The PoWs stymied guards by filling blank files in the ranks during two roll calls; the guards resorted to dividing the com-pound in two and sending PoWs from one side to the other as they counted them. PoWs slipped back and forth between the groups, while others gleefully broke from the ranks and chased footballs flipped into the compound. It took hours for guards to complete the process, and this gave the escapees more time to put distance between themselves and the camp. It did not take long for the Germans to backfill the tunnel with effluent drained from the aborts. Fred pitied the poor fellows who lived in the hut above the tunnel entrance.

The Escape Committee could not have put its plans into action without the assistance of several German guards, including Eddie Munkert, an ardent anti-Nazi who worked in the administration offices. He brought in civilian clothing for the PoWs, supplied German uniforms, and lent his identification and passes for forgers to copy whenever they needed them. Munkert traveled to Memel, Lubeck and Danzig on behalf of the PoWs to attempt contact with the underground. Another guard named Sommers worked with the Polish underground and supplied photographic materials to the PoWs. Security discovered both men and executed them. Guards at the front gates remained vigilant for PoWs attempting to walk through dressed as civilian workers or German soldiers. (Crawley 1985, 32–33, 281–84)

Gestapo Take Over Heydekrug

The Gestapo showed their disapproval of the poorly managed camp by assuming control of Stalag Luft VI. Even with their reputation for brutality they had a difficult time wresting control from the PoWs. Rayment recalled the brazen antics of one Yorkshire man who infuriated the Gestapo leader during a roll call when he mimicked the German's appearance. Many German officers wore riding britches with high boots, and resembled grasshoppers. The Yorkshire man left the ranks during an inspection and jumped about the Appel square in the manner of a locust. He earned a week's solitary confinement for his impudence.

Keep Busy, Boy!

Time passed slowly in the prison environment, so most PoWs made the effort to use their time constructively. Tradesmen and professionals volunteered to teach their skills to fellow Kriegies and if exams could be written at the end of the courses, some men received accreditation. Fred had grown up in an isolated region of Alberta and learned how to master material through self-directed study. He had a particular interest in the agricultural sciences and earned the moniker of "professor" from one Englishman because he dedicated so much of his time to his studies.

Heydekrug PoWs organized the usual variety of sporting activities: softball, soccer, cricket, rugger and skating. A year after the camp first opened the Germans permitted an inter-compound Sports Day. Prisoners from Rayment's compound moved into the adjacent enclosure for an afternoon of competitions, and he found the change of scenery spectacular, even though the views from the two compounds varied by just a few hundred feet!

A small theatre troupe performed several plays, including the musical *Cinderella* where effeminate males assumed the female roles. The camp suffered a grievous loss when fire razed the theatre in the middle of the night. In a concerted effort to save other buildings, guards unlocked the doors of the barracks and had PoWs form a line to carry water pails from the well to the fire. A pall swept PoW ranks because the loss of the theatre meant one less activity to occupy their minds.

The Germans knew that PoWs fermented dried fruits and potatoes and distilled the byproduct. They never tried to shut down the operations as long as the

Prisoners of war disrupted roll calls to delay the discovery of an escape.
(Courtesy of A.F. Rayment, *Handle with Care*)

The "cooler" or punishment cell was intended to break PoWs of undesirable
behaviour. A prisoner subsisted on bread and water, sometimes without the luxury
of heat, blankets or light. Smoking and reading were strictly forbidden.
(Courtesy of A.F. Rayment, *Handle with Care*)

" *He's been doing it all day !* "

Pipers brought the benefits of Scottish civilization to Heydekrug. (Courtesy of A.F. Rayment, *Handle with Care*)

. . . *the old-fashioned human chain* . . . "

Prisoners did their best to save their theatre. (Courtesy of A.F. Rayment, *Handle with Care*)

PoWs behaved. On one visit to the camp, SS guards were known to purchase some of the brew with German money. The Germans bent the rules and permitted a local supplier to import a few kegs of beer into camp at Christmas 1943. They even permitted the PoWs to usher in the new year outside of their barracks and stay up until two in the morning. Kriegies in Rayment's compound joined hands in a circle around the Appell square and struck up a heart-warming rendition of "Auld Lang Syne" at midnight.

Tide of the War Turns

It was obvious that the collapse of the Third Reich was imminent as Allied forces pushed on all fronts and German forces retreated to the Reich's 1939 boundaries. Artillery fire resonating from the east signaled the advance of the Soviet Army. Hopes for a quick release were dashed when the Germans evacuated the Heydekrug PoWs to Thorn, Poland, to prevent their liberation. The relentless drive by the Red Army forced the Germans to evacuate the same PoWs from Thorn to Follingbostel within four months.

While at Thorn, Rayment witnessed the evolution of long-range weapons. When the Germans test-fired rockets, PoWs gazed skyward and marveled at the wondrous devices; they learned later that they had witnessed the test firing of V2 rockets, presumably from facilities at Peenemünde, an island in the Baltic Sea. As the rockets went up out of sight they left a vapour trail that started straight but twisted with the changing winds. The PoWs never saw or heard a V2 crash because they exploded well out of range of the camp.

A Reprisal Camp

Fred Rayment felt he had little reason to complain about his existence until his arrival at Follingbostel. There he received one Red Cross parcel upon his arrival and subsisted on irregular servings of turnip soup and rye bread after that. Germans considered prisoners the lowest form of life and doled out starvation rations—the equivalent of 800 calories per day. Swallowing their pride, prisoners ignored jeers from guards as they picked through the remnants of the swill pile outside the guards' cookhouse. Starving PoWs could be forgiven for fighting each other. Fred joined a group of six other men to form a cooking unit. The group, or combine, gave each member certain chores to perform and it was Fred's job to gather whatever food he could find. He recalls one of the grandest meals he ever tasted consisted of turnip peelings cooked with onions obtained from Russian PoWs in exchange for cigarettes; a member of his combine had secured some lard for frying the two vegetables and someone else had found a charcoal briquette to heat it up. Prisoners kept physical activity to a minimum to preserve calories. In Fred's case, rations were so meagre that he managed just one bowel movement per week.

He considered the Follingbostel period the worst days of the war. No one could forget the misery of the winter of 1944–45. The Germans had designated Follingbostel as a reprisal camp for perceived "mistreatment" of German troops captured in North Africa: the Allied armies had been unable to supply mattresses to German PoWs captured in the deserts of North Africa. Admittedly, the German PoWs slept on the ground, but the Allies did not deprive them of water, rations or warmth. Follingbostel PoWs existed in damp, unheated barracks in the cold of winter, with mattresses. Body odour permeated the barracks and few men braved ice-cold showers because of the risk of hypothermia. Those who did shivered for hours and were fortunate to avoid pneumonia. On Christmas Day 1944, guards issued PoWs a few miserable lumps of charcoal to warm their food, but not nearly enough to take the chill out of the building.

The German guards remained vindictive to the end. They entered the Follingbostel compound on 14 January 1945 and ordered everyone, except the bedridden, to surrender their straw mattresses under the premise that clean ones had arrived to replace the soiled ones. The PoWs knew this was a lie and implored guards to allow them to keep their mattresses. The Germans ignored them, wheeled several heavy machine guns inside the gates of the camp as a show of force, and then marched Russian prisoners into the compound and had them remove all mattresses to a pile outside of the wire in plain view of PoWs. The Germans ordered the Russians to remove most tables and benches from the barracks and heap them beside the mattresses. New mattresses never came. The PoWs, deprived of adequate calories and bedding preserved body heat by sharing bunks, huddled under jackets and a few remaining blankets.

The PoWs drew strength from the knowledge that their liberation was not that far away. The Germans might have controlled the camp but the Allies controlled the skies. The RAF and USAAF conducted extensive bombing campaigns in and

The Germans had no transport to supply PoW camps with Red Cross parcels from England. The German rations were also cut to the minimum. (Courtesy of A.F. Rayment, *Handle with Care*)

around the town of Follingbostel. The windows in the barracks rattled every night from bombs exploding nearby. The PoWs were jubilant when Mosquito pilots unloaded their bombs with precision on the large army training facility nestled beside the PoW camp.

The Germans broke the rules of the Geneva Convention and risked the lives of prisoners by parking tanks in the PoW compound. Red Cross officials caught wind of the violations, but when they came to investigate the charges the Germans had temporarily removed the armour from the camp. The Germans failed to keep PoW camps illuminated at night because they did not want Allied bomber crews to use the camps as landmarks.

As British and Canadian forces pinched in from the west, PoWs endured another forced march, this time to the east. They scavenged turnips, sugar beets and potatoes from beneath straw piles in fields. Guards fired warning shots over the heads of PoWs who strayed too far off the road or moved too slowly. Some farmers took pity on the marchers and offered them anything they could spare: peas, barley, turnips or sugar beets, rye or vegetables. Many of the PoWs, on the verge of starvation, exercised amazing self-control by consuming minute amounts of food because they feared excruciating stomach cramps and severe diarrhea after subsisting for months on starvation rations.

PoWs Had Honour

The PoWs conducted themselves with honour in spite of their pitiful conditions. One of them had found a stockpile of peas in a barn where the column was billeted for the night. Peas are a godsend for a starving man—the stomach can digest legumes easily. The German farmer frantically appealed to Dixie Deans to have his precious peas returned to him because his family intended to sow them in the spring and they depended upon the small quantity of seeds to get them through the following winter. Deans called together the men under his command and appealed to their decency to understand the plight of this family. He calmly asked for the return of the remaining seed—and they returned them. The fact that these starving men gave up the only food they had demonstrated the high regard felt for Flight Sergeant Deans.

Hold on until Liberation

Near the end of the last forced march, Fred broke from the column and headed for a dairy farm where he hoped to acquire fresh milk. He could only dream of the taste because at no time in his two years of captivity had he had access to any. He found a dirty beer bottle in the building and set his heart on filling it by going quietly from cow to cow, while a guard stood at the far end of the barn to prevent pilfering. Fred had nearly filled the bottle when the guard spotted him. He could have shot Rayment on the spot, but dashed the nearly full bottle from Fred's hand, sending the precious milk crashing to the floor. Fred escaped with

" *Aren't men beasts !* "

A humorous side to the march. The Follingbostel PoWs were a motley lot whose rough appearance still shocked war-weary civilians who encountered them (Courtesy of A.F. Rayment, *Handle with Care*)

his life, but the thought of getting that close to a drink of milk really hurt.

Tragedy Strikes

An unfortunate consequence of war is death by friendly fire. Millions of civilians clogged the roads alongside hundreds of thousands of German soldiers under orders to fight to the end. Over one hundred thousand Allied PoWs were force-marched across Germany at the same time, and it is easy to understand why Allied pilots sometimes mistook them for enemy soldiers, especially when hundreds of soldiers marched alongside them. Six British Typhoon fighter aircraft strafed Fred's column just two days before war's end, after Dixie Deans, under the flag of truce, had received permission to pass safely through German and British lines to secure Red Cross parcels to feed the men. Just as the PoWs sat down in ditches to eat their first Red Cross parcels in months, Allied aircraft swooped down on them. The aircraft unleashed machine gun fire, cannon fire, rockets and bombs onto the men. A pilot later reported that he had believed the upward pointing drawbars of old wagons, hauled by the PoWs, were 88mm anti-aircraft guns. Hundreds of men scattered through adjoining fields during the attacks. Fred believed he was a goner when he bolted across the open field to get away from the main body of men; in the moment of terror, he looked back over his shoulder and it appeared as though one of the Typhoons was lining up on him for an attack. He threw himself to the ground as bullets from the Typhoons ripped up clods of dirt and rockets tore huge pockets in the ground all around him. Some of the men had the sense to wave the white linings of their greatcoats at the aircraft as they came in for another pass. The pilots rocked their wings in acknowledgment and flew off. The attack left nine German guards and twenty-seven PoWs dead. Naturally the pilots were distraught when they learned that they had inflicted misery and death on men who had survived months and years of captivity, only to have their lives snuffed out in the last few days of the war.

Repatriation

When the war ended one of the immediate benefits of liberation for Fred was the unlimited amount of food available for the first time since his capture. He gorged himself, became quite ill and spent the next few days convalescing. The RAF transported the Follingbostel PoWs back to Britain in Lancaster bombers. The one in which Fred flew crashed and burned on takeoff after debris littering the runway blew out a tire. The passengers escaped with their lives but lost the possessions they had accumulated during captivity.

Epilogue

Prisoners of war underwent significant psychological adjustments to survive captivity. Loss of freedom and constant hunger stood out as the two aspects of prison life most difficult to deal with. Mail and Red Cross parcels were the PoWs' only ties to the world and gave most a sense of hope. To this day, Fred Rayment is disgusted with the suffering inflicted on soldiers and civilians alike while the Germans prolonged the war as long as possible. Sadly, a few trigger-happy guards shot PoWs over insignificant issues, and many good men died needlessly from exposure, sickness, starvation and mishaps like the Typhoon incident. Rayment's pilot, George Large, survived up to the last few weeks of the war but then succumbed to complications from a hernia. His comrades left him to convalesce in a barn with intentions to return for him, but Large did not make it.

Fred Rayment graduated from the Faculty of Agriculture, University of Alberta, with a bachelor of science degree in 1950, and a master's degree in the 1960s. He dedicated twenty-five years of his life to research in Newfoundland before he and his wife Peggy moved to Leduc, Alberta, for their retirement years.

Pilot Officer Richard "Duke" Dutka, MiD

Bombers sent on operations to Berlin in mid-August 1943 temporarily benefited from new radar jamming technology, called Window, that cloaked them from attacks. It was a simple technique. Crews simply pushed millions of strips of tin foil through flare tubes, which scattered through the sky and deflected radar signals, preventing German pilots from locating them and ground technicians from ascertaining the number of bombers and their bearings. This tactic gave Bomber Command an advantage they had not enjoyed before; however, the benefits lasted for only a few raids. The Germans overcame Window's effect by modifying their defence doctrine for German cities. Previously, German fighters had flown the Tame Boar Formation (*Zahme Sau*) in which defenders stayed within a specific quadrant and waited for bombers to fly through. With the advent of Window, German ground control could no longer track bombers and advise fighters of their approach. In a new tactic, termed *Wilde Sau* or Wild Boar, ground technicians surrendered control and individual Luftwaffe pilots responded visually to incoming waves of bombers. Bomber Command's losses mounted once more.

Three raids on Berlin between 23 August and September 3 proved costly. Of the 1669 sorties flown, 125 bombers failed to return, or 7.5 percent of the total, German fighter defences around Berlin had successfully regrouped.

To counter Wild Boar formations, Bomber Command initiated "spoof" or diversionary raids to draw German fighters away from the main bomber streams sent to the primary targets. Bomber Harris also withdrew the slower Wellington bombers from the main force and relegated them to secondary duties (Middlebrook and Everitt 1985, 417–19)

On the night of 31 August/1 September 1943, 622 bombers flew to Berlin, including bombers of 428 Squadron RCAF based at Middleton St. George. The Germans were prepared. Searchlights coned many bombers, including Duke Dutka's Halifax. Duke's navigator reported in his post-war statement that he heard the sound of bullets ripping through the fuselage; a German fighter had finished them off. Dutka exited his damaged aircraft safely and landed near Potsdam. He evaded capture for three weeks in an exciting cross-country trek that took him from the Berlin area to the Belgian border. For this remarkable journey Richard Dutka was "mentioned in dispatches" during King George VI's birthday celebrations in 1945.

Skies over Berlin Were Hot

Bombers attacked Berlin in six successive waves. The bombing window for the first one hundred bombers commenced at 0050 hours on 1 September. Duke's Halifax arrived with the fifth wave; and he was awestruck by the bright orange flames already rising high above the city. This night's operation proved costly to the RAF; German defenders shot down forty-seven aircraft, or 7.6 percent of the total sent that night. They attributed this higher than usual loss to the effectiveness of parachute flares released by German fighters to illuminate bombers. Bomber Command considered the operation a failure because many bombers released their bomb loads as much as thirty miles before the intended target, on empty fields marked with target indicators placed by German aircrafts. Bombs destroyed only seven industrial buildings. However, the raid's

Flight Sergeant Richard "Duke" Dutka had his portrait taken during his last leave in London, only days before he was shot down over Berlin on 1 September 1943.

psychological effect was devastating on Berliners. Ten of thousands of children and all adults not involved in defence activities were ordered out of the city and relocated to outlying areas (Middlebrook and Everitt 1985, 427–8).

Duke's Halifax Sustains Severe Damage

Dutka knew it would be a long time before he saw England. Tracers and flak lit up the sky and downed the bomber next to his. When his aircraft was struck, he strapped on his chest pack parachute and readied himself for the evacuation order. Damage to the airframe made it difficult for the crew to wrench open the twisted escape hatch. Proper evacuation procedures slipped his mind. Duke left his intercom cable and oxygen mask attached to his flying helmet and they nearly strangled him as he dropped out of the aircraft. Instead of making a clean exit from the belly of the Halifax, he clung to the doorframe. The 200-mile-an-hour slipstream pounded his legs against the bottom of the fuselage. The sound of the wind sounded like the devil laughing! Duke lost consciousness and awoke to a cacophony of flak bursts, tracers, bombers and fighters. Searchlights swung back, and the smell of cordite permeated his nostrils. Dutka believed he would die before ever making it to the ground; even if he did survive, the fires on the ground would consume him. He made peace with God.

On the Run for Three Weeks

Remarkably, Dutka descended into a quiet field outside Potsdam and hid in forests for several days before moving southwest at night. Hunger never became an issue. The rations in his escape kit provided food for four days and he used tablets to purify slough water. The harvest season was in full swing, and he enjoyed a bounty of fresh potatoes, berries, fruits and vegetables. His confidence grew as he chose to move by day—in his uniform! He attempted his first crossing of the River Elbe near the village of Barby but it proved a formidable barrier. The Elbe stretches 1200 kilometers across Germany from the mountains southeast of Dresden to the North Sea between Bremen and Lubeck. He walked for two days in search of a boat to row across the river, then chose to traverse a train bridge in broad daylight. The two lazy sentries on the far bank did not rise from their seats to challenge Duke until he broke into a run for the trees on the far side; they did not even send a patrol after him! He believed his scruffy, unkempt appearance led the guards to take him for a foreign worker. He jumped a boxcar further up the line and rode for 450 miles through Weisenbach and Frankfurt to Neiderlahnstein, a small centre on the Rhine near Belgium.

The Rhine River was a natural obstacle, and the Germans reinforced all transportation arteries and bridges with extra security. Guards searched for stowaways on trains in the marshaling yard. Duke jumped from his car and hid from the sentries. He broke windows in buildings and smashed dashboard instruments on military vehicles parked on flatcars. French workers alerted the sentries because they feared they would be blamed for the damage. A young German sentry about Dutka's age arrested him. They walked side by side to a lock-up, carrying on a cordial conversation in English. Dutka wondered if someone might report the young German for appearing overly friendly. He thought his adversary could have made a good friend if circumstances had been different.

Dulag Luft and Heydekrug

Interrogators took a keen interest in Dutka because he was a navigator. A friendly German promised him books and writing paper if he answered their questions. Duke refused to divulge anything, and they responded by returning him to solitary for a few more days. The isolation failed to weaken Dutka's resolve and officials purged him to Stalag Luft VI. The Germans crowded forty PoWs into two sections of a drafty small boxcar; the middle third was reserved for two guards. Everyone shared water from a communal pail, and the train stopped once or twice a day to allow the prisoners to relieve themselves. Dutka felt no ill will towards the Germans. The poor conditions on the train were circumstances of war; the guards did nothing to antagonize anyone or exacerbate their conditions. During a layover, Duke witnessed Nazi barbarism first hand. The SS beat conscript workers for collecting hot water dripping from the bottom of the steam locomotive.

Trigger Happy Guards at Heydekrug

The Heydekrug camp guards had instructions to shoot any PoW who was outside his hut after curfew or during an air raid. After the Germans had confiscated all watches, two young Americans made an honest mistake one morning and paid for it with their lives. A guard in the tower shot the pair for emerging from their hut minutes before the morning curfew was lifted. Duke remembered other occasions when British PoWs died from gunshots for standing too close to the warning wire.

"Dear John"

Many a fellow received the dreaded "Dear John" letter from the girl whose undying devotion was his sole reason for existence. One girl wrote to say that she had met a new fellow; she was sorry to say that they had fallen in love and she was too weak to turn down his marriage proposal. She closed by saying she knew he was a swell guy and would understand. Rumours circulated through the camp like wildfire; one young husband incarcerated for over a year received a letter from his wife to the effect that she had found a baby and she wanted to keep it. Another letter was to the effect "I had an accident," another, "Someone left a baby on the doorstep, imagine that!" The PoWs posted their letters of woe on a

" That makes 1,500 guys in this camp with an Auntie Winnie and an Uncle Joe "

All mail in and out of prison camps was censored (*geprüft*) and read for embedded messages. Proofreaders blacked out sections before forwarding mail to recipients. Letters from every Luftwaffe-controlled camp passed through Stalg Luft III's mail room. (Courtesy of A.F. Rayment, *Handle with Care*)

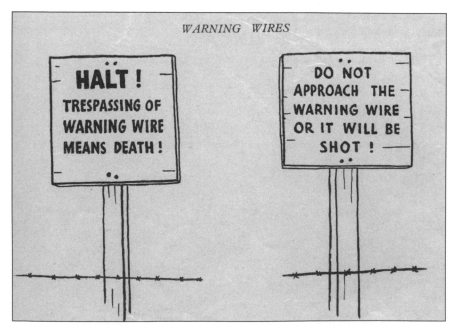

Not all signs made sense, but the Germans knew what they meant. (Courtesy of A.F. Rayment, *Handle with Care*)

wall as a warning to others. The worst letter originated from a girl in Vancouver:

Dear ———,

When you went missing, I was so sad and lonely. Your dad was great; he came over to comfort me and took me out to movies and dinners. I fell in love with him and when he asked me to marry him I accepted. Please don't be mad at me. We are so glad to hear that you are safe and well.
  Love,
  Your mom

The Invasion of Fortress Europe

The inevitability of the D-Day invasion was the worst-kept secret of the war. Bookmakers in the camp set up a pool to guess the date, and one of Dutka's two entries won the 600-cigarette pot. The news of the Normandy landings on 6 June 1944 provided a much needed morale boost and gave some PoWs the hope that they would be home by Christmas.

Heydekrug Pows on the March

The Germans evacuated Dutka and several hundred other PoWs to Thorn in September 1944. The PoWs must have appeared a miserable lot, because labourers tossed them their lunches. Starving PoWs ate livestock killed by

"... I'm sorry, dear, but I love a soldier. I know you'll understand ..."

Letters from family, wives and girlfriends kept the PoWs abreast of most events on the home front. Some letters gave the worst of all news: a sweetheart no longer loved him. (Courtesy of A.F. Rayment, *Handle with Care*)

shrapnel; men cut chunks from tainted carcasses and consumed them raw. Dutka went hungry because, to him, a full belly was not worth a bout of botulism. Poles showed their appreciation and risked their lives by lining roadways and passing over food, despite threats from guards. Hitler Youth were a menace beyond redemption; dressing like boy scouts did not mask the evil they permeated. They exhibited pleasure when they intimidated PoWs with their rifles and daggers. During the march, Dutka joined up with two Poles who relished the prospect of being near their hometown at war's end. One regularly bribed a guard and slipped out to visit his wife and family but always returned before daybreak for his family's sake. This man did not need a reminder of what the Nazis would do to him. An adjacent compound operated as a "punishment camp" (*Sonderkommando*). Air force PoWs moved in from Heydekrug were not subjected to the same rigours as those unfortunate souls in the punishment camp, but they were subject to the whims of the same sadistic guards.

Epilogue

Heydekrug PoWs were refugees, no different from the millions of civilians caught between two armies. In Dutka's estimation, the Nazis maximized everyone's suffering as long as possible. He did not expect friends and family to understand the hardships he went through, and he chose to internalize his experiences for most of his life. On his return to Canada, Dutka took up farming under a federally sponsored plan for veterans. He worked the night shift for Canadian National Railway for fifteen years and during this period typed out some of the more poignant events from his time as a PoW. Duke and his wife, Rose, are retired in the city of Wetaskiwin, Alberta.

" . . . now I wonder if I packed my tooth-brush ? "

The Heydekrug PoWs on forced march discarded most of their precious possessions in the ditches alongside the road. (Courtesy of A.F. Rayment, *Handle with Care*)

Richard Dutka's 428 Squadron earned the nickname of "Ghost Squadron" because of the high casualty rate suffered during operations. A fitting memorial dedicated to 6 Group stands at CFB Trenton, Ontario. Rose and Richard Dutka stand in the foreground. (Courtesy of R. and R. Dutka)

Flight Sergeant J. D. "Doug" MacNeill

J.D. "Doug" MacNeill passed away without leaving written memoirs of his experiences as a prisoner of war. His logbook contains numerous illustrations and bits of information that offer insight into the life of a PoW, with specific reference to his periods of internment at Heydekrug, Thorn and Follingbostel from mid-1943 to May 1945.

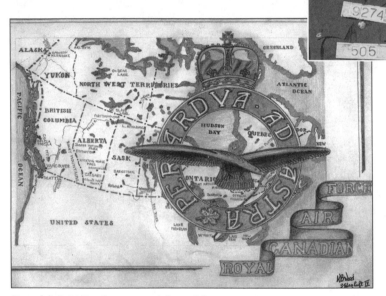

Canada's RCAF volunteers originated from sea to sea.

Doug MacNeill's Travel Log Showing Day Mileage and Food Allotments 6 February 1945 to 7 May 1945

This travel log, transposed verbatim from the original, is a valuable record of the movement of Allied PoWs from Thorn, Poland, to Follingbostel, Germany, and their liberation on 2 May 1945.

Feb. 6—Gross Tychon to Naffin	16 km
⅓ bread and 1½ Red Cross parcels per man.	
Feb. 7—Stralskenburg	28 km
Feb. 8—Roman	20 km
Feb. 9—Rest for a day	
Feb. 10—¼ bread	20 km

Feb. 11—Dorphagen (through Grefenberg)	27 km
Feb. 12—Gorke	17 km
Feb. 13—Rest	
Feb. 14—Restow (Knackerbrot 6 biscuits, $\frac{1}{10}$ meat)	6 km
Feb. 15—left to Portter, slept in the open passed through Woltin	42 km
1 Red Cross parcel and $\frac{2}{5}$ of a parcel	
Feb. 16—Dargin, crossed the Oder River	24 km
Feb. 17—Murchim	27 km
Feb. 18—Tromstow (Anklam)	18 km
Feb. 19—Seltz	30½ km
Feb. 20—Rest	
Feb. 21—Schassour	8½ km
Feb. 22—Schassour. Rest for day. $\frac{2}{5}$ loaf of bread and margarine	
Feb. 23—Tarnow	14km
Feb. 24 to Mar. 3—Rest at Tarnow.	
(Feb. 28, parcel/man. Mar. 3, bread & marg.)	
Mar. 4—Kargon $\frac{1}{5}$ bread loaf and margarine	27 km
Mar. 5—Lebbin	30 km
Mar. 6—Monchbusch	16 km
Mar. 7—Rest. $\frac{1}{5}$ loaf of bread, $\frac{1}{25}$ margarine	
Mar. 8—Zahron	22 km
Mar. 9/10/11—Rest for three days ½ bread loaf.	
Mar. 12—Lankin	12 km
Mar. 13—Through village	3 km
Mar. 14—Moduity	12 km
Mar. 15/16—Rest	
Mar. 17—Dutschon ¼ bread loaf, $\frac{1}{10}$ margarine	13 km
Mar. 18—Molenbeck	10 km
Mar. 19—Rest	
Mar. 20—Neese ¼ bread loaf, $\frac{1}{5}$ margarine	10 km
Mar. 21—Bresegard	21 km
Mar. 22—Barnity ½ Red cross parcel/man	23 km
Mar. 23—Rest $\frac{1}{5}$ bread loaf, $\frac{1}{25}$ margarine	
Mar. 24—Metzingen ½ Red Cross parcel. Crossed the Elbe River	21 km
Mar. 25—Thorndorf $\frac{3}{5}$ bread loaf, 120 gram margarine	21 km
Mar. 26—Westerweyhen	26 km
Mar. 27—Rest	
Mar. 28—Ebstsef Transport by rail 86, men per carriage. ¼ bread loaf and margarine. No windows or vent in truck	
Mar. 29—Follingbostell, Stalag 11B	
Apr. 8—Left Follingbostell	15 km
Apr. 9 to May 1—Never kept	

May 2—Liberated by 6th Airborne Division

May 3—Commandeered German canteen at Boizenburg, arrived at reception
camp at Luneburg

May 4—Left Luneburg by truck for Sulenger. 50 men per truck.

May 5—Sulenger

May 6—Left Sulenger, arrived at Emodelten

May 7—Emodelten to England

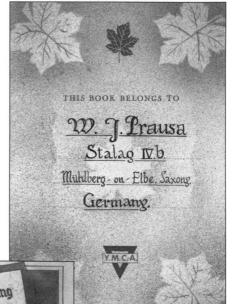

(Courtesy of MacNeill family)

Doug MacNeill had a friend
draw a front-page news
headline in his logbook to
announce his arrival in
Germany. (Courtesy of
MacNeill family)

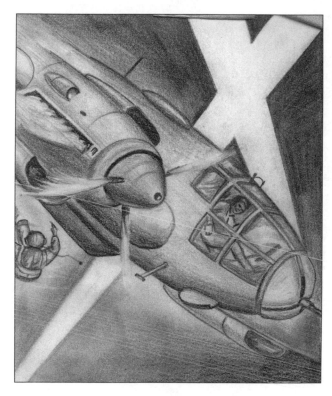

One of the lucky ones. The safe evacuation of an airman from his bomber over the night skies of Germany. (Courtesy of MacNeill family)

Daily roll calls on the *Appelplatz* became one of the mundane routines for all PoWs. Guards performed one or two head counts per day to monitor escape activities and to make announcements. PoWs could prolong the counts for hours when necessary to cover up an escape. In retaliation guards stood PoWs at attention for extended periods during roll calls. Prisoners walked the perimeter of their compounds to pass the time and to stay in shape. (Courtesy of MacNeill family)

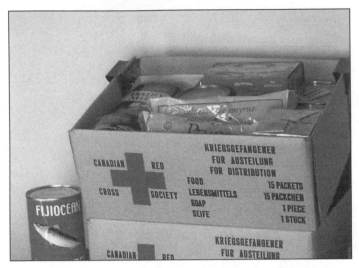

A PoW knew he was fairly safe when the Red Cross registered his identity. This card entitled the bearer to the same food as his fellow PoWs. (Courtesy of MacNeill family)

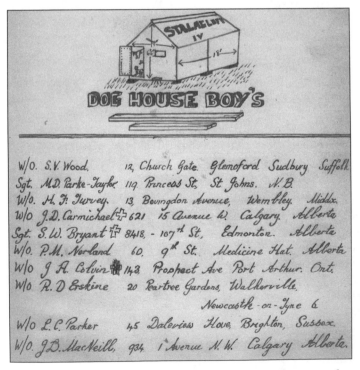

Many PoWs kept a record of their roommates in case they wanted to make contact after the war. (Courtesy of MacNeill family)

Entitled "First Blood," this drawing shows the fight could not be taken out of a PoW.
(Courtesy of MacNeill family)

(Courtesy of MacNeill family)

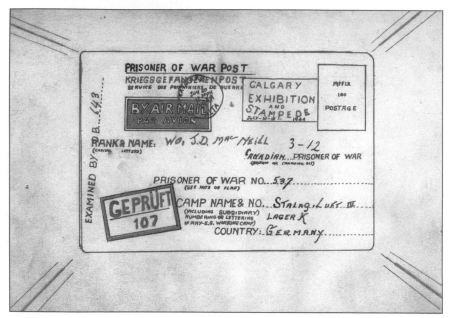

MacNeill's conception of his only connection to home—mail! (Courtesy of MacNeill family)

Flight Sergeant Frank Dunn

Flight Sergeant Frank Dunn, RCAF, was held prisoner in Heydekrug, Thorn and Follingbostel from May 1943 to April 1945. His wartime recollections here apply to the period from late 1944 to early 1945. Frank Dunn broke from the main PoW column at Follingbostel in the final two weeks of the war and moved to British lines west of Hannover.

Dunn served as a flight engineer aboard three Halifax bombers in the RCAF's 419 (Moose) Squadron. He survived two crash landings in England following operations over Germany, as well as a third crash landing in Germany on 24 May 1943. He climbed from the burning wreckage, his clothes ablaze. He evaded capture for ten days before falling into enemy hands near the Dutch-German frontier. His family was told that Frank and his crewmates had perished in the burning Halifax. They learned of his survival four months later, on 1 October 1943.

Dunn's captivity began in Stalag Luft VI. Rations, constantly in short supply, varied little from the usual fare of dark rye bread, sauerkraut and occasional pieces of horsemeat. As Allied forces tightened the noose around the Third Reich, the Germans feared that airmen liberated by the Russians could be used to defeat them. Consequently, the Heydekrug PoWs were relocated to Thorn,

Poland, in three purges, the first of which departed in July 1944, the second in September and the last in November. Frank Dunn moved from Heydekrug in the last purge.

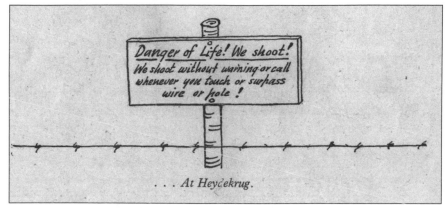

. . . At Heydekrug.

Oddly worded signs still made their point. (Courtesy of A.F. Rayment, *Handle with Care*)

Below are passages from Frank Dunn's memoirs recorded in the early 1990s.

[When] I was at HEYDEKRUG . . . the Toronto Maple leaf Hockey Team sent out complete equipment for a hockey team and the Germans built an outdoor rink as they were anxious to see the game played. It was a great diversion for us, although in our weakened condition through lack of food our performances were somewhat poorer than we wished.

[Escape Activities]
The PoWs dug tunnels in the sandy soil . . . we did all the digging at night and carried out the dirt in our pockets and . . . made a tunnel which extended beyond the barbed wire fencing around the camp. . . Thirty-five escapees made it through the tunnel, but unfortunately all were captured and returned to prison. To prevent further attempts at escape, the Germans ran all over the area with steam rollers causing the tunnels to cave in, but in spite of this the activity continued. . . Doberman Pinschers were let loose at dusk to patrol the camp . . .

Move to Camp Two, Stalag 357 After about eighteen months the entire [compound] was moved in freight cars to TORUN, Poland.We had to walk about 5 miles to get to the railway station and as I had an injured knee caused by the final crash, walking was very painful and left my knee permanently damaged.

Move to Camp Three, Follingbostel I was in Poland for thirty days and was in charge of a party of thirty PoWs who went to the forest everyday and dug out tree stumps, which was our only source of fuel in a bitterly cold winter. The next move was to Follingbostel. Thousands of PoWs were so weak that very slow progress was made . . . British Allied Intruders were shooting up the lines.

[Reprisals]

There was a good deal of tension when it was announced that as a reprisal for German PoWs in Africa having to sleep on the ground . . . the soldiers surrounded the PoWs congregated outside and guarded us with machine guns while our mattresses were dragged outside and burned in a huge bonfire.

At Follingbostel, the Russian guns were so close that it was decided to move us further from the front. The evacuation from Stamalager [*sic*] 357 began on April 6, 1945. On the day we left we were issued one Red Cross invalid parcel between every eight men and seventy cigarettes.

My partner Rex Sargent . . . suggested . . . we should plan to escape during March. Our food consisted of one half tin Nestle's milk, two ounces of Oatmeal, a few spoonfuls of sugar, a loaf of Rye bread and two pounds of margarine—rations for a week. [W]e were counted . . . and formed into parties of five hundred men! Fifty guards armed with machine guns . . . and many trained police dogs on leash completed the column, the guards march[ed] along each side about ten yards apart. We felt that the British lines were only about forty miles away. Rain had fallen daily all winter and the woods were drenched. At 9:00 pm when darkness began to fall, Rex and I worked our way to the head of the column and watched closely for a likely spot to slip away. A halt was called at 9:30 and as the column moved noisily to the right of the road with a clatter of equipment, we crawled into a ditch. One guard sat at the end of the ditch and smoked a cigarette. [W]e stopped breathing and hoped; no headlights came along; presently the order to start was given and during ensuing noise and confusion we crept into the woods and headed south by the stars into terrain almost impassable in darkness due to ditches, craters made by mortar explosions and tree stumps . . . Aircraft zoomed overhead, flares were dropped and explosions could be heard so sleep was very limited.

Saturday 7 April 1945 Everything seemed fairly quiet so we camouflaged a suitable spot for a hide-out and made a fire with ice-coated twigs and boiled some of our very small supply of tea in water we had found in a wagon rut, notched our two loaves of bread into six days rations at three slices per day. [W]e had breakfast—tea with very little milk and sugar and a slice of bread and margarine. We had not had matches for weeks . . . but as we left the prison camp I happened to see a Czech national in the German Army . . . he gave me 2 boxes—a priceless treasure! We lay low because there was heavy mortar and machine gun fire everywhere and occasionally rifle shots . . . an unpleasant reminder that the SS had warned that all escaped prisoners would be shot on sight!

Sunday 8 April 1945   Two RAF and a soldier turned up at our camp, but were very nervous . . . and decided to start on a daylight march south . . .

Tuesday 10 April 1945   [Left camp and] landed in a swamp—heavy mortar and artillery fire—aircraft dropping flares and tracer bullets roaring into the sky constantly . . . We decided to take cover and were joined by two RCAF escapees, George Fielding and David Ferguson . . . The flak was so bad that we had to stay put and we dug a trench and put heavy logs over it and crawled into it twice when things got really hot . . . We were there three days.

Friday 13 April 1945   Rex climbed a tree and reported . . . we were in a flak and Panzer school . . . Spitfires flew around and three Typhoons roar[ed] over our heads, pouring cannon shells and rockets close to our shelter about 6:00 pm. More Typhoons came over and bedlam broke loose—one burst of cannon shells set fire to the grass only twenty yards from our camp and fearing discovery if people came to extinguish the fire, we discarded all kit and greatcoats, excepting toilet articles and two blankets each, one of which we cut a hole in the centre and wore them like a cape hoping they would sufficiently resemble German Army capes to pass inspection at a distance . . . We traveled a short distance and under sparse cover saw two Germans and a concealed gun spewing tracers at Spitfires, directly in front of us . . . Heading south we were forced to rest frequently, not having eaten for two days . . . We smoked our last cigarette butts rolled in toilet tissue and finally found a road where we met a German officer who fired rapid questions to us in German . . . He gave my companions a short command in German to follow him. The officer continued on his way and we lost no time in striking out through a swamp and making ourselves scarce. Travel in the swamp was very difficult as we soon camped on a grassy ridge. Finding a patch of nettles we camped for the day, boiled and ate nettles twice, which helped a great deal.

Saturday 14 April 1945   George and Dave entered a huge barn and returned with a brown hen and nineteen eggs. We moved away rapidly . . . then found a thicket where we boiled the half-hatched eggs, removed the chickens and ate the yolks and remaining whites, which had the consistency of rubber! Dave and I picked the hen which Dave had expertly dispatched, cleaned, cut-up and stewed the hen, which we all enjoyed very much indeed. After resting all day we decided to move on, and . . . found about a dozen helmets and a loaf of bread immediately, and all forgetful of possible booby traps. We searched the area quietly and collected more rye bread, cheese, marg and one and a half packs of tobacco.

Monday 16 April 1945 We combed the German camp and found hidden shelter . . . and much personal equipment scattered about . . . We collected five loaves of bread, two pounds of sausage, cheese and tobacco . . . cigarettes, a mirror, socks and . . . rucksacks . . . I suggested staying another night—the others readily agreed, as all were suffering from stomach trouble and diarrhea, probably caused by drinking unboiled swamp water . . . Working our way over the burnt over woods we reached a paved road and Rex picked up a copy of the Daily Mirror, an English newspaper and the wrapper from an English can of beans, so we felt encouraged. We . . . continued west . . . and . . . we learned that the nearest British HQ was in Schwarnstadt 10 kilometers west, so we continued on and saw wrecked tanks, trucks and houses. The bridge across the river Aller was wrecked so we turned back after trying to cross it . . . We also drank from the river which we later learned was badly contaminated with typhoid . . .

18 April 1945 At 7:00 am a truck . . . of the British Royal Engineers . . . took us to the village where they were stationed. [They] forced the Germans to give them ham and eggs for our breakfast. . . . [and] later drove us by transport to Celle, where the Army Catering Corps were operating a receiving depot for released prisoners. We had a shower, were issued clothing cigarettes and toilet articles and have pleasant rooms in barrack buildings, the food is very good, and our stomachs recovering.

20 April 1945 More escaped PoWs are coming in every hour—dining rooms queues take ¾ hour [to get through].

Saturday 21 April 1945 About 1000 escaped and released PoWs left Celle and were moved by Army Transport to Hienstadt, a three hour journey . . . My stomach is giving me lots of trouble and I look very white and thin. We left Heinstadt on April 24 and rode in an army truck for six hours—I was very sick with chills and fever and pains. Billeted in a German school, I lay all day on a straw sack too miserable to even wash my face or get a drink of water. At 3:30 pm I was driven to the airport and took off for England in a Dakota.

24 April 1945 Driven to Army receiving centre at Aylesbury—ate little and shivered all night on a comfortable cot in a Nissen hut.

25 April 1945 Inspections, pay etc. A neat hospital camp [where] everyone [is] very prompt and kind. Left by train for London and was met and taken to a hotel. I was painfully ill so was taken to hospital with fierce pains in the abdomen, chills and vomiting.

Monday 30 April 1945 Walked outside today and feel much better. Met Peter Elko who was horrified at my awful appearance—weight 143 pounds! No luck in getting new uniform yet. Try again tomorrow . . .

Stalag Luft III, Sagan

Though Reichsmarschall Hermann Goering designated Stalag Luft III the quintessential camp for captive officers of Western air forces, its conditions varied little from other PoW camps. However, Stalag Luft III evolved into the premiere camp, because of the efforts of its occupants over three years in organizing themselves—it had little to do with the Germans who ran the camp. While the Luftwaffe retained firm control over occupants of its camps, its PoWs were given more latitude than their Wehrmacht and Kriegsmarine counterparts. Some have suggested that the Germans unwittingly contributed to an environment for so many exceptional events to occur because they assembled many of the brightest minds of many nations into one camp. Still, Stalag Luft III might have slipped into the back pages of history books after the war were it not for Operation 200, better known as The Great Escape.

Stalag Luft III grew quickly, and by war's end contained over 10,500 PoWs. East Compound received its first Allied air force officers in April 1942. Centre Compound housed non-commissioned officer prisoners until mid-1943 when the Germans moved its occupants to a new camp, Stalag Luft VI, at Heydekrug in East Prussia; United States Army Air Force officers moved into the recently vacated Centre Compound. North Compound opened in early 1943 to accommodate the ever-increasing numbers of officers falling, literally, into Luftwaffe custody. The Germans added South Compound before they began relocating hundreds of Sagan PoWs to an annex at Belaria, a compound four miles down the road, which was designated first as Stalag Luft III and later Stalag Luft IV. A separate Russian compound situated on the fringe of Stalag Luft III reminded Western PoWs just how badly their treatment could have been were it not for the existence of the Geneva Convention Relative to the Treatment of Prisoners of War.

This picture, of unknown origin, was taken from one of the guard towers at Stalag Luft III. A searchlight and machine gun stand at the ready.
(Courtesy of Davidson family)

Flying Officer Harry Newby

Flying Officer Harry Newby, RCAF No. J20835, failed to return after a raid to Bochum on the night of 13/14 May 1943. German records stated that the 442 bombers involved in that night's operation inflicted minimal damage to Bochum's military installations because German defenders successfully diverted many of the RAF bombers away from the city by firing decoy target marking flares at points outside the city's boundaries. Of the 135 Halifaxes, 104 Wellingtons, 98 Lancasters, 95 Stirlings and 10 Mosquitoes sent to Bochum, 24 bombers failed to return. Newby's Wellington was one of them (Middlebrook and Everitt 1985, 384).

Loss of Newby's Wellington

Newby and one other man survived the ditching of their Wellington Mark X and they floated about the North Sea for eight hours in a round yellow dinghy

The PoWs who survived the ditching of their aircraft became Goldfish. (Courtesy of MacNeill family)

before Dutch fishermen retrieved them from the frigid waters. Both survivors qualified for membership in the Goldfish Club, a fraternity reserved for those who lived to recount the ditching of their aircraft.

Newby Contributes to the "Wooden Horse" Escape

Harry Newby was given PoW No. 1349 and was sent to East Compound of Stalag Luft III. His arrival coincided with the "Wooden Horse" breakout and the "home runs" (safe return) of three PoWs to England. The idea to tunnel out of East Compound using a wooden vaulting horse originated with Flight Lieutenant Eric Williams, RAF, and Fleet Air Arm Midshipman Michael Codner of New Zealand. Completion of such an undertaking before freeze-up required the conscription of a third officer. Williams and Codner chose Flight Lieutenant Oliver Philpot to join them in their endeavour. Carpenters constructed the wooden horse from wood panels salvaged from Canadian Red Cross crates. They designed it so a digger could brace himself on cross pieces while several men carried it across the compound. The horse, approximately three and a half feet high, four feet long and narrower at the apex than at the base, was large enough to conceal at least two men and up to twelve bags of sand hanging from hooks nailed on the top beam. Williams and Codner made bags from pant legs sewn shut at one end. Success rested on placing the tunnel entrance as close as possible to the perimeter fence. Each time the diggers wanted to go out a willing team of gymnasts carried the wooden horse to the pre-arranged spot in the yard. Diggers went below ground when they received an all-clear signal from the vaulters. They reopened a cleverly concealed lid that covered the tunnel entrance, dug, then loaded bags of sand into the horse. Diggers then resealed the entrance with a foot of ubiquitous sand, without leaving a trace. Harry Newby and other enthusiastic gymnasts vaulted until the tunnellers signaled they were ready to be carried off the field.

Organizers took precautions to allay guards' suspicions when the new apparatus appeared in the compound. In the first week, jumpers made a point of knocking over the horse several times to show curious guards that nothing was hidden within the box. The digging team knew that the guards had inspected the horse one night because sometime between curfew and the following day when vaulters carried it out on the grounds, someone had disturbed telltale evidence planted on it.

The Luftwaffe had judiciously selected the Sagan area for a prison camp because the compounds sat over a bed of sand, which, in theory, would make tunnel excavations next to impossible to complete. Planners made provisions for the possibility of cave-ins and crack lines along the surface. Vaulters maintained a vigilant watch for evidence of sinking. One quick-thinking jumper feigned a twisted ankle to conceal a hole that opened as a result of the digging. Fears that the repeated vaulting sessions would cave in the ground on either side of the horse necessitated the shoring of the entrance with wooden bed boards and the installation of a foundation of bricks. Packing sand into the spaces around the boards prevented shifting and sinking (Williams 1951, 53–57).

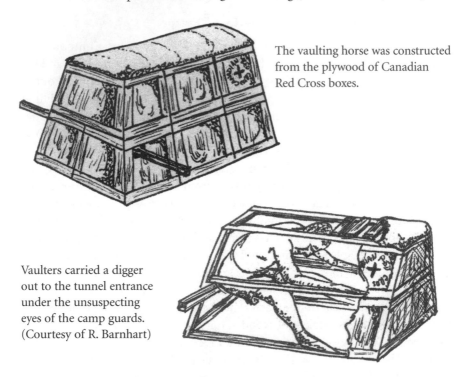

The vaulting horse was constructed from the plywood of Canadian Red Cross boxes.

Vaulters carried a digger out to the tunnel entrance under the unsuspecting eyes of the camp guards. (Courtesy of R. Barnhart)

The enterprise became arduous for all parties involved. Vaulters had to extend their exercise periods as the tunnel lengthened because diggers needed additional time to move a dozen sandbags back through the tunnel. Tunnelling in complete darkness and stagnant air slowed the digging process. They feared that guard dogs might detect their scents if they poked small holes in the top of the tunnel for fresh air. The tunnellers received extra rations for the duration. However, the vaulters continued their activities without the benefit of extra food, simply because there were not enough rations to go around; several vaulters bowed out because of overexertion and limited food intake. They also found it exceedingly difficult to carry the wooden horse when the operation expanded and a second man began to go underground. The vaulters feared that the Germans would notice the additional men carrying the horse. Remarkably, none did.

Additional Security Measures

Sergeant (Feldwebel) Glemnitz headed security for Luftwaffe PoWs from 1940, first at Barth and later at Sagan. He possessed a good understanding of PoW

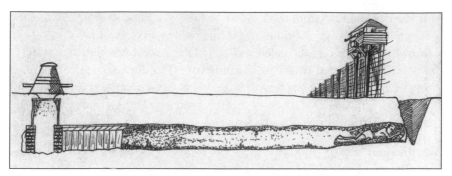

The tunnel was excavated while the gymnasts vaulted above ground. (Courtesy of R. Barnhart)

psychology and used his experience to detect illicit activities. The prisoners outfoxed Glemnitz with the ordinary appearance of the vaulting horse. All the same, they gave him little reason to scrutinize them, by going to great lengths to hide telltale signs of digging. Known for his stern demeanour, Glemnitz kept the PoWs off balance; he often made offhand quips such as "Well, why aren't you digging today? It's bad weather to be above ground," or, "I hear that the Allies have selected Sagan as the place at which to open their second front!" (Crawley 1985, 29). The Germans employed ferrets, guards who were specially trained in the art of tunnel detection, to find tunnel entrances and evidence of digging. They looked for bright yellow subterranean sand that contrasted with topsoil in the compounds. Guards conducted regular searches of barracks for cleverly concealed trap doors, false walls and contraband. Newby remembered when a German major conducting a search commended the PoWs for their exquisite taste in music because Beethoven, composer of the music blaring from the phonograph, was regarded as a good German. An unabashed PoW retorted, "Yes, that's true, but that's only because he's dead!" The Luftwaffe bolstered security with personnel of communications squadrons who sunk sounding devices into the sand at different levels to detect scraping and chiseling sounds. The pounding of vaulters' feet during jumping routines distorted sounds picked up by the monitors, and the camp's stage band practiced outside near the vaulters to cover any noise emerging from the tunnel.

Disposal of yellow sand posed a logistical problem for the disposal committee. They hid sand in the rafters of huts and even in the Germans' cookhouse. "Penguins" dispersed sand from bags concealed within their pant legs, mixing it into the topsoil with their boots. Dispersal crews spread tons of sand between the floor joists of barrack blocks and down aborts. Diggers kept the diameter of the tunnel to a minimum to reduce the volume of sand for disposal; to wiggle their way through, they stripped off their clothes. They rigged ropes to pull a pan full of sand back to the wooden horse. They widened a section of the tunnel near the exit point to store food for the escape. On the day of the escape, the three dragged out bags of clothes tied to their ankles (Williams 1951, 105–113).

According to the diggers' calculations, their excavation would open into a drainage ditch situated twelve feet outside wire. The ditch concealed the three escapees from guards in the towers as they crawled along the channel bottom before scurrying to the cover of nearby woods. (The Germans backfilled trenches at all camps following the escape.)

The Breakout

Officers Williams, Philpot and Codner designated 28/29 October 1943 as the target date for their breakout. After that, the likelihood of frost would prevent them from completing the last few meters and snow on the ground would make it easy for search parties to track them. Prisoners assisted the escapees' bid for freedom by milling about the compound during the roll call, ultimately forcing guards to make several recounts. Williams, Philpot and Codner spread pepper over their tracks to dull the senses of the tracking dogs. Embedded messages about three "home runs" arrived via PoW mail three months later.

Newby was Cognizant of Escape-Related Activities

Harry Newby offers a rare glimpse into the inner workings of the highly secretive escape organization. He roomed with the influential senior RAF officers in East Compound who directed most operations. Regular shipments of contraband, received through bogus philanthropic organizations, were directed to his roommate, Squadron Leader R.B. Abraham, RAF No. 28104, PoW No. 1446. Abe, known as "Little X," second in command for the Escape Committee, possessed an interesting assortment of useful items for escape-related activities. He showed Newby the faint outline of a greatcoat which appeared on a brown wool blanket when it was soaked in water. Escape articles were ingeniously concealed within ordinary items like crib boards, buttons, heels of shoes or toothpaste tubes. Maps were smuggled into the camp enclosed in handkerchiefs and decks of playing cards. Newby had received a tobacco pipe that contained a small compass, and he saw compasses concealed within buttons. The Germans caught on to most of the tricks, so the RAF modified designs, like changing right-handed threads to left-handed in the screw-off lids on buttons that contained miniature compasses. Some PoWs with the old style buttons resorted to stitching thread through the buttons to prevent guards from removing the covers.

German Guards Aided the "X Committee"

A German cook named Dutchy Schultz cooperated with the PoWs by using his food cart to move contraband into the camp and between compounds. He acquired radio parts for PoWs during trips to town, and they reciprocated by rewarding him with chocolate and cigarettes. Dutchy had rolls of film processed for prisoners despite the nationwide inventory controls placed on photo paper. Security forces eventually discovered the cook's activities and sent him to serve a three-year sentence in a military prison. Dutchy told a British officer in an adjacent cell that he preferred jail to the eastern front (Crawley 1985, 30).

Golfing Was a Passion

One would not associate a prisoner of war camp with a miniature golf course, but a country club atmosphere evolved for a short time at Stalag Luft III's East Compound when PoWs constructed a nine-hole par three golf course that doglegged between barrack blocks. Golfing became a passion of many PoWs and one had to choose a walking route judiciously to avoid being struck by a golf ball.

Golf clubs and golf balls were handmade until the YMCA shipped some to the camp. A few officers became experts in the design and composition of different kinds of balls. The centre of the ball began with a pebble or a ball of tin foil around which rubber was wound. Newby prided himself on his superior creation. He rolled the silver foil of a cheese package into a marble-sized ball and then cut rubber bands to wind around it. He discovered he could cut very thin strips of rubber from old football bladders by sticking a razor blade into the edge of a table and pulling the rubber bladder over the blade. Newby made the exterior with pieces of leather cut from the tongues of worn-out boots. He cut two identical leather pieces, similar to those found on baseballs, then stitched them together. He even perfected the design by punching the exact number of holes into each leather piece to make it easier for threading. Each golf ball received a smooth finish by the application of several layers of shoe polish. Rolling it around a board surface for hours gave the ball symmetry. This process produced a remarkably good ball. Harry Newby's friend, Flight Lieutenant L.E. "Lee" Usher (RCAF No. J14135, Stalag Luft III PoW No. 1352) still possesses one of these golf balls.

Flight Lieutenant J. L. "Joe" Mennill (RCAF No. J7216, Stalag Luft III PoW No. 86) made some of the first golf clubs. He attached broken hockey sticks to heads molded from soft metal. He melted the metal found in their *Keintrinkwasser* jugs and poured it into a mold carved from a large piece of pumice rock, or soap, that the Germans called *Riff*. Mennill had cut a block of Riff down the middle, hollowed out the two pieces, and put them back together. When the molten metal had cooled, he opened the mold and finished the club head by sanding down the rough surface. He affixed the club head to a wooden shaft. Flight Lieutenant Arthur Crighton's left-handed golf club was fashioned in a similar manner, except that Mennill attached it to the oak prop from the lid of the camp's grand piano.

If PoWs inadvertently played ball out of bounds they could still retrieve the ball by securing a guard's permission to cross the warning wire near the perimeter fence. In a pre-arranged system, a golfer signaled his intent to enter into the prohibited zone by waving to a guard in a tower, donning a jacket with a large red circle on the back (similar to a bull's eye target), then crossing the warning wire.

Last Months of the War

The last few months of confinement at Stalag Luft III filled Harry Newby with anticipation and dread. Fears of a German collapse started rumours that the Nazis would execute all PoWs to prevent their liberation. Senior officers devised plans to rush the guard towers and seize weapons if the Germans attempted to harm them. At the forefront of the charge would be the Poles, who had trained as soldiers before qualifying for the air force; they were versed in the art of combat and could use these skills to neutralize guards. The massacre of Russian PoWs in an adjacent compound gave credence to their fears. This murder was reiterated by Australian Flight Lieutenant Tony Gordon, RAAF, a PoW in North Compound to his son, Drew. Gordon recalled the rattle of gunfire emerging from the Russian compound before the Germans informed them of an impending forced march.

Fortunately camp commanders disobeyed Hitler's order to execute Allied air force officers and instead kept the PoWs in order to gain favourable terms of surrender with the advancing Canadian, British and American armies. In the early hours of 28 January 1945, PoWs from East Compound began a forced march to the west. They carried what they could and dragged more on sledges (sleighs) constructed from chair backs and bed boards until the weight became too great. Newby said that the woolen blanket given to him by Squadron Leader Abraham before their departure might have saved his life during the cold nights of the forced march. The first five days on the march and the four days locked in a boxcar on a rail siding are remembered as the most frightful and grueling days of Newby's time as a prisoner of war.

Epilogue

Harry Newby does not expect people to understand how the experiences as a PoW shaped his outlook on life. Six decades have not diminished memories of friends lost in war. He wonders why he was fortunate enough to survive a crash, camp life and the rigors of the winter march when so many did not. Camp life was not always deprivation, and friendships have lasted a lifetime. His six roommates provided him with some of the best memories of his life; he shared a camaraderie with them that no other life experience could parallel. He is proud of the accomplishments of one of them, Squadron Leader Sir W.D. Hodgkinson (RAF No. 39385, PoW No. 470) who became Air Marshall and Commander-in-Chief of the Royal Air Force in the post-war era. Squadron Leader Abraham, "Little X," earned the respect of fellow officers by dedicating his time in the camp to improving the lot of fellow Kriegies, building morale and leading East Compound's escape organization.

Harry was one of the founding members of the Edmonton chapter of RCAF Ex-PoWs, and he served as the organization's treasurer for many years. He retired from the banking industry and is living in Edmonton. He harbours no ill feeling for the Germans as most of them did not intentionally make life difficult for him or his fellow Kriegies. Life as a PoW gave him plenty of time to think, and Harry Newby has learned that no one should take life for granted.

Flight Lieutenant Lloyd "Hap" Geddes

Lloyd "Hap" Geddes, a native of Grenfell, Saskatchewan, spent most of his thirty-five months of captivity at Stalag Luft III. He shared a room with two of the major players of the Great Escape, Barry Davidson of Calgary and Jimmy Wernham of Winnipeg.

Early Years in the RCAF

Flight Lieutenant Geddes, RCAF No. J4773, trained as an observer in Canada under the auspices of the British Commonwealth Air Training Plan. An observer performed the duties of navigator and bomb aimer before the advent of the heavy bombers. By late 1942, the Plan's administrators divided the observer position into two separate designations because the dual responsibilities proved too demanding for one person to perform in the four-engine bombers, the Stirlings, Halifaxes and Lancasters. In Bermuda Geddes received additional navigational training to prepare him for his transatlantic crossing in a PBY flying boat supplied by the United States.

Arrival at Bournemouth

Hap Geddes' short layover at the Canadian reception in Bournemouth suggested that the RAF had few trained crews in reserve. Bomber C/ losses averaged 5 percent for most of the war, and at the time of his ran as high as 7 to 8 percent a night. Hap's operational training cor Kinloss, Scotland, in the obsolete Whitley bomber, an aircraft a

Two views of a Whitley bomber. (Courtesy of W. Prausa)

referred to as the "flying pencil" for its long slender fuselage. An antiquated aircraft by 1941 standards, it was all the RAF had to offer. Outdated navigational aids and bombing sights further restricted its effectiveness. The Whitley's lack of maneuverability and limited armaments made it easy prey for the faster, better-armed German fighters.

Active Duty

Geddes survived the destruction of three bombers. An Me109 inflicted so much heavy damage to his first Whitley that he could scarcely believe it limped home to its base in England; Bomber Command wrote it off. Hap's replacement bomber collided with a second Whitley during takeoff and neither exploded despite the fact that they were weighed down with full bomb loads and fuel tanks. Geddes underwent conversion training to a Halifax bomber at Middleton St. George in the winter of 1941–42 with 78 Squadron, one of the first outfitted with modern four-engine aircraft. He participated in the first ever 1000-aircraft raid to Cologne on 30 May 1942. Two nights later, 1/2 June, Geddes' crew participated in the RAF's second 1000-aircraft raid, to Essen. A total of 956 bombers were dispatched: 545 Wellingtons, 127 Halifaxes, 77 Stirlings, 74 Lancasters, 71 Hampdens, 33 Manchesters and 29 Whitleys. In all, 31 bombers failed to return, representing 3.2 percent of the force (Middlebrook and Everitt 1985, 274), including Geddes' Halifax, which was felled by an Me110's upward firing 20mm cannon. The destruction of his navigational aids prevented Hap from knowing on which side of the German Dutch frontier he would land. The parachute pack opened inside the fuselage, and the 'chute wound around everything. Hap tore the silk from protrusions holding it, scooped it into a ball, lay on top of it and forced himself through the tiny 18-by-24-inch escape hatch in the belly of the aircraft.

Geddes questioned the strategy of "bombing by moonlight" because the moon's light shimmered off the bombers, making them easy targets for German night fighters and flak batteries. He was unsure if he was descending into Germany or the Netherlands. The windmill towering in the distance was a common landmark in both nations. Evasion was improbable; briefings back on the squadron had suggested the Dutch underground was in its infancy. Thoughts of lynch mobs frightened him. He knew he could not travel because of his shrapnel wounds; besides, he had lost his boots in the jump. He took refuge in a stand of trees until daybreak and decided to risk contact with occupants of a nearby farmhouse. The farmer spotted Geddes coming across his field and waved him into his home. He and his wife gave no indication of their nationality and Geddes felt somewhat hopeful until a German soldier broke through the door with pistol drawn. On his heels were two little boys. He felt no malice towards the German couple; they had only protected their children. Obviously, they had sent the young lads to inform the authorities about the airman's arrival.

Lock-up

The RAF bombed Krefeldt when Geddes was locked in a cell awaiting transfer to the interrogation centre at Frankfurt am Main, one hundred miles to the south. His guards had hustled him into a bunker with irate civilians who took exception to sharing the shelter with a *terrorflieger*. Explosions rattled the thick walls of the air raid shelter as sirens wailed outside. It was pointless to run as bombs rained indiscriminately; the chances of survival were as good in the

(Courtesy of MacNeill family)

shelter as elsewhere. For the first time, Hap empathized with civilians on both sides. He is adamant that his guards prevented a lynching that night.

Geddes continued to fear reprisals from civilians as his guards drove him through the rubble of Cologne. He wondered if an angry mob would pull him out of the truck and kill him. Hostile Germans spat at him. Even his guards appeared frightened by the crowd. Geddes could understand their anger: their homes were reduced to ruins; their city was absolutely leveled. To his amazement, Cologne's trains continued to operate on time following the 1000-aircraft raid. A total of 3330 industrial and commercial buildings were destroyed, 2090 more were seriously damaged and 7420 sustained light damage; 13,010 apartments and flats were destroyed, 6360 were seriously damaged and 22,270 lightly damaged. Officials estimated 469 to 486 deaths, 5027 casualties and 45,132 bombed out of their homes. Between 135,000 and 150,000 people left Cologne as a result of the raid (Middlebrook and Everitt 1985, 272). Geddes' arrival in Cologne could not have occurred at a worse time.

Gee Box

Interrogators pressured Geddes for information about navigational equipment. He endured seven or eight days of intense questioning by an Oxford-educated German officer who alternated between the good-guy and bad-guy stereotype. At times he could be affable, and generous with American cigarettes. At other times he became aggressive and grilled Geddes on the Gee Box, a tracking system that helped crews find targets even through 10/10ths fog. The Germans wanted to know if the curvature of the earth limited the range of the Gee Box. To keep this technology out of enemy hands, Bomber Command had ordered navigators to detonate explosive charges embedded in the Box during attacks, even if crews believed they would make it home.

Stalag Luft III

Hap Geddes became Stalag Luft III PoW No. 373 in mid-June 1942. Like all new PoWs, he needed his identity verified by Kriegies in the camp because the Germans attempted to plant spies in the PoW population. Newcomers were kept under constant surveillance by the other prisoners until their identities were verified, or they were shunned if Kriegies suspected that a stoolie had been planted in their midst. PoWs occasionally froze out the wrong people. A British airman captured in the North African desert remained in virtual isolation for three weeks before other PoWs vouched for him. The multi-ethnic composition of Luft III's population, which included South Africans, Poles, Czechs, Free French, Rhodesians, British, Canadians, New Zealanders and Australians, slowed the verification process.

Geddes had a deep respect for those who had already spent up to three years in captivity. Notable people in the camp included Stanford Tuck, Douglas Bader,

"Wings" Day, 1942
(Courtesy of Barry
Davidson family)

Barry Davidson, "Wings" Day, Jimmy James, Ken "Shag" Rees and Roger Bushell. Geddes understood that routines had evolved out of necessity and that he needed to adapt quickly to be accepted into PoW circles and to cope with the tribulations associated with an indeterminate period of captivity. Camp life was unlike anything he had experienced before. Armed guards, sentry towers, searchlights, dogs, barbed wire, curfews and spartan quarters reinforced the fact of how little control he exercised over his own life. The strangeness of Kriegie culture was compounded by his first roommates, seven Englishmen—good people, but different. He found it difficult to establish a rapport with them because of their cultural differences. Geddes cautiously assumed they must have thought him the oddball. Relations were cordial, but he could not see himself wanting to spend the remainder of the war with them. When a vacancy came available across the hall in the room occupied exclusively by Canadians, including Barry Davidson and Jimmy Wernham, Geddes moved in.

Inner Workings of Operation 200

Members of the Escape Committee were sworn to secrecy, and information was disseminated on a need-to-know basis. Although Geddes roomed with major players in Operation 200 (The Great Escape), he knew very little of the group's work. Discussion of escape related activities was strictly forbidden even though the roommates were like family. Hap had the opportunity to observe how Barry Davidson gained the confidence of certain German guards and then black-mailed them. Davidson would invite these Germans to his room for coffee; he learned when they were going on leave, and gave them gifts of chocolate for their families. Some became easy marks because of their gullibility. When some signed chits for "gifts" received, Davidson threatened to expose them to their superiors if they failed to do as they were told. Once they were under his control, he requested blank paper, maps, ink, pens, buttons and other small articles

This was the room shared by Hap Geddes, Jimmy Wernham and Barry Davidson, 1943. (Courtesy of Barry Davidson family)

Jimmy Wernham (upper bunk) and Hap Geddes (lower bunk), 1943. (Courtesy of Barry Davidson family)

that might add authenticity to escape kits. The guards took great risks. Geddes remembered a German guard shook like a leaf when he turned over his identification to him, knowing that PoWs intended to use it to create duplicate copies. The guards knew that imprisonment or execution awaited them if they were exposed. The PoWs flexed their muscles as the need arose.

Flight Lieutenant James Wernham of Winnipeg led a tunnelling team during Operation 200. He often emerged after a shift underground nearly asphyxiated from the lack of good air, and looking gray and haggard from the hard work and lack of good food. He walked through the compound and released sand from long pockets sewn into the legs of his trousers, while others buried sand in small garden plots beneath the windows of the barracks.

The success of Operation 200 hinged on control over the amount of information the participants learned about the plan. The Escape Committee entrusted Geddes as a "duty pilot" and with sand dispersal. He never learned who secured cameras, film, photographic paper and chemicals for film processing, but he did have a chance to inspect forged identification cards and noted that they looked even better than the real ones carried by German soldiers.

Links to the Outside World

Secret radios provided an accurate picture of the progress of the war from the BBC perspective. The German propaganda machine distributed a news sheet, *Der Volkischer Beobachter*, to enlighten PoWs with the German perspective on the war. The PoWs assumed a version of the truth lay somewhere between what they heard over the airwaves and what the Germans told them in their propaganda rags.

An information officer distributed news to each barrack block and the barrack block commander read it out to the occupants. Information circulated between compounds on paper tied to baseballs or rocks tossed over fences.

Prussians Were Respected

Conditions within any PoW camp were austere, and Geddes knew that the Kriegies in Stalag Luft III were fortunate to have a commandant who loathed Nazism. Hap Geddes speaks well of the Camp Commandant, Baron Oberst (Colonel) von Lindeiner, a career military officer of Prussian extraction who served as aide de camp to the last Kaiser of the German Empire, Wilhelm II. A principled, highly decorated veteran of the First World War, he was brought out of retirement by the Nazis to serve as commandant of Stalag Luft III.

Every PoW knew where he stood with the security head, Feldwebel Glemnitz. Glemnitz accepted an invitation to attend an RCAF Ex-PoW Association reunion in Toronto in 1963 during the inaugural showing of *The Great Escape* with the officers whom he had once guarded. Respected for his arcane sense of humor, Glemnitz remembered faces but forgot names. He asked ex-PoWs if

A copy of the German propaganda sheet made available to PoWs. (Courtesy of W. Wanless)

Staff at Stalag Luft III. Hauptman Pieber is at far left, and Feldwebel Glemnitz at far right. (Courtesy of Barry Davidson family)

they were still digging tunnels. He remembered one of them as the "bastard" who stole his binoculars.

Geddes, like most PoWs, remembered escape as an accepted part of Kriegie culture. Everyone dreamed of escaping, principally because of the burning

Ley Kenyon, the man who immortalized the Great Escape in his tunnel drawings, drew this illustration of Stalag Luft III's security officer, Hauptmann Pieber. (Courtesy of Barry Davidson family)

desire to go home. Those PoWs caught escaping faced short stints in the cooler and most never thought they would be shot. By 1944, Geddes thought the Germans had reached the point of threats, but even then no one believed the Nazis would resort to murder to deter escapes.

Russian PoWs Not Protected by Geneva Convention

Germans usually followed the terms of the Geneva Convention when dealing with Western PoWs, but did not feel obliged to follow the same guidelines when dealing with Russian PoWs. Russians endured beatings, starvation and humiliation, and they did not have the benefit of parcels shipped to them. Western air force PoWs had little to spare but tossed cigarettes or the occasional piece of bread over the wire. Starving Russians fought each other over rotten potatoes and other spoiled food that Allied PoWs would not eat. Some even risked their lives by crossing into other compounds after curfew to scrounge for food. The Germans executed many of them, often without provocation. Geddes recalled how Russian soldiers went berserk when the first British tank arrived to liberate them at Lubeck in May 1945. When a tank ran down the perimeter fences, the Russians immediately killed a cow and devoured it on the spot. Starvation and deprivation had reduced them to a primeval state.

The Wait

For Geddes the worst part of PoW life was not knowing how long he would be in captivity. He speculates that most PoWs would have done better psychologically if they had known their release date. A Nazi victory seemed entirely possible until the end of 1943 and news of German victories in the USSR, Western Europe, the North Atlantic and Africa undermined morale. Geddes welcomed any news that indicated the war was not going well for the Nazi war machine.

(Drawing by J. Cordwell, courtesy of Barry Davidson family)

Everyone thrived on rumours and anyone could have started a rumour in a minute. Months of captivity dragged into years and conditions worsened noticeably by 1944. PoWs were grateful to the Red Cross for shipping food parcels into the camp. If the parcels did not arrive in sufficient numbers, everyone suffered. Small quantities of food were hoarded for weeks for a special meal at Christmas. A "goon" controlled by Barry Davidson grudgingly smuggled a duck into Davidson's room by flattening it out and concealing it inside his jackboot. The prisoners sewed the flattened rack back together into the shape of a duck and cooked it up for Christmas dinner. They took extra precautions to avoid having the bones discovered, by incinerating them into dust.

A copy of this picture of Hap Geddes, taken in Stalag Luft III, was mailed to Arthur Crighton in Edmonton in the mid 1980s by South African PoW Roy Wilkins. (Courtesy of A. Crighton)

Last Months of the War

The Germans prolonged the war as long as possible. The hasty evacuation of Stalag Luft III in January 1945 compounded everyone's misery. Guards, generally older or unfit for anything but light duty, were less prepared than the PoWs for the rigours of the forced march. Empathetic prisoners carried guards' rifles and transported their rucksacks on homemade sleighs. The PoWs trudged through snow and sleet and had to scrounge for food. The lowest point of Geddes' PoW experience occurred when all prisoners were crowded into unventilated boxcars for four days without food, water or heat before setting off for Trenthorst. The Germans had arranged to intern them in a camp where a typhus epidemic had broken out. Strong protests by RCAF Group Captain Wray influenced the Germans to move the PoWs to another holding area at Marlag Milag. Two months later, with the onset of warmer weather, the march resumed to the German province of Schleswig-Holstein. Long columns of PoWs were mistaken for German soldiers and strafed by Allied fighters. They spent the last weeks of the war on an estate at Lubeck, less than ten miles from the Baltic Sea.

Repatriation

Allied air forces repatriated PoWs quickly. Pick-up squadrons ferried them to England and medics deloused them as they stepped off the aircraft. Even though Hap had longed to be free, he found the initial transition to civilian life difficult. He had made real friendships in the air force and at Sagan, and these were difficult to replicate anywhere else. Six decades after the war ex-PoWs are still Hap's best friends.

Germany in Retrospect

In retrospect, camp life was not desperation one hundred percent of the time. Geddes thinks many of the men became better people because of their wartime experiences. Everyone learned the true meaning of cooperation and tolerance. Captivity and deprivation has allowed him to appreciate the quality of life that emerged in the post-Second World War era.

Before the war and during his three years of incarceration Hap knew very little about the German people. His knowledge of them was accumulated during the winter and spring marches in 1945. In the midst of the collapse of their nation, Geddes found the German people kind and generous. However, this mood did not always exist. When the course of the war had appeared to favour Germany, the majority had jumped on the bandwagon, but as the tide of the war turned, few seemed inclined to admit that they supported Hitler. Geddes does not forgive the Nazis for the atrocities committed but he is empathetic enough to understand that the German people suffered under the yoke of Nazism.

Hap remembered hearing about events in Germany on the radio in the mid-1930s and realized early that it was only a matter of time before he put his life on the line to fight Hitler and Fascism. He understood how Nazism's easy solutions to difficult problems had great appeal but he feels that many of the German people did not have a full understanding of the implications of their support for Hitler until it was unstoppable. Ignorance and short sightedness could not absolve them of their guilt, though. As a people they had to accept responsibility for the actions of their nation. The Germans began the conquest of Europe by annexing reluctant neighbors, followed by blitzkrieg. From a personal viewpoint, Geddes felt the German people were hypocritical in their disdain for bomber crews since the Germans had begun the terror bombings of civilians in every nation they subjugated. The Germans started it, the Allies finished it, and Hap is proud to have been a part of it. He feels that if the Germans had won the war, or if the Allied air forces had not brought the war to the doorstep of the German people, they might have had a difficult time understanding the misery they had inflicted on the world.

How Hap Geddes perceived the repatriation of a Kriegie after three years in a German PoW camp. (From the logbook of S. Gordon King)

Flight Lieutenant S. Gordon King

Stanley Gordon King volunteered for the RCAF in September 1940, shortly after his twentieth birthday. He earned his pilot wings in June 1942 and expected a posting to an operational squadron after gaining experience on "gardening runs," the sowing of mines in the North Sea and in the waters outside submarine pens on the coast of France, and on "nickel runs," the dropping of propaganda leaflets to people in occupied countries. Novice pilots usually flew as "second dickies," or co-pilots, before Bomber Command turned them loose with their own bombers.

King's graduation from an Operational Training Unit (OTU) coincided with the RAF's first two 1000-aircraft raids. The success of these raids on Cologne and Essen prompted Bomber Harris to plan a third raid of equal proportions on Bremen. He ordered every bomber from Bomber Command, Coastal Command and the Navy to participate in the operation but he found the number of available bombers still fell short of 1000. Hence, he pressed the worn-out aircraft and the green crews of OTUs into service. This necessitated the early return of Bomber Pilot Officer Gordon King from his leave.

The 1000-Aircraft Raid on Bremen

Pilot Officer King and his crew returned to Bassingbourne, 12 Operational Training Unit for the 25/26 June 1942 raid to Bremen. King's "Wimpy" had previously been retired from front line service because it had exceeded its operational life. His aircraft could not keep up, or fly at 20,000 feet with the other bombers; it tagged along at half that altitude and King knew he would be an easy target for a Ju88 fighter.

A Bad Premonition About This One

The RAF had chosen 25/26 June for the Bremen raid because the light of the full moon would illuminate the targets for the bomb aimers. The 8/10ths cloud cover should have obscured his bomber, but it had the opposite effect. The aircraft shimmered against the backdrop of the clouds and made it easy pickings. King's operational career was short—not quite half a mission. He recounted the destruction of his Wellington in a Loss of Bomber Aircraft Report filed on 12 May 1945, following his repatriation. He stated that a German fighter commenced its attack at 0115 hours. Its pilot fired a second cannon burst into the Wellington's port engine and raked the fuselage and cockpit with machine gun fire. Damage to the elevator controls sent the Wellington into an uncontrolled dive. King issued the order to bail out numerous times between 5000 and 4000 feet.

"Check Your Gear Before You Jump!"

Bomber pilots were trained to stay at the controls as long as possible to give the crew more time to bail out. Gordon King wore a parachute seat pack but kept

A sketch of a Wellington Bomber taken from Gordon king's logbook. (Courtesy of S.G. King)

Words heard by thousands of airmen! (Drawing by R.M. Woychuk, courtesy of H.K. Ward)

the shoulder harnesses loose because they restricted his movement. He forgot to cinch them up before jumping out at 500 feet, and gravity rolled him upside down. King locked his knees around the tether straps to keep from slipping out. Shock waves from the explosion of his bomb-laden aircraft rocked him during his descent. Luckily, tree boughs caught his parachute and kept him from landing on his head and, possibly, breaking his neck. He had no idea how far he hung above the ground. Undaunted, he severed his parachute cords with a pocketknife and fell headlong to the ground, knocking himself unconscious. When he awoke, dawn had broken and curious civilians peered down at him, with the remnants of the parachute dangling fifteen or twenty feet above their heads. Gord King became a PoW near Lingen, a centre on the German-Dutch frontier.

The Germans took King to the crash site to identify the wreckage. The charred remains of New Zealand Wireless Operator Sergeant Ali Barber and Front Gunner Sergeant Ivan Reeves were located a short distance from the burned wreckage. Barber's chute had deployed but Reeves' had not. The fate of Navigator Sergeant Main remains a mystery. His body was not recovered nor was he repatriated with other PoWs in 1945 (DHist 73/844).

Was the Bremen Raid Worth the Losses?

Bomber Command had caught the Germans flatfooted during the first two 1000 aircraft raids but they bounced back in time for the Bremen raid. The catastrophic losses suffered that night forced Bomber Command to re-assess its tactics. Of the 960 aircraft deployed, 48 bombers failed to return, including 4 that ditched in the ocean; 11.6 percent of the Whitley and Wellington bombers from Operational Training Units were lost, a staggering figure considering losses rarely exceeded 5 percent during raids (Middlebrook and Everitt 1985, 280–1). Middlebrook attributes the high losses during the Bremen raid to three factors: first and primarily, the inexperience of crews; second, planners failed to take into account that the aircraft had to fly through 200 more miles of flak and fighters than bombers sent out on the previous two 1000-aircraft raids; third, inexperienced crews expended more time locating targets in overcast conditions and fell to enemy fire. The RAF concluded that the losses did not warrant the inclusion of OTU bombers in future combat operations.

Interrogation at Dulag Luft

King rode in a passenger car for the journey to Frankfurt, site of the interrogation centre. The undisturbed German countryside did not suggest the nation was at war. Though rations were short, he remembered craving for cigarettes more than food. Interrogators at Dulag Luft seemed to know everything about him. They sent in an interrogator who had lived in Winnipeg before the war. He tried to get Gordon to open up by talking about familiar landmarks. He knew

The Transformation of a PoW into a Kriegie.

1. "On the squadron" refers to the period of active service.
2. "The chop" represents the time a flyer first becomes a PoW.
3. "40 & 8" refers to transport between camps in a boxcar intended for 40 men or 8 horses.
4. "1st Month" refers to a Kriegie's period of adjustment to camp life.
5. "1st Year" shows the transformation of a PoW into a "seasoned" Kriegie.
6. "Old Kriegie" shows the long-term changes a PoW underwent after a long stretch in the camps. (Drawing by R.M. Woychuk, courtesy of H.K. Ward)

where King had received his training in England, the courses he had taken, the names of members of his crew, and the very aircraft in which he had flown.

Stalag Luft III

King passed through Dulag Luft in a matter of days and traveled the breadth of Germany to the recently annexed Polish province of Upper Silesia. He was one of the earlier PoWs to arrive at Stalag Luft III, Sagan. The Germans bragged about the quality of this new camp, built specifically for Allied air force officers on orders from Reichsmarschall Hermann Goering. Goering had thought members of Western air forces would bond with members of the Luftwaffe, because of their flying background. He hoped a "special" camp would accelerate the bonding process. Evidently, Goering had overlooked a simple fact— Allied air force officers had volunteered to defeat tyranny, not join it. The PoWs never warmed to Nazism. Stalag Luft III became the Luftwaffe's showcase camp built for the benefit of Red Cross inspection.

Captives Contributed to the War Effort

Many PoWs coped with the indeterminate period of incarceration by convincing themselves that the war could not extend another six months. Pragmatists and those longing for home thought otherwise and turned their thoughts to escape. Escape served two purposes: first, planning breakouts helped time to pass; more importantly, the possibility of breakouts forced the posting of German military personnel around PoW camps, away from the front lines. German authorities declared a *Grossfahndung*, or national emergency, when 76 officers broke out of Sagan in March 1944. This order drew 100,000 soldiers into a nationwide manhunt for the escapees. Civilian police and hundreds of thousands of workers left jobs to join in the search. The Nazis decreed another *Grossfahndung* when five high profile British PoWs broke out from Sachsenhausen in September 1944. The escapes accomplished exactly what was intended: they drew heavily upon the human resources of the Reich.

King's Contribution to PoW Life at Stalag Luft III

Gordon King had been a sports enthusiast before the war and understood the

Kriegie Joe. A Kriegie, or prisoner of war, adapted to his loss of freedom and made do with the few resources at his disposal. It often became necessary to mix military dress with clothing sent from home. Note the symbols of PoW life: the Red Cross food parcel supplemented meager rations. The Kriegie made his own utensils, cups and plates from tin cans enclosed in the parcels. (Drawing by R.M. Woychuk, courtesy of H.K. Ward)

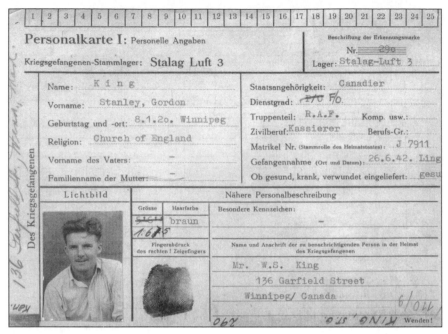

The RCAF recovered this prisoner of war identification after the war and forwarded it to Gordon King in 1947. It is just one of 400 recovered. (Courtesy of S.G. King)

positive effects of physical fitness and sports promotion in building morale. He received the YMCA's coveted Sports Badge in October 1944 for his contributions to the sports program at Stalag Luft III, an honour bestowed on less than 2 percent of PoWs. King drew up rosters, kept records, organized tournaments and sports days. He helped the Sports Committee secure equipment from the Red Cross, YMCA, and the Salvation Army, and he promoted physical fitness and team sports.

Prisoners of different nationalities organized the sports they had enjoyed before the outbreak of the war, including soccer, English rugger, volleyball, basketball, track and field, cricket, gymnastics, boxing, hockey and fastball. Equipment shortages were endemic in every camp and PoWs relied on the generosity of outside sources like the YMCA. They resorted to making some of their own gear from resources available in the camp; for example, Gordon King used cricket pads when he played goalie on an ice hockey team.

Canadians Bring Hockey to Luft III

Cold Sagan winters suited Canada's national game. Hockey enthusiasts flooded a part of the compound and received permission to maintain the ice surface at night. King's parents sent over his ice skates from Winnipeg. Players carved goalie sticks from pieces of wood, built nets, and substituted cricket pads for

Canadians preferred to use the cricket bat like a fastball bat to add a little excitement to a sport dominated by the South Africans. (Courtesy of S.G. King)

Hockey was a passion of Canadian officers in the camp. Gordon King is shown sprawling across the ice to make another goal-mouth save! (Courtesy of S.G. King)

goalie pads. King's experience as a star junior hockey goalie before the war earned him a position on the first string team. The Germans even permitted games between the teams of North and East Compounds. The inter-camp rivalries allowed players and spectators the rare opportunity to scan the landscape from another compound. Sadly, ice hockey came to an abrupt end when the Germans confiscated all skates after learning that some PoWs had fashioned the hard steel blades into wire cutters.

Fastball in Luft III

Because fastball required a minimal amount of equipment and almost anyone could throw a ball, it evolved into Luft III's most popular sport. The Sports Committee organized three leagues. Gordon King took on the dual role of captain and manager of the tier-one "Tiger" fastball team. He traded players to other teams in the genuine attempt to "level out" the talent pools. He admits he accepted the occasional gifts of chocolate and cigarettes in return for making certain trades. Bookmakers took bets from Kriegies, using cigarettes and chocolate bars as currency.

Caber Tossing and Other Sports

Sports reflected the ethnic composition of the camp. English rugger was a tough game dominated by the Welsh and South Africans. Canadians excelled at this sport because they had perfected "tackling" in Canadian-rules football. Everyone despised the English custom of jumping on opponents' backs when they were down. Games often degenerated into mayhem when the British took to the fields. The Welsh and English dominated soccer. Track and field days proved popular and athletes took to the "field" under homemade banners of their own nations. The Scottish introduced caber tossing and spectators soon realized they were safer if they participated! Basketball did not enjoy popularity until the influx of large numbers of Americans to Centre Compound in 1943. The Germans balked at PoW requests for gravel or tar to make a hard surface, so players improvised by tamping the ground until it was hard enough to bounce a basketball.

Construction of the Theatre in North Compound

German authorities at Stalag Luft III consented to PoW requests for the construction of a multi-purpose building to stage musical events, wrestling and boxing matches, theatrical productions and gymnastics. Commandant Oberst von Lindeiner agreed to supply materials if PoWs designed and constructed the building themselves. They excavated a few hundred metres of dirt by hand to provide a sloping floor from the rear to the front of the auditorium. They laid a brick foundation and painted walls with whatever colours were available. Carpenters fashioned 350 theatre seats from Canadian Red Cross food crates.

Gymnastics was a regular part of the sporting routines at Stalag Luft III. The man second from right is Flight Lieutenant Tony Gordon of Melbourne, Australia, 1942. (Courtesy of A. Gordon)

Dramatic Arts

When various productions demanded female actors, smaller PoWs assumed the role of young women. Gordon King's small stature made him an ideal candidate as he rarely exceeded the 110-pound mark during his incarceration. Makeup artists transformed him into a passable female with makeup, false eyelashes, a wig and falsies. From the back of the theatre, he did not look too bad. The Germans sometimes arranged costume rentals from suppliers in Berlin.

In the three years of the theatre's existence the PoWs produced such well-known London West End plays as *Arsenic and Old Lace*, Noel Coward's *Blithe Spirit*, *Design for Living*, *Macbeth* and George Bernard Shaw's *Pygmalion*. They produced two farces called *Thark* and *At Home* and other plays and skits. A pit orchestra provided incidental music for the performances. Most PoWs supported theatrical productions in other ways. Electricians designed sophisticated stage lighting systems, carpenters and artists designed sets.

Home Brew

Resourceful PoWs produced potent batches of hooch with the sixteen-ounce packs of dried fruit enclosed in Red Cross food parcels. Distillation, an imperfect science without the luxury of thermometers and hydrometers, occasionally resulted in the production of methyl alcohol and ethyl alcohol; some revelers lost their eyesight, temporarily. They cut the medicinal taste of the moonshine with powdered orange and lemon crystals. Some batches were distilled enough

The excavation of dirt and the construction of the theatre's foundations were projects eagerly undertaken by Kriegies during the summer of 1943. (From *Wirebound World*, H.P. Clark)

An interior view of North Compound's theatre, with 350 seats constructed from Red Cross boxes. (From *Wirebound World*, H.P. Clark)

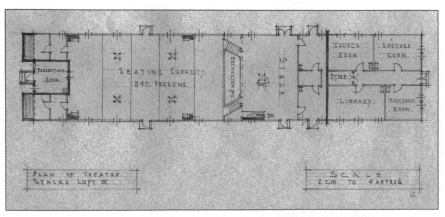

The theater was a multi-use facility where church services, theatrical productions, concerts, educational classes and reading were held. (Courtesy of S.G. King)

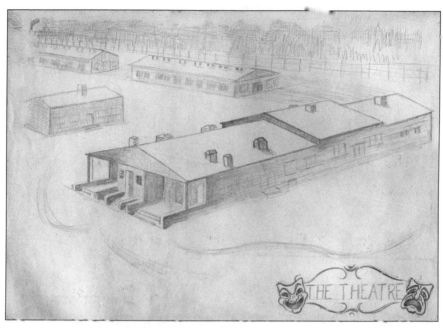

The theatre built in North Compound, Stalag Luft III. (Courtesy of Barry Davidson family).

Gordon King played many female lead roles in plays produced in the theatre. Cartoon by Bill Fordyce of Melbourne, Australia. (Courtesy of S.G. King)

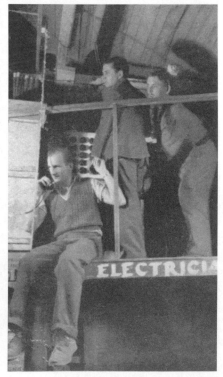

Tradesmen of every sort contributed to the operation of the theatre, including electricians, carpenters, bricklayers, painters, set designers, tailors and makeup artists. (From *Wirebound World*, H.P. Clark)

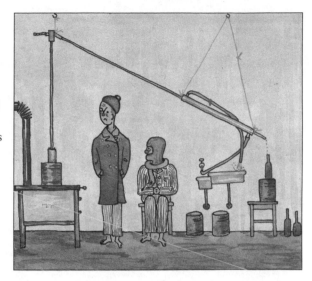

Tiger Brandy. Being a PoW did not restrict Kriegie access to alcohol. Dried fruit was fermented in homemade vats and then distilled in containers made by tin bashers in the camp. (Courtesy of S.G. King)

to produce nearly pure alcohol, confirmed by the burning off of a teaspoon of moonshine and by the burning sensation in one's belly. Some men went a bit crazy. German sentries who contended with rowdy PoWs became more tolerant if the prisoners allowed them to imbibe, too. Hooch served as a suitable replacement for lighter fluid.

Three Christmases

No celebration tugged at the heartstrings and made the PoWs long for home more than the Christmas season. Despite the loneliness, they made the best of a difficult time by preparing lavish dinners from the delicacies enclosed in Red Cross parcels. Gordon King never would have believed he would celebrate three Christmas seasons in a PoW camp—1942, 1943 and 1944. Note the improvement in fare in 1944 (see menus, next page).

Tunnelling

Tunnelling was the preferred method of escape. Early escape attempts were haphazard until the arrival of Wings Day and Roger Bushell. Diggers made minimal efforts to conceal their activities; light-coloured sand on the dark surface soil was a dead giveaway that someone was in the process of digging a tunnel.

One often had to question the sanity of going underground. Early efforts involved excavating under the compound as quickly as possible before the tunnel caved in or before the Germans detected it. Gordon King worked just once with a Czech pilot named Cenek Chaloupka on a "blitz" tunnel. Gord's job was to scoop the sand to the mouth of the tunnel, but he could not keep up with the Czech excavator. The men worked in complete darkness or illuminated the tunnel with margarine lamps that burned precious oxygen, usually causing the

CHRISTMAS 1942

MENU

Hors d'oeuvres Royals
Consommé Julienne
Viande all tin Canadien
Crème de Pommes de Sagan
Reichs Carrottes all Fromage
Plum Pudding
Sauce Speciale de la Maison
Fromage et Biscuits
Corbeille de Fruits Americaines
Moica de l'Afrique du Nord
Desert de la Croix Rouge
Cigares et Cigarettes variées

SAGAN STALAG LUFT 3, 25·12·42

CHRISTMAS 1943
Menu

HORS D'OEUVRES ROYAUX
POTAGE REIN DE TOMATES
VIANDE D'INVASION IMAGINEE
POMMES DE TERRE IMAGINES À LA TIMOSHENKO
PETITS POIS ET LÉGUMES DE SAISON D'ESCAPE
PLUM PUDDING M'NEPHARTO
SAUCE TEKPEARL
CAFÉ GLACE
SAUCE DE CHOCOLAT SUAVO
BISCUITS ET FROMAGE
CORBEILLE DE HAUTS VARIES
ORDENATS DE LA CAUX ROUGE
MOKA ET CREMO
LIQUEUR DE PERMO
CIGARETTES ET QUELQUES CIGARS

STALAG LUFT 3

(Courtesy of S.G. King)

CHRISTMAS
1944

F/Lt. S.G. King
R.C.A.F.

STALAG LUFT 3

(Courtesy of S.G. King)

BREAKFAST
1000 HRS

Porridge
Toast & Butter, Jam, Honey
Tea

LUNCH
1230 HRS

Vegetable Soup
Toast & Butter, Cheese, Ham
Coffee

TEA
1430 HRS

Christmas Cake
Tea

DINNER
1700 HRS

Rose Mill Soup

Cheese Entree

Turkey, Vienna Sausage
Creamed Potatoes, Carrots

Christmas Pudding & Sweet Sauce

Pumpkin Pie

Cherries & Cream

Coffee, Fruit, Nuts, Candies, Orange Cordials, Cigars

SUPPER
2100 HRS

Christmas Cake, Cheese Sandwiches
Tea

diggers to suffer terrible headaches. Sweat and sand irritated the tunnellers' eyes; some stripped in an attempt to stay cooler. Ferrets usually detected tunnels soon after they were started, but held back to allow the diggers to work themselves to exhaustion before they drove over the tunnels with heavy vehicles or back-filled them with raw sewage.

Except for the "Wooden Horse" episode of 1942, which resulted in the successful escape of three prisoners, no other tunnelling projects in Stalag Luft III were successful until Operation 200 in March 1944.

Return to Canada

British forces liberated Gordon King on 2 May 1945 near Lubeck after three years of captivity. Within ten days he found himself in England and on a ship to Canada. Veterans who served ninety days in an operational squadron in Europe qualified for the Air Crew Europe medal. King did not qualify, even though he had spent three years in an air force PoW camp.

Gordon married June Rutherford in 1946. They had corresponded since his departure for England in 1940. He resumed his clerical job with the City of Winnipeg but left the job for private business when a friend employed with W.G. MacMahon Floor Coverings of Winnipeg encouraged him to join his sales team. Business in the post war era boomed after years of rationing and consumers bought everything despite premium prices. The company wisely chose to cross-market and began to sell farm and home supplies. In 1964, Gordon accepted the manager position offered at W.G. MacMahon's Edmonton branch where he worked until his retirement in 1984.

Gordon and June raised three sons, Robb, Chris, and Richard, and a daughter, Cathy. In the early 1970s, Robb and Chris won the Canadian Men's High School

Kriegies often wondered how well they would fit in to civilian life after the war. (Drawing by R.M. Woychuk, courtesy of H.K. Ward)

Curling Championship twice. Cathy was skip of a team of Canadian Women's Curlers who were twice national champions. She skipped the Canadian Women's Curling Championship team at the 1998 Brier and later that year won the bronze medal at the world championships held in Brandon, Manitoba. In January of 2002, Cathy King won the Ladies' Alberta Curling Championship again. Mr. and Mrs. Gordon King have nine grandchildren.

Gordon remains active in the community. He curls twice a week and works out regularly at the YMCA where he was awarded a life membership after fifty years of continuous support. He continues to hunt big game and waterfowl. Gordon is president of the Edmonton branch of the RCAF Ex-PoW Association and stays in close contact with friends he met in Europe sixty years ago.

Epilogue

Gordon King performed an important role during the war by making sure the morale of fellow officers did not falter. He helped to keep the spirits and bodies of his fellow officers healthy, which in turn, contributed to the healthy return of fellow officers to Canada after the cessation of hostilities.

This is the underside of the compass manufactured by PoWs in Stalag Luft III for use in the Great Escape. It is stamped on the back "Stalag Luft III Sagan Germy" with a swastika emblazoned in the centre. (LaGrandeur collection)

Flight Lieutenant Arthur B. Crighton

Article 17 of the Geneva Convention of 27 July 1929 Relative to the Treatment of Prisoners of War specified that PoWs were entitled to organize intellectual and sporting pursuits. The Germans usually encouraged such activities because busy PoWs were less inclined to escape. Athletic, dramatic and musical programs sustained morale and provided thousands of hours of enjoyment in an environment otherwise devoid of stimulation.

Flight Lieutenant Arthur Crighton assumed a leading role in Stalag Luft III's music program. He was a paradox of sorts. Though dedicated to flying when he joined the RCAF in

1940, he was equally devoted to teaching band music in the eastern Ontario towns of Maxville, Finch and Cornwall. After completing pilot training and receiving his commission, he exchanged musical instruments for the controls of a Wellington bomber.

Pilot to PoW

During Crighton's eighth raid, in this case to Hamburg on 8/9 April 1942, the tired engines in his Wellington X3467 failed, and he jettisoned the bomb load to maintain altitude. A fire in the port engine was extinguished with compressed

Pilot Officer Crighton in Calgary, 1941. (Courtesy of A. Crighton)

The squadron crest of 419 "Moose" Squadron RCAF. (Courtesy of A. Crighton)

Q, "Queenie," the Wellington bomber flown by Flight Lieutenant Crighton in the early years of 419 Squadron RCAF. (Courtesy of A. Crighton)

nitrogen and the engine restarted. Then the starboard engine overheated and started to burn. After Crighton suppressed the flames and feathered the starboard propeller, flames broke out in the port engine again. The fire spread quickly into the canvas stretched over the Wellington's geodetic frame and Crighton ordered the crew to abandon the aircraft. Crighton's Wellington crashed between Roggenburg and Barssel, Germany. Grievously mourned was the death of the crew's rear gunner, Pilot Officer Ernest Richard Howard, RCAF No. J15150. His loss was especially sad to Crighton because they had grown up together as brothers, under the same roof, in Calgary. Ground crews who performed routine service and maintenance to bombers were resigned to the probability that aircraft were undergoing repairs for "one more flight" as resources were continually stretched to the limit.

Arrival at Stalag Luft III

During the first year of captivity Crighton was first interned at East Compound of Stalag Luft III, Sagan then at Oflag XXIB, Schubin, Poland, then again at East Compound, followed by a "posting" to North Compound in April 1943. He dispersed yellow sand under barracks and "stooged," or kept watch, during various tunnelling activities in East Compound and Oflag XXIB before resolving to contribute to the betterment of his fellow Kriegies by resuming the activities of his peacetime occupation of teaching and performing music.

Musical and theatrical programs in PoW camps reflected the ambitions and skills of leaders and participants. John Marshall formed the first band in 1941 at Stalag Luft I and conducted four concerts before the camp's closure and the PoWs' move to Stalag Luft III in 1942. Roy Wilkins reorganized the stage band at Sagan in 1942. Wilkins, a South African, had organized a stage band, "Roy's Zulus," and Crighton joined the trumpet section shortly after his arrival in the camp.

Oflag XXIB, Schubin, Poland

Two hundred air force officers, including Crighton, voluntarily transferred from Stalag Luft III to Oflag XXIB at Schubin, Poland, in September 1942, optimistically looking forward to a change of scenery. Crighton established a music program with a concert stage, a stage band and chamber music groups. A January 1943 concert included overtures by Gluck and Stradella, a waltz by Strauss, and excerpts from *The Mikado.*

Return to Stalag Luft III's East Compound

The escape of forty-three PoWs from Oflag XXIB in April 1943 prompted the SS and Gestapo to take control of the Schubin camp and return all PoWs to East Compound of Stalag Luft III, where Luftwaffe guards, more familiar than the Wehrmacht with recognizing the signs of escape, would be in control once again. A north compound added to the camp during Crighton's absence provided accommodations for the growing PoW population. Roy Wilkins, one of several hundred PoWs moved into the new North Compound in March 1943, persuaded German authorities to "post" Crighton from East to North Compound as the orchestra needed an expert trumpet player for an upcoming concert. Crighton looked forward to performance opportunities in the newly constructed theatre building. He suggests he was the only PoW "posted" to a camp at the behest of fellow PoWs. Shortly after his arrival, he assumed responsibility for the musical program and became conductor of North Compound's orchestra. Concerts included the overtures "Light Calvary" and "If I were King," the Strauss waltz "Vienna Life," and Ketelby's "In a Persian Market," Schubert's *Unfinished Symphony* and Beethoven's first and fifth symphonies.

In August 1943 Bruce Organ, a pre-war producer at the Stratford theatre at Stratford-on-Avon, prepared and directed an open air performance of *A Midsummer Night's Dream*. Crighton conducted the orchestra that provided incidental music drawn mainly from "Weber's Overture" and "Oberon," and excerpts from Elizabethan composers and Henry Purcell. Though PoWs had no knowledge of the Holocaust they understood that the traditional music by Felix Mendelssohn for *A Midsummer Night's Dream* was not acceptable for racial reasons in a German-controlled camp. Crighton wrote a simple composition, "Titania's Lullaby" for that performance, his only original score. The singer for this first performance was Bruce Adinsell, a relative of Richard Adinsell, composer of the Warsaw Concerto.

A "glee club" with soloists and chamber music groups performed at concerts. Over time enough musical instruments arrived to give PoWs the opportunity to form a full forty-two piece orchestra, courtesy of the YMCA and other philanthropic groups. Crighton filled the months playing and conducting. An education program existed in which many subjects were taught including music theory and the rudiments of wind instruments, taught by Crighton.

The standard of performance steadily increased as more instrumentalists were shipped to the camp, and the American YMCA supplied more instruments. The orchestra performed three concerts by Christmas 1943, including overtures to *Light Cavalry*, *Pique Dame*, and *Danse Macabre*; ballet music from Faust; and the string serenade "Eine Kleine Nachtmusik." Crighton conducted the camp's first full symphony, Schubert's *Unfinished Symphony*, along with Beethoven's *Egmont* Overture, from 16 to 19 July 1944. Baritones Roland Stamp and Glen Gardiner shone in the all-male chorus directed by Arthur Loveland. From 15 to 18 July 1944, an orchestral extravaganza, assisted by the male chorus, performed the Blue Danube waltz by Strauss and "On the Trail" and "Mardi Gras" by Ferde Grofe. The male chorus sang spirituals and suites of well-known arrangements by W.A. Fisher, Arthur Sullivan, Edward German, Steven Adams and Eric Coates. On 31 October 1944 Crighton conducted Mozart's overture to *The*

Marriage of Figaro, Bach's "Jesu, Joy of Man's Desiring" from Cantata No. 147, Beethoven's Symphony No. 1 in C Major, as well as five other major concert pieces—an evening of accomplishment for Stalag Luft III's orchestra!

The musicians formed the Happy Valley Silver Band for an inter-compound sports day in May 1944. The Happy Valley euphemistically referred to the Ruhr Valley, dreaded by air force bombers for the concentrations of exploding flak that "rose like geysers from hell."

Last Performance in Stalag Luft III

The PoWs sensed that the 22 December 1944 performance of Handel's *Messiah* signaled their last Christmas in captivity. Arthur Loveland transcribed Handel's original score for an all male chorus. The original orchestral score, limited to strings, trumpets and timpani, underwent a transformation thanks to the dedicated efforts of musicians who listened carefully to phonograph recordings, adding parts for wind instruments as required, transforming Handel's version of the *Messiah* into a full Mozart score. The group lacked a tenor soloist and the Germans obliged by downing Edward Thorn in time for him to learn both the soprano and tenor parts. Ley Kenyon performed in the second violin section. Arthur Crighton supplied the trumpet obbligato for Gardiner's performance of "The Trumpet Shall Sound." (After the war, Crighton acted as best man at Gardiner's wedding into Toronto.)

The thermometer plunged below zero outside. Freezing temperatures during the performance of the *Messiah* did not diminish the magnificence of the moment. Members of the audience came prepared, bundled into their overcoats

Roy's Zulus performing in East Compound, Stalag Luft III in 1942. The violin soloist is Melville Carson. (Courtesy of A. Crighton)

Arthur Crighton's stage band at Oflag XXIB. (Courtesy of A. Crighton)

Stalag Luft III's orchestra with Arthur Crighton as the conductor, 1943.

Arthur Crighton conducting the orchestra, 1943. Ley Kenyon, famous for his artistic depictions of the tunnelling activities of the Great Escape, is the light-haired violinist on the left. His illustrations were hidden away in Tunnel Dick and retrieved by a PoW after the camp's evacuation in January 1945. Ley Kenyon later received international attention for his photographic work during 25 years of deep sea diving with Jacques Cousteau.

The Happy Valley Silver Band in North Compound, 1943. (Courtesy of A. Crighton)

The pit orchestra provided incidental music for drama productions. (Courtesy of A. Crighton)

and their best clothes. Musicians donned greatcoats and fingerless gloves and provided the most awe-inspiring performance, with a cacophony of Russian guns fifty miles distant across the River Oder as a fitting backdrop for the last concert in Stalag Luft III. Arthur Crighton's musical accomplishments are not forgotten by fellow Kriegie Gordon King, who commented nearly sixty years later, "Art Crighton should have been given a medal for playing so much beautiful music and making the camp a better place." In 2003, Arthur Crighton received a Queen's Jubilee Medal for his contributions to PoW life and his lifetime commitment to music.

Epilogue

Arthur Crighton is intensely aware of his good fortune in being able to pursue music during his three years as a PoW. After the war he earned a doctorate in Church music at the University of Southern California, and became Professor Music at the University of Alberta. He continued to serve in the Canadian

Reserve Air Force. As a lieutenant-colonel he commanded the Regular Officer Training Program and the University Reserve Training Plan, programs that prepared young Canadians to assume leadership positions in the Canadian Forces by combining academic studies with officer training.

Crighton acknowledges that Stalag Luft III was a model camp, set up with the intent of impressing officials of the Red Cross and neutral nations about the quality of care provided to prisoners of war. He was able to share his passion for music with others, teaching them the rudiments of music and how to play instruments. Crighton's selfless dedication to his comrades helped many of them get through an ordeal that otherwise might have consumed them. The PoWs chose to learn music and develop their minds, ultimately returning to a peaceful world.

Flying Officer W.D.J. "Wally" MacCaw

Wally MacCaw's school principal and teacher, the Honorable John Sturdy, a veteran of the First World War and later a Cabinet minister in the Saskatchewan government, influenced him profoundly in his formative years. Sturdy was a veteran of trench warfare on the Western front. He immigrated to Canada in the interwar years and settled in Qu'Appelle, Saskatchewan where he taught in a one-room school. The Englishman recited countless acts of heroism and sacrifice by British soldiers during the Great War. Sturdy brought a world of experience to the small rural community, and his stories instilled in his students an interest in world news and a sense of patriotism, while emphasizing the need for young Wally's generation to prepare for new threats, especially those of Nazi Germany. Wally MacCaw developed a desire to fly at a young age and dreams became reality when he and another local boy travelled to England to commence pilot training with the RAF in August 1938. Leaving Canada seemed reasonable, as job prospects during the Depression were scarce.

The British Empire neglected to initiate a program of re-armament even when Hitler's aggressive posture foreshadowed the inevitability of war with Western democracies. Britain looked overseas to fill the ranks of its armed forces, especially after the Nazis re-affirmed their sovereignty over the Rhineland in 1936, annexed Austria in 1938, absorbed Sudetenland in the same year and clamoured to reclaim the Polish Corridor. MacCaw joined countless other Canadians who volunteered for five-year short service commissions in the RAF. Flying Officer MacCaw, RAF No. 41397, flew routine patrols over the North Sea in search of German supply ships. In 1941, a German fighter escort intercepted and inflicted heavy damage on his Beaufort, forcing him to ditch it in the ocean. Rescued from the water by the German Kriegsmarine, MacCaw spent four years in German hands, first at Stalag Luft I, Barth, and then at Stalag Luft III as PoW No. 630. The Escape Committee in North Compound assessed MacCaw's dependable and meticulous nature as the qualities needed to head security in Hut 104, the starting point for one of three tunnels used in the escape of 76 fellow PoWs on the night of 24/25 March 1944.

Four Years of Captivity Lay Ahead

MacCaw flew a Beaufort bomber with the RAF's Coastal Command. The aircraft had been modified to carry a single 2000-pound torpedo. On 2 June 1941, his torpedo bomber dropped to just fifty feet above the water as he commenced an attack on twelve cargo vessels off the Dutch coast. His actions were tantamount to a sacrificial charge as ship batteries unleashed murderous fire pointblank towards the Beaufort. MacCaw aimed for the centre of the convoy and released the torpedo. To his disbelief the trail of the torpedo disappeared, and he assumed it must have lodged in a sandbar. Two Messerschmitt fighters swarmed in from the port aft and fired on his aircraft. He attempted to lose the faster, more maneuverable fighters by climbing into the clouds, but failed; their bullets ripped into the Beaufort's fuselage and set the aircraft on fire. Unable to regain sufficient altitude to glide his aircraft over to the continent where the crew might parachute out over land, he concentrated his energies on ditching his Beaufort into the icy water near the Frisian island of Terschelling. (MacCaw received recognition for making a perfect landing in an aircraft renowned for remaining afloat for a perilously short period.) The ditched aircraft stayed afloat a few seconds longer than usual, giving the crew a chance to throw out a life raft and scramble out before it sank below the murky waters. MacCaw's navigator, Sergeant O'Brien, slipped in and out of consciousness from the shock of a 20mm shell ripping through his body. The frigid water revived him, and he managed to pull himself through the escape hatch in the roof of the cockpit and slide into the open sea. Two others crawled out before the aircraft disappeared beneath the waves, in less than thirty seconds.

Fire and machine gun bullets had destroyed the rubber dinghies and the survivors floated in the frigid North Sea. Mae West life vests kept their heads above

Art Johnson and Wally MacCaw at South Cerney Training School before the outbreak of hostilities. (Courtesy of W.D.J. MacCaw)

Wally MacCaw's PoW identification card. (Courtesy of W.D.J. MacCaw)

water, but two of the crew succumbed to the cold almost immediately. Bleeding profusely, the navigator passed out again. MacCaw swam to a remnant of the bomb bay door and partly hoisted himself out of the water. Taffy Edwards, the wireless operator, died of exposure before MacCaw could reach him. Gunner Sergeant Woodland and MacCaw clung to the debris for an hour and a half before a German flak ship pulled alongside and fished them from the water. One of the two German fighter pilots who had pursued Wally's Beaufort had saved their lives by radioing in their position. This rescue was exceptional for wartime because captains of vessels knew that they would become sitting ducks for submarines or attack aircraft if they stopped to pick up survivors. MacCaw was grateful for receiving a second chance at life.

Prisoners of the Germans

MacCaw and Woodland began their captivity in Den Helder, the most northerly mainland port in the Netherlands, sixty kilometers from Amsterdam. Interrogators at Dulag Luft incorrectly presumed that Wally had flown one of two Bristol Blenheims that were shot down during an attack by 44 Blenheims on German shipping along the Frisian Islands around the same time that his Beaufort had been lost. He did nothing to discourage their confusion.

First PoW Camp, Barth

MacCaw arrived in Stalag Luft I in early July 1941 and concluded that the camp had the makings of the League of Nations. Though most PoWs originated from Britain, Canada, Australia and New Zealand, nationals from France, Czechoslovakia, Belgium, Poland, the Netherlands, Norway and Denmark had become German prisoners after escaping their homelands and volunteering their services to the Royal Air Force. MacCaw remembered the shock of seeing so many thin PoWs in loose-fitting uniforms. Some had already spent two years behind barbed wire and Wally shuddered at the prospect of spending a comparative period in custody. It took time for him to adapt to his loss of freedom, and his first winter at Barth seemed to drag on forever. Boredom dulled the soul; infrequent delivery of Red Cross parcels affected his health. The cool, damp Baltic wind chilled him to the bone. Naturally, MacCaw's thoughts turned to escape. His captors caught him dispersing sand beneath the raised floor of a hut and locked him in solitary for a few weeks, where he subsisted on bread and water without the luxury of a blanket or cot. In May 1942, the Germans relocated air force officers and NCOs of Barth to East Compound of Stalag Luft III at Sagan to alleviate crowded conditions.

Tunnelling Broke the Monotony

Machine guns in towers, searchlights, dogs and fear of anti-personnel mines outside the fence made tunnelling the preferred method of escape. German guards (ferrets) often let would-be escapees dig themselves to the point of exhaustion before they destroyed the tunnel. Diggers who attracted too much attention found themselves purged to another camp. Repeated failures to escape only intensified PoW frustration levels. Flight Lieutenant Barry Davidson stated that he knew of forty-seven tunnels dug at Barth during his time there as a PoW, from the middle of July 1940 until his relocation to East Compound of Stalag Luft III on 10 April 1942 (DHist 181.009[D624]).

MacCaw's Role in Operation 200

By earning the trust of Roger Bushell and the X Committee, MacCaw became security head "Little S" for Hut 104, the barracks from which Tunnel Harry, used in the Great Escape, had originated. The responsibility of security head required him to check all possible spots where a German guard might lie in wait for PoWs to slip up during their clandestine activities. Wally coordinated security in and around the hut and personally checked the attic and the space between the floor and the ground for ferrets before the diggers started. Members of PoW security teams conducted thorough searches of the fifteen barracks of North Compound after each *appell*, or roll call, in case a guard had slipped in unseen and planted himself somewhere in the compound. When each block had been secured, an "all clear" message circulated through the camp and each group would commence its escape-related activity; forging, tailoring, map or compass making, digging or sand dispersal.

MacCaw recalls that the tunnelling could have been completed in a matter of a few weeks, but Bushell insisted on caution. He did not want the Germans to have reason to step up searches after finding obvious deposits of light-coloured sand.

The Night of the Great Escape

MacCaw's account of Operation 200 is as vivid now as it was sixty years ago. Through the cracks in a shutter, he watched shadowy figures move their way to Hut 104 at predetermined intervals. Blackout conditions were imposed over Stalag Luft III the night of the Great Escape, for the first time since late January because of intense RAF bombing of the German capital. The Germans extinguished lights in all compounds to prevent Allied aircrews from using the PoW camp for navigation, a remarkable feat considering Stalag Luft III's proximity eighty miles southeast of Berlin. MacCaw was amazed to learn that the explosions and rumbling from bomb blasts in the capital shook the barracks at Sagan. The ultimate effect of the imposed blackout on escapees in Luft III was the reduction of potential escapees from 200 down to 76, a blessing when one considered the horrible toll exacted on those who made it through the tunnel.

The escape operation continued until four in the morning when a guard making water spotted figures emerging from the exit point of the tunnel. Gunshots alerted the camp to an escape in progress, but the Germans had no idea of the magnitude of Operation 200 for several hours. Officers slated to escape but not in the tunnel scurried out of Hut 104 and made their way quietly back to their barrack blocks, keeping to the shadows. They burned forged travel papers and disguises; no one wanted the Germans to find any incriminating evidence. Guards who had supplied maps, copies of passports, travel documents and pieces of uniforms feared for their lives. A German NCO crawled back through the tunnel to find where it originated. Guards were astounded by the complexity of the operation. Under their noses, PoWs had incorporated railcars, an air circulation system, shoring and electric lighting into a complex tunnel system over the previous year. German reinforcements manned extra machine guns in the compound to keep order. Gestapo arrived in their long coats and felt hats and ordered rations reduced for PoWs, a terrible blow for men already existing on minimum rations. Freedom to move about the camp was abolished. Security men stormed barracks at any time of the day or night to conduct searches. The Germans thought harsh actions might deter further escape attempts.

A Twist of Fate

Wally MacCaw's dedication to the operation had earned him an early position in the escape order, but he chose to pass up his opportunity because of a premonition. Sensing that the escape would not go well, he withdrew, and James Wernham of Winnipeg went in his place. The Gestapo executed Wernham and forty-nine other officers as a reprisal.

A New Tunnel Completed

Senior British officers approved the immediate construction of a new tunnel after the Great Escape because many PoWs believed a point would come when the Germans might execute them all instead of allowing them to be repatriated. The Escape Committee enlarged the crawl space below the theatre and used it as a command post and gathering point in case of a premeditated attack on PoWs. A new tunnel originating from the crawl space crossed beneath the wire, emerging in the guards' compound beneath the shed that housed their small arms. The prisoners hoped to surprise its occupants and seize weapons to prevent their annihilation. Many, including MacCaw, organized themselves into platoons and received commando-style training from Polish PoWs. Fortunately, the occasion never arose for the Sagan PoWs to defend themselves.

Flight Lieutenant W.A. "Wilkie" Wanless, MiD

To survive two dozen operations as a rear gunner, nearly two years in a PoW camp, and weeks traversing Germany in a forced march is nothing short of miraculous. Statistics speak for themselves. A single night's loss of twenty heavy bombers normally resulted in 100 to 140 casualties, and losses were more horrific on many operations. The loss of over 100 bombers during the 1000-aircraft raid on Nuremburg in March 1944 claimed the lives of over 500 men of Bomber Command. In comparison, these casualties were more than double the losses incurred by the Canadian Army during the D-Day assault on the Normandy beaches. In total, 50,000 officers and men of Bomber Command lost their lives during the Second World War. Training accidents claimed close to 10 percent of them. One veteran says he could not recall a day passing without funerals for comrades killed in training accidents or takeoffs. Once a bomber crew became operational, they ran gauntlets of steel fired from German flak ships in the English Channel, the North Sea and inland anti-aircraft batteries. German interceptors, assisted by ground units, shot down thousands of bombers. Unpredictable weather, mechanical problems, structural fatigue, and navigational problems contributed to these astounding losses. Consequently, crews thought in terms of operations completed instead of a full tour of thirty operations completed.

Wanless flew thirteen operations with his original crew and eleven more with six different crews. His original crew failed to return from operations while he had a brief stint in hospital. He never knew the names of the men with whom he flew as a spare gunner, not even the names of those men he replaced. The squadron was perpetually short of gunners, and he only learned at the briefing before an operation that he would go out on a particular night. Wilkie detested the mid-upper gunner assignment because it required him to leave his guns to throw Window out the flare chute every minute, which increased the bomber's vulnerability. He was very unhappy when he had to fly with a green crew just out of OTU for an operation to Mannheim. Their inexperience made Wanless nervous; two or three of the crew chattered incessantly over the intercom about the explosions, flashes and tracers around the aircraft. He refused to f with them again. Sadly, those novices joined the long list of casualties wit a few weeks.

This picture, taken at Spalding Moor after his original crew went missing, shows Wanless (second from right) with a crew he knew from training; all of them ended up at 76 Squadron. He chummed around with them between operations. (Courtesy of W.A. Wanless)

Wilkie Wanless cites his participation in the attack on the V2 rocket facilities at Peenemunde as the most noteworthy of his operational experiences. Crews were not privy to the details of the raid on the Baltic island, but all understood the significance of their objective because their commanding officers told them they would return again and again until they obliterated their target. Analysts estimated that a single V2 rocket had the potential to inflict 4000 casualties, a staggering estimate considering 3000 RAF bombers loaded with 8300 tons of bombs delivered the same damage. Fortunately, the crews found their mark during their initial run on the rocket facilities. This set back the V2 program for several months, and delayed implementation of this weapon (Chorley, 84–5).

Wanless went missing in action after a raid to Kassel on 3 October 1943. His family learned of his survival two months later when Red Cross officials added his name to a list of new arrivals at Stalag Luft III. He spent just five months in North Compound before guards purged him along with suspected organizers of the Escape Committee to Stalag Luft IV at Belaria.

On the Squadron

Wanless was posted to the RAF's 76 Squadron based at Holme on Spalding Moor on 18 February 1943 and his first two operations were to Cologne and St. Nazaire on 26 and 28 February, respectively. On 14 April 1943, near Stuttgart, received credit for downing one of two Ju88 interceptors engaged in a simultaneous attack on his Halifax. Their gunfire tore the astrodome off the top of the bomber and rendered the hydraulics and wireless unit unserviceable. With the flaps and landing gear down and the bomb doors open, Wilkie wondered how his crippled aircraft would remain aloft for the two-hour journey to England. His bomb aimer died of wounds, and the funeral had a sobering effect on the crew. Six months later a single Me110, armed with an upward firing 20mm cannon, downed his Halifax near Detmold, claiming the life of the mid-upper gunner and the pilot. Damaged hydraulics trapped Wanless in the cramped compartment at the back of the bomber. He cheated death by turning his turret by hand 180 degrees and falling backwards into the night sky. Fearing a bomber in the stream would fly into him, he freefell before deploying his parachute.

Parachuting into Germany

Following his short-lived freedom of three days, the Gestapo took Wanless into custody. He learned that his four crewmates had survived because their parachutes and Irving flight jackets were in the same room in which he was locked. The evil work of Nazi Propaganda Minister Joseph Goebbels had its desired effect on the German people. During his transfer to the Luftwaffe interrogation centre in Oberursel, an angry mob descended on Wanless and his single escort. The guard commanded him to run and jump aboard the moving train at the far end of the platform if he wanted to live!

Dulag Luft

The walls of Dulag Luft protected Wanless from angry civilians. He collapsed into a deep sleep after his captors locked him in isolation. Rejuvenated by the rest, he went over what he had learned about Luftwaffe interrogation procedures from an RAF sergeant who had escaped custody in Germany. The sergeant had warned crews to expect their morale to take a plunge before the Germans began any questioning. Interrogators would probably place him in a "dinky, ungodly uncomfortable cell" with the heat turned up to an intolerably hot temperature, where hunger and loneliness would consume him. He should expect a shock because "the Germans know everything about you!" They would attempt to disarm a PoW with promises of cigarettes and escorted walks into town if he cooperated. The sergeant warned the crews to be on the watch for imposters. Wilkie felt disgust when an interrogator, masquerading as a Red Cross official, entered the room with a clipboard of questions, supposedly to facilitate contact with his family. Wilkie also readied himself for a visit from a particular squadron leader thought to be a collaborator. He did not know it at the time but MI9 had exonerated this officer after his transfer to Luft III, after he had improved conditions for new arrivals. A board of inquiry, convened by senior British officers at Stalag Luft III, concluded that this squadron leader had performed his duties with distinction by securing good treatment, exercise outside cells and medical attention for them (MI 9/S/P/G (G) 1316).

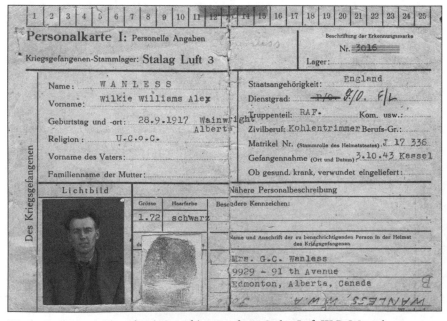

To Mrs. George Cuthbert Wanless

I have learned with deep regret

that Pilot Officer Wilkie William Alexander Wanless,

has been reported missing. R.C.A.F.

The Government and people of Canada join

me in expressing the hope that more favourable news

will be forthcoming in the near future.

Charles G. Power

Minister of National Defence for Air

This letter of regret was received by Flight Lieutenant Wilkie Wanless's mother after he was reported missing in action over Germany in 1944. (Courtesy of W.A. Wanless)

Wanless's German identification card is one of 400 Stalag Luft III PoW cards recovered. (Courtesy of W.A. Wanless)

Following ten days of isolation and interrogation, Wanless's captors released him into the general PoW population. Before shipping him on to a permanent camp, the gaolers fed him well and issued a great coat, new army boots, toiletry items, towels and other necessities.

Stalag Luft III

Kriegies at Stalag Luft III scrutinized new arrivals to make sure moles did not enter the PoW population; Wanless needed someone in the camp to verify his identity. Group Captain Wilson and Jimmy Carey, a friend posted in East Compound, vouched for him and his navigator, Flying Officer Philip J. Suzor, a citizen of the island nation of Mauritius in the Indian Ocean. Wanless met Kriegies who had been shot down in their antiquated Fairey Battles before the fall of France in June 1940. Some fighter pilots went by the nickname of "Scruffy" because of facial scarring; they had suffered burns to their faces and hands because the fuel tanks, mounted in front of the cockpits, ignited before they bailed out. A badly burned Canadian fighter pilot named Donnie Foster had drawn three hundred cigarettes from the Canadian Communal Fund and left them on Wilkie's bunk so he could barter for food and other scarce commodities before his first Red Cross parcel came through.

Wilkie's first night in North Compound was an event to remember; two PoWs used his room in an escape bid because it was situated close to the perimeter fence. Armed with homemade wire cutters and burlap to cover the strands in the perimeter wire, they crawled out his window after curfew. They took only a few steps before a guard fired on their silhouettes. At least one round whizzed through the wall of Wilkie's room. The pair thrust their arms high in the air and one man shouted, *Nix schiessen, nix schiessen!* (Don't shoot, don't shoot!) Guards wheeled a heavy machine gun into the compound to deter unruly behavior. Wanless never thought he would be shot at once he was in a PoW camp.

The Red Cross added Wanless's name to their PoW list. He received blank postcards and sent the first to his mother. His second went to the Irving Parachute Company in England to request the coveted Caterpillar lapel pin, a memento supplied by the manufacturer of the parachute that had saved his life.

Transfer to Belaria

The Germans suspected that a group within North Compound was in the final stages of an escape plan when they singled out nineteen PoWs during roll call, including Wilkie Wanless, and purged them to Belaria just three weeks before the Great Escape. The intent of the transfer on 2 March 1944 was to remove leaders of the Escape Committee. Ironically, Wilkie knew nothing of the inner workings of the organization but he believes the Germans included him because he had frequently acted as lookout or duty pilot.

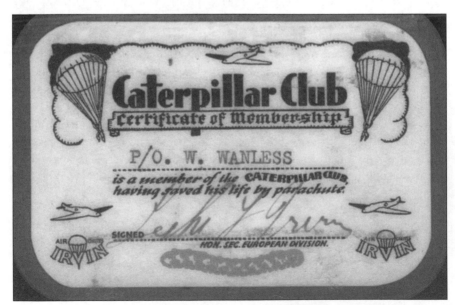

Air force PoWs often used their first postcard to notify the Irving Parachute Company that their product had saved their lives. Survivors received the coveted Caterpillar lapel pin, a badge ex-PoWs and Evaders have worn proudly all their lives. Note the date on the postcard, two months after Wilkie Wanless's capture. (Courtesy of W.A. Wanless)

Survivors of a parachute jump eagerly applied for membership in the Irving Parachute Company's esteemed "Caterpillar Club". (Courtesy of W.A. Wanless)

The comforts of Belaria were exaggerated. (From "The Log," courtesy of W.A. Wanless)

The forced march from Belaria, although difficult, was welcomed by PoWs because they were outside the confines of a camp, some for the first time in years. (From "The Log," courtesy of W.A. Wanless)

Luckenwalde PoWs banded together to complete the most basic tasks, in this case, hauling water. (Courtesy of W.A. Wanless)

Satellite Compound of Stalag Luft III

The Germans listed Belaria, a satellite camp of Sagan, as Stalag Luft IV. Popular misconceptions had some believe that "Belaria on the Hill" was an officers' rest camp with hot baths, comfortable lounges and spacious living quarters. Nothing could be further from the truth. Wanless attests the only advantage associated with a posting to Belaria was that just ten men lived in a room instead of the eighteen he lived with in Sagan.

News of the Great Escape Reaches Belaria

Three weeks after Wilkie's transfer to Belaria, the mass breakout of seventy-six PoWs from North Compound of Stalag Luft III occurred. When the news about the murdered officers trickled into camp, PoWs cut black diamond patches from the end of their ties and sewed them on the sleeves of their uniforms as a symbol of mourning. Senior officers held a special memorial service to honour the dead on 13 April 1944 in the Belaria compound (Cousens 1947, 4).

Belaria to Luckenwalde, Stalag IIIA

Belaria's population of 750 officers, including 200 Canadians, was evacuated in January 1945. Despite cold weather and food shortages, the marchers preferred the arduous cross-country trek to the mundane routine of camp life because the forced march afforded them the first real change of scenery in years. The Belaria group arrived in Luckenwalde nine days later, where the general population of the camp surpassed 25,000 PoWs before war's end.

Liberation

The Red Army rolled its tanks over the perimeter fences of Luchenwald on 21/22 April 1945. All able-bodied Russian PoWs were given rifles and ordered into battle. The senior British officer forbade anyone under his command to join in the offensive and ordered all weapons accumulated by Allied soldiers to be tossed in the cooling pond. The Soviets invoked martial law and delayed the repatriation of Allied personnel to the west. Wilkie Wanless and two friends, Alfie Stevens and Mark Laloge, grew weary of the Russian stalling tactics and slipped away from the camp on 4 May, contrary to the orders of the Russian commander. They took advantage of the permission granted to PoWs to go outside the camp to collect food during daylight hours, in order to put as much distance between them and Luchenwald before curfew. They headed for the American lines at Wittenberg. Travel was dangerous—the Germans, and now the Russians, were the enemy.

The trio moved uncontested until their arrival at Altaas Lager, once a formidable brick-walled Wehrmacht stronghold, similar in size to Currie Barracks in Calgary or Namao Air Base in Edmonton. The Soviet army had commandeered the garrison as a command post while they hunted out sporadic pockets of German resistance. The guards mistook the haggard figures for enemy soldiers and threw them into a barbed-wire cage with German PoWs. A wounded Luftwaffe pilot resigned to his fate muttered, "Englanders good, Russians swine!" With no way to communicate with the Russian guards, the three Allied airmen became very worried about their plight. A female Russian officer walking by the cage stopped when they hailed her in broken German. She ordered one of the guards to release them but issued a stern warning to leave the Lager immediately before someone else decided to return them to the cage.

Wilkie, Alfie and Mark could hardly believe the chaos unfolding outside the Lager. Discipline in the Russian army was disintegrating. Soldiers brandishing bottles of vodka seized anything motorized and tore wildly across roads and fields. When the inebriated fell from the vehicles, their drivers barely noticed. A few pulled over and indicated that they wanted the westerners to imbibe with them. The sight of rifles slung over their shoulders compelled the three airmen to oblige and swallow copious quantities of vodka.

The Soviets had waited four years to get their revenge on Germany, and German civilians paid dearly. Two older women, who disguised the beauty of a young girl by dressing her in rags and smearing dirt over her face and hands, approached Wilkie, Alfie and Mark and asked them to protect their honour from Russian soldiers. Fearing accusations of collaboration, the men left the women and pushed on, all the while wishing they could have been in a position to do more.

The three ex-PoWs sought shelter in a train station before dark because they knew the Russians would not hesitate to shoot anyone out after curfew. They found living quarters on the upper floor recently abandoned, apparently in haste because a warm meal remained untouched on the table. For the first time since their capture, the men could enjoy beds with sheets, pillows and real mattresses, but gunfire and exploding mortar shells from a nearby firefight prevented any chance of sleep. Wanless and his comrades moved on at first light and found German bodies littering the roadway a short distance up the road. The Russians continued to encounter resistance everywhere they went and they would shoot first without a thought. The three Allied flyers knew they could not avoid Russian soldiers and moved cautiously as they came to a Russian field kitchen. Soldiers paid little attention until Alfie spoke to a cook in German and asked for water. Mistaking them for German troops, the cook pushed Alfie and hollered at him to move on. Alfie stood up and told him he was an American officer. Two or three Russian officers instantly leapt to their feet, shook hands with the airmen and offered them food. A large porcelain commode brimmed with sugar. When their hosts offered cups of tea sweetened with sugar scooped from the commode they gulped down the contents without batting an eyelash!

Contact with Americans Did Not Bring a Quick Conclusion

The fluid nature of the front line made it difficult to figure out which army controlled a region. Apparently, the Russian zone extended to the point where American positions began. The airmen realized that making contact with American troops would be more difficult than originally anticipated, and Russian authorities had bigger issues to deal with than worrying how three westerners would go home. Fortunately, an empathetic Russian nurse knew that American trucks moved through the area and she arranged their transport to a former Luftwaffe air base that was being used as a collection point by the Americans to move ex-PoWs to LeHavre. Wanless, Stevens and Laloge were shocked and dismayed by the indifference the Americans showed for them. The Americans told them that they had no obligation to assist them because they were not from the U.S. The three airmen watched from the sidelines as planeloads of recently liberated Americans flew out to Belgium. The American commander remained unsympathetic as the men pleaded their case. Stevens must have hit a nerve when he said he longed to get back to England to see his wife and a child he had never seen, and "We've walked this far, so we can walk a little farther." Softened by that comment, the commander put the three RAF officers on a Dakota transport to Brussels where British authorities could get them to London.

The Belgians went wild because the war ended that day. After receiving new army uniforms and drawing pay, Wanless, Stevens and Laloge joined in the revelry. Wanless's 600 Belgian francs disappeared quickly and he returned to the pay clerk for more. The clerk advised Wanless to save his money and swap free cigarettes from the canteen for drinks with war-weary Belgians who had gone without tobacco for years. Wilkie filled his tunic with packages of cigarettes and partied into the early hours without spending a franc. Wanless, Stevens and Laloge nearly missed their repatriation flight to England. An irate group waited in a DC 3 parked on the end of the runway. Wilkie thought of Luchenwald. He had slipped away just six days earlier and was going home. Others who stayed in the camp had their repatriation delayed for weeks.

Wilkie arrived in England the day after VE Day to find the country had drunk itself dry. He found it impossible to find a single drink at Bournemouth, the reception centre for Canadians. He went to Scotland to reclaim his kit from his cousin, to whom it had been given by the RAF when Wilkie had failed to return from action eighteen months earlier. While there, Wilkie received a telegram instructing him to return early to catch the first vessel bound for Canada, the *Louis Pasteur*.

Wilkie's adjustment to peacetime and his restoration to full health did not come easily. He checked himself into a Calgary hospital because of difficulty adjusting to a balanced diet. Hospital staff decided that the surest cure for his stomach ailment was confiscation of his uniform in order to keep him in at night. Several days of uninterrupted rest and proper meals contributed to a full recovery. The RCAF promoted him to flight lieutenant, and discharged him in the fall of 1945. He returned to the family lumber business in Edmonton before joining the paper giant MacMillan Bloedel. Wanless retired in 1982 and remains involved in many activities in Calgary.

Flight Lieutenant Barry Davidson

The Directorate of History at Canada's Department of Defence possesses a statement written by Flight Lieutenant Barry Davidson in December 1945 that outlines his experience as a prisoner of war (DHist 181.009[D624]). Davidson became a prisoner on 6 July 1940 after an emergency landing on the French coast midway between Calais and Dunkirk. Initially, he entertained the prospect that his aircraft had crossed the English Channel before touching down on the beach, but the quick appearance of German troops confirmed his worst fear;

he had landed in France. He and his crew, Sergeant Gilmore, Observer and Sergeant Fiske, Wireless Air Gunner did not have enough time to destroy the aircraft and its contents.

Crew Became PoWs on Inaugural Flight

Davidson piloted a Blenheim bomber of 18 Squadron, 2 Group RAF that departed West Raynham in a mid-afternoon operation for a target over the continent. After completing the operation, he set a course for his base in England but, short of fuel, he had to touch down in France. A swarm of German soldiers descended upon them from the cliffs and moved the captives inland. The prisoners spent their first night in captivity in a barn between the coast and St. Omer. The following day a car transported them to Brussels airport where a transport aircraft ferried the trio east to Münster, Germany. They boarded a train for a 400-kilometer journey south to the Luftwaffe Interrogation centre at Oberursel. The guards placed the three in solitary before putting them through three days of interrogation. The Germans purged Davidson to Stalag Luft I at Barth. During his sixteen months there, he remembered at least forty-seven separate tunnelling efforts, with none resulting in successful escapes. He contributed to the efforts of the escape group by securing road maps, railroad timetables and other important details from guards. It was in Barth that Barry earned his reputation for procuring items to facilitate escapes. On 10 April 1942 he was moved to Sagan, where he became known as the "Scrounger"; his character was immortalized in the 1963 movie *The Great Escape*.

Three Years at Sagan

North Compound's Escape Committee recognized Davidson's procurement skills. Barry used guards with strong anti-Nazi sentiments to supply contraband. His best contact was a German *Obergefrieter* named Fischer. Other guards fell into Davidson's control through manipulation. He used his strong interpersonal skills to draw them into his room with offers of supplies from Red Cross parcels, and then, after several such occasions, he began to demand items for escape kits. He even "borrowed" guards' identification papers for forgers to copy. If they did not cooperate, he threatened to expose them. His roommate, Hap Geddes, marveled over how easily Barry took control of his "contacts" despite the fact that he never learned to speak German. Even after the Great Escape, Fischer supplied Davidson with written information from the Vorlager about the fate of several of the fifty executed men. Davidson passed the information on to Squadron Leader Walters, the officer who replaced Squadron Leader Roger Bushell as operation officer of the Escape Committee.

Winter March

Davidson recalled the period referred to as the "winter march," starting in

January 1945, as the most gruelling period of his five-year captivity. Ill-prepared PoWs in poor health after months and years of captivity did not have stamina for a forced march, especially in the cold of January. The Germans failed to arrange for shelter or rations. The PoWs ate the frozen food from the contents of Red Cross parcels carried on their backs, and dysentery set in after a few days. Some officers slept outside or took turns resting in a church too small to hold them all at one time. The first five days of the march wound through Preibus to Spremburg, followed by three horrendous days aboard cattle cars bound for Tarmstadt. Davidson's health deteriorated to the point that his comrades dragged him aboard one of the last cars; his recollections of this period are scant because of the delirium. The train unloaded its human cargo at Marlag Milag, where they remained from 5 February until 20 April 1945. Word circulated that eight officers had died in the two weeks since they departed Sagan.

Spring March

The Sagan PoWs received orders to move out of Marlag Milag as British and Canadian troops closed in from the west. The prisoners refer to this period as the "spring march" and remember it as relatively easy compared to the winter march of January and February. The Germans routed the columns of PoWs to a Stalag on the outskirts of Lubeck. Typhus wracked its population, and RCAF Group Captain L.E. Wray protested strongly against the placement of PoWs in the camps as it was tantamount to a death sentence. Instead, the Germans placed the marchers on a huge estate outside of Trenthorst, where they remained until their unceremonious liberation by two Scotsmen in a jeep who simply declared the PoWs "liberated" and moved on.

Epilogue

Barry Davidson witnessed the evolution of the Luftwaffe prisoner of war system during his five years in captivity. He became a PoW before the Germans built separate camps for the air force, army and navy prisoners. He chronicled his PoW history in a logbook supplied to him by the YMCA, including photographs, stories, artwork and commentaries about Kriegie culture, from 1940 to 1945. Davidson kept his book through the forced marches of 1945, and it survives as one of the best testaments of PoW life. He identified five commanding officers in his time at Stalag Luft III: Wing Commander H.W. Day, RAF; Group Captain Massey, RAF; Group Captain Kellett; Group Captain D.E.L. Wilson, RAAF; and Group Captain L.E. Wray, RCAF. The Escape Committee in North Compound, under the leadership of Squadron Leader Roger Bushell, achieved a higher degree of sophistication after his arrival in March 1943. Davidson, member of the inner circle, was privy to events preceding the Great Escape, and to its aftermath. In his December 1945 statement to the RCAF, he recounted information told to him about the fate of the fifty. Interestingly enough, no one realized the scope of the murder conspiracy because most believed that the fifty condemned officers met death by a variety of means: hanging, poisoning or shooting. The findings of the RAF War Crimes tribunals proved that the mass killing had originated from the highest levels because the reports filed on the killing of each escapee were identical. Each of the fifty officers died from gunshot wounds to the head at the hands of the Gestapo, under the pretense that they had been shot while attempting escape.

Barry Davidson closed his 1945 testament by declaring: "Since my liberation I endeavoured to forget all that transpired during my incarceration. The two forced marches we made, however, will not be easily forgotten, and on the first I was in such a weakened condition, there are some details I could not remember if I wanted to." Barry Davidson passed away in Calgary in 1996 at the age of 82.

Flight Lieutenant A.B. "Tommy" Thompson

The war in Europe lasted a total of 2058 days. Canadian Flight Lieutenant Alfred B. "Tommy" Thompson, Can No. 097013, RAF No. 39585, was lost over Germany the very first day of the war, near Weimar. Luftwaffe Reichsmarschall Hermann Goering personally interrogated Thompson and his co-pilot, Squadron Leader Murray, on 10 September 1939, but Thompson thought that Goering was more interested in meeting the Reich's first RAF PoWs than in discussing anything of importance.

Tommy Thompson was the 68th man out of the tunnel during the Great Escape, and the Gestapo spared his life, probably because he was the first RAF PoW of the war. They spared the lives of Thompson, Keith Ogilvie and William Cameron. Thompson reported in a post-war attestation taken in Toronto on 12 March 1946 that the Gestapo and the Kriminal Polizei threatened to kill him several times before returning him to Stalag Luft III (DHist 181.009[D1229]).

Captivity Begins

When Flight Lieutenant Thompson and Squadron Leader Murray bailed out of their Whitley Mark III bomber over Germany, the aircraft spiraled out of control and came close to striking Thompson twice during his descent. He and Murray came down near the crash site and dutifully crawled into the wreckage to burn documents and destroy the instrumentation before civilians arrested the pair and turned them over to the local constabulary. Luftwaffe officials transported them to Berlin by car, where overzealous interrogators had no idea how to conduct interrogations.

Thompson's PoW history revealed that the Germans imprisoned air force, army and navy PoWs in the same camps until the Nazi High Command acquiesced to Hermann Goering's demand to allow the Luftwaffe to set up their own camp for air force officers at Stalag Luft I, Barth, in July 1940. The number of new air force PoWs exceeded Stalag Luft I's capacity to handle them, and consequently Thompson lingered between medieval fortresses at Spangenburg, Thorn and Warburg before the Luftwaffe opened East Compound at Stalag Luft III near Sagan in April 1942. The Germans recorded him as PoW No. 59 at Stalag Luft III. Between 12 September 1939 and 29 January 1945, Thompson's captors transferred him between eight facilities.

1. Oflag X   Itzehoe   12 Sept 1939–6 Oct 1939

2. Oflag IX   Spangenburg   6 Oct 1939–6 Mar 1941

3. Stalag XX(A5)   Thorn, Poland   6 Mar 1941–5 June1941

4. Oflag IX   Spangenburg   5 June 1941–10 Oct 1941

5. Oflag VIB   Doessel-Warburg   10 Oct 1941–12 Jul 1942

6. Stalag Luft III   Sagan   12 Jul 1942–9 Sept 1942

7. Oflag XXIB   Schubin, Poland   9 Sept 1942–10 Apr 1943

8. Stalag Luft III   Sagan   10 Apr 1943–29 Jan 1945

9. Forced march ahead   29 Jan 1945–10 Feb 1945
   of Russian advance

10. Marlag Milag   Bremen   10 Feb 1945–19 Apr 1945

11. Forced march ahead   19 Apr 1945–End of April 1945
    of British advance   to near Lubeck

12. Lubeck   End of April–2 May 1945
    Freed by British Second Army   2 May 1945

Arthur Crighton lived across the hall in the same barrack block in East Compound as Tommy Thompson. Thompson had been a captive for three years before Crighton's arrival and he took an immediate interest in him because they were both Canadians. Thompson was incredibly hungry all the time and he wanted Crighton to write home and ask anyone he knew to send him food. Crighton never forgot Tommy's prophetic summary of captivity: "Arthur, it's not the days, it's not the weeks, it's not the months; it's the yearrss!"

Thompson's Involvement in Escape-Related Activities

Thompson joined escape committees and dug numerous tunnels between 1941 and 1945. His only successful escape transpired during the Great Escape, and his short bid for freedom nearly cost him his life. The Gestapo returned him to Sagan and camp administrators locked him in the cooler as punishment. Within a month of the 50 killings by the Gestapo, a Swiss legation visiting Stalag Luft III interviewed Thompson and recorded his testimony. It was remarkable that the Germans permitted the Swiss to interview the Canadian in light of the fact that he could provide crucial evidence at post-war criminal tribunals. Already the Nazis had sent 5 of the 26 survivors of the Great Escape to Sachsenhausen, a death camp outside of Berlin. Information contained within Thompson's statement reached the British government within a month and prompted authorities to formalize the proceedings for bringing the conspirators to justice in the post-war era. In June 1945, Thompson appeared before war crimes tribunals to confirm the contents of the Swiss report that was offered to the British. His crucial testimony provided clues to link the conspirators to the murders; ironically, the decision by Gestapo leaders to spare Thompson's life contributed to their identification, capture and conviction.

Tommy Thompson died in 1984. His six years of captivity was the longest term of imprisonment served by a Canadian combatant in the Second World War.

Flight Lieutenant James Chrystall Wernham

The Gestapo murdered six Canadians after the Great Escape: Flight Lieutenants Birkland, Kidder, Langford, McGill, Wiley and Wernham. Through Hap Geddes I had the opportunity to correspond with and meet James Wernham's niece, Diane Bates who explained how her uncle's senseless murder had a lasting impact on her family.

Jimmy Wernham's parents, James Chrystall Wernham Sr. and Flora Murray, moved from Scotland to Canada in September 1913. Their allegiance to the United Kingdom remained strong, and the call to serve king and country resulted in their return during the war years. Following the defeat of the Kaiser's Germany, the Wernham family, with their children Florence Elizabeth and James Chrystall Jr. returned to Canada.

Intelligence, athleticism, good looks and charm indicated a promising future for young Jimmy. He worked with the John Deere Company until he enlisted in the RCAF in October 1940. The Depression precluded any opportunity for university, but Wernham excelled in navigational studies, earned his observer wings and received his air force commission in August 1941. Before going overseas, Jimmy proposed to Dorothy Bain.

The RCAF posted Pilot Officer Wernham to 405 Squadron after his arrival in England. When his bomber failed to return from an operation on 8/9 June 1942, the Wernham family believed they had lost their beloved son. They rejoiced when the International Red Cross informed them that their son had survived the downing of his aircraft, though he was a prisoner of war in Germany at Stalag Luft III, near Sagan. As unfavourable as it was to have their son in enemy hands, they believed he would return home after the war, largely because Germany was a signatory nation to the 1929 Geneva Convention Relative to the Treatment of Prisoners of War. Contrary to international protocol, Hitler issued secret orders to shoot PoWs involved in any mass escape attempt, and the Gestapo took the lives of six of the nine Canadians recaptured outside of Stalag Luft III in March 1944, including Jimmy.

At Stalag Luft III, Jimmy was active in many PoW activities. He participated in ice hockey, fastball and drama productions. He played female roles, and from the back of the auditorium, he appeared a passable substitute.

Jimmy was a dedicated officer who continued the war effort from within the confines of Stalag Luft III. During Operation 200, he led a tunnelling team and dispersed excavated sand above ground. The mass breakout fulfilled one of its intended results by disrupting the German war effort, though at an unanticipated cost. Close to one million Germans were involved in intensive manhunts across the nation, drawing badly needed troops off front lines and from support positions.

Flight Lieutenant Wernham's family had difficulty bringing finality to their

Jimmy Wernham (front center) is kneeling beside his best friend Hap Geddes (front left) in Stalag Luft III. After the war, Hap returned Jimmy's gold ring to the Wernham family in Winnipeg where, in a chance meeting, he met his future bride, Dorothy Bain, formerly Jimmy's fiancée. (Courtesy of D. Bates)

Wernham playing hockey (above), and playing a woman (far left) in *Between Ourselves*. (Courtesy of D. Bates)

His Majesty, King George VI, posthumously awarded Flight Lieutenant Wernham a Mention in Despatches for distinguished service. (Courtesy of D. Bates)

son's death. His parents moved in with their daughter Florence and her family after the war. Diane Bates remembered that discussion of her uncle's death was forbidden in the presence of her grandparents because of the grief it caused.

Jimmy's spirit lives on in the hearts and minds of those who knew him and in the minds of an appreciative nation. Selfless efforts of young men, such as James Wernham, promoted development of a Canadian value system that included respect for human rights, the rule of law, and accountability in the post-war era. By supporting war crimes tribunals, rewriting international law and arresting leaders of rogue states for crimes and human rights violations, Western nations, like Canada, have sent a strong message that perpetrators will face justice.

Operation 200, The Great Escape Sagan, 24–25 March 1944

The mass escape of seventy-six officers from Stalag Luft III in March 1944 was the largest breakout of PoWs in the history of modern warfare. The plan, code-named Operation 200, involved six hundred officers who tunnelled, procured supplies, mass-produced forged documents and maintained security during an eleven-month period. The simultaneous construction of three tunnels, "Tom, Dick and Harry," was a marvelous engineering feat. The PoWs shored tunnels with wood, built railcars, installed lighting, built air ducts, while concealing tunnel entrances so ingeniously that the Germans discovered only one of the tunnels. The retaliatory murder of 50 Allied air force officers by the Gestapo moved the heinous crime into immortality. Up to that point of the war, escape was an accepted part of PoW culture and the usual punishment for attempting a breakout was a few weeks of isolation in the cooler. Though word had circulated that the Germans might make examples of those participating in a mass breakout, none of the PoWs in Stalag Luft III believed the Nazis would actually resort to murder.

Bushell, Mastermind Tunneller

Squadron Leader Roger Bushell became a German PoW in early 1940 after his Spitfire engaged Messerschmitts in a dogfight over the French coast. He was mastermind of the Great Escape. Shortly after his arrival at North Compound in early 1943, he proposed the breakout of two hundred officers. He earned a reputation for escape during his first year of imprisonment at Dulag Luft. His fluency in German helped him to make his way to a Czech town called Lidice, where he hid out with a family for a year. His recapture coincided with the fatal wounding of Deputy Reich Protector of Bohemia and Moravia, Führer Reinhard Heydrich, by a British-trained Czech assassination squad on 29 May 1942. The SS rounded up Bushell during a sweep for the assassins and executed the family harbouring him, along with most of Lidice's inhabitants. The Gestapo suspected him of playing a role in the assassination of Heydrich and shipped him to Berlin for intense interrogation before returning him to the custody of the Luftwaffe. No one knows why the Luftwaffe placed Bushell in North Compound of Stalag Luft III. Many thought the Nazis would have taken him to the high security fortress of Colditz in Saxony, a Special Camp (*Sonderlager*) created under Article 48 of the Geneva Convention for "undesirables" like Bushell.

Bushell's Presence Was Felt Immediately

Before Bushell's arrival, PoWs invariably started most tunnelling projects from

St Clement Danes
London
Central Church of the Royal Air Force

MEMORIAL SERVICE
FOR
THE FIFTY
MEMBERS OF THE
ROYAL AIR FORCE, DOMINION, AND
ALLIED AIR FORCES WHO LOST THEIR LIVES
IN ACTION DURING OPERATION ESCAPE 200,
24TH MARCH 1944 FROM STALAG LUFT 3,
SAGAN, SILESIA, GERMANY

Friday 25TH March 1994
at 3.30 pm

FIFTY YEARS ONWARDS

The cover of the program from the memorial service held for "The Fifty" on 25 March 1944 at the RAF cathedral in England. (Courtesy of A. Crighton)

under their barracks. They lifted floorboards and slipped between the joists to the two-foot open space between the floor and the ground. Boards were re-laid to appear as if they had never been disturbed. Some energetic tunnellers might hide a false trap door under a thin layer of dirt. Crews brought yellow sand to the surface, smoothed it out under a barrack block, then attempted to camouflage it with darker soil. The large floor area under the hut provided ample storage, but where the space between the floor of the hut and the ground narrowed, the Germans became vigilant in their searches for elusive tunnel entrances. Trucks, or "putt-putt tractors," were driven through the compound to collapse any excavations, and guards buried microphones in the soil to detect the sounds of digging. Bushell concluded that the Germans had little difficulty detecting tunnelling efforts because most tunnels originated in sand beneath barrack blocks.

Bushell ended all freelance tunnelling projects and embarked on his plan for a mass breakout. The plan involved the simultaneous construction of three tunnels. At his behest, PoWs devised three novel starting points for tunnels. Workers chipped through the three-foot-square cement supports beneath stoves in Huts 122 and 104; they hid a third tunnel entrance below the shower drain in Hut 123. All tunnels descended thirty feet below ground to minimize the chances of having German sounding equipment detect the digging. At thirty feet, the tunnels turned 90 degrees and ran parallel to the surface to points outside the compound. Bushell insisted that dispersal crews dispose of sand where the Germans would least expect to find it: in ceilings of huts, in aborts and the cavities beneath barrack blocks. In a 1995 interview, Barry Davidson stated that the dispersal crews even filled Red Cross boxes with sand and stacked them in their barracks. Guards were furious when they learned of the deception, but as Davidson noted, this sand removal managed short and long-term disposal problems because the Germans hauled the sand away (Matheson 1999, 86–7). Alternately, PoWs filled bags with sand, hid them inside their pant legs, and then kicked it into the surface soil as they walked about the compound.

The Escape Committee formed four departments: Engineering, Supplies, Sand Disposal and Security. The inner circle of the Escape Committee included Stanford Tuck, Wings Day, George Harsh, Wally Floody, Shag Rees and "Hornblower" (a nickname given to Fleet Air Arm pilot, Doug Pointer). They never referred to Roger Bushell by name; instead, they called him "Big X." The "X" Committee code-named the plan Operation 200 because they slated 200 officers for escape. They decided at the onset to give those officers with fluency in German (namely the Dutch, Polish, French, Czech and Norwegian nationals) early positions in the escape order because they had the best chance to cross enemy-held territory. Those officers also received complete sets of forged documents and the best hand-tailored clothes. Tunnellers, tailors, forgers and members of the sand dispersal crews drew the next hundred spots from a hat.

They received complete sets of maps, travel papers and identity cards. The remaining slots were filled by "hard arsers," those recognized for their contributions but unable to speak German. Gordon King earned the 148th position for excavating sand and operating the bellows pump.

Security Department

Flight Lieutenant George Harsh, RCAF No. J7795, headed the 150-man security department. Everyone referred to Harsh as "Big S," never by his name. The X Committee selected him for his prison experience, his understanding of prison psychology and his ability to go about his business without attracting attention—skills acquired during twelve years of hard time in the United States. Born into an influential and wealthy Atlanta family, Harsh had grown restless with the privileged life and had turned to armed robberies for thrills. A botched robbery resulted in the killing of two men, and he received a death sentence in 1928 at age nineteen. With his death sentence commuted to life imprisonment, Harsh worked in the prison infirmary and assisted the doctor during surgeries. His fate took a turn for the better when an inmate suffered an appendicitis attack during a raging snowstorm. Blocked roads prevented the doctor from reaching the prison, and Harsh saved the prisoner's life by performing the operation himself. For this, he received a pardon from the Georgia governor in 1940 and was released. Before anyone could reverse the decision, Harsh moved to Canada and volunteered for duty in the RCAF in May 1941. He trained as an air gunner and became a PoW during a raid to Cologne on 5/6 November 1942.

At Sagan Harsh's routines ensured that surreptitious escape activities went undetected for an entire year. Everyone avoided words like "tunnel" and "sand" and used the tunnels' names. He prohibited the discussion of escape plans, except while walking circuits around the camp perimeter, because ferrets might accidentally overhear conversations. Participants were given information only as they needed it, and very few knew the complexity of the operation. Adherence to rules was enforced by the head of security for each hut, a designation referred to as "Little S." Flying Officer Wally MacCaw of Regina was Little S in Hut 104, the building that contained the entrance to Harry, the tunnel used for the Great Escape. The PoWs used hand signals and hung towels to inform other PoWs about the movement of ferrets. These specially trained guards looked for telltale signs of yellow sand on clothing, in the fluctuating ground level beneath barracks, and by pushing thin metal rods into the ground. Lookouts, known as stooges or duty pilots, yelled "Goon up!" or "Goon in the block!" to give diggers, forgers and tailors time to conceal their activities behind false walls. Lookouts kept a "duty log," or written record, of every guard in the compound, where he went, as well as the times he entered and left. The system prevented Germans from slipping around the compound undetected. Sweeps of the entire compound, block by block, occurred after each roll call to ensure a guard had not

Guard dogs kept escapers at bay at Stalag Luft III. (Courtesy of Davidson family)

concealed himself in one of the huts or under the floor in hopes of discovering a digging operation. Diggers waited for the all-clear signal before they began excavating. Gordon King recalled his shifts as duty pilot. The guards knew PoWs were constantly engaged in surreptitious activities and thought King's job was one of a series of jokes. On one occasion he fell asleep, and a guard crept up to the open window and tried to pull the duty log from King's hands. The guard had no intention to take the book; he simply laughed and said, "Just checking to see if you are on the job!"

The discovery of the Tom tunnel did not result from an indiscretion by a PoW (DHist 181.0091[D624]). There are two versions about how the Germans discovered Tom. One story contends that the tunnel was accidentally discovered when a guard dropped a pickaxe on the cement finish of the shower drain. Another version suggests that the ferrets heard digging from below a floor drain during a random search (DHist 80/514). Because Bushell believed that the Germans would eventually discover the remaining two tunnels, he ordered the discontinuation of all digging in Dick tunnel and directed all efforts into the completion of Harry. The Escape Committee used Dick to store the hundreds of items used in the Great Escape, as well as sand dug out of Harry. Some documents were often stowed in the watertight false bottoms of barrels or the false backs of shelves.

Supplies Department

"Dean and Dawson Travel Agency: Master Forgers": An Englishman, Flight Lieutenant G.A. "Tim" Wahlenn, set up a forgery section of the supplies department to produce documents to assist escapees in their movements across Germany. His forgery operation earned the moniker "Dean and Dawson" after a noted travel agency in London. The department produced 200 hundred sets of identification and travel papers that could pass cursory inspection by German officials. Forgeries were painstakingly reproduced by hand with supplies originating outside the camp. To ensure accuracy, the forgers needed the most up-to-date versions of Nazi documents. The department ended up destroying many of their perfectly crafted forgeries when the Germans updated and changed the appearance of all their documents for security reasons. Hundreds of hours had been spent for naught. Forgers did much of their work in the canteen because the venue provided a perfect cover for them. Crates and small items for sale such as pens, small pads of writing paper, rulers and erasers normally filled shelves in the room and on a moment's notice the workers could slip their work among them with little risk of discovery. Forgers alternately worked behind false walls or in darkened rooms, and for some, months of tedious work in poor lighting led to a deterioration of eyesight.

Original documents needed for reproduction were hard to acquire, but some guards sold identification cards of dead family members or provided their own as samples in exchange for the coveted chocolate and coffee from Red Cross parcels. Forgers reproduced four categories of documents needed by escapees: a pass to get out the front gate; a travel permission letter; a military identification card; or a civilian identification card. Most documents took a few weeks to produce. In the nine months before the Great Escape, the forgery department produced 450 complete sets of papers for escapes, of which 250 were produced by hand and 200 on a typewriter. One resourceful PoW built a wooden-boxed camera and an enlarger capable of reducing or enlarging negatives to the standard size found on German identification cards. The forgers never needed to use the device because a German guard supplied a 35mm camera (Crawley 1985, 43–54).

Understandably, multiple copies of maps of Germany and adjacent nations were unobtainable, so forgers traced over fifteen hundred copies of such maps onto onionskin (Crawley 1985, 55–57). Gordon King still possesses his map as well as a handmade compass made from the black vinyl of a phonograph record, glass cut from a window, and a needle cut from a razor blade; the needle was magnetized by repeated stroking over a few days.

The Escape Committee relied upon the skills of resident tailors, hat makers, leather workers, carpenters, electricians, engineers and air conditioning engineers. Tailors altered uniforms and blankets into rough German uniforms or civilian clothes. Skate blades and hinges were sharpened into wire cutters; steel bands on water barrels were made into good knives, saw blades, and jigs to hold blades. Bellows, made from canvas kit bags, pumped fresh air the length of the tunnel through pipes made from Klim cans connected end to end. The PoWs made lock picks and keys that enabled access to many locked buildings in the compounds. Tin bashers converted cans into digging tools for the diggers.

Electric lights in the tunnel brought the operation into the twentieth century. Incandescent bulbs replaced margarine lamps, which had smoked and consumed precious oxygen (Martin 1989, 139). Canadians Gord King and Ted White had procured a spool of electrical wire when a German electrician, Obergefreiter Lubos, left it unattended at the base of his ladder while changing a bulb at the top of a pole. King slipped the spool under his Polish greatcoat and ran into his hut. Joe "Red" Noble took the wire down into Harry. Gord King and Ted White were not credited with that feat in Gwyn Martin's book, *Up and*

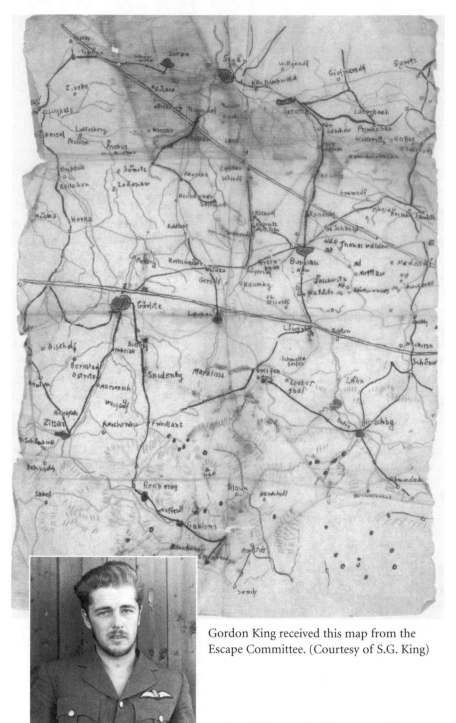

Gordon King received this map from the Escape Committee. (Courtesy of S.G. King)

Undated photograph of Barry Davidson, Stalag Luft's "scrounger." (Courtesy of Davidson family)

Gordon King's RCAF identification tag, German-issued tag and the compass made by PoWs for the Great Escape. (LaGrandeur collection)

Under, and she made amends in a 1991 note to King:

> To "Gordie" with my unreserved apologies for having attributed the theft of the wire—so crucial to the success of the tunnel Harry in Luft III—to "Red" Noble and not to "Gordie" and Ted White (p139) I regret the agonies and suffering that this unforgivable error has caused to "Gordie" and Ted in their declining years.
>
> [signed] Gwyn Martin
Warwick, August 1991
>
> P.S. Also, my best wishes and my thanks for a life long friendship. GM

The German electrician responsible for the lost wire was so terrified that he did not report the theft to authorities. When the wire and spool were later found in the tunnel, authorities prosecuted him for his negligence and sent him to prison.

Bribing of Guards

Officers in the Supplies Department covertly exchanged chocolate, coffee and cigarettes from Red Cross parcels for pens, ink, cameras, film, train timetables, identity cards and more. Unwary guards even signed receipts for goods received from PoWs. Once PoWs had control of them, these guards continued to supply more contraband out of fear of exposure; they knew collaboration could result in the firing squad, the Russian front or, at minimum, a prison term. Chief scrounger Flight Lieutenant Barry Davidson confined his "contact work" to two strongly anti-Nazi guards, Obergefreiters Fischer and "Dutchy" Schultz (DHist 181.009[624]). Fischer reproduced documents for Davidson on his own time. When asked why he took risks, Fischer said he could do more to help the Allied war effort in the Luftwaffe than from a concentration camp. Schultz moved contraband between compounds on his food wagon and was rewarded with food from Red Cross parcels (Crawley 1985, 48).

Other Germans assisted the Escape Committee. A corporal named Hesse, who was called Harry, did whatever he could to hasten the collapse of Nazism. He obtained the services of a German photographer during leaves. Through his access to the camp adjutant's office he was able to provide valuable information about the latest orders from Berlin, regulations for those entering or exiting the gates of Stalag Luft III, railroad timetables and alterations to identification cards. Hesse stole security cards and provided the forgers with a typewriter and authentic Dutch identity cards. He was cunning enough to turn in other guards who cooperated with PoWs. There was a humanitarian side to Hesse: he smuggled food from the RAF compound to feed starving soldiers in the Russian compound. Hesse received documents signed by the British senior officer of Luft III, stating that his collaboration warranted certain considerations if he were taken into custody. Everyone hoped that the British, Canadians or Americans would capture him, and not the Russians.

An unnamed Luftwaffe sergeant smuggled radio parts into the camp and arranged with friends in Dresden and Leipzig to type forged documents and develop photographs. A camp administrator named Rickmers provided needed information. A Hanoverian named Karl Pilz, nicknamed "Charlie," traded his services for chocolates, coffee, sugar and cigarettes. Charlie framed other guards to deflect suspicion away from himself, thus ensuring that his share of contraband remained uninterrupted. Another, named Rudi, hated the Nazis and supplied rubber stamps and parts for a printing press (Crawley 1985, 25–33, 43–54).

Engineering Department

Roger Bushell appointed Flight Lieutenant Wally Floody, a Canadian Spitfire pilot, to head tunnelling activities because of his pre-war mining experience with Lakeshore Mines of Kirkland Lake, Ontario. Two-man digging teams passed the pale yellow sand to another team who loaded it into handmade trolley cars. The contents were rolled over 348 feet back to the bottom of the tunnel entrance. The trolley wheels had been handmade, and they rolled effortlessly over rails that days before had served as studs in barrack block walls. Gordon King stated the walls of the barracks were just "hanging on by their teeth" because so much of his hut had been taken below ground! The PoWs cringed when someone from the supplies department showed up to requisition more bed boards for the tunnellers. Tunnellers faced frequent cave-ins and used the 30-inch boards to shore up the walls and ceiling.

Sand Disposal Department

Peter Fanshawe coordinated teams in the sand dispersal department. From the outset of Operation 200, Roger Bushell had insisted that all sand be dispersed cautiously to ensure that the Germans were unaware of tunnelling activities. By January 1944, the dispersal team was running out of hiding places for the light-

It seemed the only factor limiting a PoW's ability to escape was his imagination. (Courtesy of S.G. King)

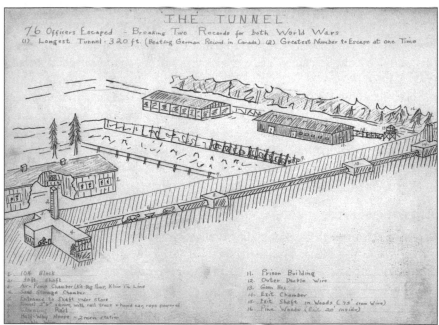

A copy of an original sketch in the logbook of Gordon King. (Courtesy of S.G. King)

coloured sand. Peter Fanshawe approached Squadron Leader Jimmy James and asked him to lead one of the two six-officer teams to carry the sand into the theatre at night and stow it below the floor of the auditorium. The secret entrance to the hollow spot was beneath seat 13. James recalled that though he was rarely superstitious, he felt that number was a bad omen for the entire operation (James 1983, 100–1).

Tunnel Tom

The PoWs had the last laugh after the discovery of Tom beneath Hut 123. The demolition "expert" brought in from Berlin collapsed the tunnel but lifted the roof off the building at the same time! The miscalculation produced a wild chorus of guffaws as lumber rained down across the compound. Rattled by the 500 jeering officers, the mood of the guards deteriorated quickly, and the ill-humoured squad outside the hut cocked their rifles and awaited an order to fire. Sergeant Glemnitz, infuriated by the laughter, spouted a statement immortalized in the annals of North Compound Kriegies: "You, you Englander offizers think that I, Glemnitz, knows bugger nothings. But I know bugger all!" It was just too much for the PoWs (Martin 1989, 136).

German surveillance teams headed by Sergeant Hermann Glemnitz maintained an observation post outside North Compound, hidden in trees beyond the wire. Three weeks before the breakout, security head Hauptmann Pieber purged nineteen suspected tunnellers from North Compound to the Teilager at Belaria, an annex to Sagan four miles down the road. The authorities had guessed correctly when they transferred four ring leaders, Wally Floody, George Harsh, Bob Tuck and Peter Fanshawe. Roger Bushell's decision to maintain a low profile paid off as he remained in North Compound after the purge to Belaria (James 1989, 103).

Producers of the 1963 movie *The Great Escape* hired Floody as a technical consultant for the film. He and ex-Sergeant Hermann Glemnitz met at the movie's Toronto premiere, nearly twenty years after the escape, and Glemnitz asked Floody if he still dug tunnels (Brown 1989, 100–2). Glemnitz was an American of German origin who had visited Germany in 1938 and then was denied permission to leave the Reich.

Nazis Sought Retribution

In 1943 the Nazi High Command had tired of escapes from camps and decided the most effective method to deter further attempts was to make examples of the next group of escapees. Stalag Luft III's Commandant, Baron Oberst von Lindeiner, received orders from High Command as early as October 1943 to liquidate escapees. When a Gestapo agent told him that he would be ordered to conduct the executions of escapees, von Lindeiner told a subordinate that he would rather shoot himself (James 1983, 94–7). In February 1944, the Nazis issued *Stufe Romisch III*, an order directing that all recaptured PoW officers and non-commissioned officers, other than British and American, be turned over to the Security Police and all evidence related to their capture and demise be erased. In early March, the Gestapo revised the directive and ordered that *all* officers and NCOs detained under *Stufe Romisch III* be secretly turned over to them and the records of their detention and fate destroyed. This top-secret bulletin was called Operation Bullet (*Aktion Kugel*). The Chief of PoW camp security for the Berlin region, *Kriminal Direktor* Brunner, told von Lindeiner that a large breakout at Sagan was anticipated and it would be advisable to take the necessary actions to avoid it (James 1983, 103). Commandant von Lindeiner called together the senior British officers and chaplains in Luft III in hopes they would use their authority to dissuade PoWs from carrying out escape plans. Hauptmann Pieber warned Flight Lieutenant Harry Marshall that an escape of over six officers would result in severe reprisals (Andrews 1976, 38–9). The PoWs did not know the Nazi High Command had replaced the usual punishment of two weeks of solitary confinement with an order for the mass execution of escapees, and they continued with their tunnelling activities.

Considering the anxiety created by escape activities, it seemed incredible that the German staff had turned off the seismographic equipment outside Hut 104 during the winter of 1943–44. It was the detection of digging sounds under Hut 123 that had led to Tom's discovery (James 1983, 238). Did the disabling of seismographic equipment under other huts suggest that the Germans wanted to have a mass breakout so they could carry out a mass reprisal? It is difficult to think otherwise.

Hitler's Reaction to the Great Escape

Adolf Hitler flew into a rage at the news of the mass breakout and ordered the execution of *all* escapees. Security chief Heinrich Himmler, the Nazi second-in-command, and Reichsmarschall Hermann Goering pleaded with Hitler to reduce the numbers. Hitler relented but demanded that at least half of them be executed. Field Marshal Wilhelm Keitel, Hitler's Chief of High Command, decided on fifty and issued an order to that effect (Andrews 1976, 16). The Gestapo carried out the shootings. All deaths were reported to have occurred under identical circumstances: "shot while trying to escape," despite the fact the killings occurred in different regions of Germany. British MP Anthony Eden broke the news of the murders to British Parliament in July 1944, and six full-time RAF investigators gathered evidence for post-war criminal proceedings. The investigators used the identical death reports as the basis for their murder conspiracy theory. Twelve Germans received the death sentence, and six other conspirators received prison sentences for their roles in the murders and cover-up.

In a war that claimed 80 million lives, the taking of fifty lives seemed relatively insignificant. Jimmy James, one of the twenty-three officers who escaped execution after the Great Escape, believes that the executions gained notoriety only because they involved the killing of RAF officers. The killings came as a shock because the Germans had violated the Geneva Convention, having used the protocol as a guideline for the treatment of prisoners for most of the war.

Night of the Great Escape

The night of 24/25 March was chosen for Operation 200 because there was no moon. The PoWs followed the usual lockdown procedure at curfew, except that many would-be escapees exchanged places with the regular occupants of Hut 104. One hundred officers assembled in the hut with forged documents, maps, compasses, concentrated food made of fruit, cereals and chocolate, and German money obtained from guards in exchange for chocolate, coffee and cigarettes. One escapee who was dressed as a German soldier, and outfitted with a helmet and a replica wooden rifle, even fooled his comrades; they actually believed they had been discovered!

Flying Officer Wally MacCaw of Regina had a gut feeling that something bad was going to happen and gave his spot in the escape order to Jimmy Wernham.

After hearing the weather bulletin, he believed his chances to evade capture were minimal. The light skiff of snow would make it easy for Germans to track him. Jimmy Wernham must have had a similar premonition, for he requested his good friend Hap Geddes to deliver his ring to his parents in Winnipeg. (Hap never forgot how Wernham's eyes gleamed.)

Disappointment

Problems plagued the escape from the outset. Johnny Bull lost an hour of valuable time chopping through frost in the last few feet of the tunnel. Next, the diggers discovered that the tunnel's exit point fell thirty feet short of the woods. Instead of a steady flow of officers emerging from the tunnel, each departure was delayed until the sentry patrolling outside the fence had strolled to the far end of the compound. As the moonless night made it difficult to see, escapees strung a rope between the tunnel exit and the edge of the trees. The tunnellers feared a guard within the compound would spot the steam rising from the tunnel exit. Electric lights in the tunnel, so necessary for a smooth escape, were extinguished because of an RAF air raid over Berlin, 80 miles distant. Planners had failed to consider the possibility of blackout conditions because Allied bombers had not targeted Berlin before. Using margarine lamps in the tunnel, cave-ins occurred as men moved blindly through the tunnel, and a few officers panicked and nearly suffocated in the confusion. More valuable escape time slipped away, and it became evident that two hundred would not get out before daybreak.

Flight Lieutenant James C. Wernham of Winnipeg was murdered on 31 March, a week after the Great Escape. (Courtesy of D. Bates)

Sagan train station is the same today as it was on the night of the Great Escape in March 1944. Pictured here is Drew Gordon of Melbourne, son of Flight Lieutenant Tony Gordon, Stalag Luft III PoW. (Courtesy of D. Gordon)

Only a Matter of Time

A guard patrolling outside the perimeter fence eventually stumbled across the tunnel entrance. Of the seventy-nine officers who had slipped into the woods, three were immediately recaptured. They were the lucky ones because they did not fall into Gestapo hands. Over 120 officers remained in the tunnel or in Hut 104. Months of work "went up in smoke" as PoWs burned all their paperwork in stoves before the Germans got them. They wolfed down their escape rations before the Germans could confiscate them, but the concentrated food blocks caused most of the men to vomit because their stomachs were unaccustomed to the richness of the mixture.

Guards kicked down the door of Hut 104 and ordered the remaining PoWs into the compound. A thin layer of snow blanketed the ground, and the guards ordered the PoWs to strip. The Germans had their machine guns trained on the prisoners and would have shot anyone who moved. The PoWs whispered warnings to one another to stand perfectly still and do exactly as they were told. This was the only time Gord King thought he was going to be shot. The Germans brought out boxes of identification cards and performed a photographic verification of all PoWs during roll call. It was then the Germans became aware of the number of officers who had escaped. By that time a sentry had crawled back through Harry, and the complexity of the tunnel system left the guards dumbfounded. How could an operation of that magnitude have gone undetected?

The Aftermath

Hitler went berserk, and the SS took control of the camp. The camp commandant and nine other officers at Stalag Luft III were court-martialled for dereliction of duty. Evidence brought forward during their trials suggested that camp staff should have been more diligent in their search for tunnels, especially when large quantities of materials that were useful for tunnelling had disappeared between January 1943 and March 1944 (James 1983 238–9). These materials included:

1699 blankets	52 tables for two men
192 bed covers	76 benches
161 pillowcases	90 double tier bunks
165 sheets	246 water cans
3424 towels	1219 knives
655 palliasses	582 forks
1212 bolsters	478 spoons
34 single chairs	69 lamps
10 single tables	30 shovels

Many speculated that von Lindeiner would face the firing squad, but a military

Flight Lieutenant Tony Gordon, 455 Squadron RAAF is pictured with Squadron Leader James Catanach, RAAF, DFC. Catanach was one of the fifty officers murdered after the mass breakout. (Courtesy of D. Gordon)

"The Vault" (Courtesy of S.G. King)

This memorial cairn and the vault built for the urns of the fifty murdered officers still exists, and the site is maintained by a committee from the neighbouring town of Sagan, Poland. Except for a few foundations, Stalag Luft III has long since disappeared. (Courtesy of D. Gordon)

court imposed a one-year sentence in a military prison. Before beginning his sentence he suffered a heart attack and a nervous breakdown and avoided incarceration (Andrews 1976, 43). After the war, von Lindeiner's interrogation provided details that led to the arrest and conviction of some of those responsible for the murder of the fifty escapees.

Luftwaffe reaction to the murders varied, but many guards appeared shaken by the deaths. No German knew specifically about the construction of Harry, but evidence assembled proved beyond any doubt that many had suspected the existence of a tunnelling operation, all the while supplying contraband. The Gestapo ransacked homes of guards for evidence of their collaboration with PoWs during the tunnels' construction. Unfortunately the Gestapo found chocolate bar and coffee wrappers unique to Red Cross parcels. Guards guilty of collaboration were demoted, transferred to the Russian front, or worse. Most Luftwaffe guards at Stalag Luft III regretted the executions of "the fifty" but directed blame elsewhere as bloodstains were on Gestapo hands, not theirs. The guards feared reprisals as much as the PoWs did.

Knowledge of the fate of the fifty escapees "shot while trying to escape" filtered back to Stalag Luft III within days. Six Canadians were among the murdered. Flight Lieutenant Hank Birkland, 26, from Calgary, was murdered at Hirschberg. Flight Lieutenant Pat Langford, 24, from Field (British Columbia), best remembered for designing the trap doors, and Flight Lieutenant George McGill, 25, from Toronto, a digger team captain, were recaptured close to Sagan, then murdered. Flying Officer Gordon Kidder, 30, from Toronto, who served as a penguin, and Flight Lieutenant George W. Wiley, 22, a tunnel excavator, were shot at Görlitz. Flight Lieutenant Jimmy Wernham from Winnipeg, a tunneller and penguin, was executed on 31 March at an unknown location.

The nationwide manhunt for the escapees was successful. Only 3 of the 76 men who passed through the tunnel reached England. One was Norwegian Flight Lieutenant Jens Muller, the 43rd man out of the tunnel; he had helped to design the air conditioning system that pumped air through the tunnels. Norwegian-born Flight Lieutenant Peter Bergsland, the 44th man to leave, oversaw the manufacture of the civilian wear and replica German uniforms worn by the escapees. Netherlander Flight Lieutenant Bram Van der Stok, master forger, passed through Belgium, France and Spain before reaching British officials in Gibraltar. All three spoke German fluently. Roger Bushell, the brilliant organizer of the Great Escape, escaped through the tunnel with Flying Officer Danny Krol, a Pole who had joined the RAF after Poland's collapse. An alert Gestapo agent on the Swiss frontier suspected that they were two of the escapees as they made their way to the bridge to that would take them to freedom. He tripped up Krol with a casual salutation in English and arrested them. A French informant at the German port city of Stettin turned Wings Day and Paul Tolbolski, a Polish pilot in the service of the RAF, over to the Gestapo. The French informant was of no further value to the German police, who then informed his comrades of his activities so that they would eliminate the collaborator themselves.

Investigators believed that General Nebe, a senior Gestapo official, had drawn up the names of the fifty officers for execution. He spared twenty-three lives. Wing Commander Harry Day, Major Johnny Dodge (Winston Churchill's cousin), Sydney Dowse, and Jimmy James went to Sachsenhausen, a notorious death camp near Berlin. With Peter Churchill they dug their way out of Sachsenhausen in September 1944 but were recaptured. Fifteen others from the Great Escape returned to Stalag Luft III, including Flight Lieutenant A.B. "Tommy" Thompson of Toronto. Thompson's damning testimony helped convict several conspirators after the war. Two Czechs ended up in Colditz, and one officer went to Stalag Luft I at Barth.

Wally MacCaw believes that permission to build a stone memorial at Stalag Luft III with materials supplied by the Germans originated from the highest

To all Prisoners of War!

The escape from prison camps is no longer a sport!

Germany has always kept to the Hague Convention and only punished recaptured prisoners of war with minor disciplinary punishment.

Germany will still maintain these principles of international law.

But England has besides fighting at the front in an honest manner instituted an illegal warfare in non combat zones in the form of gangster commandos, terror bandits and sabotage troops even up to the frontiers of Germany.

They say in a captured secret and confidential English military pamphlet,

THE HANDBOOK OF MODERN IRREGULAR WARFARE:

". . . the days when we could practise the rules of sportsmanship are over. For the time being, every soldier must be a potential gangster and must be prepared to adopt their methods whenever necessary."

"The sphere of operations should always include the enemy's own country, any occupied territory, and in certain circumstances, such neutral countries as he is using as a source of supply."

England has with these instructions opened up a non military form of gangster war!

Germany is determined to safeguard her homeland, and especially her war industry and provisional centres for the fighting fronts. Therefore it has become necessary to create strictly forbidden zones, called death zones, in which all unauthorised trespassers will be immediately shot on sight.

Escaping prisoners of war, entering such death zones, will certainly lose their lives. They are therefore in constant danger of being mistaken for enemy agents or sabotage groups.

Urgent warning is given against making future escapes!

In plain English: Stay in the camp where you will be safe! Breaking out of it is now a damned dangerous act.

The chances of preserving your life are almost nil!

All police and military guards have been given the most strict orders to shoot on sight all suspected persons.

Escaping from prison camps has ceased to be a sport!

A poster removed from the wall of a barrack block at Stalag Luft III by Gordon King in January 1945. (Courtesy of S.G. King)

levels of the German military. Officials "paroled" two dozen PoWs to work in the small cemetery outside the wire, and permitted an honour guard of PoWs for a short memorial service in June 1944. Arthur Crighton, trumpeter, played the Last Post. At the end of the war the Polish government moved the urns of the fifty men to the Poznan community cemetery. The stone vault exists today in the memorial garden near the remains of Stalag Luft III.

"Escape Is No Longer a Sport!"

German authorities posted warnings that PoWs would be shot if they attempted further escapes. Allied authorities also sent messages into each camp to discourage them because the risks were too high. The outcome of the war was clear; the defeat of the Nazis was just a matter of time. Relations between guards and PoWs deteriorated.

Post-war Investigation Impeded by Soviets

Cold War politics hindered the murder investigations. Soviet officials impeded RAF investigators who asked to interview one of the major conspirators, Dr Absolon, who had fallen into Russian hands at the end of the war. The Russians reacted with indifference to the murders, probably because they suffered staggering losses at the hands of the Germans. To them, the fifty deaths paled when compared with the twenty million Soviet deaths.

Note that the epitaph does not indicate the year the war ended. (Courtesy of D. Gordon)

Dulag Luft and Prisoner Interrogation

Dulag Luft is a contraction for the German word *Durchgangslager* which roughly translates to *entrance camp*—a suitable name considering Dulag Luft was the first place air force personnel were taken after their capture. Dulag Luft consisted of three compounds in the Frankfurt area, a hospital at Hohemark, an interrogation centre at Oberursal, and a transit camp at Wetzlar.

Though it served as the primary interrogation facility for air force PoWs, Dulag Luft also served as a permanent camp in the early stages of the war until Stalag Luft I was opened at Barth in July 1940. The central interrogation centre consisted of four wooden buildings. Two buildings were each divided into about a hundred small isolation cells. The Germans converted some cells into hot-boxes where PoWs were subjected to intolerably high temperatures in an effort to make them more cooperative for interrogation sessions. Members of the Luftwaffe conducted most sessions but representatives of the SS and Gestapo participated in the interrogation of some PoWs.

In 1945 the RCAF obtained from the British a copy of a translated Luftwaffe document that outlined, in great detail, the organization of, and methods used by, interrogators at Oberursal and later at Auswerterstelle West, the two Luftwaffe interrogation centres in the region. The captured German document entitled "Prisoner Interrogation and Documents Evaluation and Their Intelligence Value to the Higher Command," outlined Luftwaffe policy regarding interrogation techniques and procedures as well as the evolution of the interrogation units into fifteen separate sections.

Analysts of British intelligence suggested that its German authors created the elaborate document of nearly fifty pages to impress the German High Command. The British also contended that its authors knew Germany had lost the war and that the creation of such an elaborate summary of interrogation practices might help German interrogators avoid war crimes trials by asserting that the Luftwaffe made it a policy to treat PoWs well. Assuming it would fall in the hands of Allied authorities, the authors suggest treatment of PoWs was civilized, and the use of psychology was preferred to force or coercion while attempting to gather intelligence from captives. After the war, Commandant Erich Killenger, Major Heinz Junge and a junior officer were found guilty of war crimes for mistreatment inflicted on PoWs.

The Luftwaffe established regional interrogation centres to allow for the efficient analysis of intelligence in that specific theatre of war. They understood that information had more value if put to use early. Dulag Luft became the Luftwaffe's primary interrogation centre for air force personnel captured in Western Europe. The Luftwaffe set up separate interrogation centres in other theatres, including the Eastern front, Italy and North Africa.

Dulag Luft was designed to process several hundred air force PoWs at one time. The Germans concluded they would obtain better results if new arrivals were isolated before and during interrogation. Fifty of Dulag Luft's two hundred sound proofed cells were equipped with listening devices. Electric heaters were installed in each cell, instead of hot water pipes, to prevent communication between PoWs tapping out Morse code. The Luftwaffe felt their interrogations were compromised because they could not control what PoWs discussed amongst themselves during their journey to the interrogation centre. The sheer volume of new arrivals exceeded Dulag Luft's ability to process them. Interrogators made on-the-spot decisions about whom to isolate and whom to place in large common areas with other new PoWs.

The interrogation unit kept meticulous files on every aspect of enemy air forces. A card index arranged alphabetically included names of personnel attached to each unit, squadron histories, aircraft types, equipment on board, location of bases, photographs of airfields, markings of the unit, and protocols in each unit. An interrogator familiarized himself with the details of a new PoW before an interrogation commenced. The Germans hoped to demonstrate to the captive that the Germans knew as much or more about his unit than he did, and therefore he did not need to hold back information.

Interference by German Officials

Interrogators expressed concerns about what transpired between a PoW and his captors before his delivery to Luftwaffe officials. They seethed with anger about German personnel who spoiled a new PoW with "amateurish sleuthing techniques" before a proper interrogation could be carried out by trained Luftwaffe staff. Luftwaffe interrogators ordered the discontinuation of the practice of returning captives to their crashed wreckage to verify it as theirs or to identify dead crew. Officials found they lost an advantage if PoWs had first-hand information about the aftermath of a crash site. They ordered guards to leave the crash site intact and to prevent looting by civilians. Luftwaffe officials were also concerned about conversations between guards and PoWs in transit to Dulag Luft. Many guards unwittingly bolstered the confidence of a new PoW by expressing a disinterest in, or a frustration towards, the war.

Progress of an Interrogation at Dulag Luft

New arrivals were subjected to a strict regimen. Each PoW went through a thorough search for compasses, maps, files, money, keys and any other article which could be used for escape. Front and profile photographs of each PoW were taken, and a description made of his physical features, which could be used to help locate him in the event of an escape.

If a large group arrived then officials divided up the men by crew or separated them into officers and NCOs. The Germans concentrated on navigators and wireless operators because they possessed the most intimate knowledge of the latest technologies, routes flown during operations, and procedures used by squadrons. Remarkably enough, interrogators dedicated less time to questioning pilots because a pilot "merely flew the aircraft and went where the navigator told him." Then guards began by isolating PoWs in cells with nothing more than a bed, and sometimes a table and chair. They placed members of the same crew at different parts of Dulag Luft to prevent chance encounters in the hallways or communication with Morse code. Each cell window was opaque or painted over, barred up and locked.

The initial contact with a PoW was considered pivotal by interrogators. Staff made on the spot psychological assessments to determine who might talk. Interrogators confronted those selected with a written questionnaire about their personal and military history. They gauged PoWs' reactions to determine suitability for further sessions. Interrogators placed PoWs in tiny, drab, stuffy rooms, and guards received instructions to minimize interaction with them. Loneliness and uncertainty often weakened their resolve. The PoWs could not wash, shave or have ready access to lavatories. Without reading materials, a PoW's thoughts turned to home. PoWs were kept hungry. Interrogators found that hungry PoWs often showed their "gratitude" for additional rations by revealing more than they originally intended. However, the failure to recognize a prisoner's status as a PoW proved most effective. Accusations that downed airmen had engaged in espionage and sabotage before their capture were especially unnerving, even more so when the men heard they could be shot.

The Germans found wounded PoWs in hospitals to be less receptive to interrogation because they received more food and comforts than PoWs at Dulag Luft. Hence, interrogators had hospital staff place wounded PoWs in isolation wards with nothing to do. After this change, some PoWs became very receptive to the company of the interrogator.

The Interrogation

German interrogators learned that a standard rule for interrogation did not exist. The success of an interrogation depended upon how well the PoW understood the interrogator's intentions and techniques. Germans learned that the initial shock of becoming a PoW did not work to their advantage because PoWs followed a code of silence. Instead, the interrogator would attempt to start conversation by subtly dropping details of what they knew about the squadron and avoided using "legal cross examinations" to pry out information. The aim of the interrogation was not to determine if information was truthful but to open a line of communication that would later lead to "guided questions."

The interrogators recognized they could not control PoWs from Canada, the United States or the Dominions because they were immune to the notion of class structure. North Americans, for example, placed little value on class distinctions and usually did not respond to questioning based upon one's station in life. Therefore, the interrogator analyzed a PoW's intelligence, education levels, biases and youthfulness. To sum up, the willingness of a PoW to talk was determined more by his personality than any other factor.

Methods of Interrogation

There were two ways used to extract information from PoWs. The less successful method involved constant grilling and confrontations. The preferred method of interrogation involved subtle questioning and conversation. The interrogation officer might begin a session on a friendly note, interspersing jokes with inquiries about a PoW's wounds, his mother and his family. The officer even resorted to flattery if he thought this worked to his advantage. The interrogator used reverse psychology by telling the prisoner important information about squadrons, flight paths or equipment to make the prisoner believe he already knew everything, anyway. A skilled line of questions could lead a prisoner to think there was nothing he could betray as the belligerent air forces shared so many similarities.

If a prisoner did not respond to gentle questioning, then an interrogator resorted to sternness, sarcasm or cynicism. The PoWs might be provoked with a statement such as "You wouldn't know anything about the matter in question because it is too difficult for you to understand." The interrogator would become friendly again and offer cigarettes without making them appear to be bribes. Repeated rounds of questioning were intended to wear down a PoW's resolve. An experienced interrogator knew how many sessions to conduct, based on his perception of the prisoner's intelligence, resolve and maturity.

A successful interrogation required the interrogator to familiarize himself with as much information as possible about the prisoner ahead of time. The Germans amassed the following details in their files:

Ration cards	confiscated from captured personnel
RAF identity cards	confiscated from captured personnel
False passports	prepared for crew who might need one to evade
Meteorology	weather forecasts to determine to which unit the aircraft belonged.
Characteristics	facts assembled to create a profile of a unit
Raid routes	burnt maps and records that pinpointed corridors and tactics against defenses

Places	names, places, station, motor routes, theatres, laundries in the area of bases
Airfields	the name of all airfields and the squadrons posted to them
Facts	the latest information on any subject
Target day book	the coordinates of all targets
Abbreviations	A quick reference for all abbreviations
Air Force slang	A quick reference for slang terms
List of Rendezvous points	code letters for assembly points
Main file (huge)	any subject, listed for quick reference
Summary files	A condensation of all captured documents

Flying Officer William Dunwoodie

Bomber Command dispatched 408 Squadron to destroy a major concentration of Me110s, Me109s and Ju88s parked on runways at the Lohausen airfield on Christmas Eve 1944. Germany's last ditch offensive on the western front, known as the Battle of the Bulge, had started ten days earlier. The Wehrmacht had caught the Allied armies off guard by breaking the line at Bastogne. It was imperative to destroy the German aircraft before the overcast lifted and they could be used against Allied ground troops.

As a pilot regularly assigned to nighttime bombing runs, Bill Dunwoodie looked forward to his first daylight raid. He never made it to the target. A flak round exploded in his cockpit, and the blast knocked him unconscious. Revived by the cold air, he awoke to the realization that the explosion had blinded him and caused serious wounds to his legs. He thought he could escape through the hatch in the belly of the Halifax, but the slipstream sucked him through a side window when he undid his seat belt. Dunwoodie survived his descent into enemy territory and soldiers placed him under arrest immediately. He spent three months in an SS hospital at Krefeldt for treatment of his wounds. A sadistic nurse exacted a horrible vengeance. He never reached a prisoner of war camp; the war ended while he was at the Luftwaffe interrogation centre, before he could be moved to a permanent camp.

Christmas Eve Raid During Battle of the Bulge

Bursts of flak filled the sky as Bill Dunwoodie's Halifax bomber approached the Luftwaffe airfields and hangers at Dusseldorf, Germany, on Christmas Eve 1944. Strong defences ringed the base. The Germans utilized two types of 88mm anti-aircraft guns against incoming waves of bombers; one type of gun fired with radar guidance; the other fired repeated volleys to the same altitude. Dunwoodie watched flak explode directly in front of his bomber, and he thought he might be lucky enough to fly his aircraft between the repeated bursts, just as the aircraft in front of him was doing. Besides, it made no sense to break from the approach, as the Halifax was only minutes from the target.

As quickly as he had made the decision to maintain his bearing, an 88mm shell tore through the floor of the cockpit between his legs and exploded just above his knees, shattering the perspex in the window frames, obliterating the control column in front of his seat and blinding him. His head thudding against the armour plate behind his seat revived him. So much raced through his mind simultaneously: the fate of his crew, his blindness, his throbbing legs and the condition of his aircraft. The explosion ripped off his oxygen mask and microphone and prevented him from communicating with his crew. Dunwoodie depressed the warning button mounted to the left of his seat to activate red warning lights in the fuselage. He flashed the Morse code letter "P" for parachute, an indication that all were to bail out of the aircraft immediately. Unbeknownst to Dunwoodie, five of the six crew members had already left the aircraft. Rear Gunner Flight Sergeant D.A. Chaisson remained trapped in his turret; he frantically worked the manual armature to rotate the turret enough to throw his parachute into the slipstream. He intended to use the force of the wind to expand it and pull him out. Chaisson failed to pull both feet clear of obstacles around the seat, and he found himself hanging upside down by his boot as his Halifax plummeted to earth.

Dunwoodie Struggles to Save Himself

Dunwoodie intended to feel his way to the escape hatch in the belly of the fuselage. If he went through the cockpit window, he ran the risk of hitting the propellers, the antennae wires or the tail plane. As he undid his lap belt to cinch up the parachute harness, the wind sucked him through the jagged perspex, around the propellers and tail plane. He deployed the parachute, and the force of the wind yanked the slack from the harness. The flash burn, blindness, broken bones and shrapnel took a back seat to the excruciating pain emanating from his groin. No amount of struggling did anything to relieve his agony. The descent lasted forever, and Dunwoodie believed "Newton's law of gravity was repealed!" He landed in the soft ooze of a pigsty; the smell of German swine permeated the air! German soldiers following his descent jumped on him immediately. Unable to convey the cause of his agony to his captors, he continued to wrestle with the release mechanism on his harness to relieve the pressure on his groin. The harder he struggled the more forcefully they pinned him to the ground. Dunwoodie assumed they must have thought that the plunger on the front of his harness was attached to explosives. Eventually the guards caught on and stood back to allow him to get out of the webbing.

Independent Verifications of Dunwoodie's Account

Cliff McManus of Minnedosa, Manitoba, corroborated Dunwoodie's interpretation of events in a report filed after the operation. McManus was directly behind Dunwoodie's Halifax when the shell hit the bomber. He saw five chutes open almost immediately after the aircraft veered off to the right. McManus stated he did not see Flight Sergeant Chaisson hanging out of the rear turret. Crews in other bombers saw five parachutes open. Based on McManus's eyewitness testimony, the commanding officer of 408 Squadron listed Dunwoodie and Chaisson as missing in action after air operations. The squadron revised Dunwoodie's status to "assumed killed" some weeks later. The Germans reported that they had captured Chaisson, and the RCAF had no reason to believe Dunwoodie had survived. His status remained unchanged until his liberation at Dulag Luft in April 1945. After his liberation, Chaisson told authorities that he saw Dunwoodie whisk by him with an extended, but unopened, parachute.

Squadron Account of the Operation

Details of the raid recorded in the Operations Record Book of 408 Squadron outlined the demise of Dunwoodie's Halifax.

> Sixteen Halifax aircraft of this Squadron were detailed to attack DUSSEL-DORF/LOHAUSEN airfield. All aircraft took off. Thirteen aircraft claimed to have attacked the target between 1450.5 and 1457.5 hours between 15 to 18,500 feet. Two aircraft abandoned mission due to engine trouble. One aircraft, NP 781 "U", failed to return from this operation and nothing has been heard of, or from this crew, since take off time. Weather was reported as clear with some slight haze over the target. The target was identified by most crews by the TI's and runways. Bombing was carried out on Red TI markers and runways. All crews were unanimous in the decision that this attack was successful and very concentrated. Ground defenses consisted of heavy flak bursting between 16 to 18,500 feet. A number of our aircraft were damaged by flak. All aircraft were diverted. While our aircraft were out wishing Hitler a "JERRY" Christmas, the orderly room staff were guests of the former Commanding Officer.

Missing crew is listed below:

Pilot	Canadian	J37475	F/O W.H. Dunwoodie
Navigator	Canadian	J13140	F/L H.L. Fricker
Aimer/Bombardier	Canadian	J38411	F/O D.G. Keller
Wireless Operator	Canadian	R212809	F/Sgt Tonkin, D.
Mid Upper Gunner	Canadian	R274509	F/Sgt D'Amour, G.R.A.
Rear Gunner	Canadian	R88187	F/Sgt Chaisson, J.A.
Flight Engineer	Canadian	R208171	Sgt Allan, W.B.

Dunwoodie learned after the war that vengeful civilians murdered five of his crew after they parachuted safely to earth. One of the bereaved families told him that a German padre wrote to express shame for the actions of his countrymen. The padre hoped they, and the other families, had the heart to forgive the German people for what was done to those five young Canadian boys.

Christmas Eve 1944 in an SS Hospital

Dunwoodie's captors tossed him into the back of their truck and drove him to a hospital in Krefeldt. Doctors delayed surgery until Christmas morning and, in the interim, placed him in a hospital ward with German wounded. An unparalleled sense of loneliness swept over him. Earlier that day, Dunwoodie had envisioned spending Christmas on a base in England, reading letters and thinking about loved ones in Canada. No one in the hospital spoke English or even took the time to acknowledge him. Civilians milled about the ward, singing Christmas carols in what seemed a lacklustre attempt to cheer up the patients. He heard the distinctive clinking of bottles and he could smell beer. When all had left and the patients had fallen asleep, Dunwoodie drank two bottles of beer intended for the German in the next bed. He awoke to a verbal tirade and smiled as he received his first German language lesson, complete with expletives.

Hospital staff operated on his shattered legs without giving him an anesthetic and set them in split casts that allowed nurses access to change the dressings on his wounds. Gauze dressings covered his eyes. Blindness from shell flash was often a temporary condition, and Dunwoodie regained partial vision in his right eye after several weeks of convalescence. In his exuberance he hailed a German nurse to tell her the good news. She appeared pleased and returned with a small vial and dropper that he believed to contain antiseptic. She smiled as she doused his good eye with a caustic substance which burned the pupil and eyelid, causing permanent blindness. This nurse had perpetrated an act of barbarity! When vision returned to his left eye a few weeks later, Bill kept quiet about it. The medical staff thought he was blind, and he used this to his advantage. He hobbled around the ward at night and ate sweets and cookies while everyone slept. He threw wrappings under the beds of other patients and enjoyed the excitement when someone awoke to find his treats missing and the evidence below someone else's bed. They never suspected Bill because heavy casts encased his legs and they thought he was unable to see. Dunwoodie lost fifty pounds during his four months in the hospital, going from 160 to 110 pounds. He existed on starvation rations: turnip soup and fish-flavoured cheese.

Allied aircraft bombed many targets close to the hospital, and Dunwoodie prayed the bomb aimers were good at precision bombing. Explosions rattled the building day after day. When air raid sirens started to wail, the staff evacuated the wounded to the relative safety of the basement, but they left Dunwoodie on his bed next to a window. He implored the staff to at least swing the panes open to lessen the danger of flying shards of glass. He protected himself by pulling his body to the underside of the bed frame. He lifted his plastered legs from their supports and hoisted his body with casts off the end of the bed. During one raid he jerked his damaged legs from the casts and pulled himself below the mattress just seconds before an explosion blew out the window and turned the room to shambles. The incessant bombing drove Dunwoodie to the brink of collapse.

An English-speaking German pilot-in-training ended up on the ward after surviving the destruction of his third aircraft. He was yet to earn his wings despite being shot down twice and bailing from a third aircraft before an American pilot could finish him off. Dunwoodie learned from him that the SS operated this particular hospital, which explained the calloused attitude of the staff.

A wounded British marine named Powell, a survivor of Arnhem, was brought to the hospital, and the gritty Brit proved good company. The pair conspired to escape during an air raid when everyone went to the basement. They stumbled out of the hospital in casts and bandages and headed toward Holland or Belgium. The German sentries who arrested them laughed at the pathos of the situation and returned the pair to hospital.

Relocation to Dulag Luft

The hospital transferred Dunwoodie to Dulag Luft at Frankfurt am Main after learning he had regained sight to one eye. He and two wounded Americans were loaded into a boxcar attached to a locomotive. The Allies controlled the skies, and fighters strafed the locomotive several times. The crew jumped from the train each time an attack commenced but left the PoWs behind. At least they had the decency to leave the door of the boxcar unlocked in case the locomotive exploded. During one attack the PoWs broke for the cover of woods, even at risk of getting shot in the back. Train wrecks clogged the lines, and the PoWs had to walk most of the distance from Krefeldt to Frankfurt. Dunwoodie's muscles had atrophied during three months of convalescence and poor diet, and he could not manage under his own strength. A guard kicked him in his ribs and head to make him get up. The wounded Americans slung him over their shoulders for the five-day march to Frankfurt. At no time did the Germans provide food or water. The PoWs bartered wristwatches and any other personal items for morsels of food. One of the Americans stole back a watch he had traded to a guard and sold it to another for more food. Fighting erupted between the two guards over ownership of the watch, and that brought some comic relief to a dismal situation.

The awesome power of Bomber Command struck home when Dunwoodie moved through the medieval city of Cologne. Bombs had reduced everything to rubble except the medieval cathedral whose spire rose several hundred feet above the ruins. An unexploded 2000 lb bomb had become embedded in the ground beside the train station and Dunwoodie assumed it was still armed. The shell had created a massive impact crater in the street. Smell permeating from open sewers was nothing like the cologne he used in Canada. One tired old guard left his rifle with the PoWs when he went in search of food. He muttered, "Be good, boys, look after this for me until I get back." He returned with nothing but stagnant water. Guards added twelve more PoWs to the original group of three. After the PoWs resumed the march they believed their time had expired when a demented guard herded them into a gravel pit. With their backs to him, they heard the guard pull back the hammer of his machine gun and then release a salvo of gunfire. Bullets ricocheted off the rocks and Dunwoodie felt two or three bullets penetrate his back. He writhed in pain, fell to the ground and looked over to see the guard and a PoW laughing at him. His imagination had got the better of him—the guard was just scaring them and had shot the rounds over their heads.

The Uncertainty of the Last Days

Guards at Dulag Luft locked the fifteen PoWs in solitary confinement for three more days without food or water. Idle threats and intimidation had little effect on Dunwoodie at that point. He had absolutely nothing to say. A man in an RAF officer's uniform entered the room with a heaping plate of food and stuffed his face in front of Dunwoodie. A true comrade would have shared his food. Between mouthfuls of food this imposter fired off a battery of questions about Dunwoodie's squadron. Disgusted, Dunwoodie retorted, "I know what I can tell you, I'll tell you what my religion is." The interrogator barked back, "I'm not interested in your damned religion!" Dunwoodie retorted, "Okay, that's about the end of our conversation."

Conditions in Dulag Luft were unnecessarily miserable. The Germans kept 250 PoWs on the verge of starvation even though a warehouse in the compound contained an estimated 150,000 Red Cross parcels. Dysentery ran rampant, and the abort consisted of a log stretched over an open ablution pit. Unheated barracks chilled everyone to the bone, and poor health prevented many from leaving their bunks and reporting for roll calls. The guards ordered able-bodied PoWs to prepare for evacuation as the American army closed in from the west. The commandant assembled the PoWs in the small compound before they left.

He informed them that the Nazi High Command had ordered their execution but he chose to disobey the directive. Whether guided by morality or fear of retribution, the commandant surrendered to the PoWs. Prisoners manned the guard towers but agreed to return the rifles to the guards when columns of retreating Germans passed by the camp.

Liberation by the U.S. Army

The Americans liberated the camp that night. Medical corpsmen loaded Dunwoodie and three other seriously wounded comrades into an ambulance and transported them to an Allied hospital at Liege, Belgium. An RAF group captain convalesced in the adjoining bed. The hospital scoffed at his claim to be the commanding officer of an operational squadron, because standing orders prohibited senior officers from flying. This group captain had broken the rules by flying an operation and had become a PoW on his only raid over Germany. He asked Bill to call his squadron headquarters in Brussels to have a car sent over to pick him up. The medical staff was shocked when an entourage entered the hospital to claim their leader. Bill went with the captain to Brussels and was repatriated to England quickly.

Bill's wife, Cecilia, knew that he had survived the downing of his aircraft back in December and refused to give up hope, even though the RCAF had changed his status from "missing" to "presumed killed." His survival was confirmed after his repatriation on 9 April 1945. A padre at Taplow Military Hospital wrote to Cecilia to inform her that her husband needed several operations to reconstruct his face; he warned her to prepare for the worst. Dunwoodie underwent several surgeries at Taplow between 9 April and 23 May 1945. The surgeon who removed his eye confirmed that a caustic substance had burned his eye, eyelid and the surrounding skin.

Repatriation

Flying Officer Dunwoodie sailed into Lachine, Quebec, on 16 July and the RCAF discharged him on 21 September 1945. He dove under the kitchen table the first night he arrived home at Rivers, Manitoba: a Greyhound bus had backfired in front of his house when he sat down to supper with Cecilia. He needed time to adjustment to peacetime.

War crimes investigators captured the SS nurse responsible for robbing Dunwoodie of his eyesight. Officials laid many criminal charges against her because she had mistreated numerous PoWs who had passed through the hospital. The prosecution at the Nuremberg War Crimes Trial asked Bill to testify against her, but he declined for two reasons: he did not believe he could identify her because he had seen her only a few times; second, his return to Germany for the trial would have been too traumatic. Dunwoodie was content to have come home alive and to be with the woman he loved. Other captives supplied

Flight Sergeant William Dunwoodie is shown here walking down a street in Edmonton before his overseas deployment. (Courtesy of W. Dunwoodie)

Bill and Cecilia Dunwoodie celebrated their sixtieth anniversary in 2003. (Courtesy of W. Dunwoodie)

sufficient evidence to convict the same nurse of war crimes.

After the war, Bill Dunwoodie did his best to get on with his life and raise his family. He continues to experience nightmares and live with guilt because he lived and five men in his crew died. However, he has enjoyed every day of the past sixty years. He always believes that a good person will not be held back, regardless of life's circumstances. The cruelty inflicted on him made him more determined to succeed. As his family grew, Bill volunteered in home and school associations, led cub and scout groups and served on the executive of Edmonton's Pleasantview Community League. Professionally, he sat on the executive of the Accounting Society. At the age of 57, Dunwoodie retired from the position of the Chief of Appeals for Revenue Canada. When asked by the Province of Alberta to come out of retirement and establish a new corporate taxation department and appeals procedure for the province, he worked for another five years. For the past twenty-four years, he and Cecilia have enjoyed time with their family and friends. Bill kept his pilot's license until a few years ago and amazed his grandson when he landed his aircraft at the Edmonton International Airport in 10/10ths cloud cover using instrument flight rules. Membership in the RCAF Ex-PoW Association brought him together with other men who had experienced hardship as prisoners of war. This camaraderie has allowed Bill Dunwoodie to find resolution for wartime trauma and has contributed to an inner peace that eluded him for much too long.

Part B
RCAF Evaders

This form was issued by MI9 to William Poohkay after his repatriation to England in September 1944. (Courtesy of W.M. Poohkay)

The British government created an organization to oversee the establishment of escape networks on the continent after the fall of France in June 1940. The original mission of MI9 was to assist in the repatriation of soldiers stranded at Dunkirk. It expanded its scope of operations to assist aircrews shot down over Europe. Underground networks needed financial, technical and logistical support if they were to assist any number of evaders making it back to England. Inadequate funding hampered MI9's efforts. In June 1942, MI9 created SI9(d), a School of Intelligence, to train agents to go behind enemy lines to assist evaders. An ultra-secret organization, SI9(d) started with three officers and two secretaries. British officer Airey Neave headed the group because of his escape experience. Neave had broken out of the high security Colditz prison and reached Gibraltar by crossing through Switzerland, France and neutral Spain. Unfortunately strict security measures kept senior bureaucrats in MI9 from learning of SI9(d)'s existence, which created a Catch-22 situation. Its clandestine nature precluded any chance of SI9(d) receiving adequate financial resources, radio sets, aircraft and watercraft, and the benefit of MI9's ability to expand its networks on the continent.

Escape lines existed in all nations under Nazi control. They began as unsophisticated cells that the Germans infiltrated easily. Direct communication with London was virtually impossible because workers in the escape lines lacked the training to use field radios. Most cells were afraid to use radios because the Germans had a knack of locating transmitters by using a system of triangulation. Despite the inevitability of capture, the underground valiantly kept open lines for most of the war. The Danes moved evaders to the island of Zealand, where the narrowest stretch of water between Denmark and neutral Sweden was no more than three miles. The Belgians ran three lines: Comet, Shelburne and O'Leary. The landing of Allied forces in France rendered their services redundant after August 1944. Political intrigue compromised the effectiveness of French escape lines; British and American intelligence networks viewed the French as less reliable than their Belgian counterparts. The Dutch failed to establish escape lines until late in the war; however, Dutch citizens sympathetic to the Allied cause moved evaders to the Belgian frontier where contact was established with an escape network. Several thousand evaders sought sanctuary in Switzerland during the war. Evasion on the Italian front had a twist: sympathetic officials within the Vatican allowed MI9 to operate from their offices, but they would have claimed ignorance if the Germans had swarmed the Holy See. Approximately 1000 soldiers trapped on the beaches of Dunkirk returned to England via escape lines. Though less than one percent of flight crews became evaders, over 2000 evaded capture and returned to England. In the last year of the war, an evader stood a 50 percent chance of getting home.

Evasion came with a price. Germans infiltrated most escape lines and tortured operatives into revealing the names of their associates. They were executed or sent to concentration camps. The Germans accused captured military personnel of sabotage and espionage as an excuse to deny them their Geneva Convention rights. Evaders captured by Gestapo, Abwehr or Field Police could expect more brutal treatment than if they were captured by the Luftwaffe.

Flying Officer David High

The Gestapo arrested Flying Officer David High, RCAF No. J92346, in Paris in July 1944 while he was attempting to escape to Spain via the Comet line. They had been tracking High's movements for several days before apprehending him on the Champs Elysées. They tortured him for three weeks at Fresnes prison before deporting him to Buchenwald concentration camp with twenty-six other RCAF personnel. Buchenwald was one of three concentration camps opened when Hitler invoked emergency powers and suspended civil liberties in 1933. Over 238,000 prisoners passed through its gates in twelve years. Its compounds held up to 45,000 prisoners at a time—Jews, Gypsies, Poles, Yugoslavs, French, Dutch, Belgians, Danes, Russians, Canadians, British, and Americans, as well as German dissidents. Sometimes the population exceeded 58,000. Buchenwald evolved into a temporary holding area for condemned inmates who were slated for labour battalions and the death camps—Bergen-Belsen, Auschwitz and Dachau. Crowded, unheated barracks with up to four lifts of bunks contributed to outbreaks of typhus and dysentery. Inmates rarely survived beyond nine months because of starvation and beatings. The deceased and those too weak to work were thrown into ovens, and the smell of burnt flesh permeated the area around the camp.

New arrivals had their heads shorn to control lice. Slavic and Jewish prisoners wore striped pajama-like uniforms or burlap sacks. Guards terrorized inmates with indiscriminate beatings and savage dog attacks. Elsewhere in the camp SS "research" physicians used Jewish inmates to evaluate reactions to pain during an operation without anesthetic, cold weather survival tests, and for experiments with typhus. Most realized that the only other way out of Buchenwald was up the smokestacks of the crematoria. The SS took great pride in their ruthless efficiency and profited from the sale of slave labour to nearby factories owned and operated by prominent German industrialists. After the war, these industrialists faced war crimes tribunals but most of them escaped punishment.

Flying Officer High believes he owes his life to a fellow PoW, Wing Commander Forest Frederick Yeo-Thomas, the most senior British Special Operations

Executive (SOE) agent arrested in France during the war. Both Yeo-Thomas and High were betrayed by rogue members of the underground in Paris in 1944. They shared nearly identical experiences from the time of their arrests in Paris to their incarceration at Buchenwald. David High found it too difficult to elaborate on the haunting memories of the camp. To clarify events and to provide a broader context, references to Yeo-Thomas' 1952 biography, *The White Rabbit*, are used here.

How David High Became an Inmate of Buchenwald

On the night of 4/5 July 1944, David High's Lancaster attacked the railroad marshalling yards at Villeneuve-St. Georges, a suburb of Paris. The operation was of vital importance to the success of the D-Day landings because destruction of transportation links would impede the movement of enemy reinforcements to the Normandy beaches.

Twenty-millimetre cannon fire from two Fokke-Wulf 190s raked the fuselage of High's Mark X and sent shards of shrapnel into his back. He went into shock, and believes he might have gone down in the crash if someone had not pushed him through the escape hatch. High was knocked senseless when his head struck the doorframe, and he is unsure how his parachute deployed. The jerk of the parachute harness worked the pieces of metal further into his back, and the tightness of the harness around his wounds created excruciating pain. He landed heavily in a field near Pitre, a small town about 50 kilometers from the English Channel and 150 kilometers west of Paris. He buried his parachute, extra equipment and insignia and then hid in underbrush for the night.

Flyers Were Briefed on Escape Lines to Spain

By that point of the war, aviators received briefings about the existence of escape routes in the areas over which they flew. The British, in concert with Dutch, Belgian, French and Spanish resisters, had worked hard in the previous two years to establish extensive escape networks through to Gibraltar. Organizers possessed enough confidence in the sophistication of the escape links to dare to reveal considerable details to air crews, to facilitate their evasion of capture and movement through enemy territory. Airmen relied on instinct and luck, more than any other factors, to avoid capture. German patrols scoured the countryside and an evader would not know if the Frenchmen he encountered were supporters of the resistance or collaborators. High's limited knowledge of the French language did not bolster his confidence, especially when underground networks would dispatch him if they thought he posed a threat to their existence.

A resistance organization took High into its confidence after he made contact with a local farmer. The underground, or Maquis, went to great lengths to protect its members' identities in case members of a cell fell into German hands.

Each Maquisard, or member of the underground, including High, remained nameless and used a number for identification—nothing more. The Maquis moved High between several cells in the few weeks he worked in the Chartres area because the Germans, who knew of their presence, were hunting for him and other evaders.

High Becomes a Radio Operator for the Maquis

High's expertise proved indispensable because few Maquisards possessed the skills needed to operate the radio units dropped into France by the British. Through most of the war, resistance leaders were understandably reticent to use radios because the Germans had the technology to pinpoint the location of radio transmitters. Instead, the Maquis preferred to use couriers to deliver messages, despite the inefficiencies. In 1943, the Maquis and the Free French Forces of the Interior integrated radio units into their regular operations after relenting to pressure from the British SOE and British military intelligence (MI9).

The underground warned High of the consequences of being captured with members of the Resistance. The Germans infiltrated most cells in well-coordinated sweeps because of the duplicity of French collaborators who sold their services for money and food, and the fighting between groups posturing for power or coercion. Frequent breaches in the escape lines earned the French resistance a reputation for being less reliable than its counterparts in Belgium and the Netherlands. British SOE agents in the Chartres area had liquidated two collaborators only a few days earlier. Regardless of the risks involved, David High volunteered his services to the Maquis immediately. He was ecstatic to learn that the invasion had started. He had contributed to Operation Overlord by bombing the marshalling yard near Paris on the night his bomber was lost. During his first five nights with the underground, High helped to blow bridges and railway lines to impede the movement of German soldiers and supplies. He conveyed messages about the group's activities to London and the reply gave instructions to destroy other installations. In London, military intelligence protected High's identity by assigning him a contact number, and an experienced wireless operator verified his identity each time by his signature style of Morse code communication.

Increased radio traffic in the Chartres area prompted the Germans to expand their searches for saboteurs and downed wireless operators like High. The Maquis moved evaders out of the region and put them in contact with members of the Comet escape line who could help them evade capture and reach neutral Spain. On 28 July David High, Harry Bastable of Winnipeg, and Alex Smith of Trenton, Ontario, were transported to Paris by a distinguished-looking couple in the back of their Black Maria. The trio of evaders took refuge in a flat along the Champs Elysées, two blocks from the Eiffel Tower. They felt indescribable elation when a car arrived three days later driven by people who would set them on their journey to freedom. The three evaders climbed into the back of the car, which traveled only a few blocks before several vehicles closed in around them and forced them to stop. Gestapo agents ordered the evaders out of the car at gunpoint, searched them and pushed them back into the car. The two people in the front seat drove them to Fresnes Prison, a notorious centre of torture owned by the Gestapo. The Germans must have had them under surveillance for days. High later learned that the man and woman who had picked them up in the country were collaborators.

The PoWs Should Have Been Placed in Luftwaffe Camps

The Gestapo and the SS kept the arrests of the three men secret. High realized the precariousness of his situation because the RCAF had no indication that he had survived the bombing raid. Their captors asserted that they had forfeited their stipulated Geneva Convention rights by collaborating with members of the French underground. Hitler's October 1942 "Commando Order" had dictated the execution of any saboteur or commando caught in Western Europe in or out of uniform. The Germans knew that the Maquis had helped the three men, but they did not have the evidence to link them to incidents of sabotage occurring in the Chartres area. They attempted to coerce confessions from High and his comrades with torture. High knew he had to reveal absolutely nothing because, the moment he did, the Gestapo would kill him. Until he admitted it, the Gestapo could only suspect he was one of the illicit radio operators they had monitored in the past few weeks. What the Gestapo knew for sure was that radio traffic had ceased when they captured High and a few other wireless operators.

The Gestapo understood how to use psychological aspects of torture. To break his will, they moved High to a cell adjacent to a woman undergoing torture. High could see the woman's feet suspended from a ceiling hook. They lowered her face down into a tub of ice water and held her down until she stopped thrashing about. She was then revived, and the process was repeated. The Gestapo insinuated they knew everything about High and therefore he should answer their questions to avoid similar treatment. They told him where he was born, where he lived, where he went to school, how long he had been in the air force and what he did in the air force. High kept reminding himself to remain silent. He took extraordinary measures to avoid reacting or responding to anything, because that would give his interrogators provocation to beat him more. The Germans made mountains from molehills.

Two weeks of intense battle school training in Dalton, England, did nothing to prepare High for what he endured. His tormentors stripped him and locked his hands behind his back. They thrashed him with rubber hoses and kicked him about. Between beatings and interrogations High returned to a pitch-black, stone dungeon four feet long, three feet wide and four feet high with a small steel grate as the only source of air and light. Solitary confinement, screams from other cells, poor food and the cold drove prisoners to despair.

Gestapo collaborators were of many nationalities—Czech, Polish, French, Belgian, Dutch and Yugoslav. These sadistic tormentors wore plain clothes, spoke good English and were thirty to thirty-five years of age. Many of them had also suffered brutality at the hands of the Nazis and had switched allegiances to protect their families. High thought that more than fifty percent of his interrogators were of nationalities other than German.

In defiance of their tormentors, Fresnes prisoners communicated by tapping on the walls and pipes. Echoes of Morse code resonated through the fortress. Members of the French underground crawled into the sewers and subterranean passages around the prison to convey messages and to give them hope. Prisoners knew of the progress of the Normandy invasion and the news gave High the inner strength to hold on. When the Nazis knew the war was lost, they stepped up reprisals against saboteurs and resistance fighters. They ordered the mass executions of all spies and saboteurs and accelerated the liquidation of concentration camp inmates to prevent their liberation.

Experience of Yeo-Thomas, Captured SOE Agent

David High attributes his survival to the heroic efforts of Wing Commander Forest Frederick Yeo-Thomas, a principal of the SOE who was arrested on Avenue Victor Hugo in Paris on 24 March 1944. Yeo-Thomas, code-named the White Rabbit, managed to conceal his identity from the Gestapo the entire time he was in their custody. He survived unimaginable brutality at Fresnes Prison before the Germans sent him to Buchenwald for extermination. They hurled him against walls and over desks and trampled him under their jackboots. He was stripped and handcuffed to a chair with his arms locked behind him, while tied to the chair he was kicked in the groin and knocked across the room. They slapped, punched and kicked him repeatedly about the face. Handcuffs were left on his wrists for days and cut deeply into his flesh; infection set in. His grotesquely distorted face became a bloody pulp. His purple eyes ballooned shut, his lips split, his nose flattened and his teeth loosened. Gestapo guards held Yeo-Thomas' face under water in a tub until he passed out; they pumped water from his lungs, resuscitated him and then repeated the process. He hoped for death and swallowed water to speed it up (Marshall 1952, 110–131). David High could not bring himself to discuss the mistreatment he suffered, but he said it varied little from that of Yeo-Thomas.

Deportation to the Third Reich

The advance of Allied forces on Paris in August 1944 expedited the evacuation of the German forces and their prisoners, including the 1500 at Fresnes. Among them were 167 British, Canadian, and American air force personnel and SOE agents arrested by the Gestapo. Testimony gathered in post-war trials suggests the Germans planned to execute the prisoners in Fresnes if they had enough time to shoot and dispose of the bodies, because those prisoners were material witnesses to horrors of the Nazi regime and could have provided damning evidence at war crimes trials.

High initially believed he was destined for a Luftwaffe-controlled PoW camp when he left Paris in a cattle car. The PoW train was not marked with large white P-O-W letters, and it was subjected to attack from roving bands of Allied fighters. Bullets ripped through the walls and roofs of several wooden boxcars, setting some of them ablaze. SS guards unloaded the prisoners and marched them down the tracks to another train waiting up the line. They crammed High into a car designed for eight horses or forty men, with 90 other prisoners. One resourceful prisoner had grabbed a steel bar from the track bed and used it to pry three planks from the floor of his boxcar once the train ride resumed. Five men slipped through a hole between the axles of the car; one of them slipped beneath the undercarriage and the wheels crushed him. Guards at the rear of the train spotted his remains. The train screeched to a stop and a search commenced for other escapees and the car from which the man had fallen. When the SS found the car, they slid open the side door and the Hauptmann sprayed the interior with automatic fire. One Frenchman hollered when a bullet pierced his hand. The Hauptmann motioned the wounded man out of the boxcar, asked his name and nationality, directed him to the front of the train for medical attention and shot him in the back as he walked away. Dave High and a French-Canadian airman were ordered out of the boxcar and told to bury the corpse in the gravel bed of the train track. They stuffed the body into a gunnysack and covered it with eighteen inches of gravel. The remaining men in High's rail carriage were stripped naked to deter further escape attempts. One of the four surviving escapees, Flying Officer Joel Matthew Stevenson of 419 Squadron, RCAF, reported in his Account of Escape of September 1944 that he was the man who pried a hole in the floor while the train traveled at about twenty-five miles per hour. He and two French officers managed to clear the wheels, and they hid in the undergrowth adjacent the tracks. Stevenson estimated that they had escaped from the train forty kilometers east of Paris. The reported day of the escape was 18 August. The trio then walked to Mezy-Moulins and hid in a house for two nights. Locals moved Stevenson to Chateau Thierry and hid him above a shop until 28 August 1944, then turned him over to American forces when they moved into the area (Ref.79/507 DHist MI9/S/PG(F)2812).

Misfortune Adds to the Misery

When Fresnes prisoner records burned in one of the cars attacked by the Allied fighters, the SS guards made an on-the-spot decision to send all prisoners to Buchenwald. These new arrivals could not fathom what lay behind the tall gates of Buchenwald. The naked men from High's boxcar marched from the terminal into the camp. High remembers how his feelings of indignity dissipated when he saw what he would become: starving men in striped uniforms moved listlessly about their enclosures; heads were bald; mottled sores oozed pus. The new arrivals could not believe the smell, the lice, and the emaciated bodies. High wondered why the guards even sent the newcomers to the showers for fumigation. He might have experienced brutal treatment in Fresnes, but nothing prepared him for what he witnessed during the next three months.

Inmates wore identifiable coloured triangles and letters on their pajamas that denoted their classification of crime and country of origin. Black and green triangles denoted criminals, pink denoted homosexuals, and violet indicated Jehovah's Witnesses. Prisoners were labeled with an F (French), R (Russian), T (Czech), P (Polish) and S (Spanish). Every day three hundred died from starvation or beatings inflicted by the SS or the Jewish guards, called Kapos, who exchanged their dignity for an extra piece of bread, warmer clothing or improved shelter. The SS derived pleasure from driving the work gangs mercilessly, bludgeoning out brains or releasing attack dogs on stragglers (Marshall 1952,180–4). High remembers a horror that was repeated each day: a guard randomly selected one person for extermination from each group of PoWs.

Prospects of survival appeared bleak. Prisoners had been sent there to die, and guards made everyone suffer in the process. The 1500 new arrivals wasted away on a rocky slope in the elements for two weeks before enough room opened up in barrack blocks. Yeo-Thomas used his connections in the Russian compound to secure blankets for them. The Russians actually lived better than the Western PoWs because they had managed to establish underground links to the outside world (Marshall 1952, 194). David High woke one cold morning to the vacant stare of an open-mouthed corpse on the ground beside him. Germans subjected inmates to roll calls in wind, rain or sleet conditions, often leaving them to stand in rows for three or four hours at a time.

Dreadful conditions promoted the spread of disease. The ablution pit was an open filth hole. David High and an American, Glenn Harwich of San Diego, succumbed to dysentery three days after their arrival at Buchenwald. The Germans moved the pair into an isolation hut, where they lay on a bare wooden bunk with five others under one ragged and dirty blanket. Columns of bunks extended to the roof. For some imbecile reason the Nazis created a façade that sick people received medical attention. At least five corpses were removed from the "hospital" each day and taken on a two-wheeled hand-drawn wagon to the furnaces. Execution squads killed many more. Value on life did not exist.

German civilians knew of the genocide occurring around them. Boxcar after boxcar brought in thousands and smokestacks belched out the putrid black ash of the dead. Farmers working in adjacent fields could look through the barbed wire into the compounds. Civilians witnessed the throngs of slave labour walk between Buchenwald and adjacent armaments factories every day, for years. Germans were complicit in the crime, High feels.

Sentenced to Death

After David High's first month in the camp, the Gestapo demanded that all surviving airmen from Fresnes sign interrogation forms. High and ten others who refused were condemned to death. SS guards took them to a holding pen on the edge of the parade square to await execution. High believed they were going to die because the SS had just killed twenty-two SOE agents, including at least one Canadian, named Pickersgill, by hanging them from wires attached to meat hooks. A sickening fact about these executions was that these men had wandered freely through the Buchenwald compound during their weeks of captivity and reported for execution when they heard their names bellowed over the public address system. They had no choice; if they did not comply, they would still be rounded up and others would die in addition to them as a reprisal.

As High and the other condemned men awaited death, a sadistic woman in an SS uniform, with two Rottweilers, strode across the square to their holding pen. Evil burned in her eyes as she sized them up. She said nothing and moved on. High learned that this woman was the sadistic Ilsa Koch, better known as the "Bitch of Buchenwald." Apparently she liked to make a cursory inspection of the condemned to see if they had tattoos, and then would have their skin peeled off to make lampshades and wallets for her personal collections. After liberation, the Americans found Koch's quarters adorned with a collection of ornaments made from human skin thought to have been harvested primarily from Russian cadavers. Koch's husband, *Standartenfuehrer* (Colonel) Karl Koch, was a Commandant of Buchenwald. The pair amassed a huge fortune supplying slave labour to owners of munitions plants. Herr Koch was of such dastardly character that the SS placed him on trial and executed him for corruption. Somehow, Ilsa Koch evaded the hangman's noose. She was convicted of mass murder by the American military court after the war and sentenced to life in prison but the court reduced her sentence to just four years. Many attribute this leniency to information received by the American tribunal that while in U.S. custody she had given birth to a child fathered by an American guard. The West German government could not stomach this. She was re-arrested, convicted and sentenced to life in prison in the early 1950s. She killed herself in 1967 in Spandau Prison.

High and the ten other condemned airmen had their lives spared that day. They endured two more months in Buchenwald before the Luftwaffe rescued the surviving airmen from the clutches of the SS. Apparently, Yeo-Thomas had enlisted the services of an anti-Nazi guard, Hans Baumeister, who was willing to smuggle out a letter, inside the cover of a book to a nearby Luftwaffe base; the letter bore information about the fate of the air force officers in the SS-controlled camp. Luftwaffe Reichsmarschall Hermann Goering received confirmation of the air force personnel in Buchenwald and dispatched a delegation to the camp to secure their release. The airmen were dispersed to various Luftwaffe-controlled camps throughout the Reich.

Stalag Luft III for Two Months

David High, on the verge of death, arrived at Stalag Luft III on 18 November 1944. The PoWs there could not comprehend the enormity of the crime committed against High and the thousands of other inmates of Buchenwald. Prisoners of war had no knowledge of the concentration and death camps. Claims of conspiracy and genocide were incomprehensible, especially to those PoWs who had experienced years of incarceration. Besides, no one could accept the accusations that the Germans could commit such atrocities against fellow human beings.

Post-war Tribunals Reveal How the Comet Line was Compromised

What events led to David High's arrest in Paris in July 1944? Evidence presented at the Nuremberg War Crimes Trial in 1946 by Major Airey Neave, Chief Commissioner for Criminal Organizations, outlined the events and named the alleged traitors who had compromised the escape routes in France at the time of Flying Officer David High's arrest. The Gestapo had overseen the roundup of helpers in the escape line, local cells of the Maquis, and the evaders in their protection. The political wing of the Nazi Party Security Service directed by Reichsfuehrer Heinrich Himmler, the Gestapo consisted of the *Geheime Staatspolizei* and the *Sicherheitsdienst* (SS Security Service). On 1 June 1944 the Gestapo absorbed the Abwehr after Admiral Canaris had fallen into disfavour with Hitler. The Abwehr consisted of two groups, the *Geheime Feldpolizei* (Secret Field Police) and the *Feldgendarmerie* (Field Police). The judges at Nuremberg declared the Abwehr and the Gestapo criminal organizations. These organizations had employed every means to destroy the escape lines in Western Europe. According to Neave, they had enlisted Roger Leveneu, a French national, to compromise the O'Leary and Shelburne escape lines in 1943. The Maquis captured and executed Leveneu for treason shortly after the liberation of France in 1944. Neave claims the treachery of Prosper Desitter and Jacques Desoubrie compromised the Comet escape line in July 1944, which resulted in the arrests of the three Canadians, David High, Harry Bastable and Allan Smith.

Neave stated that the single man who masterminded the infiltration of the escape networks was an Englishman, Harold Cole. Cole had been stranded at Dunkirk in 1940 and worked quite successfully as a British agent until the Abwehr captured him in December 1941. In exchange for his life, he agreed to work for them. Neave suggested that Cole's actions resulted in the death of 150 French resisters between late 1941 and 1944. With the withdrawal of German forces from France imminent, the Gestapo rounded up all resistance workers under their surveillance. David High's arrest had coincided with this Nazi sweep. Harold Cole was seen leaving Paris in a high-ranking SS uniform during the evacuation. (Neave 1969, 303–311).

Success of the Escape Networks

Until their compromise, the escape networks helped repatriate 1000 Allied soldiers who had escaped from Dunkirk and about 3000 airmen shot down before D-Day. After D-Day, 600 other airmen found their way back to England with the assistance of brave helpers in the network. Another 5413 air force personnel escaped to Switzerland, where they waited out the duration of the war. During the Second World War over 135,000 Allied prisoners of war were incarcerated in Nazi Germany, and fewer than 150 escaped to freedom, or "hit a home run" (Neave 1969, 19–20) . By late 1943 Allied statistics showed that an airman stood a 50 percent chance of getting back to England with the help of a network once he successfully parachuted to earth. Unfortunately, David High was among the 50 percent who fell into German hands.

High refused to discuss his mistreatment in German custody after his repatriation because most people would find his experience incredible. Even David's father could not accept the extent of the brutality he endured. In October 2001, fifty-seven years after the end of the Second World War, David High received $5446 compensation from the German government for the suffering he had endured at the hands of the Nazis. He asserts that the Canadian government's failure until 1985 to acknowledge his suffering and that of twenty-six other RCAF officers and men who survived Buchenwald has been a grave insult. High mentioned that the federal government paid Buchenwald survivors only $156 Can. for their pain and suffering. Comparatively, the U.S. government paid its Buchenwald survivors up to $100,000, U.S. for their suffering. However, payment for his suffering has never been the central issue for David High. Public acknowledgment of his treatment at Fresnes and Buchenwald is the most important issue. He states that a lawsuit settled in the mid-1980s verified beyond any doubt the incarceration of Allied airmen in various concentration camps.

Others Evaders Captured in France Experienced Hardships

A PoW's experience during captivity depended on which agency arrested him, where he was captured, the stage of the war when his capture occurred, and where he was sent by his captors. David High's experience was not unique. Flying Officer Donald Alexander Lennie, RCAF No. J24617, bailed out of his damaged Halifax on a supply-dropping mission northwest of Poitiers, France on 9 May 1944, and subsequently joined with the Maquis. On 12 May a division of the Waffen SS rounded up most members of the cell with whom he operated. Lennie reported that the SS and Gestapo interrogators beat him. The beat-

Ordered By:

INTERNATIONAL ORG FOR MIGRATION
GERMAN FORCED LABOUR COMPENSATION
CASE POSTALE 71 CH-1211 GENEVA 19
SWITZERLAND

Beneficiary:

DAVID HIGH
IOM Claim Number: 1012887

000024-01/01-83286 CA006171 20050511-L.0000097412
HIGH, DAVID

CLIENT ID:	83286
REF. NUMBER:	L.0000097412
ISSUE DATE:	MAY 16, 2005
CHECK NUMBER:	028957760
AMOUNT DUE:	CAD ************ *6,058.81

NOTICE OF PAYMENT (Instalment 2)
IOM German Forced Labour Compensation Programme

Award for Forced Labour/Slave Labour

Awarded amount: DEM 15000.00   (EUR   7669.38)

Previously received compensation from a German company/
Austrian Reconciliation Fund, deducted from this award:
DEM   0.00   (EUR   0.00)

Net awarded amount: DEM 15000.00   (EUR   7669.38)

First instalment amount already paid: DEM   7500.00   (EUR   3834.69)

Second instalment amount paid through the attached cheque:
DEM   7500.00   (EUR   3834.69)

Please cash this cheque promptly upon receipt.

David High received monetary compensation for his slave labour during his time
at Buchenwald Concentration Camp. Note payment was made 6 decades after the fact.
(Courtesy of David High)

ings ceased when he showed them his dog tags. They moved him to St. Michel
Prison at Toulouse where twenty-three other airmen were already locked up. On
15 June the Germans moved nineteen of them out, presumably to Germany.
Lennie received word that one of the four men left behind, Flying Officer
Charles Hespic, RAF No. 146167, was executed by the Germans. In previous
conversations, Hespic had told Lennie that he worked as a secret agent and had
already spent many months in captivity. On 19 August with the fall of France
imminent, the German guards abandoned St. Michel Prison. The Free French
Forces liberated Lennie and had him repatriated to England. Luck had spared
Lennie's execution or evacuation to Buchenwald, the fate of the 1500 prisoners
from Fresnes Prison.

Flying Officer Harold Bastable

Flying Officer Harold Bastable, RCAF No. J27478, was one of 168 officers and men of Western Allied air forces condemned to Buchenwald concentration camp in August 1944. The Gestapo initially held this group in Paris but relocated them to the Nazi concentration camp to prevent their liberation by Allied forces encircling the French capital. The Gestapo considered a mass execution but realized that disposal of 1500 detainees at Fresnes, including the air force personnel, was impossible on short notice. Instead, the Nazis put the entire prison population in cattle cars and moved them to the Reich for disposal.

The inevitably of the German collapse in France had compelled the Nazis to round up and arrest all known covert operators in early July, and the capture of evaders like Bastable had been a bonus. The Gestapo had tracked his movement from the Chartres area to Paris before arresting him. Collaborators made it easy—they betrayed Bastable for just a few hundred francs. They took Bastable into their confidence under the pretence of smuggling him to Spain via the Comet escape line. The Gestapo held him for six weeks before deporting him on the last train to leave Paris, just days before Allied forces took over the city.

Evasion Begins near Chartres

Bastable's Halifax heavy bomber, LK866 of 640 Squadron RAF, was lost during a bombing operation to the St. Cyr rail yards at Versailles on 8/9 June 1944. The only other Canadian on board, Pilot Officer Ian MacKenzie Hamilton of Toronto, RCAF No. J19966, stayed at the controls of his aircraft to the end to give his crew maximum time to evacuate. Hamilton and the rear gunner, Sergeant Bill Lane, are buried at Soulaires, the French village closest to the crash site. Though authorities failed to recover the remains of the other crew, Bomber Command considered them killed (Allison and Hayward 1996, 296). Bastable evacuated safely through the aircraft's belly but suffered a broken ankle upon landing. He landed on the side of his boot and could hear and feel the bones fracture as the full weight of his body came down on his foot. After burying his parachute and spending a wet, cold night on the outskirts of Soulaires, Bastable realized he had little chance of evasion without assistance. He dragged himself to the shoulder of a nearby road, leaned against a stone wall and waited. The first and only passerby was an elderly French woman. She pretended not to see him but soon returned with six or seven men. His injury waylaid their suspicions about him. They carried him off to the cover of a nearby house, gave him a bed and tended to his swollen ankle. After cutting away his boot and sock, an old man massaged horse liniment over the area of the fracture and attempted to work the bones back into place with his two thumbs. The excruciating pain created by the rubbing action made Bastable flinch but he refused to utter a sound. He had gone without water since the previous night and asked his hosts for something to drink. Bastable learned the French bathed in water but rarely drank it! Their idea of quenching thirst involved drinking a copious amount of cognac—with enough burn to raise him from the bed, a feat the ankle massage had failed to do minutes earlier. His protectors wanted to recover his parachute because silk was a valuable commodity in a wartime economy. Bastable obliged by drawing a rough sketch indicating where he had buried it in relation to the spot where they found him, but after an extensive search, they failed to uncover it.

The locals hid Bastable in a greenhouse at Emance. A brave young couple graciously shared their food and shelter with the evader even though the Germans would shoot them, along with their baby, if the enemy discovered him. For two weeks Harold hid beneath the greenery growing over the sides of the hothouse tables. Tiny green lizards ran along the irrigation pipes that hung just inches above his face. It seemed everyone in the village knew about him. Despite his hosts' pleas for him to remain with them, Bastable set out for Spain, all the while leaning on a crutch. Villagers helped alter his appearance by turning his uniform inside out after cutting off all identifiable insignia. They packed boiled eggs and fresh cherries for his journey. He carried his map and several compasses cleverly hidden in buttons, a zipper and a pipe.

A hobbled man does not go far on three legs. Harold was still in town when he heard the clanking of enemy tanks just over the hill. Lead tanks of a Panzer column, moving northwest to reinforce German positions at Normandy, had mistakenly turned off the main road into Emance. Having no time to seek cover, Harold dove into the ditch and crushed the boiled eggs and cherries that were tucked in his tunic. One tank rumbled to a stop beside him. He could have touched one tank's track rollers and grabbed the boot of the officer bellowing to the crews to return to the main road. The officer would have spotted Bastable lying in the ditch bottom if he had turned around. Bastable knew from months of training in England that Sherman tanks could only change directions by circling about, so he naturally assumed the Panzer would do the same. He counted off the seconds before the Panzer, towering above him, would roll down the embankment on top of him. Instead, it engaged reverse gear and backed out of the village. That was Bastable's first experience with the Germans, and he was still in town!

Bastable waited for nightfall before moving to Galardon, the first village down the road. His nerves were raw; the sounds of animals lurking in the trees might just have been German soldiers. Like all villages in France, the predominant landmark in Galardon was the Catholic church. The rural French appeared poor but each community had the means to raise a beautiful house of worship. Harold hoped the Christian principle of finding sanctuary in a church would hold true for him, and he waited inside for the arrival of a clergyman. To his dismay, a priest barely acknowledged him as he lay on the pew. Harold could not believe it. He moved outside and used the cover of a funeral procession moving through the churchyard to make good his escape from Galardon. A horse pulled an old-fashioned, glass-encased hearse containing an ornate casket and was followed by a column of mourners. Bringing up the rear was the same priest who had ignored him earlier!

In with the Maquis

A more hospitable welcome awaited Bastable in the next village. An older couple, well in their eighties, keen to his predicament, took him in. Despite membership in the Maquis, their reckless actions exasperated the Canadian. He was mortified when the elderly woman once stood boldly in the window to curse and shake her fist at a German soldier walking by with a young woman in tow. She refused to budge despite Bastable's pleas. He feared the German would kick down her door and find him inside. He was not sure if her defiance was an act of bravery or an act of stupidity. He later assumed the main reason the German ignored her was that he knew the war was lost and he would gain nothing by terrorizing her. Bastable knew that the young girl hanging off the German's arm would be punished for her collaboration once the Boche were driven out of France and the underground rounded her up.

Bastable found the old woman's son equally brazen. He insisted Bastable ride with him on a tandem bicycle through the town and country, and he took him to an unexploded 500-pound bomb embedded in a field. Apparently it had skip-bombed over a bridge after a pilot of an American P-38 Lightning had missed his mark. The cavalier Frenchman "cowboyed up" on back of the bomb and "put the spurs" to his iron bronc. Harold cringed. He knew the explosive capability of 500 pounds of TNT and assumed the detonator was still armed. He yelled at the boy to end his foolishness. He hoped someone in the village could disarm the bomb before it exploded. The boy and his parents intended to fight to the death if the Germans raided their house; they kept a loaded Sten gun concealed in a basket of baguettes in their kitchen.

Bastable could not stay with them, so they moved him to a house occupied by a major Maquis leader. People came and went at all hours of the day. By contrast, this Maquis cell operated in a more disciplined manner. The leader relied on the expertise of his two sons, graduates of the French military academy, to organize attacks against German positions and strategic targets. Harold's broken ankle prevented him from actively participating in operations, but he assisted by making bombs from plastic explosives. A typical bomb consisted of five inches of plastic shaped like a sausage, which had the explosive power to blow a two-foot piece of rail from a train track, just as if someone had cleanly sawed it away. Yet, the stability of the plastic explosive amazed its handlers. A lighted match failed to set it off, as did throwing it against a wall. Only a chemical reaction could ignite it. The process was simple: an aluminum stick contained a chemical that ate through the thin tube after its user pinched it off. Marks on each aluminum stick or fuse indicated the number of minutes that would elapse before the chemical ate through the stick and set off the explosion. Bastable knew the saboteurs had succeeded when he heard distant explosions in rapid succession.

The two sons acted with impunity against Germans. They liquidated a German officer recently posted to the local garrison. Bastable knew they had completed this job when they returned with a new silk map. When he inquired about its origin, one son replied, "From the German officer," as he drew his finger across his throat in a quick slashing motion. Bastable believed that he risked the same fate if he showed any signs of weakness. They issued Bastable a revolver and expected him to carry it with him at all times. When he stashed it under his pillow in his bedroom, the old man flushed with anger because he felt Harold failed to appreciate the dangerous situation in which he existed. The leader wanted him to have the weapon at the ready; he knew Harold would be unable to react quickly enough if Germans broke into the house during a surprise sweep. To prove his point, the old man crept into Bastable's room that night and held a gun to the Canadian's head before he had time to reach for his handgun. Afterwards Harold even slept with it in his hand under the bedding despite fears he would roll over and accidentally shoot himself—the gun did not have a safety catch!

Rendezvous with an Escape Line

The underground arranged to move Bastable and two other Canadian evaders to Spain via the Comet escape line. Organizers rendezvoused with a French man and a Belgian woman going to Paris. The group spent the night in the home of a wealthy woman whose role for the underground involved the retrieval of weapons and explosives dropped at night by British Lysander aircraft. It was a risky job and the three bullet scars in her legs proved it! The Germans had an uncanny ability to know the location of the drop zones and they would lie in wait for the supplies and the Maquis to arrive. No one knew for sure if the Germans deciphered coded messages sent from London with the details of the drops or if collaborators tipped off the Gestapo. Even though the Germans shot at her, this woman managed to recover many of the bundles. The risks failed to deter her, and she continued to serve France fearlessly.

Evaders like Bastable were in the unenviable position of having to place their lives into the hands of people they did not know. In retrospect, Bastable said he ignored the obvious signs of collaboration that cost him his freedom. For instance, movement by car into Paris was too easy. The Germans had check-points set up at virtually every intersection, yet they always waved through the black car containing the three evaders. The driver had a bountiful supply of petrol. After a brief stay at a safe house in Paris, his new driver managed to end up at a roadblock manned by Gestapo with British Sten guns. Obviously the underground was compromised. Bastable learned after the war that the female who accompanied him into Paris was a known collaborator but she avoided prosecution. Years later, Bastable returned to France. Survivors from the French underground took him to the establishment where she worked. He intended to confront her but thought better of it, at the last moment, fearing his emotions might overwhelm him.

Incarceration

Harold Bastable knew his status as a prisoner of war was tenuous at best, considering he had disposed of his military identification and dog tags back at Emance. Secondly, the Gestapo could take him to be a saboteur and a spy because of his association with the Maquis. Despite the loss of freedom and the uncertainty of his predicament, the six weeks in Fresnes Prison proved to be "relatively" uneventful. He spent most days in a small cell with a French Jew, who, upon his departure, gave Bastable a small piece of his bread despite his own precarious future. Harold assumed this octogenarian did not live to see the year 1945.

Deportation to Buchenwald

On 16 August 1944, the Gestapo emptied Fresnes Prison and herded its 1500 prisoners through the streets of Paris to the marshalling yards. Emotions ran high. Defiant citizens lined the streets, flashed a "V" for victory, shouted words of encouragement to the prisoners and handed over bits of food even when the German guards waved machine guns at them. The SS divided the men into groups of 80 or 90 before crowding them into boxcars meant to hold forty. A small pile of raw potatoes lay in the centre of the floor, along with a washtub intended for use as a toilet. Already weakened by poor nutrition, dysentery and mistreatment, prisoners defecated where they stood. Many vomited on the floor. The rocking of the boxcar rolled the potatoes through the train car, and within minutes the men had trampled the potatoes underfoot, amidst the feces and vomit. The boxcar stank just miles into the trip; the floor was slippery and the food was spoiled. The 168 anxious PoWs assumed they were going to PoW camps somewhere in the Reich. None of them had heard of concentration or death camps.

The trip proved precarious. The train crew often had to stop beneath the canopy of forests to hide from roving Allied aircraft. Prisoners hoped the Resistance would ambush the train to free them. In Bastable's car, guards neglected to return for the hammer that had been used to nail barbed wire over the small opening in the side wall. Some PoWs used it to pry up floorboards and escaped through the hole on 19 August. Pilot Officer Joel M. Stevenson of 419 Squadron RCAF and two French officers made for the cover and undergrowth. The Maquis helped Stevenson evade and had him repatriated to England by 4 September 1944 (Stevenson 1944, 2–3). It took no time for the guards to zero in on the offending car, beat and strip the remaining men, then announce they intended to shoot 16 English and 16 French prisoners in the morning, as punishment. The train rolled on through the night. Men jostled for position to the far ends of the car but no one would budge. Those nearest the door resigned themselves to the eventuality that the Germans would select them for execution in the morning. The train stopped in a gully at sunrise. Guards slid back the door and ordered 32 prisoners out. A big American muttered, "If we are going to die then let's die like men!"

The presence of French civilians standing along a rail and looking down upon the hapless group of naked men most likely saved their lives. The officer in charge did not want witnesses and he attempted to disperse the crowd with a volley of gunfire. Bastable expected a bullet to rip through him momentarily. He looked down the barrel of a rifle held by a soldier, just feet away, and thought, "That bastard is going to kill me!" The rifle muzzle looked like a cannon. The officer went through the motion of ordering the squad to aim but at the last second told the firing squad to stand down. Guards pushed the naked men back into the boxcar and the train continued into the unknown. Bastable remembered one man inside the car, in particular. This fellow had a Bible in his hand and chanted prayers during the ordeal. He wanted to know if Harold thought of God in his last few seconds. Bastable retorted, "I was so mad, I did not think of God, not even my family!"

Allied aircraft continued to attack the train. Guards warned prisoners to stay clear of the windows but an impetuous French teenager pulled himself up to find out why the train had stopped. Shots rang out and one round tore through the boy's hand. Bastable never forgot the expression of sheer terror on the lad's face. Pressing the wound to stem the blood flow, Bastable pulled him to the door and pounded on the door until it opened. An SS officer questioned the boy and ordered him to walk down the line. The door slammed shut, the officer barked an order and shots rang out. Witnesses looking through cracks in the wall saw soldiers shoot the French boy in the back. The officer drew his Luger from its holster and fired two shots into the boy's head.

Arrival at Buchenwald

The train stopped in a rail yard about a mile away from their destination and the SS ordered everyone to form up on the rail siding. Trouble began as soon as the door of Bastable's boxcar slid open. A guard viciously beat a prisoner for failing to stand at attention properly. He wanted the new arrivals to stand like German soldiers, with their fingers outstretched along the seam of their pants, not like the British who turned their fingers into the palms of their hands. If the SS brute wanted to instill terror, he succeeded. A sign erected over the front gates of Buchenwald revealed the future: "Abandon all hope, those who pass through these gates." The arrivals had their heads shaved with blunt electric shears that tore out chunks of flesh and then painted with a purple liquid applied by a mop. Each new prisoner received wooden shoes and striped pajamas emblazoned with a large red circle in the middle of the shirt back to give guards a good target to shoot at. If one found humour in those circumstances, it began when the 168 airmen were herded into the rocky compound where they would spend the next two weeks. Enough time had passed for the purple coating to penetrate the wounds opened by the blunt shears. Every man hollered and jumped around the compound until the burning subsided. Resigned to their predicament, men created spots on which to lie by moving rocks and lying down amongst them. Fortunately the weather remained relatively warm until barracks became available. The previous occupants were Gypsies, deported to Auschwitz. The PoWs learned to tolerate the poor quality food after the first day. The slices of dark bread looked so unpalatable; yeast sank to the bottom, and the wood fibre stayed on the top. Moldy, soft potatoes and smelly cheese rounded out the diet. Communal kitchens supplied pails of soup made with weeds and the occasional chunk of meat of uncertain origin. Other prisoners scooped up the food and devoured it before the new arrivals had time to change their minds.

Everyone suffered the effects of dysentery. If one were fast, he might manage to lower his pants before he emptied his bowels. Inmates squatted on a poplar over an open cesspool. Many slipped on the feces and urine splattered on the ground or the log, or fell down into the open pit. Sleeping arrangements were equally degrading—four men huddled on each rack. Without room to turn, all slept on their sides. Four-tier bunks stacked men to the ceiling. Inmates on the top bunk were luckier than the ones below because human waste dripped between the cracks unto those in the lower levels. Each morning prisoners hosed down their bed frames with cold water. It may have washed off the feces and urine but the moisture kept the racks cool, contributing to innumerable cases of pleurisy. Corpses were collectedly daily and hauled to the "ice house" to await cremation.

The SS ran the camp but they relied on kapos to do their dirty work. Prisoners elevated to junior guard status, the kapos received more food, warmer clothing and a clean barracks for their troubles. Most importantly, they had a chance to live longer than those they oversaw. Bastable believed most kapos were German communists. They saw value in protecting the air force PoWs because they assumed the airmen would have useful skills if the general population rebelled. The kapos kept most of the airmen in the barracks instead of assigning them to labour battalions where they would be worn down by back-breaking work and frequent beatings. Bastable remembered that most Germans demonstrated indifference to prisoners but could be brutal if an inmate failed to remove his hat in the presence of a guard.

The camp was a paradox. A traveling dentist periodically worked on inmates' teeth in an office equipped with sixteen modern chairs. Bastable went once for treatment but declined further "appointments" because procedures were performed without the luxury of anesthetic. The Germans designated one building as a hospital, but substandard facilities and supply shortages limited its ability to improve the health of "patients." A third barrack block contained a grisly collection of artifacts crafted from human remains. Lampshades and book covers made from skins of the deceased, and shrunken heads of Polish men were testaments to the fetishes of sadistic Nazis. Buchenwald was also a center for ghoulish experimentation on people.

Slave labour stacked corpses in a building called the "icehouse" until they cremated the backlog. Bastable went regularly to view the deceased until he spotted two fellow airmen among them. He told MI9 of the deaths of his comrades at Buchenwald in his 5 May 1945 Evasion and Capture Report, confirming the cremation of Flying Officer P.D. Hemmens, RAF No. 152583, in September 1944 and Lieutenant L.C. Beck, USAAF No. 0.736945, in November 1944.

Bastable suffered from pleurisy, sinus problems and a severe infection in his right leg. What originated as a simple bite by a flea on his shin festered into a gaping wound into which he could push his finger. He believed it would be gangrenous within days. With assistance from a Russian prisoner, Bastable limped to an aid tent for medical attention. They heard screaming from within. Apparently a Dutch surgeon, also a PoW, was performing surgery on one of the airmen without anesthetic. Bastable considered his options. Hospital treatments were primitive, maybe even barbaric. Alternatively, amputation of his leg was a real possibility. He took his place in a long queue. He never forgot the image of the old man lying on the ground inside the tent. Shallow breathing moved his threadbare cotton shirt ever so slightly. He was close to death. He failed to flinch when flies crawled in and out of his mouth and nose and over his eyeballs. Bastable pitied this man; he imagined he was probably a proud grandfather who had rocked his grandchildren back and forth on his knee, just months earlier.

Bastable could not understand how sick people could recover in such filthy surroundings. A German opened up "hospital" beds by singling out those considered too sick for further treatment and sending them to the ovens. Fellow patients removed a gravely ill airman from the building each time this merchant of death made his rounds. Bastable received white pills the size of quarters from orderlies. He assumed the pills had some effect because the infection cleared up enough that he no longer feared amputation of his limb.

Harold Bastable's short stay in the hospital coincided with the unanticipated relocation of 160 of the 166 airmen in Buchenwald to prisoner of war camps run by the Luftwaffe. On 2 November 1944, Luftwaffe representatives unknowingly left Bastable and five other airmen in Buchenwald's hospital. Subsequently, his value to the kapos was reduced and they turned him into the general prison population. Guards relocated Bastable into the main compound where, to his amazement, all buildings were constructed of cement. Though the rooms were drier than the wooden barracks, the cement barracks were colder. He slept on a metal bunk under a thin blanket. He rose at 4:00 a.m. to stand on the parade square at attention, rain or shine, while guards conducted roll calls, sometimes for several hours, before he went out to repair area highways under a civilian contractor out of Weimar. It seemed to rain all the time. Fortunately the German guard watching Bastable's section left the prisoners alone. However, he would release his attack dog if anyone strayed too far. The prisoners feared Ukrainian, Polish and Russian volunteers who worked for the SS. These guards wore lighter grey uniforms than their German counterparts did. They also stood out for their sadistic demeanour. Bastable remembered one SS guard chastising an ethnic guard for the brutal treatment of one man in Bastable's gang. Exposure and hard work weakened Harold quickly.

If the Luftwaffe had not returned to claim the remaining airmen in Buchenwald, he believes he would have died from exhaustion.

In Luftwaffe Custody

Bastable's last day in Buchenwald began on the parade square. After roll call, a guard ordered him to the Vorlager. Guards humiliated him one last time by stripping him naked before marching him into the commandant's office where junior officers and two females stood around and leered at him. They wanted to hear him say that they had treated him well during his stay at Buchenwald, even though they saw the exposed bone on his leg and heard his raspy breathing. Their arrogant smirks made Bastable hope that the Russians would liberate this camp. After he told them what they wanted to hear, they returned his clothes, and Bastable was hustled outside the front gate into the custody of a well-dressed Luftwaffe officer in his mid-twenties. The officer stood elegantly in his high black leather boots and wrapped in a dark green cape with a shiny white velvet lining.

Bastable was astounded by the civil treatment he received from this English-speaking German who demonstrated a genuine interest in his well-being. He is convinced this German might have known that camps like Buchenwald existed but had not encountered one before. Bastable gave details about the poor food, the labour gangs, people dying en masse, and the crematoria. The German wretched when Bastable lifted his pant leg to show the rotten flesh and the exposed bone. He gave Bastable warm clothing and then told him that he had orders to escort him to a Luftwaffe-controlled camp, Stalag Luft III.

Even though the journey by train would be arduous by most standards, at least Bastable was out of Buchenwald, and alive. Frequent Allied air attacks slowed the trains; rain and snow made the trip miserable. In contrast, the respect shown to him by this officer made the trip tolerable. During one stopover, the officer *asked* Bastable if he wanted to go into a terminal building to warm up and get hot soup. Harold could not believe that a German would exhibit so much courtesy. He sat down at a table with him and the two guards as he ate his potato soup. Bastable believed he was in heaven. So engrossed in his meal, he failed to notice the crush of hostile onlookers closing in around them. Understanding the gravity of the situation, the Luftwaffe officer ordered his two soldiers to face the mob, with their rifles at the ready. Retaining his composure, the Luftwaffe officer politely asked, "Sir, would you mind coming outside, again?" as he pointed to the throng of civilians. "Those people know who you are. I do not want to order my men to shoot my own people. If they move any closer then I'll have to give the order to shoot." Bastable respected this man and obviously wanted to avoid a confrontation. The civilians retreated when they went outside. They shivered for hours waiting for their connection to arrive.

Stalag Luft III

Flying Officer Harold Bastable joined the officers in Stalag Luft's North Compound in late November 1944. They failed to comprehend what he told them about Buchenwald because no one had heard of concentration or death camps. Bastable felt out of place. He needed time to adjust to a camp where Germans demonstrated restraint. For the first few mornings he *ran* to the parade square. He stood at attention and could not believe it as the other officers sauntered out. He suffered from pneumonia and spent most of his time in the infirmary while at Stalag Luft III. Compared to Buchenwald, here the food was excellent. He received warm clothes, clean blankets and clean living quarters. Conditions deteriorated when the prisoners were force-marched from Stalag Luft III in January 1945. This proved a very difficult time, but after surviving Buchenwald, he could survive anything.

Conclusion

Harold Bastable returned to Canada in relatively good health. The most apparent evidence of his captivity was the loss of weight. He noted that a few

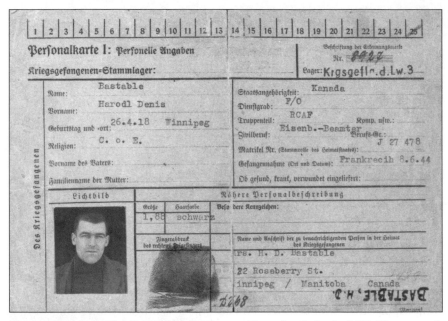

Flying Officer Bastable's PoW identification card issued at Stalag Luft III. (Courtesy of H. Bastable)

additional weeks of hard labour and poor diet in Buchenwald would have claimed his life. Fortunately the Germans did not subject him to torture, and he avoided a firing squad twice, in Gestapo custody and en route to Germany. He understood the mentality of his captors and kept a low profile to avoid drawing attention.

Bastable speaks freely about his personal experiences as well as the mistreatment and demise of thousands during his captivity. He feels no animosity towards the German people, but he loathes Nazism and the existence of other extremist movements. He does not find solace in religion and he challenges the faith of others by asking them how a God would allow the mistreatment and murder of millions of innocent people and the destruction of many nations on several continents. He is proud of his service to Canada and for his role in the preservation of democracy. In his 88th year he continued to make presentations to students in public school and university and to the Jewish community in Winnipeg. Nearly sixty years after the war, the German government compensated Harold Bastable with close to $7000 from a fund paid into by German businesses that benefitted from conscript labour supplied by camps like Buchenwald.

Flying Officer William M. Poohkay

If there ever was a man who derived much glee from his wartime evasion experiences, Bill Poohkay should come to mind. This Canadian landed in eastern France after bailing out of his Halifax near the city of Reims shortly after D-Day. During his recollections, one could observe a twinkle in his eyes after he recounted stories of sabotage and tales of evasion from the German patrols sent out to find him and his French companions. Poohkay survived his time as an evader because of his innate ability to read people and gain their trust. He did not waver when the local cell of the Maquis exhibited reticence when dealing with him. Flying Officer William Poohkay, RCAF No. J19530, fought alongside the resisters for two months before connecting with U.S. General George Patton's army on the French-Belgian border.

Ack-Ack was Effective

In the briefing before his thirty-eighth operation, Poohkay and his crew were informed that aerial reconnaissance could not spot any German anti-aircraft batteries along the route of their next mission. Actually the reconnaissance had failed to detect them because the Germans had effectively camouflaged the gun placements. Near Metz a cluster of ack-ack filled the night sky and laid an effective field of fire in front of Poohkay's Halifax. Bill recalled how easy it was at 20,000 feet to follow the orange streaks emerging from the barrels of anti-aircraft guns. He had no time to warn the pilot to take evasive action; in a few seconds, shells had holed the starboard wing and set the starboard engine on fire. The flight engineer attempted to suppress the flames with fire extinguishers built into the engine cowling, but failed. The pilot tried to extinguish the flames by pushing the aircraft into a steep dive. Flying at over two hundred miles per hour and losing altitude at close to five hundred feet per second, and only a minute or two from impact, the skipper issued the order to bail out. Poohkay exited from the belly of the aircraft. The contrast between the chaos aboard the crippled aircraft and the silence of the night amazed him.

"I Wished I Had Paid Closer Attention During Parachute Training!"

One component of Poohkay's air training had been an intensive but brief course on the use of a parachute. Poohkay recalled the parachute lectures were one aspect of the training no one wanted to think about; it was like thinking about death. Now he wished he had paid closer attention to the finer details of the lecture. He was not able to recall how to stop his parachute from swaying in an erratic circular motion, nor could he recall how to direct his movement to the left or right. He needed to direct himself away from the white reflection below, which he took for a large body of water. It would be easy to drown beneath the weight of the harness and canopy. Hundreds of soldiers from the United States 82nd and 101st Airborne Divisions had been found dead in just a few feet of water after their drop into the flooded fields of Normandy during the night of 5/6 June 1944. Poohkay had the luxury of a "Mae West," a personal flotation device, capable of keeping him afloat long enough to cut himself out of his harness before the weight of his gear pulled him down. As it turned out, the crests of water were stalks of barley waving in the wind. Poohkay landed safely, then rolled his parachute into a ball and stuffed it below the sea of grain. He had no doubts that the German pilot who had just flown over had seen him struggling with the outstretched white parachute and radioed in his location. Poohkay

Flying Officer W.M. Poohkay carried this 1250F standard RCAF identification card. Note his date of birth is written as 1905 instead of 1915. (Courtesy of W.M. Poohkay)

A 1943 picture of a Wellington flight crew that included Sergeant Harry Holland, center front, and Navigator Sergeant W.M. Poohkay, right front. (Courtesy of W.M. Poohkay)

knew from the drone of aircraft that a German airbase was very close and a patrol could be upon him in minutes.

Feet Firmly Planted on French Soil

Poohkay had a good fix on his location. His bomber had been equipped with H2S radar, a system that reproduced details of the landscape on his radar screen. He had recognized landforms near Reims before bailing out. Flying Officer Poohkay decided to outfox German patrols by moving in the direction they least expected—towards Switzerland. That was a wise choice. Three hundred and fifty thousand German troops retreated from the Falaise pocket two weeks after he bailed out over France, and Poohkay would have found it difficult to evade them as they retreated. He stumbled into a battery of well-camouflaged anti-aircraft guns that the RAF reconnaissance flights had missed. He understood why: they were impossible to spot on the ground, let alone from the air.

Poohkay believed the conservative rural farmers of France were sympathizers to the Allied cause and would help him evade. The first man he encountered turned out to be a conscript worker from an eastern European nation, who flew into a rage when he spotted the Canadian making his way towards him. He frantically motioned the aviator to go away. One could hardly blame him; the Germans shot those who assisted the enemy. Poohkay retreated to the edge of the hollow, with revolver in hand, and prayed the man did not make a break to alert the Germans. His second encounter was better. A farmer leapt from his tractor and relished shaking the hand of a man who was fighting to rid France of the Boche. Poohkay's high-school French still allowed him to convey the idea that he needed to link up with the underground. This Frenchman had waited a long time to do his part for France. Poohkay told him to resume his work to avoid drawing suspicion and to return at the end of the day. The man concurred. Not fully convinced of the farmer's trustworthiness, Bill hid elsewhere and waited. The man returned later in the evening to the pre-arranged location and appeared disappointed that the evader had moved on. Convinced a rear guard of German soldiers had not followed him, Poohkay emerged from the underbrush and waved the Frenchman over. Poohkay's extra precautions impressed the Frenchman.

The pair's arrival was the worst-kept secret in Juzancourt, a small village in the French Ardennes. Sixteen villagers cheered his arrival. A Frenchman asked, "Will you fight for us? Do you fight for our country?" The Canadian responded, "Yes!" to a chorus of cheers. These unsophisticated people seemed to take him at face value. They ignored the threat that he might be a plant sent to ferret out an underground cell. However, his freedom nearly ended the following morning when a German army officer randomly chose to stop, at the very house where he was hidden, to buy some eggs for his breakfast. The officer did not enter the house; rather, he took his eggs and moved on. The farm wife nearly collapsed after the German's departure but the chance appearance of the officer appeared to dissipate suspicions about Poohkay. To celebrate their near brush with death, the family slaughtered the largest rooster in their brood and hung it in the sun, all day, to "cure." Remarkably, Poohkay's iron stomach withstood the bacteria test.

The underground remained guarded in their estimation of Poohkay and relocated him to a remote part of the Ardennes forest for a final evaluation of his allegiance. It did not take him long to realize they still had qualms about his identity. They placed him under surveillance for three or four days, during which time the underground had to make a decision to shoot him or let him live. Poohkay remains convinced that his single act of "defeating" a challenger in a session of hand-to-hand combat won over their support. Maybe he exhibited moves typical of those taught to RCAF personnel in self-defence classes, or maybe they thought his prowess at pinning his adversary to the ground was impressive. He was unsure. What mattered was that the Maquis accepted him as a member into their cell of twenty men. Poohkay earned the monikers "General Foche" and "*état-major*" from his French compatriots.

Operations of a Local Cell of the Maquis

The sophistication of the underground impressed Poohkay, although it appeared to operate in a haphazard manner. Local cells worked in groups of a few dozen men. Through tragic experience, the cells learned to operate in small groups because the Germans had little difficulty detecting large groups of resisters. Poohkay's group did not light fires because the enemy would see the smoke above the trees. Farmers acted as the eyes and ears of the underground; they relayed messages and cached food and cognac along the routes traveled by the Maquis. The Resistance did not seem to be short of funds. The cells secured money from two sources. The British SOE smuggled in millions of francs overland through Spain and Portugal, or by air drops at night. The second source of money was intriguing. Sympathetic officials in Vichy France told the Maquis when to hijack shipments of money from trains and trucks, and gendarmes stayed away. Poohkay still has the 400 French francs the Maquis paid him for his work.

Poohkay joined a cell near the French city of Metz, a significant distance from the coast and too far inland to receive regular supply drops from the SOE. The group had been parachuted a radio, a bazooka, some explosives, anti-tank mines, and a rifle for each man, but nothing more. The British made a concerted attempt to supply Poohkay's group from a Lysander, a sturdy, single-engine supply aircraft. Once, these Maquisards illuminated a landing strip with two rows of pot fires, but they aborted the rendezvous when a number of German soldiers appeared in the area.

Poohkay's group roamed the countryside cutting phone lines, blowing up sections of road and draining canals. Assassinations and ambush of German patrols were generally discouraged because patrols were equipped with radios and could call in reinforcements before their attackers could melt away into the woods. Instead, the Maquisards inconvenienced and harassed local units of the German military. Their physical presence was small, but the occasional ambush and killing discouraged German troops from venturing off the main roads.

Bill Poohkay found these French pragmatic, especially an older man in the cell who was a veteran of the Great War. This man had a peculiar habit of shielding the orange glow of his cigarette inside the palm of his hand. He picked up this habit during the stalemate on the western front in the First World War because German snipers picked off careless smokers on the front line. The same man had disposed of his wife because she had collaborated with the Germans. With an absence of emotion, he told Poohkay how he took her out for a walk and "put her away." She was expendable; he put the safety of the group above her life. A young French boy befriended Poohkay. He told Bill that the Germans had deported him to Frankfurt to work in an armament factory. Allied bombers were constantly bombarding the city and the boy realized it was just a matter of time before he would be killed in an air strike. He slipped away and made his way back to France to join the Maquis, knowing that if the Germans recaptured him he would be tortured and killed. The boy pointed to Poohkay's Colt revolver and made the Canadian swear to shoot him if the Germans captured the group.

The Germans knew that Poohkay's cell of Maquisards was operating around Metz and that a Canadian was among them, which forced the cell to keep on the move. They inadvertently took refuge in a village at the same time the Gestapo were conducting an intensive door-to-door search for them. They were lucky on this occasion. Poohkay and another resister had just walked around a corner when two Gestapo cars, with eight men, pulled away in the opposite direction. Poohkay's cell moved west to Charleville in late August to meet up with the Americans. Strong pockets of German holdouts manned the lines but not all the Germans were willing to die. Two Belgian schoolchildren alerted Poohkay to the presence of two young Wehrmacht soldiers who had deserted their unit and had hidden themselves in a potato field. The Canadian beckoned them to throw out their weapons. Up rose the two heavily armed soldiers equipped with rifles, potato masher grenades, rucksacks and supplies. Some members of the cell wanted to execute these two prisoners on the spot. Poohkay saved their lives when he intervened and demanded that full protection of the Geneva Convention be extended to them.

Nazis Pillaged France

The Germans looted France of its wealth and treasures even as they retreated into the fatherland. In the Charleville area Poohkay and his group watched an American fighter bomber swoop down and destroy a train destined to the Third Reich. The train's engineer and fireman died; the cargo of champagne remained relatively intact. The Maquisards scooped up as many cases as they could carry and made their way to a castle called Chateau Mon Dieu, an estate coincidentally managed by a couple from Saskatchewan. The resisters had subsisted for weeks on slabs of salt pork and rye loaves that were so tough a hammer could not dent them. Their gracious Canadian hosts welcomed them into their chateau and served up a bounty of twelve courses, complete with the champagne recovered from the train wreck. It was a meal most of these Frenchmen had not enjoyed for four years. After hours of levity the Canadian hosts revealed that a German commander had previously visited the castle and had informed its occupants he intended to commandeer it as headquarters for a German division when troops moved into the area. The Maquisards sat stunned, realizing the Germans could appear at any time, especially as their armies were in full retreat. They made an immediate break for the surrounding hills and rendezvoused at a predetermined location with one of their group who had chosen to act as a lookout. Sadly they discovered their comrade dead at the base of a waterfall; a bullet had dispatched him. They laid him to rest in a nearby copse of trees before continuing west to join up with the Americans.

A Mosaic of France's Political Culture

Poohkay observed serious political rifts among Maquisards and had the sense to stay clear during heated arguments. These Frenchmen spent too much time squabbling amongst themselves when they should have presented a unified front to the Germans. Fractured politics weakened their effectiveness. Members of Poohkay's group represented the political stripes that had undermined successive French governments in the 1930s, pitting left against right and labour against business. Pre-war French politics had three main divisions: conservative Royalists; radical Communists; and the Popular Front; a coalition of socialists, liberals, moderate communists, labour, some of the middle class, and anti-fascists who supported progressive change within the established democratic process. The leader of the Popular Front was a Jewish socialist, Leon Blum. The anti-Semitic feelings of the era did not bode well for Blum's coalition government.

Dogged by internal strife, successive French administrations lacked the resources to address the issue of German re-armament with a pragmatic defence strategy to protect against German aggression. The French hid behind the Maginot Line on their eastern frontier and shored up their northern flank, along the borders with Belgium and Luxembourg, with eighty divisions. The military, like the government, lacked effective leadership, and France cloaked itself in a false sense of security. The Little Entente, a confusing collection of alliances between France, Czechoslovakia, Yugoslavia, Poland and Romania, only served to antagonize Germany. When pressed, France refused to support its allies even though it had instigated the alliance. The terms of the Treaty of Versailles, the French occupation of the Saar and the Ruhr, and the loss of German sovereignty over Rhineland set up France for a drubbing. France might have had the strength to repel an invasion but it lacked the unity to withstand the Nazi juggernaut. The French stood idle when Germany reasserted its control over the Rhineland in 1936, annexed Austria in 1938, and took over parts of Czechoslovakia in two thrusts, once in 1938 and again in 1939. France's policy of non-intervention in the Spanish civil war reduced support for Blum's left wing government in Paris while signaling to the world that western liberal democracies, through the inaction of the League of Nations, were unwilling to assert themselves. After the declaration of war in September 1939, the French still remained divided. When France signed the armistice in June 1940, Marshal Philippe Pétain further demoralized French nationalists when he agreed to the German plan to partition France. Northern France was ruled by French leaders who cooperated with Hitler; Pétain ruled Vichy France, for which he earned the label "collaborator." Rifts found their way down to the smallest factions of French society. Had these Maquisards not had a common enemy, they might have destroyed each other.

By default, a new leader, General Charles de Gaulle emerged as a force in French politics after the collapse of France in 1940. He led the Free French from exile in London and inspired them through the BBC. He gained the confidence of different underground organizations, the Free French in North Africa and subjects in the French colonies. De Gaulle's stature rose with his appointment as provisional leader of a French government in exile in 1943. Many French citizens began to view him as the last gasp of hope for France. De Gaulle foresaw the possibility of civil war or a communist takeover in France after the war. He forged an alliance with the resisters who were called French Forces of the Interior (FFI), and used his close links with the British Special Operations Executive (SOE) to strengthen them. The FFI consisted of many soldiers who had been released after the fall of France, who had already undergone extensive training and who understood discipline and organization. They trained in secret until D-Day. The British were able to provide them with radio sets, weapons, supplies and money, and parachute in operatives to assist in their training. De Gaulle hesitated to arm the Maquis because many bands of Maquisards had earned a reputation as opportunists out to establish fiefdoms. Some cells operated recklessly, gaining notoriety for robbery, extortion and murder. Therefore, a real dilemma existed. De Gaulle decided that the resisters were to be lightly armed only, and the Allies would do most of the fighting to minimize the quantity of weapons in the hands of rival resistance movements.

The Maquis was much less sophisticated in its operations than the FFI for a number of reasons. Most Maquisards consisted of young Frenchmen who had fled from authorities rounding up conscript labour. They had little or no formal military training and discipline. Their groups were under equipped; anyone who intended to join the Maquis brought his own supplies—shirts, pants, socks, sweaters, a beret, a jacket and cooking utensils. De Gualle's supporters wore armbands bearing the Cross of Lorraine. In heated discussions they ripped off their armbands, only to reattach them days later when emotions had subsided. As an outsider, Poohkay viewed the divisiveness of the Maquis as its major limitation, but any notion about its ineffectiveness was dispelled after D-Day when the isolated groups stepped up acts of sabotage. They blew up railway lines and bridges and held back German reinforcements from reaching the Normandy beaches for two weeks. The Maquis fought bravely without proper weaponry and suffered heavy casualties against Wehrmacht and Panzer divisions. Poohkay directed all his energies into the defeat of Germany and remained above the petty divisions, which had contributed to the fractured nation of France in the first place.

Last Days of German Occupation

The liberation of Paris finally came on 23 August 1944. A half-million Allied troops advanced beyond the capital and had crossed the Seine River by 30 August. Patton's Third Army moved forward from south of Paris, crossed the hilly forests of the Ardennes, encircled Metz and advanced to the Meuse River, liberating the Charleville area. Poohkay bade farewell to his Maquis friends and hooked up with an American tank regiment, whose commander revealed that shortages of fuel, ammunition and food had slowed his advance since breaking from the beachhead in Normandy. The commanding officer requested Poohkay to accompany him to the front because he had operated behind the lines for weeks. They observed German troops set up a new line of defence, just across the Meuse. Poohkay moved to the American encampment in the rear, where word circulated about the surrender of 3000 German soldiers. The Americans were arranging to take them from the battlefield to cages behind the lines. Poohkay rode shotgun at the front of thirty transport trucks, each containing a hundred German prisoners. He knew that every German was happy to have survived and would not present a problem.

The Process of Repatriation Begins

Poohkay was reunited with RAF officials in Paris at the Hotel Maurice, the former headquarters of the Gestapo. They issued him an American uniform to replace his tattered flying suit, and American military police stopped him several times because his uniform lacked rank and insignia. When he presented his papers, the MPs came to attention and smartly saluted the Canadian officer. Bill took in the sights of Paris for a week, waiting for the inclement weather to break.

William Poohkay was one of a few officers who experienced good fortune for the duration of his service. There is no doubt he evaded capture and survived because of his common sense and his ability to assess and understand people. His original plan to escape east to Switzerland had paid off. He gained the trust of Maquis leaders who could have just as easily shot him if they had suspected he was a German spy. He demonstrated his bravery during sabotage operations against the Nazis.

Return to Civilian Life

The RCAF discharged Bill Poohkay on 28 February 1945. Like so many of his fellow Canadian service personnel, he quietly returned to civilian life after the war and adjusted well to peacetime Canada. However, after his four years of service in the RCAF, Poohkay found a limited number of employment opportunities available to veterans. He had grown up on a farm, but his services were redundant because Canadian farming had undergone the transition to large-scale operations and mechanized production. A friend who operated a pharmacy suggested that he apply to the University of Alberta for entrance into the Faculty of Pharmacy. Poohkay had earned an entitlement from the Department of Veterans' Affairs that paid for tuition fees and living expenses.

In 1946 he entered the Faculty of Science at the University of Alberta and in 1948 graduated with a bachelor of science degree in Pharmacy. In 1951 he married Mary Symotiuk of Edmonton, and they raised two daughters, Patricia and Sandra. During his professional career Bill Poohkay was a partner in two Edmonton drugstores. In 1966, Mr. Poohkay sold his share in his drugstore

ROYAL CANADIAN AIR FORCE
CERTIFICATE OF SERVICE

ISSUED TO OFFICERS

This is to Certify THAT (Rank) *Flying Officer* (Number) *CAN. J 19530*

(Name in full) *Poohkay, William Burke*

was appointed to Commissioned Rank

in *the Special Reserve, General List, Air Border Branch,*

of the

ROYAL CANADIAN AIR FORCE on the *sixth* ....day

of *December* 19 *43*

and was STRUCK OFF STRENGTH on the *twenty-seventh* ....day

of *February* .... 19 *45* by reason of *K.R.(Air) 141(1)(b) On retirement.*

Transferred to Class "E" of the General Section of the Reserve

PARTICULARS OF SERVICE

Countries *Canada: 1 December 1941 to 4 January 1943.*

United Kingdom: 4 January 1943 to 9 October 1944.

Canada: 9 October 1944 to 27 February 1945.

Orders, Decorations, Medals, Mentions and Commendations *Operational Wing,*

Canadian Volunteer Service Medal and Clasp, Air Border's Badge,
1939-43 Star.

Wounds *Nil.*

Dated at *Calgary, Alberta* this *twenty-seventh* ....day

of *February* .... 19 *45*.

for Chief of Air Staff

R.C.A.F.—R. 183
50M—11-44 (4551)
H. Q. 885-R. 155

This certificate was a temporary identification issued to Flying Officer Poohkay after British Military Intelligence, MI9, confirmed his identity. (Courtesy of W.M. Poohkay)

when his partner passed away, and went to work at another store. For a short time he operated a wholesale supply to hospitals, and in 1982 he retired from business.

Bill Poohkay joined the Royal Canadian Legion, Montgomery Branch, in 1945 and became a charter member of the Norwood Legion in 1948 where he remains a member to this day. He is active in the Strathcona Seniors' Center and the Lions' Club, where he pursues his lapidary passion. In December 2002, Bill suffered a serious stroke and is presently a resident in a veterans' home in Edmonton.

Flight Lieutenant
J.G. "Mickey" Middlemass, DFC

Flight Lieutenant J.G. "Mickey" Middlemass, DFC, RCAF No. J5097, enjoyed a distinguished military career in Bomber Command and MI9. From 19 November 1942 to 12 September 1943, the Italians had Mickey imprisoned near Sulmona, thirty miles north of Rome. He and twenty-two other Canadians were among 2400 Allied PoWs who walked out of Prigionieri di Guerra Campo No. 78 as Italy descended into anarchy in the last days of Mussolini's regime. These men dispersed into the hills around the camp, then moved south towards Allied lines. Hundreds of men, including the Canadians, reached the safety of the Allied lines between October 1943 and the spring of 1944. The mass breakout is recorded as the single largest escape of Allied personnel from one camp (DHist RAF 6G/S 230/3/INT IT/AF/298).

Welcome To Italy

Unusual circumstances contributed to the capture of Mickey Middlemass near Turin, Italy, on 19 November 1942. The crew evacuated their Halifax at 18,000 feet when smoke billowed through the entire aircraft. Assuming his aircraft had suffered irreparable damage, Wing Commander B.V. Robinson had issued the evacuation order, then engaged the plane's autopilot, before moving to the escape hatch. As he positioned himself over the hatch and prepared to drop into the night sky, he took one last glance through the fuselage and saw the smoke dissipating and flames receding. He spied the remnants of a flare smouldering in the bomb bay; apparently it had lodged in the bomb rack instead of falling from the plane. Robinson returned to his seat, disengaged the autopilot and returned the crewless bomber to his base in England.

Italians Capture Middlemass

Winds dispersed the crew over a wide area. Middlemass's heavy landing in a dense thicket alerted every Italian soldier within a half mile. They had no difficulty spotting his light-coloured parachute in the dark and yelled into the bushes for him to show himself. The excited tone of their voices prompted Middlemass to call back before he moved. He did not want trigger-happy soldiers to start shooting blindly at him. His captors transported him by truck to a

Flight Lieutenant Mickey Middlemass (second from left) with Pilot Wing Commander Robinson (fourth from left) and other unidentified crew standing in front of their Halifax bomber in 1943. (Courtesy of Middlemass family)

"All our planes returned."—Air Ministry communique after Wednesday night's raid on Turin.

"The British have made a mistake. Some of the crews have been made prisoner after their planes were brought down."—Rome radio.

But the communique was right. All our planes DID return. The Italians were right about the prisoners, and guessed the rest of the story—wrongly.

One man, flying a huge 30-ton Halifax bomber single-handed for over 500 miles made them wrong. This is how:

Soon after the Halifax, captained by Wing-Commander B. V. Robinson, D.S.O., D.F.C.,

Plane left its crew behind

dropped its heavy load, fire broke out in the bomb bay, caused by a powerful flare which had "hung up."

Flames spread and there was a violent explosion. The captain had the bomb doors opened to release the burning

flare—but it failed to drop.

In front were the Alps, the ground only a thousand feet below. The captain could not maintain height. It seemed that the bomber must hit the peaks. He ordered the crew to bale out.

They did so, and he was preparing to follow when the fire ceased as suddenly as it began.

Robinson stayed with the plane, and crossed the Alps attending to the navigators' and flight engineers' jobs himself.

... ould have been helpless against attack by fighter planes, but fortune favours the brave; there was no attack, and—

All our planes return.

The fate of Middlemass's crew was reported in the English newspapers. (Courtesy of Middlemass family)

resplendent villa north of Rome, where a high-ranking Italian officer asked a few questions before guards locked Middlemass in the comfortable surroundings of an adjacent room. Staff left an array of fresh fruit and canned products on the table. Middlemass respected the Italians for the civil treatment he received. Within a few days an escort moved him 150 kilometers south. He underwent additional interrogation before being taken to Sulmona, a PoW camp nestled along the base of the Apennine mountain chain north of Rome.

Prigionieri Di Guerra Campo No. 78

The charm of the picturesque valley surrounding Prigionieri di Guerra Campo No. 78 would have made the region an idyllic vacation spot in another era. The camp administration imposed very little of its authority over the PoWs who filled their days basking in the hot Mediterranean sun. Some actually looked forward to the daily "work parties" to alleviate monotony. The "royalist" guards displayed indifference to PoWs and avoided contact with them as much as possible. Hard-core fascists, the fanatical Blackshirts and the truncheon-wielding Squadistri, rarely visited the camp; consequently guards feared little repercussion for their lackadaisical attitude. No one could accuse the Italians of fraternization, but they frequently crossed the line by competing in friendly Sunday soccer matches with English PoWs. These games diffused tensions between adversaries and built morale in the British ranks because they usually trounced the Italians. Guards took PoWs on strolls through the town, but they insisted that the PoWs spruce themselves up first to ensure they left a favourable impression, especially among the young ladies. The Red Cross forwarded twenty percent of a PoW's pay, in cash, from the British government. The Italian camp staff, eager to earn extra money, bought fresh fruit and vegetables for PoWs. This occasional civilized treatment was unheard of in German camps. A black market made confinement more tolerable. Nonetheless, Middlemass emphasized his gratitude for Red Cross food parcels because levels of rations fluctuated.

Canadian prisoners made up one percent of the camp's 2400 rough, battle-hardened officers and troops who had been captured in Greece and North Africa. Though Mickey Middlemass had lived in England for some time, he did not adapt to the idiosyncrasies of its working class backgrounds and entrenched British class system, both of which he felt restricted individuality and free thought. The existence of Sulmona's two compounds reinforced the British notion of class hierarchy. Officers resided in the upper compound; NCOs stayed in the lower compound. Guards initially placed Middlemass with twenty British soldiers in an overcrowded, spartan room of the lower compound. He wanted to move to the upper compound where conditions were better. Senior officers shared quarters with just one other person and they ate meals in their rooms. The senior officers even organized NCOs to wait on them through the day. Mickey did not expect those genteel privileges to be extended to himself but a

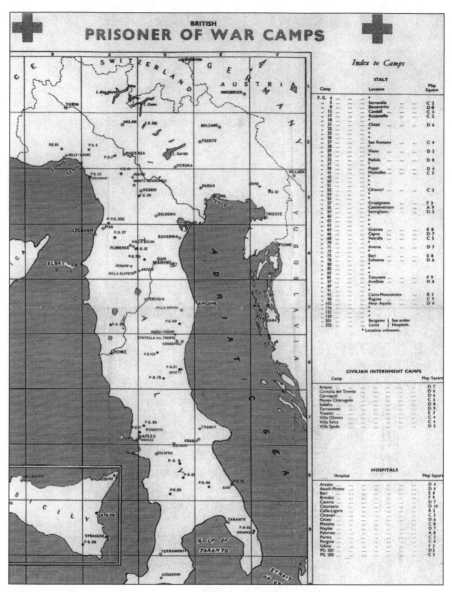

This Red Cross map was supplied to families of Canadian PoWs interned in Italy. (Courtesy of H.K. Ward)

move to the upper compound would alleviate overcrowding and the banter associated with the lower compound.

Allied Invasion of Italy

The Allied invasion of Italy in July 1943 accelerated the demise of Mussolini's

Artist's conception of the upper and lower compounds of Prigioneri Di Guerra
Campo No. 78 at Sulmona, Italy. This was a Christmas card sent to the Middlemass
family in 1946 by a fellow PoW interned at Sulmona. (Courtesy of J.G. Middlemass)

regime. Operation Torch originated in Sicily, and within weeks the British and
the Canadians had ploughed through Italian defences to the mainland. As
Italian resistance melted, German forces insisted on the relocation of the
Allied PoWs interned in Italian camps to Stalags in Germany to prevent their
liberation by forces advancing from the south. The Italians purged 190 British
and Dominion officers from the Sulmona camp north to Rimini on 25 July.
They told the 30 remaining officers (Canadians, South Africans and one
Briton) to prepare for evacuation on 28 August. Whether or not the destruction of the local train station on 27 August by 70 to 75 American Liberators
and Flying Fortresses was coincidental, it resulted in the postponement of the

remaining PoWs' evacuation. A second bomber force pummelled the rail lines again on 3 September (MI9/S/P.G. (-) 1526). Italian conscript guards used the hasty withdrawal of German armoured columns outside the camp as a pretext to desert en masse. After the war, Sulmona PoWs testified that the Italian commandant handed control of Prigionieri Di Guerra Campo No. 78 to senior British officers in the camp on 10 September 1943. Those officers formed a de facto administration and posted PoWs into the hills to act as lookouts. They believed the Germans planned to return and relocate them to Germany before the advancing Allied forces could liberate them. On 12 September at 1800 hours the 2400 PoWs broke into three groups and moved to the mountains overlooking their camp.

German alpine troops descended on Prigionieri Di Guerra Campo No. 78 the following day and initiated an operation to round up the escapees from the surrounding mountains. The swiftness of the German advance surprised the 300 PoWs still in the base camp. Five officers—Flight Lieutenants Middlemass, Chappel and Derek, Flying Officers Patrick and Hare—and two NCOs managed to flee into the subalpine during the melee. Well-conditioned foot patrols overtook Middlemass' group on 15 September, and the evaders hid among the rocks and trees while soldiers combed the mountain paths. Middlemass was adamant that soldiers spotted him crouched behind a boulder but for reasons unknown, left him. After what seemed an eternity, the shrill blast of a whistle signaled the end of the search, and the mountain troops retreated to their assembly point. Reports estimated that the Germans rounded up and sent between 700 and 1500 of the camp's 2400 PoWs to Stalags in the Reich.

Italians Assisted Evaders

Empathetic Italians assisted Middlemass and six evaders to move south. Palestinian shepherds slaughtered a sheep for them and provided valuable information about the frequency and location of German patrols in the mountain passes. A young Italian guide explained why he risked his life to help the ex-PoWs. His emotional story began during his service with the Italian army in North Africa. He had received word that his wife had borne another child, and under Italian law a father with five or more dependent children could receive a compassionate discharge from the military and return home to care for his family. Somewhere in the North African desert he fell into British hands, but they released him after listening to his story. That young guide repaid this act of kindness by helping the seven Canadians make their way through German lines.

Escape Networks Established

Most Italians had grown weary of fascism and welcomed the collapse of Mussolini's regime in July of 1943. The collapse resulted in temporary lapses of security in Italian-run PoW camps and gave up to 50,000 prisoners the opportunity to flee. To assist the 50,000 Allied PoWs who had broken out of Italian camps, MI9 parachuted agents behind enemy lines. One former PoW, Lieutenant Colonel S.I. Derry, established an escape line through German lines with the support of Allied sympathizers in the Vatican. A November 1945 memorandum identified Derry as head of Section 19(a-g), the wing of MI9 that oversaw most aspects of escapes and evasions (DHist 181.009(618)). In the first week of October, two British paratroopers intercepted Middlemass and instructed him to move south quickly before an Allied offensive started on 9 October. Middlemass, Patrick, Hare and Chappel headed southeast through the villages of Guardlagrele, Casoli and Villa San Maria. Middlemass and Patrick left on their own about 13 or 14 October and crossed the Sangro River at the village of Salcito. On 15 October, the pair made contact with a British operative, who hired an Italian guide to secrete them and two Americans, Robert Williams (U.S. Army) and Albert S. Romero (U.S. Army Air Force), across the Tringo River, around the town of Salciata on 21 October. On 23 October they met two Canadian soldiers of the Royal 22nd Regiment across the Bifferno River. After Middlemass and his companions verified their identifications with dog tags, the soldiers led the group to the Canadian headquarters. They provided a detailed report of their escape at British Advance Divisional Headquarters in Campo Basso.

In his MI9 Evader Statement, Middlemass credited several Italians, including Signora Jessidia Alberico, Vecci Florino and Sckiavi Abrusso, for helping him evade (DHist RAF 6G/S 230/3/INT - IT/AF/298). The Germans exacted a deadly revenge on villagers who harboured evaders. An Evader Statement filed by Flying Officer Raymond J. F. Sherk, RCAF No. J15237, on 13 November 1943 described the machine-gunning by German soldiers of the inhabitants of Campo Di Giove on 15 October in retaliation for assisting evaders (DHist RAF 6G/S 230/3/INT MI9/S/ P.G. (Italy) 1581).

After debriefing, the evaders moved through Lucero and Foggia. A British plane ferried them to Bari, a port city on the east coast of the Italian peninsula and then they flew on to Cairo, Egypt. Squadron Leader Lawson at British Headquarters, Middle East, arranged transport to Gibraltar on 29 October (MI9/s/P.G. (-) 1526). The RAF granted Middlemass a two-week furlough home to Edmonton, Alberta, in time for Christmas 1943. Several of the twenty-three Canadians who evaded capture in the hills around Sulmona hid in mountain retreats over the winter and found their way to Allied lines the following spring. Reports filed with MI9 suggested that several hundred Allied evaders behind German lines purposely avoided the operatives sent in to rescue them because they either fell in love with Italian women or established roots in villages. The thought of returning to war discouraged them from seeking repatriation.

Middlemass Recruited By MI9

Mickey Middlemass served with MI9 (Military Intelligence) and IS9 (Intelligence School 9 Section W) upon his return to England. His first-hand experience as a PoW, escapee, and evader provided invaluable insight to the intelligence community (DHist 181.009 (D618)). He interrogated British and Commonwealth escapers and evaders and, later, repatriated ex-PoWs. Middlemass also interrogated Allied PoWs suspected of collaboration. Their peers had reported their activities to Allied authorities via secret radio communiqués from within the camps. Middlemass committed to memory six pages of names of suspected collaborators so he would know if they passed through his office. Some ex-PoWs admitted their guilt and were dishonourably discharged or jailed. Most avoided incriminating themselves and returned home under a cloud of suspicion.

Epilogue

Flight Lieutenant Middlemass received a Distinguished Flying Cross for meritorious service. King George VI bestowed the honor in a ceremony at Buckingham Palace after the war. Mickey Middlemass passed away on 13 July 2002 after battling throat cancer. Friends in the RCAF Ex-Prisoner of War Association spoke very highly of him, recalling his positive nature and good humour. Mary, his wife of nearly sixty years, survives him.

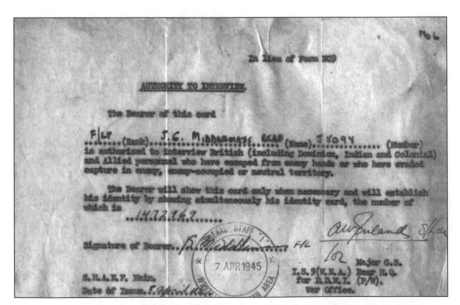

A letter of authority from Supreme Headquarters Allied Expeditionary Force giving Flight Lieutenant Middlemass the right to interrogate escapees and evaders suspected of collaboration. (Courtesy of Middlemass family)

Flight Lieutenant Middlemass is shown near Oldenburg, Germany, as the war winds down. (Courtesy of Middlemass family)

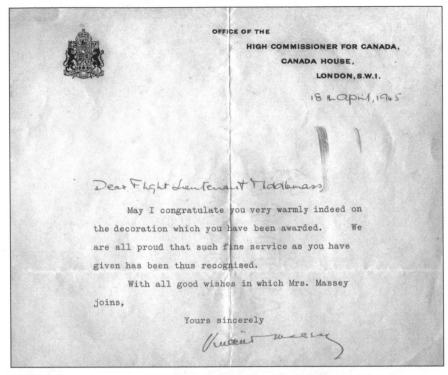

Middlemass received a letter of commendation for his DFC from the Governor General of Canada, Vincent Massey. (Courtesy of Middlemass family)`

Mickey Middlemass outside Buckingham Palace after receiving his DFC from the King of England, May 1945. (Courtesy of Middlemass family)

Flight Lieutenant Barry Chaster

Barry Chaster's repatriation began in the Netherlands. Sympathetic Dutch civilians assisted him to cross the border into Belgium, where helpers in the underground smuggled him through to neutral Spain via the Comet escape line. His escape was even more remarkable considering that the escape line was collapsing around him. The Gestapo had managed to infiltrate cells in the Comet line immediately preceding and just following his movement through Belgium and France. At least four of his helpers went to concentration camps.

Experimental Operation to Essen

Lancaster pilot Flight Sergeant Chaster went missing during a raid to Essen, Germany, on 3 January 1943. He had participated in an operation that tested the effectiveness of blind bombing. Crews dropped bombs at night through 10/10ths cloud with guidance from Mosquitoes equipped with the new navigational device, H2S. The success of the tactic resulted in its immediate adoption by Bomber Command.

After completing the run, Chaster's squadron set a course for Bottesford/ Swindesby. German ace Oberleutant Manfred Meurer, a pilot with sixty-nine kills to his credit, intercepted the Lancaster at 18,000 feet and finished it off in three attacks. Twenty-millimetre cannon shells pierced the starboard wing, ignited fuel in the tanks and silenced both starboard engines. Four of the crew perished in the attack—Bill Moger, Ken Pugh, Walter Harris and Ivan Lineker— their remains lie near Nijmegen, Holland in the Jonkerbos War Cemetery. The navigator, Gordon Marwood, and the bomb aimer, John Banfield, sustained serious injuries but lived. They failed to spring the hatch in the belly of the fuselage, but were able to escape through a gaping hole. Banfield descended into trees and hung just above the ground for hours, suffering desperately from wounds. A Dutchman and two members of the Luftwaffe found him hanging from his parachute the following morning. Ground troops captured Marwood immediately. A wall of flames had trapped Chaster in his cockpit. He smashed the jagged perspex from one window frame, tore his parachute pack open and shoved the canopy out. The slipstream filled the silk canopy like a sail and pulled him into the sky. Miraculously, he cleared the two spinning propellers and the tail plane.

Stealth Was Chaster's Only Weapon

Getting to Belgium posed a significant challenge for Chaster because a Dutch escape network was not in existence. However, brave Dutch citizens led him to the border and helped him to cross. The family who made initial contact with Chaster removed shards of perspex from his scalp, bandaged his head and gave him an overcoat to cover his uniform before sending him on his way. He had to leave their home because Gestapo agents were billeted in the adjacent house. Chaster walked through his first checkpoint unchallenged, and after impersonating the mannerisms of a deaf mute, he convinced another German sentry to let him pass. Tight border security eliminated any chance of slipping into Belgium. Frightened customs agents who worked alongside German officials found Chaster huddling in the shrubbery outside their post, but they risked their lives to summon a Dutch police chief named Odekeren to assist him. Odekeren used his connections to smuggle Chaster across near Weert in the Dutch province of Limberg.

The Comet Escape Line

The Comet escape line, Belgium's most profiled escape network, came into existence through the heroic efforts of a Belgian schoolmaster and his teenaged daughter, Mademoiselle Andree "DeeDee" de Jongh. Inspired by her father, Frederic de Jongh, DeeDee organized several escape routes from Belgium to Spain and personally escorted close to 120 men to freedom. An unfortunate consequence of operating an underground network is the eventuality of infiltration by traitors. Sadly, collaborators compromised the Comet escape line about the time Chaster entered Belgium, and brave citizens on both sides of the borders paid for their heroism with their lives. The Belgian underground assumed that the Gestapo knew of Chaster's presence, so they undertook extra precautions by relocating their "package" from Liège to a safe house in the country under the care of Joseph Heenen, once an officer in the Belgian army. Heenen had escaped from a PoW camp after his country's capitulation in 1940, and he resumed the fight against the Nazis by smuggling evaders out of the country. DeeDee remained steadfast to her cause even with the line collapsing around her. The Gestapo arrested and executed her father in mid-1943. They rounded her up some months later but refused to believe that a petite, young teenager was the mind behind the network, even when she confessed! Instead, the Gestapo sent her to languish in Ravensbrück concentration camp in January 1944.

Chaster marveled at the efficiency of the resisters. His handlers provided him with identity papers almost immediately. Chaster, like many airmen at that stage of the war, carried passport photos inside the lining of his jacket in case he needed one for a forged identity. He chose the name "Knut Rockney" for the Swedish passport issued by the underground. The cell arranged a meeting with a British SOE agent who suggested Chaster might have a chance to return to England aboard a Lysander making a nighttime supply run. This escape option failed to materialize, perhaps because, as Chaster speculated, repatriating a flight sergeant from enemy territory did not warrant the risk. The underground moved Chaster into Brussels to connect with Albert Grindel, a revered Belgian nobleman whose brother Jean oversaw operations of the Comet escape line. Albert, who went under the aliases of "Johnny" or "Adolph," escorted Chaster from Brussels to Madrid, Spain. Their closest brush with fate occurred during a train ride to Paris when two German soldiers strode down the aisle towards the pair and ordered them out of their seats. Chaster could not follow the conversation but assumed the Germans had placed them under arrest. Grindel nudged him along and whispered, "They only wanted our seats." In Paris Grindel took possession of four additional packages: two American evaders, Second Lieutenant John Spence and Technical Sergeant Devers, an Englishman, and a Belgian. Handlers in Paris provided Chaster with new shoes and clothing because Germans agents looked for travelers with scuffed footwear and an unkempt appearance—clues of someone on the run. Grindel escorted all five evaders through to Bayonne, and they detrained at a predetermined point near the French-Spanish border. He guided the group over the steep, rocky trails of the Pyrenees under the cover of darkness. The new shoes blistered Chaster's heels and made him regret ever receiving them! The Englishman and the Belgian bid farewell to the group after deciding that they stood a better chance of evasion if they left the group of six.

Spain did not accept evaders with open arms. Franco had been smart enough to keep his country out of the war, and despite its pro-Nazi sympathies, he went to great lengths to uphold its image of impartiality. Spain's border guards and police arrested, and often shot at, anyone suspected of entering the country illegally. On 15 February Spanish civil guards arrested Chaster, Spence and their guide in a taxi cab en route to the British Consulate at San Sebastian, a mere twenty-five miles away! The guards took them for French citizens fleeing the Vichy regime and treated them more harshly than British subjects or Americans in the same circumstance. The Spaniards jailed them in a windowless cell at Elizondo without food and the comforts of blankets and heat, even though snow carpeted the ground outside. Their guards were more than happy to rid themselves of the additional responsibility when the evaders suggested they transfer them to a prison in Pamplona. The evaders agreed to cover the costs of the taxi. Chaster and his comrades tolerated the minor inconveniences of poor food and overcrowding at Pamplona, knowing that this treatment paled beside imprisonment by the Gestapo. However, after three weeks of captivity they began to wonder if they would remain in Pamplona indefinitely. Fortunately the

Englishman and the Belgian who had split off from the group at the Spanish border had made inquiries about them when they failed to show at the British Consulate in San Sebastian. The British Consulate in Madrid tracked them down, arranged their release and spirited them to the embassy in Gibraltar, where arrangements for their passage to England were finalized on 4 March 1943.

Resistance Organizations

Evaders, like Barry Chaster, owed their freedom to men and women who risked everything to defeat Nazi Germany. Members of the underground, as well as their immediate families, often faced execution. Even though the Germans exacted a terrible toll to discourage citizens from operating against them, the opposite effect prevailed. For example, Dutch officials at the Customs House at Weert hid or moved evaders while working side by side with Germans in the same building. These Dutch citizens acted bravely for months and years without detection (Ref. 181.002[D68]DHist).

The Nazis rounded up Chaster's helpers in Belgium in the sweep of January-February 1943. Joseph Heenen survived two years of brutality, privation and disease in Dachau concentration camp; he received recognition for assisting seventy-eight Frenchmen as well as twenty-one Allied aviators to escape the clutches of the Nazis. The three women who assisted Chaster in Brussels, Mesdames E. Warnon, E. Leigois and Paulsen, also spent two years in German concentration camps. The head of the Comet line, Jean Grindel died in Nazi custody.

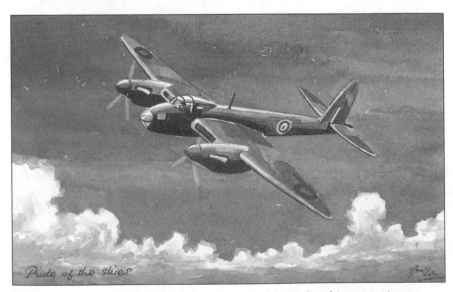

Prude of the skies

The Mosquito two-engine bomber proved its value during bombing operations.
Its speed allowed it to outrun German aircraft and mark targets for other bombers.
(Courtesy of W. Prausa)

Without the personal sacrifices of these civilians, Barry Chaster and hundreds of other evaders would have spent the duration of the war in PoW camps. The question often arises, then, were the risks associated with helping evaders worth the lives of so many helpers and their families? Over 100 of the 1000 civilian helpers in the Comet line met death at the hands of the Gestapo by war's end. The answer is an emphatic "yes!" First, the escape lines drew German manpower from the front lines. Second, the underground organizations buoyed the morale of civilian populations under the yoke of Nazi occupation. Third, escape networks and their associates provided Allied intelligence with information about German operations in occupied territories. Fourth, German knowledge of the existence of escape lines strained resources and demoralized German military personnel. Last, knowledge that escape organizations helped evaders gave Allied air force personnel faint hope in the event they were shot down.

(Courtesy of B. Chaster)

Flying Officer Ross Wiens

Flying Officer Ross Wiens, No. J27503, and three members of his crew hold the distinction of being the only members of a Pathfinder squadron to evade capture and return to England during the war.

The Stettin Raid, 16–17 August 1944

Bomber Command considered the August 1944 Stettin operation, which was Ross Wien's last, a resounding success. German authorities reported 1508 houses and 29 industrial sites destroyed and over 1000 houses and industrial sites partially destroyed. Five ships, totaling 5000 tons, went to the bottom; eight more with a total tonnage of 15000 were badly damaged. Casualties included 1150 killed and 1654 injured. The British Air Ministry discontinued the enumeration of bomber losses in subsequent raids because losses were so low and had no bearing on the planning of future operations. The night's loss represented one percent of the aircraft dispatched, a stark contrast to the 5 percent average incurred by Bomber Command during most of the war and the horrendous 13 percent lost at Nuremburg on 30–31 March 1944 (Middlebrook and Everitt 1974, 569). Coincidentally, Wiens's bomber was one of five that failed to return from that Stettin raid.

Flying Officer Wiens's Pathfinder led the bomber stream to Stettin that August night. He recalled the calmness of the European skies until the first bombers reached the outer perimeter of the Baltic city. Thousands of flak rounds lit up the sky. Wiens's Pathfinder bomber emerged unscathed after dropping marking flares over the docks for other bombers and Pilot Bud Walter set a return course to England via the south shore of the Baltic. They had instructions to fly around the northern tip of Denmark, then turn south over the North Sea. Not long after leaving Stettin, an explosion interrupted the drone of the Lancaster's engines. Shrapnel caused some minor malfunctions, but things looked promising as the flight engineer managed to keep the bomber aloft for close to an hour before the inner port engine burst into flames. Evacuation of the aircraft was moments away. Wiens stared into the image projected on his H2S screen and concluded his Lancaster had crossed over the shores of the Danish island of Zealand. He relayed the good news to the crew. He rehearsed the evacuation procedures before slipping through the hatch. His freefall towards earth resembled a plunge into a plush livingroom chair. Except for the orange flame of his aircraft disappearing on the horizon, then a flash (which he assumed to be its explosion), the night sky remained black and quiet. A general blackout existed over the continent. As a result, Wiens could not ascertain his altitude above land or water. He had continued to clench his parachute D-ring for several minutes before dropping it. He hoped he would hear it hit the ground or splash into water but he heard absolutely nothing! Gradually the sky darkened and he knew he had dropped below the tops of the surrounding hills. Ross expressed his thanks to the Almighty for his safe delivery to Denmark.

The sudden stop on Danish soil could not have been gentler! Wiens buried his parachute, flying helmet, Mae West and all identifying insignia. He believed his sidearm would bring misfortune and buried it, too. Ross' immediate goal was to put as much distance between him and his landing spot before dawn. Bundles of grain dotted Denmark's rolling landscape and he sought refuge in one of them as the sun crept over the horizon. The bundles proved a terrible place to hide because they prevented him from stretching out and sleeping, and he could have knocked one over if he were not careful. To make the situation worse, he needed to remain vigilant for Danish farmers walking about the field and collecting them with their shiny pitchforks under the watchful eyes of a German sentry. Fortune remained with Ross that day; darkness descended across the field before workers retrieved the bundle in which he hid.

Move North to Copenhagen

Ross moved north in the direction of Copenhagen by night and continued to hide in grain bundles during the day. They offered little protection from the elements and the speed of the harvest eliminated his hiding spots quickly. Wiens knew he was in trouble as he watched a large Danish farm labourer working towards his hiding spot. As the man prepared to plunge his fork into the bundle, Wiens parted the stalks of grain to uncover his face and said, "Hello!" The Dane's eyes bulged but he did nothing to alert anyone about the man in the stook. In English he commanded Wiens to stay hidden until dark, at which time he would return and take him to the safety of his home. The Dane proved as good as his word and returned later that evening. He introduced himself as Neils and apologized for his deplorable American English, acquired while fighting alongside doughboys in the trenches of the Western Front, in the First World War. For the first time in several days, Wiens enjoyed a real meal; bacon, potatoes, bread, butter and coffee. He understood the urgency to move on, because the Germans conducted regular sweeps in the area for downed aviators. Neils suggested that a sympathetic fisherman at Copenhagen might ferry him across the narrows of the Baltic Sea to Sweden.

Wiens trekked north for seven nights, past Helsingor to the coastal town of Hornbaek. As risky as it was, he walked into the centre of the seaside town, still clad in his uniform, strode along the beachfront and sat near a group of Danish

women eating lunch during their break from a nearby factory. He boldly initiated a conversation in English and requested one of them to buy him a suit with
the money he held in his outstretched hand. The women acted as if nothing out
of the ordinary had happened, despite the danger that could have befallen them.
Before long, the entire community knew about him. A leading citizen named
Manual Andres stepped forward and took the evader into his home. Andres
acted cautiously as the Germans often planted their own agents, posing as
evaders, to weed out underground networks. He arranged for Wiens to play a
round of golf with an American golf professional who had been stuck in
Denmark at the onset of the Nazi occupation in 1940. Apparently, the Danes
trusted the American and had utilized his services before to determine if a
stranger in air force uniform was truly an evader. Sufficiently satisfied, Andres
invited Wiens and the American to his home, where thirty-five community
leaders gathered to meet Wiens. They bombarded him with questions about the
progress of the war and wanted to know why Eisenhower had made certain
decisions. During their meeting Wiens regretted not having paid closer attention to Winston Churchill and Franklin Roosevelt.

Finally, Contact with the Underground

Aksel Petersen, the chief detective for the Helsingor Police Force and the head of
the underground for that area, arranged for Wiens's transportation to
Copenhagen. Wiens handed over three passport-sized photographs sewn into
the lining of his battle dress. Petersen returned the following evening with a
forged Danish passport in the name of Peter Schmidt, endorsed with an official
looking Nazi stamp and a label that explained the bearer was "deaf and dumb."
He used a police cruiser to transport Wiens to the train station where Petersen's
son, Knud, waited to accompany him on the trip to Copenhagen. A young
Jewish lad evading the holocaust joined Knud and Ross.

Escape to Sweden

Two other operatives, who avoided using their names, took control of Wiens
and the boy in Copenhagen. Armed with pistols, they informed Wiens that none
of them would fall into German hands under any circumstances. The underground relocated Wiens and the boy between three different safe houses while
they finalized travel arrangements aboard a Swedish-bound vessel. Events
unfolded without incident. Danes moved Wiens and the boy into the dock area
and instructed them to hide in the coal bin of the ship until they heard the pre-
arranged signal that indicated the ship had passed into international waters.
Russian PoWs who came below to level out the coal ignored them. After twenty-four hours below deck, the pair heard the pre-arranged signal and emerged
from the compartment. Naturally the captain exclaimed in complete surprise
when the two "stowaways" appeared. A sympathetic supporter of the Allied war

An excellent view of the rear turret of a Lancaster. A rear gunner would sit in the cramped compartment for the duration of an operation. (Courtesy of R. Wiens)

Ross Wiens' Pathfinder crew pose in their Lancaster. Phil Musgrave (centre) was the only casualty. He died as a result of a parachute failure after baling out. (Courtesy of R. Wiens)

Wiens offered the use of his MG to his ground crew when he went out on operations. The only condition was to have the gas tank filled by the next morning. (Courtesy of R. Wiens)

Ross Wiens sporting a new suit after his harrowing evasion through Denmark. (Courtesy of R. Wiens)

effort, he maintained a cover of impartiality in front of his crew in case one of them was a Nazi collaborator. After issuing a stiff rebuke against his "unwanted" passengers, he had the pair cleaned up and extended an invitation for them to join him in his cabin for a good meal. The ship's captain demonstrated a genuine interest in their health and wished them success for the remainder of their journey. He revealed that he had taken the same risk many times before, as part of an elaborate network of sea goers who had helped 7000 Jews escape the tyranny of the Nazis.

A final hurdle for Wiens and the boy remained. A remote possibility existed that a German patrol boat might board the Swedish vessel in one last search for interdicts before it entered Swedish waters. As a precaution, the Swedes rendezvoused with a small motor launch capable of outrunning the fastest German boats.

Safe Arrival in Sweden

Protocol required Flying Officer Wiens to appear before the chief of police at Trelleborg to declare himself a "non-combatant" of British origin to avoid internment for the duration of the war. The British Consulate arranged for Wiens to stay in Trelleborg's best hotel. He found it exciting to stroll through a brightly lit city after dark. Ross received a tremendous morale boost when he was reunited with three of his crew in Stockholm—Bud Walter, Ralph Rafter and Denis Budd.

Overcast conditions delayed their return to England until 8 September 1944. Twenty-one Allied service personnel traveled on the same un-armed DC-3 to Leuchars, Scotland. The RAF prohibited Wiens and his three crewmates from going back into action because they possessed intimate knowledge of Danish escape organizations. Wiens took a thirty-day furlough to Lachine, Quebec, and married his fiancée, Peggy. The RCAF encouraged him to submit his resignation because the RAF had six people in reserve for every operational position. In February 1945, Ross Wiens left the air force and returned to civilian life.

Epilogue

A total of 400 Allied airmen parachuted into Danish airspace during the war, and a remarkable 25 percent of them were repatriated to England through the bravery of Danish men and women. The Germans knew of these covert operations but could not eliminate them. Relations between Denmark and Nazi Germany had deteriorated by 1943, and the Germans sent 1500 members of the Danish constabulary to various prison camps, including Buchenwald, as punishment. This unfortunate turn of events for the Danes benefited evaders, like Wiens, because the Germans had less manpower to round up evaders. In the last days of the war, with defeat imminent, the Nazis exacted a tragic toll on the brave members of the Danish underground in their custody, including Knud Petersen,

Three evaders in Stockholm, Sweden, September 1944. Left to right: Ross Wiens, unknown RAF evader, Denis Budd. (Courtesy of R. Wiens)

Reunion of an evader and his helpers from the Danish underground in 1995. Though 50 years have passed, the bond between these men remains strong. Manual Andres (left) opened his Hornback home to evader Ross Wiens (centre). Aksel Petersen, chief detective for the Helsingor Police, doubled as local underground leader responsible to move Wiens to Sweden. (Courtesy of R. Wiens)

the Dane who had accompanied Wiens on his train journey to Copenhagen. On 11 April 1945, just three weeks before the unconditional German surrender, the Nazis executed over 100 Danes for their underground activities.

Denmark Commemorates Bravery of Evaders

In May 1995 the Danish government invited evaders from Allied nations to attend celebrations on the fiftieth anniversary of the end of the war. Ross Wiens received an official invitation to represent Canada from Sore Haslund, Deputy Director of Protocol, Ministry of Foreign Affairs, at celebrations hosted by Frederick, Crown Prince of Denmark. The Wienses visited Knud Petersen's brother, and the veterans and their hosts made a symbolic crossing of the Baltic from Denmark to Trelleborg, Sweden, where Ross had landed.

Flying Officer A.C. Denis Budd

Flight Sergeant Denis Budd, RCAF No. J88181 manned the rear turret of a Lancaster that was shot down following an operation to Stettin on 16/17 August 1944. Budd and fellow crewmen Navigator Ross Wiens, Pilot Bruce "Bud" Walter (RCAF No. J85083) and Wireless Operator Ralph Rafter (RCAF No. R84923) parachuted onto the island of Zealand, evaded captured and returned to England safely via the Danish underground less than one month after the downing of their aircraft. The four men evaded separately and were reunited in Sweden. Budd's evasion account illustrates the extent and sophistication of the Danish underground network during the Nazi occupation, and when compared to Wiens's account, shows how crew of the same aircraft remembered differently the events surrounding the downing of their bomber.

Budd stated in his MI9 evasion report that he had landed ten kilometers south of Tollose, Denmark, and then walked to Roskilde where he approached a farmer only after his wounds became unbearable. A fortunate turn of events kept him out of Nazi hands and put him in the care of the underground. Resisters hid him for a week before moving him to a safe house in Copenhagen on 21 August 1944. A policeman smuggled him aboard a Swedish-bound ship on 25 August. Danes also smuggled Budd's crewmates Ralph Rafter and Bud Walter aboard, and the trio sailed across the Baltic Sea to freedom. Their navigator, Ross Wiens, joined them in Stockholm.

The Stettin Raid

Flight Sergeant Budd maintained a vigilant watch in his rear turret for German fighters. Pilots of the German Nachtjagd used the cover of darkness to approach unseen and to shoot upward-firing 20mm cannons into the belly of bombers. The RAF had developed "Fishpond" to track these intruders. Unfortunately the wireless operator was receiving transmissions from his Bomber Group headquarters in England and had momentarily deactivated Fishpond to listen to orders. A Me110 managed to close in undetected and fire its cannon into the rear turret and the underbelly of the Lancaster. Budd returned fire and radioed to the pilot to initiate evasive corkscrew maneuvers.

Two more attacks finished off the Lancaster. Each crewman was in his own private hell. At least one 20mm shell struck the port upper gun and dislodged the turret from its rails. It prevented Budd from rotating the turret forward or back. He lifted the turret back onto its rails and rotated the apparatus far enough for him to squeeze out of the back of the bomber. His leg caught in the frame and he hung upside down in the slipstream. In a superhuman effort, Budd twisted his body back into the turret and unzipped his flying boot. He fell into the night and descended into a remote field in one of the narrowest points on the island of Zealand. Destruction of the ailerons prevented Pilot Walter from undertaking evasive actions, and damage to the throttle controls made it impossible to reduce the speed of the three remaining engines. Flight Engineer Jim Umshied attempted to suppress flames in the inner port engine with compressed nitrogen gas. The aircraft continued to tremble even after he feathered the propeller. Wireless Operator Ralph Rafter missed Walter's first order to bail out so Navigator Ross Wiens tapped him on the shoulder and motioned for him to move to the exit hatch. Rafter switched over to the intercom in time to hear the second command to evacuate. He released the trailing antenna and detonated the IFF device tied on his chute and slid through the partially blocked escape hatch at 15,000 feet. Walter stayed at the controls until 13,000 feet, then moved to the hatch and bailed out between 10,000 and 11,000 feet. The aircraft exploded in midair and once again on impact. The winds scattered the evacuees across a wide area.

A severely bruised leg restricted Budd's chances of making good his escape across Denmark. He convalesced in a wooded area for a day, sullied his uniform with dirt and removed all insignia. Armed with canvas runners, small amounts of food, a compass, a silk map and a few fishhooks, Budd decided to head northeast to Copenhagen. He began his walk with trepidation. The first German soldiers he encountered on the road simply ignored him. Budd approached a farmhouse for help and it nearly cost him his freedom. The farmer appeared sympathetic and ushered Budd into his barn to conceal him from German soldiers. In reality, the Dane was a collaborator and locked him up. The farmer attempted to place a telephone call to the local authorities but the communication lines crossed and the call rang the neighbour, Magnus Neilson. Neilson threatened to report his neighbour for harbouring an evader if he breathed a word of Budd to the Nazis. Denis Budd learned of the collaborator's fate after the war: he disappeared, presumably because of his treachery.

Taken in by the Danish Resistance

Magnus Neilson assumed a huge personal risk for crossing a collaborator and

The crew of Lancaster PA988, 405 City of Vancouver Squadron. Left to right: Bud Walter, Ross Wiens, Bruce Durfee, Ralph Rafter, Denis Budd, and Jim Umschied, before a German Me110 fighter shot them down over Denmark. The photograph is assumed to have been taken by Philip Musgrave, the only casualty from the crew. (Courtesy of Budd family)

harbouring an evader. As a precaution, the Resistance placed Budd at a relatively isolated Danish farmstead and began the process to verify his identity. His hosts, the Poul Tholstrup family of Roskilde, spoke good English and quizzed him about his squadron and personal life. Resistance leaders Major Tage Fischer Holst, code-named Joseph, and Hakon Mielche visited the Tholstrup farmstead several times to interview him. Budd learned that Holst had verified his identity by comparing what Budd told them with what Holst had gathered from officials in London. Holst offered Budd three choices: he could surrender to the Germans and spend the war in a PoW camp; he could attempt to slip into Sweden entirely through his own efforts; or he could entrust himself to the Resistance to smuggle him to Sweden on the condition he followed every order they gave him.

Budd agreed to the third choice and assumed the identity of a deaf mute named Albert Denis Jensen, a name closely resembling his given name—Albert Charles Denis Budd. The Trolstrup family continued to act as his host while the underground arranged to move him up the island. The children helped him pass the time by escorting him to local points of interest, despite the presence of German soldiers. Within a week Budd moved into the Copenhagen home of a Jewish family waiting out the war in Sweden. Major Holst communicated with England via a wireless unit hidden in the house. Budd learned that someone in London contacted Budd's mother in Vancouver, British Columbia about his status before the RCAF told her he had gone missing.

Budd appreciated the personal sacrifices made by the Danes. Helpers imperiled their lives and those of their families by assisting evaders. People made do with less so he could eat. He was amazed to eat fresh eggs, even ice cream—commodities scarcely seen in England for years! The Danes provided him with cigarettes and a bottle of Canadian Club whisky, a rarity even in Canada during the war years.

Smuggled Aboard a Swedish Vessel

Without the assistance of the Danish police, Budd would have had a difficult time leaving the country. Officer O.B. Bertelsen of the Copenhagen police escorted him into the dockyards and directed him to the ship that would take him to freedom. Budd experienced a few anxious moments when plans changed. A delay in the ship's departure forced his removal to a safe house where Danes reunited him with his pilot, Bud Walter. Their reunion was tempered by news of the death of Mid Upper Gunner Philip Musgrave as well as the capture of Bruce Durfee and Jim Umschied. The Resistance smuggled Budd and Walter aboard another vessel within days, where they were delighted to find Wireless Operator Ralph Rafter already aboard. Rafter had walked for five days before the underground took him in at Helsingor. He arrived in Copenhagen on 24 August.

Pilot Officer Philip Musgrave.
(Courtesy of Budd family)

Police in Malmo, Sweden contacted the British legation on behalf of the three evaders. Budd, Walter and Ralph met their navigator, Ross Wiens, in Stockholm. Budd recalled the strong ideological split that existed in Swedish society. One establishment displayed a portrait of British Prime Minister Winston Churchill in its lobby while an adjacent hotel demonstrated it pro-German sympathies with a picture of the Führer!

Repatriation to England

The Danish underground had done an amazing job of repatriating four members of one crew. On 9 September 1944 the Canadians provided intelligence about the escape networks to MI9 and Danish officials in London. Denis Budd tipped his parachute packer five pounds when he returned to 405 Squadron at Granston Lodge in Bedfordshire, England. The RCAF offered him three choices: he could be released from the air force, become an instructor or he could resume operations in another squadron. After a thirty-day leave to Vancouver, British Columbia, he elected to return to Leeming, England in April 1945. Promoted to flying officer, he joined 427 Lion Squadron to assist in the repatriation of air force officers recently liberated from the continent to the British Isles.

Flight Sergeant James L. Umschied, RCAF No. C88014, became PoW No. 684 at Stalag Luft VII at Bankau, and the RCAF promoted him to pilot officer during his internment. Flying Officer A. Bruce Durfee, RCAF No. J28938, ended up in Stalag Luft III as PoW No. 7729. Gunner Philip Musgrave, RCAF No. J88134, received a posthumous promotion to pilot officer. Apparently his parachute had failed to open. The Germans took Jim Umschied to the crash site the following morning, and he identified Musgrave's remains. Musgrave's hand still clutched the D-ring of his unopened parachute. His body displayed no evidence of bullet or shrapnel wounds, and the only noticeable mark was a bruise to his forehead. He is interred in the Commonwealth Memorial Cemetery thirteen miles northwest of Svino, Denmark.

Epilogue

Denis Budd returned to Denmark in 1962 to visit with those brave Danish citizens who had helped him evade the Germans in August 1944. They returned Budd's gold ring, pocketknife, wings, compass and silk map. He remained eternally grateful to the men and women of Denmark who selflessly risked their lives for him. Denis Budd passed away in May 1990 at the age of 77 in Victoria, British Columbia.

Sergeant James Flick

Sergeant Jim Flick's Halifax was lost during the Battle of Berlin, a series of nineteen raids between 23 August 1943 and 26 March 1944. His crew was more fortunate than most because they managed to keep their damaged bomber aloft for an hour after engaging two fighters over the German capital. They ditched their aircraft into the Baltic, coming to rest on a sand bar, and evacuated safely to life rafts. They waited for a Swedish patrol vessel to rescue them in the morning.

Under the terms of the Geneva Convention, military personnel of belligerents taken into custody by a neutral nation, like Sweden, were to wait out the war in an internment camp. Inundated with crews landing on their shores and ditching in their coastal waters, the Swedes negotiated with the Axis and the Allied Powers to repatriate many of them before the cessation of hostilities. The British and Germans asked for the return of pilots and navigators first. Flick remembers his "internment" as the best part of the war. He divided his time between skiing at a resort and traveling with a hockey team that played twenty-six exhibition hockey games for the Swedish/English Club. An unarmed BOAC Dakota ferried Flick and other internees to Leuchars, Scotland, in the spring of

1944. He completed thirty-two more combat operations before returning home to Canada as a seasoned veteran at the age of nineteen.

Overture to Berlin

Sergeant Jim Flick flew his inaugural operation to Nuremburg on 10 August 1943 with 405 Squadron of 6 Bomber Group (RCAF), and his second operation to the Italian city of Turin on 12 August. When his original pilot took ill, the crew missed five operations over the next ten days while the new pilot, "Snuffy" Smith familiarized himself with his new bomber. During this period, the navigator, Flying Officer Davies, insisted the crew complete dry-land dinghy training in case they crash-landed in water.

Flick and his crew returned to operations for a raid to Berlin! He recalled how his stomach twisted up when the operations officer unfurled a wall map of the target area. His Halifax bomber departed Gransden Lodge at 2000 hours with 335 Lancasters, 250 Halifaxes, 124 Stirlings and 24 Mosquitoes (Middlebrook and Everitt 1974, 425–6).

Baptism by Fire

Pathfinders marked the approaches over Berlin with flares at seventeen minutes before midnight. Crews relying on visual confirmation undershot their intended targets because German defenders had lured the attackers away by dropping their own flares over empty fields, miles away from industrial areas. Flick radioed to his skipper that he spotted red target indicators falling through the sky approximately five miles behind him. In a post-operation summary, the squadron confirmed the accuracy of Flick's message. They determined that the Germans had succeeded to divert most bombers by at least five miles. Lo and behold, Flick's navigator had performed his job admirably by taking his crew right over the target!

The Germans lay in wait for bombers drawn to the area around the empty fields. A bank of searchlights coned Flick's bomber as Pilot "Smokey" Smith began his approach. He attempted to break clear from the blue glare of the lights by dropping his right wing and sending his aircraft down into an aggressive corkscrew maneuver. The G-forces caused Flick to black out. He regained consciousness to see the nose of a Messerschmitt firing its cannon and machine guns pointblank into the Halifax's fins and rudders. At least one 20-mm cannon shell ripped through Flick's turret, just inches from his head. Shards of metal ripped into his shoulder. In a duel lasting just seconds, Flick destroyed the Me109 in a blaze of glory from his four machine guns. Flick's mid-upper gunner, Sergeant John Gates, firing on another Me109 crossing from the port aft, turned his machine guns across Jim's rear turret and believed he accidentally shot Flick. Fortunately fire interrupters in the electronic circuits silenced the guns before hot steel tore into the rear turret.

Bombers rarely escaped the silent death of searchlights, let alone simultaneous attacks by two fighters. Flick's Halifax flew out of the Berlin area with fuel tanks holed by machine fire, the electronics shot out and the engines stalling. The bomb aimer jettisoned the four remaining bombs and target indicators, and the navigator set a course for Sweden, a few hundred miles north. Returning to England was out of the question.

Martin Middlebrook and Chris Everitt's *Bomber Command War Diaries* reveals that the 727 aircraft on that night's raid to Berlin inflicted limited damage because the master bomber failed to pinpoint the intended target. Bombers approaching from the west and north overshot the city even though Mosquitoes guided them with flares along the air corridors. Aircraft that circled back missed their targets. Conversely, the raid had a substantial psychological impact on the German people that exceeded all expectations. A British spy in Berlin, Arno Abendroth, reported that the Third Reich's Propaganda Minister, Josef Goebbels, who had openly bragged of Berlin impregnability, "nearly went nuts" after the attack. The raid destroyed 2611 buildings. Most of the 854 Berliners who died had made the choice to stay outside bomb shelters despite instructions to the contrary (Middlebrook and Everitt 1974, 425).

Ditched in the Baltic

While Sweden served as a haven for service personnel of both sides the Swedes made it a matter of practice to appear more sympathetic to the Nazi cause because of geographic proximity. Swedish anti-aircraft batteries regularly

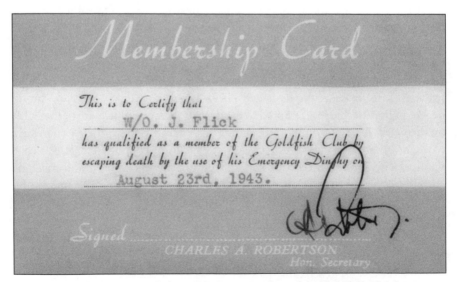

This card certified that Jim Flick qualified as a member of the Goldfish Club by escaping death using his emergency dinghy. (Courtesy of J. Flick)

Cramped conditions in the rear turret allowed the rear gunner little movement. The compartment was not heated, and gunners relied on electric flying suits and thermal boots to stay warm. Many gunners say they still froze, with some experiencing frostbite in the colder months. (Courtesy of J. Flick)

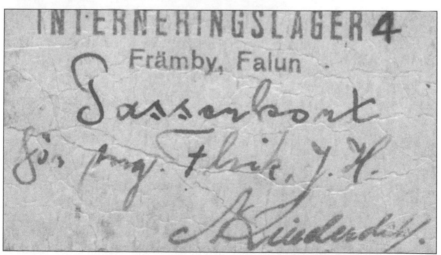

The pass card issued to Sergeant Jim Flick by Swedish authorities. It gave him freedom of movement with the hockey team and identified him as an "internee" of No. 4 Internment Camp at Falun. (Courtesy of J. Flick)

opened fire on any aircraft passing through its airspace. Whether the flak gunners truly attempted to destroy bombers is moot but their repeated poor aim suggest otherwise. Flick's Halifax drew flak from Swedish guns as it lost momentum and flopped onto a sand bar in the Baltic three miles off the coast, near Ystad at 0300 hours. Its fins and rudders remained visible above the water-line. Everyone on the crew survived and counted their blessings for being crewed with a navigator who insisted they undergo dry land dinghy training before they resumed operations. They inflated their dinghies and discovered what the air force, no doubt already knew: they could not paddle round dinghies in any direction. They rode the waves for six and a half hours before a Swedish patrol boat came to their rescue.

Internment in Sweden

The high costs of internment (an unwelcome cost of neutrality) encouraged the Swedes to find ways to return internees to their homelands without drawing the ire of either side. Both sides tacitly agreed to repatriations as long as both sides received equal numbers of men.

Briefing back on the squadron had forewarned crews to stay clear of a Swedish officer named Captain Jacobie, purportedly a Nazi sympathizer. Jacobie made his appearance and attempted to pry information from Flick's crew with ciga-rettes and beer.

The Swedes attended to the wounds of Rear Gunner Flick and Bomb Aimer

Members of James Flick's crew soon after their internment in Sweden. Left to right: Flight Engineer Catling, Mid Upper Gunner Gates, Wireless Air Gunner O'Toole, Bomb Aimer Cassidy, Pilot Smith, Navigator Davies, and Rear Air Gunner Flick in 1943. (Courtesy of J. Flick)

Sergeant Lorne Cassidy at hospital facilities in Gothenburg before transporting all of the crew to Interningslager 4 at Framby, 160 miles northwest of Stockholm. They were billeted in luxury hotels at ski resorts because internment camps brimmed with internees. The Swedes provided the new arrivals with civilian apparel and fine food as well as sports equipment such as skis and skates. Life in Sweden continued to improve after a reporter from Stockholm spotted the Canadians playing hockey on a lake near the lodge. The journalist offered to pay their expenses if they agreed to tour the country and play twenty-six games against Swedish teams.

Repatriation to England

Flick's pilot, Snuffy Smith, and his navigator, Sergeant Davies, returned to England two months before the end of the hockey season. The five others

Flick and Cassidy found themselves hard pressed when the Swedes interned them here. (Courtesy of J. Flick)

How could internment get much better? These Canadian internees toured Sweden
over the winter of 1943–44, and their Swedish hosts ensured their stay was
comfortable. (Courtesy of J. Flick)

returned to England in April 1944. These internees did not qualify as evaders or
PoWs because their only contact had been with authorities of a neutral country,
so the RCAF returned them to active duty. After repatriation and a five-week
leave, Jim crewed up with 432 Squadron in Yorkshire, on 27 May 1944 and flew
thirty-two more operations by November. He flew with a Pennsylvania Yankee
whose ancestors had left a chateau in the Netherlands that had been expropri-
ated by the Germans in 1940. The Yankee deviated from flight plans to bomb it
with two other crews. His third crew, including Flick, warned him to stick with
the intended operation or he would be looking for a fourth crew.

Flick noticed the decline in German defences between mid-1943 and May
1944 when he resumed operations. German fighters posed a formidable threat
to bombers during the Battle of Berlin but after D-Day the number of German
aircraft dwindled to the point where they could only maintain a defensive posture. The Luftwaffe lost pilots more quickly than they could replace them. Flick
flew several missions during daylight hours because the risks associated with
daylight operations had diminished considerably. Flick recalled a lone Ju88
chose not to pursue them after a bombing run to Brest, France.

An Old-Timer Before Twenty

Warrant Officer First Class James Flick retired from operational duty and returned to Canada in November 1944 to instruct at an air gunnery school. He finished the war with the rank of flying officer. Engrained in Flick's memory was his Aunt Theresa's comment after the completion of his tour. She asked, "Jimmy, what is it like to live to the old age of nineteen?" She knew that Flick and a boyhood friend, Jim Lynch, had joined the RCAF together at the age of sixteen after altering the dates on their birth certificates.

After a brief stint in civilian life, Flick remustered to serve the RCAF and Canadian Armed Forces, a total of thirty-two years, as a weapons technician (air) with an explosive ordinance detonation (EOD) specialty. During the 1960s Jim Flick was called upon several times to disarm bombs planted by FLQ radicals. He retired to Regina, Saskatchewan and now lives in Sundre, Alberta.

Part C
The Forced Marches

A Stalag Luft III PoW's depiction of the forced march from Sagan in January 1945. (Courtesy of Barry Davidson family)

Hitler's determination to prolong the war as long as possible resulted in unnecessary destruction to much of Germany, as well as untold suffering to the German people. In his madness the Führer ordered the liquidation of prisoners to prevent their liberation. The SS and the Gestapo accelerated their program of extermination in concentration and death camps, but guards of PoW camps disobeyed the order to execute PoWs. Allied PoWs sensed the possibility of mass executions and made contingency plans to rush guards and seize control of camps if they believed their lives were in jeopardy. Fortunately camp staff understood the war was lost; they marched west with PoWs, evidently preferring capture by Western forces to capture by the Russians.

The Germans confined Canadian PoWs in at least sixty-two PoW camps in Germany and German-controlled areas. They evacuated approximately 90,000 PoWs from at least twenty-two different Stalags, Oflags, military prisons and work battalions between 16 January and 16 February 1945 before the Soviet armies could liberate them. The PoWs knew that the mass evacuations signaled the imminent collapse of Nazi Germany, but other clues had emerged in the previous few months. Sagan prisoners heard the roar of Russian field guns at Poznan, fifty miles to the east of Stalag Luft III, before Christmas 1944. Prisoners noted that squadrons of German airplanes, which required two hours to make a round trip to attack Russian front lines, returned in less than half an hour. The Wehrmacht depleted guard details in the Stalags to fight the Red Army in the east and the Allies in the west. Deliveries of Red Cross parcels and mail stopped as Allied air forces decimated transportation links.

Below is a list of camps and the dates when evacuations started in early 1945.

Camp	Report Date	PoWs Involved
Stalag IIB Hammerstein	3 February	All Americans, 25 British
Stalag IID Stargard	3 February	1090 Canadians
Stalag Luft IV Gross-Tychow	3 February	828 British; 6165 American NCOs
Stalag IIIA and Work Camps at Luckenwalde	No movement	1438 prisoners
Stalag IIIB Fürstenberg	16 February	American Camp, ? British
Stalag IIIC Alt Drewitz	6 February	986 Indians
Stalag IIID Berlin/Zerndorf	No movement	217 prisoners
Stalag Luft III Sagan	6 February	2000 to Marlag-Milag, some to Luckenwalde, 3240 others moving to central Germany
Stalag Luft VII Bankau	6 February	1407 near Spremberg
Stalag VIIIA and Work Camps at Görlitz	nd	3204 marching to central Germany
Stalag VIIIB Teschen	nd	8000 marching to Stalag 344 and Nuremburg across Bohemia
Stalag 344 Lamsdorf	3–6 February	20,000 marching to Görlitz and Theresienstadt
Work detachments at Gleiwitz and Kattowitz	18 January	14,000 moving to Stalag 344

E. 715 (Stalag VIIIB)	17 January	643 moving to Stalag 344
Auschwitz		643 moving to Stalag 344
Sosnowitz		530 moving to Stalag 344
Res.Laz.Laurahuette	17 January	26 evacuated
Res. Laz.Emanuelleagen		
BAB 20 and 21	22 January	Move to Stalag 344
Blechhamer		1123
Heydebreck		1190
Also to 3.711 and 711A		2114
Work detachments North		
Linebrieg to Woldenburg	3 February	Marching northwards
Stalag VIIIC Sagan	6 February	5109 to central Germany
Stalag XXA Thorn	16 February	4858 and another 7600
Stalag XXB Marienburg	16 February	9073 and another 3000
Military Prison Graudnz	1 February	309 towards Wehrreis II
Oflag 64 Schubin	6/16 February	266 officers to Stalag IIIA
		200 left on roadside, remainder moved west

The Luftwaffe evacuated air force PoWs from Follingbostel, Lamsdorf, Bankau, Sagan and Belaria starting in January 1945. Rumours of forced marches circulated for weeks before PoWs set out, and they took measures to prepare themselves for the rigours of winter and imminent hardships. They made sleighs from chairs, Red Cross boxes and bed boards to carry their possessions; packed and repacked their meager possessions; decided what to take and what to leave behind. In most cases, PoWs received just a few hours' notice to break camp. Ten-pound Red Cross food parcels were distributed to most PoWs as they walked out of the gates. On the march frozen food left lesions in their mouths; shrunken stomachs caused many to vomit up their contents. The extra few pounds of food proved too much to carry, and many dropped rations on the road after years without enough food to eat. They traveled light, keeping only their chocolate, dried fruit, cigarettes and instant coffee packets. They regretted leaving blankets and extra clothing behind when heavy, wet snow and sleet soaked through the weary marchers' layers of clothes. The PoWs' youthful vigour and knowledge of their impending liberation gave them strength to continue. The generosity and goodwill of German civilians averted a higher death toll.

Despite their own hardships, the PoWs showed empathy for the guards who were leaving wives and families in towns adjacent to the camps. The guards lamented over their fates, knowing the Russians would soon occupy their homes. The German army placed little value on these guards. Most were unfit for service—able-bodied soldiers were at the front. The PoWs often pulled the guards' packs on their own sleighs and even carried their rifles.

First Mass Evacuation of Air Force PoWs: from Heydekrug

The first mass evacuation of Allied PoWs began at Heydekrug in July 1944 when the Germans moved them from Stalag Luft VI to Bankau (Stalag VIIB) or Thorn (Stalag XXA). The continued advance by Red Army troops forced a second relocation of the Thorn PoWs in October 1944; they were force-marched north and west through Bromberg and Stettin to Follingbostel (Stalag 357), a camp thirty miles north of Hanover. The Follingbostel experience was horrific. The Germans designated it a reprisal camp; they confiscated all mattresses and most pieces of furniture from the barracks and cut back rations to starvation levels in the middle of winter. Follingbostel is remembered as the "belt-tightening camp."

Bankau PoWS

Bankau (Stalag Luft VII) PoWs marched 240 kilometers between 19 January and 5 February 1945. Captain D.C. Howatson, Camp Medical Officer, and Pilot Officer Peter A. Thomson, Camp Leader, filed a joint submission on the condition of the Bankau marchers for the attention of the Swiss Commission acting as Protecting Power:

> As a result of this march and the deplorable conditions, the morale of the men is extremely low. They are suffering from an extreme degree of malnutrition, and at present, an outbreak of dysentery. There are numerous cases of frostbite and other minor ailments. They are quite unfit for any further movement. Food and better conditions are urgently required. We left Bankau with no Red Cross supplies and throughout the march all the rations were short issued, the most outstanding being bread.

The Germans sorted Bankau PoWs into two groups at Spremberg. American PoWs went south on trains towards the American armies under General Patton's command. The remainder, Canadians, British, Australians, New Zealanders, South Africans, Rhodesians and other nationalities boarded northbound trains. The PoWs initially believed that rail transport would bring some relief to their wretched conditions. Instead, the guards crowded fifty to ninety men into each carriage, leaving them insufficient room to sit or lie down. Then the trains stayed parked on sidings for up to four days. Most carriages had a single window cut into the wall all covered by barbed wire. Modesty became a thing of the past. Prisoners wracked with dysentery shared one pail and the man closest to the window threw the contents outside. Once underway, trains stopped occasionally to allow PoWs to stretch their legs, and some grabbed a mug of warm water from the locomotive boilers. They feared their own fighters would strafe them since the roofs of the cars were not painted white and emblazoned with a red cross.

Bankau PoW Warrant Officer Kenneth G. Taylor recalled an inspection of PoWs at Luckenwalde by the Swiss legation. Two Swiss nationals walked through a small barn filled with 1500 men. The inspectors stopped and asked Taylor and a friend to stand and lift their shirts. Appalled by their shrunken frames, one exclaimed that the men were slowly starving to death. The Russians eventually liberated Luckenwalde's 25,000 men on the last day of April 1945.

Departure from Stalag Luft III

Group Captain Wilson, senior British officer at Stalag Luft III, reported that when the Red Army had advanced to within 140 kilometers of Sagan on 19 January, the PoWs prepared for the eventuality of evacuation. American PoWs left South and West Compounds of Stalag Luft III on 27 January. British and Dominion PoWs departed North, Centre and East Compounds between 0100 and 0700 hours on Sunday 28 January. Prisoners left the Belaria Compound at 0600 hours on 29 January. The marches began with six inches of snow on the ground, and PoWs recalled several snow squalls during the first five days. On the sixth day the weather warmed, and PoWs trudged through rain or wet snow. Each man left Sagan with a single ten-pound Red Cross food parcel. Wilson reported that at least 23,000 Red Cross parcels and an estimated 2 million cigarettes (less than 200 per man) remained behind in the camp. The North Compound column marched 28 kilometers to Freiwalden the first day but inadequate accommodations and protests from local military and civilian authorities forced them to march a further six kilometers to Leippa. A barn could shelter only seven hundred men. Boots froze in the slush; PoWs downed cold rations, and most went without water. Luftwaffe Major Rostok allowed them to find their own shelter for the night if they gave their word to return to the column in the morning. Melville Carson saved Arthur Crighton's life that night by allowing him to crawl under his single wool blanket to conserve body heat.

The march resumed at 0800 on 29 January and the columns marched until the noon hour. Locals supplied water to the PoWs at Prebus. Marchers subsisted on cold Klim. They reached Maskau at 1800 hours, where the Germans had made arrangements to billet 300 officers in a theatre, 600 in a glass factory, 400 in a riding school, 150 in a stable, 80 in a laundry, 100 in a pottery and 300 in a French PoW camp. Civilians attempted to make the marchers as comfortable as they could under the conditions. The majority of men suffered the effects of dysentery. Another 1500 Sagan PoWs arrived at Maskau on 1 February. Over 500 USAAF PoWs broke off and joined another American column moving west. The column of 1920 Dominion officers resumed its muddy march west at 2245 hours. Sleds were abandoned in the mud and packs were transferred onto men's backs. A few men traded cigarettes for baby carriages, wagons and a wheelbarrow. Many suffered from vomiting, frostbite and dysentery. At Jamlitz the column met members of a German Panzer unit who shared their accommodations and food with the marchers.

On 2 February the cold weather began to break. The PoWs had slogged for most of the day and at 1500 hours the column of hungry men arrived at Spremberg where soup and hot water were served them at an army depot. They resumed the march an hour later, moving three kilometers to the railroad marshaling yard where the men were crammed into soiled cattle cars bound for Marlag Milag. After thirty-six hours aboard the train the Sagan officers were delirious with thirst. On 4 February the PoWs disembarked at Tarmstadt and marched to Marlag Milag, an army camp which served as their home until the first week in April.

The Germans then moved the Sagan PoWs north to a camp near Lubeck where its inhabitants were wracked by typhus. The senior Canadian officer, Group Captain Wray, mounted strong protest and guards moved them into area barns instead. Fortunately the spring weather made this segment of their journey bearable.

The Sagan PoWs embarked on the final leg of their forced march northeast towards Kiel, as the British Army closed the juggernaut around the Germans and the PoWs. Long columns of PoWs endured attacks from their own air forces whose pilots mistook them for columns of German soldiers. It had been decided to stop at a large estate on the outskirts of Trenthorst and wait for the war to end. The estate had a pond stocked with fish. The PoWs borrowed hand grenades from guards and threw them into the water. Dead fish floated to the surface, and the PoWs ate well in the last days before liberation. A jeep manned by two soldiers of the Scottish Firth of Forth Armoured Regiment drove to the estate on 2 May and unceremoniously declared the men liberated. Ex-PoWs celebrated their freedom by expropriating German vehicles and driving them wildly around the area. They found it odd to be in a position of power. Most of the guards feared what would happen to them when the PoWs left; they did not want to fall into Russian hands. Hostilities ceased within a few days, and trucks moved the ex-PoWs to Brussels where Lancasters flew them to England the day after VE Day.

The senior British officer from Stalag Luft III, Group Captain D.E.L. Wilson, stated in his comprehensive summary of the forced march that the Germans had no destinations as they moved PoWs through Germany. In the Report on the Forced Evacuation of Allied Officer and Other Rank Prisoners of War from Stalag Luft III, Sagan, Germany (January/February 1945), Wilson stated that the effects on the prisoners were catastrophic, especially when they were already in a weakened state, brought on by starvation and harsh treatment. For many of these men, the march was a death sentence. Some died of exposure or lost the will to go on. A few German guards remained brutal and sadistic to the end, shooting or beating stragglers who fell out of line.

The last few months of the war proved harsher than any other period of captivity. Chronic food shortages posed the most significant threat to existence. (Courtesy of S.G. King)

(Courtesy of S.G. King)

Sick and Disabled Abandoned When Camps Evacuated

The Russians showed great compassion for the disabled and sick RAF and Dominion air force PoWs liberated in their path. They fed the prisoners nutritious food and gave them good medical care. Soviet officials moved 60 officers and 2000 men to a transit camp at Odessa on the Black Sea before repatriating them to England by ship. Group Captain Wilson compiled the names of 60 officers left behind at Stalag Luft III on 27 January 1945 (Wilson 1945, 14). The Russians liberated another 3400 British and 600 Americans at various locales throughout Poland, Germany and Czechoslovakia in February 1945.

Evacuation from Lamsdorf

Over 20,000 PoWs departed the Lamsdorf compounds of Stalag 344 (formerly Stalag VIIIB) on 22 January 1945, including the PoWs from the RAF compound. By mid-April 1945 the RAF PoWs had marched 500 miles before

Prisoners of war were put up in barns outside Lubeck.(Courtesy of A. Crighton)

Prisoners outside Lubeck feared they would be caught in the crossfire, so they erected signs to warn combatants. (Courtesy of A. Crighton)

Group Captain Wray, RCAF, is shown walking alongside other PoWs in April 1945. Many PoWs grabbed carriages and wagons to haul their few possessions. (Courtesy of A. Crighton)

With smoke rising in the background from Allied bombs, PoWs cut out the letters P O W and laid them in fields to inform pilots they were not German troops. (Courtesy of A. Crighton)

The estate at Lubeck where Stalag Luft III PoWs waited out the last few weeks of the war. (Courtesy of A. Crighton)

German soldiers were much friendlier as the war wound to a close. (Courtesy of A. Crighton)

American forces liberated them near Cologne. Prisoners stopped to rest at Görlitz (Stalag VIIIA) after ten days on the march. Russian amputees and tubercular Italian troops already occupied the camp. After a few days' rest, the march was resumed. Hank Bertrand of Rocky Mountain House, Alberta, recalled the guards were under orders to execute anyone who attempted to escape. Fellow

Albertan Bill Jackson, author of *Three Stripes and Four Brownings*, told Bertrand that he was going to leave Görlitz with a column of French PoWs instead of the RAF PoWs because he had been caught attempting an escape and Jackson's captors had slated his execution for the following morning. German civilians grew weary of the thousands of refugees, PoWs and political prisoners whose movement through their towns stretched their generosity to the limit and the PoWs scrounged to survive.

Stalag Luft I (Barth) and Stalag IVB (Mühlberg)

Internees in Barth and Mühlberg were fortunate enough to avoid forced marches because of their locations. The Russians liberated Mühlberg in late April and Barth in early May 1945. For further elaboration on the winter marches, refer to the biographies herein of PoWs evacuated from Lamsdorf, Heydekrug, Bankau and Sagan.

Have We Learned from History?

The rise of extremist political movements during the interwar era was a direct result of the poor decisions made and reflected in the Peace of Paris, the five treaties that concluded the Great War. The British and the French contributed to the rise of Hitler by imposing vengeful terms in the Treaty of Versailles. The "war guilt" clause proved most troubling to Nazi Germany because all the powers of Europe had contributed to the outbreak of the First World War in the fifty years preceding 1914. The blueprints for a lasting peace as outlined in Wilson's Fourteen Points were largely ignored by the reactionary victors who viewed the Wilsonian principles as too idealistic. It seemed that those peacemakers were less worried about the implications of an unjust peace; the young would fight their battles. French President Clemenceau quipped, "God gave us Ten Commandments; Wilson gives us fourteen!" The decisions at the Paris conference did not seek solutions to the century old problem of nationalism but, instead, contributed to a new breed of dictator whose nationalist overtures and militarism sent the next generation of men off to war.

Europe's diplomats in the 1920s declared that they had learned from their past mistakes. The powers attempted to create an air of optimism in Europe by signing a plethora of empty treaties during the interwar era. These included the Covenant of the League of Nations, the Washington Naval Treaties, the Locarno Pact, the Kellogg-Briand Pact and a series of Geneva Protocols. The Kellogg-Briand Pact was probably the most absurd as signatory nations renounced war as a tool of foreign policy. Perhaps the lesson learned was that an agreement is only as good as the men who keep them.

Nonetheless, poorly scripted documents do not absolve nations of their responsibilities to check the rise of extremist movements. Ardent fascists and militarists alerted citizens of their intentions before they assumed power in their respective nations. When Hitler failed to seize power in his 1922 Beer Hall Putsch, he worked within the existing political system and the German people voted him in. Hitler and others solidified their control over governments by using propaganda, force and terror, indoctrination and direction of popular discontent to seize control of the minds and bodies of enough people to expand their aggressive programs of re-armament and expansionism. They directed popular discontent against discernible minorities or foreign powers. Once in power, the Nazis indoctrinated the youth, took control of the courts, jailed dissidents and used force and terror on the rest. They understood the propaganda value of music, sports, education and drama activities to cultivate the illusion of the master race. The silent majority of the people ignored the cloud of hate spreading through Europe, and those who did speak out were ignored or brutalized.

A second war engulfed the world in a conflagration of unprecedented devastation. Mechanization, weapons of mass destruction, genocide and total war made the Second World War different from all others. International agreements, like the Geneva Protocols, intended to establish some stability but they proved difficult, if not impossible, to enforce. Adherence to rules is what separates democracy from dictatorship. Ironically, many barbarities resulted from the actions of well-educated leaders.

Militarists knew propaganda could have as much impact as munitions. Nazi propagandists attempted to justify the air war by accusing Bomber Command of starting it. This is nonsense! In fact, the Germans had used Blitzkrieg to destroy the resistance and morale of civilian populations in Spain before the war, then in Warsaw and Rotterdam, before they blitzed British cities. On 9 October 1939 Hitler told his High Command that "the ruthless employment of the Luftwaffe against the heart of the British will-to-resist can and will follow at the given moment." Propagandists blamed the British, many times, for bombing the German city of Freiburg on 10 May 1940 when, in fact, Heinkel III crews mistakenly bombed their own people instead of a target in France. Goebbels encouraged German civilians to direct their anger on downed Allied aircrews. The British government did not start the war, nor would the British people permit it. The horrors of the First World War remained etched in the psyche of the English people, and the British government avoided conflict through diplomacy. Democratic traditions in England would not permit militarism to guide public policy. The RAF did not start the bombing war, but the British public supported an all-out offensive for reasons of self-defence and survival. (Barker 1965, 15–20) Fascism was an evil that had to be stopped, there was no doubt about that.

Analyses of economic crises during the 1930s in the United States, the former USSR and Nazi Germany illustrate how democracies and dictatorships dealt with depression and political instability. Decisions made by Roosevelt, Stalin and Hitler reflected the differing value they placed on life, freedom and quality of life. Franklin D. Roosevelt introduced the New Deal economics during the depression, and despite its flaws it outlasted its ideological counterparts. Why? Simply, the drastic economic measures of Keynesian economics gave Americans hope—not much more—just hope. Ironically, it still took a war to bring the world out of the depression. Stalin and Hitler trampled individual rights to strengthen their states. It took several more decades for soulless communism to collapse under its own weight in the Soviet Union. People had no incentive to support a system where the state constantly held a gun to the collective head of the nation. The fall of Nazism occurred more quickly but it took the world six years to defeat it.

Greed between nations has been replaced by a new master—a faceless beast that places profits above the dignity of the individual. Corporate interests are loyal to no national entity and the power they wield is considerable. The ten largest corporations produce more wealth than 140 nations in the world. People in developing regions want their entitlement, they want empowerment. This is called the revolution of rising expectations. Like people of earlier generations, they turn their ears to those who promise simple solutions to complicated problems. Hence, we see a new blend of politics mixed with fundamentalism, and all variations claim correctness. We give causes of conflict new names, but we do not always look at how to solve them.

Are world leaders willing to learn from patterns of world history? Unfortunately real statesmen rarely possess the political clout to improve international relations. Leaders with the power are not particularly adept at diplomacy. Symptoms of conflict are addressed, but the root causes are sidestepped. Maybe we have to resign ourselves to the fact that conflict is in our nature.

Appendix 1

Geneva Convention 1929 Relative to the Treatment of Prisoners of War

The 1929 Geneva Convention stipulated that prisoners of war receive humane treatment when captured by enemy forces. Captives were entitled to the same standard of care as the local garrison troops in all matters and not excepting the quality of food, clothing, shelter and protection. The 1929 Convention stated that all PoWs be protected from torture, threats and reprisals.

To ensure the standards of the Convention were upheld, neutral nations would assumed intermediary roles. In Europe during the Second World War, Switzerland and Sweden acted as intermediary powers. Their delegates moved unhindered through belligerent nations and occupied territories to monitor the treatment of prisoners of war. The International Committee of the Red Cross received recognition as the predominant humanitarian organization overseeing the provision of care to PoWs. It compiled lists of all prisoners and their personal information pertinent to the establishment of identity and facilitation of communications with family, friends and philanthropic organizations as well as the nation with which the individual served.

The neutral agency observed treatment of PoWs to ensure that their captors abided by the rules of the Geneva Convention.

The Geneva Convention of 1929 Relative to the Treatment of Prisoners of War was divided into six sections, three of which affected PoWs directly:

a) Treatment of Enemy Prisoners of War
b) Rights of Prisoners of War
c) Treatment of the Wounded and Sick

The other three sections outlined treatment of civilians and the special protection given to representatives of the Red Cross and those acting on its behalf. Below are abridgements of the prominent portions of the three sections dealing with the treatment of PoWs and are relevant to accounts given by PoWs in this book.

Treatment of Enemy PoWs

- PoWs are to be treated humanely and protected against acts of violence, intimidation, insult and public curiosity. They are entitled to respect for their person and honor.

- PoWs are regarded as being in the hands of Power, not individual units.
- No reprisals are to be taken against PoWs.
- A PoW is required only to give his name, rank, service number and date of birth. He is to produce his identification card on request and it is never to be confiscated.
- No physical or mental torture, coercion or disadvantage may be inflicted on a PoW at any time.
- PoWs are to be allowed to keep personal effects. Looting of PoW property is forbidden.
- PoWs are to be evacuated to safe areas as soon as possible and not to be used as human shields.
- PoWs can be called upon to perform work, and none that is unhealthy, dangerous or humiliating.
- Use of weapons/force against PoWs must be preceded by appropriate warning, especially in escapes.

Rights of PoWs

- Treatment of PoWs must be as favorable as the treatment of enemy forces in the area.
- Premises must be adequately heated, lighted and protected from dampness. Premises for eating, religious services, intellectual and recreational pursuits must be provided.
- There must be medical facilities, proper hygiene, baths or showers, toilet and washing facilities, and a canteen where soap, foodstuffs, tobacco and items for personal use are available.
- Food must be in sufficient quality, quantity and variety to maintain good health and to prevent loss of weight or the development of nutritional deficiencies.
- Sufficient clothing, underwear and footwear for protection against the elements as well as replacement and repair facilities should be available.
- PoWs should have access to adequate medical facilities. They must be admitted to sufficient civilian or medical facilities if additional care is needed.
- In the event of transfer a PoW is entitled to pack his personal belongings.
- All PoWs, except officers, may be compelled to work but not in any job contributing to the war effort. Officers can work if they request to, but under no circumstances are they compelled to work.
- PoW workers are to be paid at an agreed rate, no less than one quarter of a Swiss franc for a full work day.
- A PoW has the right to inform his family of his capture within one week

of his capture. A PoW is permitted to write two letters and four post-cards each month. Every correspondence is subject to censorship.

- The senior officer in the camp is to be recognized as the camp leader.
- In NCO camps, a camp leader is elected by his peers.
- PoWs are subject to the laws, regulations and orders of the armed forces of the detaining power and if convicted are subject to one of four disciplinary punishments, none of which are to exceed thirty days.

  a) a fine not exceeding fifteen days' pay
  b) discontinuances of privileges above the minimum treatment outlined in the Convention
  c) fatigue duties, not exceeding two hours per day
  d) confinement

**Escapees are subject to *disciplinary punishments* only.

Appendix 2

War Claims Commission Report

The following comments made by War Claims Commissioner T.A. Campbell in his report to the Privy Council in 1953 summarize the seriousness of the maltreatment endured by Canadian PoWs held in German custody in the Second World War.

On the whole, there is an almost universal complaint, supported by credible evidence, that (with the few exceptions) the European prison camps provided their prisoners of war with extremely inadequate food, sanitation, medical care and living conditions. The German prison rations seldom rose above 1500 calories per day and were deficient in proteins, oils, and vitamins. The most conservative deposition on this point is to the effect that "From beginning to end of the period of imprisonment, the basic rations as supplied by Germans was by no means equal to that supplied to base troops of German forces as required by the Geneva convention." It also seems clear that the general prison ration was considerably below that of German civilians, especially since the latter received supplementary rations when working, whereas prisoners of war frequently had to perform heavy and sustained labour with no additional rations.

The basic rations provided, with the addition of a normal supply of Red Cross parcels, combined to form a bare subsistence nutrition, which prevented the occurrence of wholesale starvation and widespread deaths. During the numerous periods when Red Cross parcels were inadvertently delayed or were purposely held up or reduced by the captors, the prisoners suffered seriously "from malnutrition and especially from protein deficiency which was damaging to their health and lowered their resistance to disease."

In addition to the inadequacy of the food it was generally far from palatable, and frequently repulsive and nauseating. Staple items appear frequently to have included soup made from mangold tops or turnip tops, or occasionally from beans infected with weevils, or occasionally from horse heads with teeth and eyes left in; horsemeat stew; sour black bread; ersatz coffee or black mint tea; and a foul-smelling and foul-tasting cheese which came to be known among the prisoners as "fish cheese." Making all due allowance for the merely exotic nature of some of these items, one can only conclude that the menu had usually no appetizing quality to make up for its caloric and protein deficiency. Dysentery and stomach ailments were common results, and loss of weight was often formidable.

As to heating, there was very rarely an adequate provision of fuel. In cold weather, prisoners had to sleep with all clothes including great-coats—often two or three together to pool their single blankets and their body heat. In some camps they spent cold days in bed to keep warm, in some they were denied this privilege. At certain periods, allegedly by way of reprisal for treatment of German prisoners in Africa, all mattresses were taken away, and the prisoners had to sleep on the bare boards. These boards at first numbered from 8 to 10, but many had to be burnt as fuel, and the remaining 4 or 5 made exceedingly uncomfortable sleeping accommodation.

Toilet and sanitary facilities were usually quite inadequate particularly at night, when the men would be locked in and prevented from access. The supply of water was usually inadequate or drastically curtailed: the water would be turned on for a short fraction of the day, and there was such a rush to get enough water for drinking and cooking purposes that frequently no opportunity was left to get water for washing of the person or clothes. Scant provision was made to combat the hordes of lice, fleas, bedbugs, mice, rats and other vermin which in most camps seemed to operate unmolested.

Available medical supplies "varied from fair to zero." Apparently, as a rule, medical attention could be had only for serious illness or injury, and then frequently after undue and dangerous delays. The authorities failed to make use of talent available among the prisoners themselves.

Work parties, even when based on an exceptionally good camp such as Stalag IID, were often overcrowded in their sleeping quarters, worked long hours on inadequate rations, and in many cases [were] treated brutally. The German authorities deliberately resisted efforts to have custodians of such parties familiarized with the governing regulations, preferring that the custodians should be more free to enforce their own discipline, severe and often brutal as it was.

Though the Gestapo and kindred organizations directly operated only a small proportion of the PoW camps, they apparently exercised a considerable degree of indirect influence in most of the camps by means of either permanent or casual representatives. Thus, the official security officer of a camp might be under the actual domination of an NCO. By this means even the best intentioned efforts of official camp authorities to improve the lot of their prisoners were often frustrated. During the frequent visits by Gestapo representatives and other outside inspectors the prisoners were kept on parade for long periods, while their personal belongings were ransacked and pilfered, and food taken or destroyed.

Reprisals on individuals and groups were frequently out of all proportion to trivial offences or gestures, and consisted of such punishments as standing at attention from 2 to 14 hours, solitary confinement for long periods, and withholding of mail and food and Red Cross parcels.

On occasions all the valuables possessed by groups of prisoners were confiscated and never returned.

Though sheer physical brutality was not common, the prisoners felt themselves subjected to a variety of more subtle forms of mental cruelty, apparently designed to weaken their morale. Family correspondence was frequently suppressed, and false rumours and threats systematically circulated.

Under a directive issued by Hitler many Allied "Commando" troops, and other military units operating independently, were shot even if they attempted to surrender; others who were executed later in concentration camps were never given a trial of any kind. Prisoners were particularly affected (in varying modes) by the day-long tolling of a bell in an asylum adjoining their camp, on each occasion when the Germans executed a mental patient unfit for work. Brutal floggings and even shootings were carried out in view of PoWs with the apparent intention of terrorizing them. By such and other methods, the mental and moral resistance of the prisoners was attacked, and many insanities and mental breakdowns resulted.

It is the contention of the National Council that the inadequacies of rations, as well as many other deprivations, were deliberately imposed by the Germans, partly with a view to lowering prisoners' morale and partly with the object of conserving their own food reserves. This contention is supported by the fact that numerous offers of preferential treatment were officially made to Canadian PoW's in certain camps, but were always refused when it was learned that all prisoners were not to share in the offers.

The basic ration would appear to have been deliberately fixed at a point where, supplemented by normal Red Cross parcels it would reach a subsistence level. Any interruption or partial stopping of the parcels resulted in serious malnutrition and suffering.

Such is the general picture of life in the European prison camps as painted by the depositions before me. But the most cogent complaints voiced by claimants are not so much against their regular treatment in established prison camps as against special incidents such as the shackling of prisoners captured at Dieppe, transportation in cattle cars under unspeakably horrid conditions, and particularly against the "hunger marches" of the winter and spring of 1945.

The shackling of prisoners inflicted by the Germans in the fall of 1942 was in force as long as 13 months. During the first 4 months, the tying up was extremely severe and oppressive, cords and ropes frequently being used in the absence of conventional shackles. This treatment caused painful sores on the wrists of many prisoners, and was exceedingly distressing at times of prevalent dysentery and other such ailments. For the remainder of the period the performance became gradually more perfunctory, and sometimes merely symbolic. The British Prisoners of War Department reports that the ill-effects were on the whole surprisingly small. It is apparent, however, that such unjustifiable treatment with its accompanying humiliation and discomfort, may be presumed to have resulted in some incapacity, even as late as the time of liberation, a year and a half after the discontinuance of shackling.

The so-called hunger marches took place in the winter and spring of 1945, shortly before the end of hostilities in Europe. Prisoners were moved by forced marches often through cold regions. Though there is no general evidence or physical brutality, it appears that little attention was usually given to the rations, sleeping quarters, clothing, or physical condition of the men. In fact, practically no rations were issued by the Germans, and the prisoners were obliged to rely on the scanty food which they could obtain by foraging for themselves. No replacements or clothing were available and sleeping quarters and other living conditions were usually deplorable. The actual duration of the journeys were not often over two months, but the rigours of the marches were aggravated by the reduced vitality or the men, consequent upon a preceding period of malnutrition and poor living conditions. Many had to drop out, and the rest were kept going by the hope of early liberation. In many cases, immediately before liberation the prisoners were confined in the worst camps of their experiences. Fortunately, the hunger marches were almost immediately followed by the release of the victims. Otherwise serious permanent disability would have undoubtedly prevailed. As it was, they were taken to England and most of them were reconditioned by proper rations, rest, and hospitalization where necessary. It would appear that the participation in the hunger marches was one of the principal causes of the almost universal incapacity to work noticeable in Canadian prisoners of war liberated from German custody.

Another feature which appears to have increased the hardship of many PoWs in Europe was the atrocious conditions under which many of them were transported by rail. In numerous cases the prisoners were so crowded into cattle cars that they could not lie down or even sit for journeys lasting days or weeks. Rations and drinking water were almost non-existent or extremely deficient. Prisoners were seldom allowed out of the cars, and toilet and sanitary conditions were most nauseating.

From the material before me, I have no difficulty in concluding that many of the conditions and deprivations imposed on Canadian prisoners of war in Europe constituted maltreatment and though not universal, it was so general that practically every Canadian PoW must have undergone some degree of maltreatment during his course of internment.

Of a group of over 3500 Canadian servicemen liberated from captivity in Germany in April and May 1945 (apparently a representative cross-section) it was found that approximately 90% had at least some degree of incapacity, in the sense of "loss of lessening of the power of the will and to do any normal mental or physical act." This incapacity was relieved, in the majority of cases, after periods ranging from a fortnight to six months.

In my opinion, the number of PoWs in Europe who did not suffer some measure of maltreatment, with consequent incapacity subsisting after liberation, was a negligible fraction of the total number.

Appendix 3

Aircraft Designs and Combat Hazards

Crews and repatriated PoWs who had survived the destruction of their aircraft contended that aircraft design impacted survival rates of crews. Bomber Command compiled statistics on crew losses for Lancasters, Stirlings, Halifaxes and Wellingtons starting in January 1943. Between January and June 1943, 6498 airmen failed to return from operations; 1203 of them, or just 19 percent, were known to have survived. In its report, Hazards of Escaping from Aircraft in Combat, the RAF randomly selected the data of 144 men from a pool of thousands of air force ex-PoWs, enough for an accurate statistical representation of factors influencing survival rates. Researchers concluded that Lancaster crews had the lowest survival rates, followed by Stirling crews, then Wellington crews. Halifax crews had the highest survival rates.

Researchers concluded that aircraft design impeded escapes. Twenty percent of the survivors reported that twisted front escape hatches in the belly of their aircraft had "seriously impeded" their escapes. Another 25 percent reported their exit "delayed" by a jammed escape hatch. Twenty percent reported they slipped into unconsciousness or suffered disorientation from a lack of oxygen, a frequent problem for crews attempting to bail out at high altitudes. Sixteen percent of survivors reported having to clear the aircraft due to explosion or disintegration. Twenty percent reported injuries incurred during evacuation. The committee concluded that the design and arrangements for escapes were inadequate and that all bombers needed radical alterations to facilitate escape. They recommended incorporation of new safety measures.

Surviving Aircrew Members for Each Aircraft Type

	Lancaster (365 crews missing)		Stirling (161 crews missing)		Halifax (274 crews missing)		Wellington (157 crews missing)	
	Survivors	%	Survivors	%	Survivors	%	Survivors	%
Pilot	35	9.6	12	7.4	57	20.8	25	14.6
Navigator	50	13.8	32	19.8	99	36.2	33	21.0
W/Operator	43	11.9	32	19.8	89	32.5	29	18.5
Engineer	45	12.4	31	19.2	93	34.0	-	-
Aimer	48	13.2	22	13.6	86	31.4	29	18.5

	Lancaster (365 crews missing)		Stirling (161 crews missing)		Halifax (274 crews missing)		Wellington (157 crews missing)	
	Survivors	%	Survivors	%	Survivors	%	Survivors	%
M/U Gunner	31	8.5	30	18.6	75	27.3	-	-
Rear Gunner	25	8.0	32	19.8	64	25.4	23	14.6
	277	10.9	191	16.9	563	29.4	139	17.5
Independent Passengers	2 out of 27	7.4	9 out of 36	25.0	22 out of 41	53.7	2 out of 26	7.7

1. The researchers stated that different crew members had different survival rates and the chances of survival varied by aircraft type.
2. The researchers found little difference in survival rates for aircraft that crashed over England except that survival rates for the Halifax were three times that of the Lancaster. It is assumed the evacuation procedures used over enemy territory were the same as those used by crews abandoning aircraft over England.

Source: An Examination of the Emergency Escape Arrangements from Bomber Command Operational Aircraft, p. 3

The Lancaster

The cramped space within the Lancaster's fuselage prevented the rapid movement of crews to the forward escape hatch behind the cockpit. The small escape hatch slowed the exit of survivors. Based on information gathered from survivors, 30 percent of hatches on Lancasters jammed. Even if a hatch was forced open, its small size made it difficult for airmen wearing bulky flight suits and parachute packs to exit the aircraft. The slipstream impeded the opening of the Lancaster's rear starboard door. Crew suffered serious injuries because the slipstream propelled evacuees into the tail plane. Statistics revealed a lower survival rate and a higher injury rate for rear gunners and correspondingly dismal rates for mid upper gunners. The emergency evacuation procedure in the Lancaster specified that the bomb aimer, flight engineer and navigator escape through the front hatch, in that order. The mid upper gunner, the rear gunner and wireless operator had instructions to leave through the rear starboard door, in that order. Statistics showed that crew members who exited through the front hatch of the Lancaster stood a better chance of survival than those expected to use the starboard hatch. Survival rates for pilots were usually lower than for other crew members because they were the last to abandon the aircraft. Fires in the Lancasters broke out in 91 percent of lost aircraft while fires occurred in other heavy bombers at a rate of about 85 percent. Survivors from Lancasters indicated that explosions occurred in 18.5 percent of lost aircraft. Fires originated with the fuel tanks, oil leaking from hydraulic lines, or bombs.

Defences aboard bombers were inadequate. Two major deficiencies existed. The .303 calibre machines had limited effective range, outside of which German fighters, armed with 20mm cannons, could commence firing on bombers. Bomber Command began equipping heavy bombers with .50 calibre guns after D-Day. Second, the design of the Lancaster aircraft created a blind spot on the underbelly of the fuselage. The Luftwaffe used this deficiency to their advantage by equipping the Me110 fighter with an upward firing 20mm cannon, called Slanted Music. An extra gun turret in the belly of the aircraft would have allowed a gunner to watch for, and fire upon, incoming German aircraft equipped with upward firing 20 mm cannons. The mid upper gun turret was considered relatively useless during night operations, and its size increased drag, slowing the Lancaster by 50 mph.

The Stirling

Intercom problems frequently plagued the Stirling heavy bomber more than other aircraft. Officials concluded that some crews missed the verbal command to evacuate, as well as the red flashing light, the backup signal for evacuation. The Stirling recorded higher incidences of wing fires than other aircraft. The RAF installed nitrogen tanks to suppress flames. Stirling bombers flew lower and slower than Lancasters and Halifaxes. Bomber Command withdrew the last 250 from front line service during the Battle of Berlin.

The Halifax

The front escape hatch on the Halifax bomber jammed for 17.5 percent of the crews. The force of the slipstream was the primary reason for the hatch to jam. Engine fires caused Halifax wings to fall off.

The Wellington

The geodetic design of the Wellington aircraft could sustain heavy damage, including repeated hits from flak, bullets and cannon fire but its wooden frame and canvas skin made it more susceptible to fires. The two-engine Wellington medium bomber had a single escape hatch located in the floor behind the pilot. Designers expected crews to use the rear turret as the alternative escape port. Experienced crews and survivors of the abandonment of any make of aircraft stated that the use of the rear turret as an exit point was unrealistic.

Changes to Escape Policies

Many crewmen lost vital seconds strapping on their parachutes. The RAF issued 92 percent of crews with the "Observer" or chest pack, and most chose not to wear it because it impeded movement. Pilots wore seat packs for convenience. All they needed to do was cinch up the harness straps before exiting the aircraft. Many crew lost valuable seconds because they could not locate their parachutes after an attack commenced. The RAF began experimenting with a back-type parachute for all crew, to encourage wearing it at all times with maximum comfort. Widespread use of the new parachute design became a post-war reality.

In an addendum dated 19 May 1945 information showed a marked increase in survival rates for crews between January and September 1944. The committee attributed this to several reasons. Crews underwent more practical survival training including strapping on parachutes, moving through the aircraft, keeping the ripcord handle in one's hand at all times, and simulating jumps from a stationary plane into a net. The use of training films became mandatory. Oxygen tubes and radio wires attached to helmets underwent modifications to allow a quick release if any became entangled. Wearing the helmet offered protection against fire and bruising. Crews received instructions to bail out head first from the hatch so the slipstream would catch their backs, and reduce the chances of hitting the bottom of the aircraft or experiencing injuries by striking the exit frame on the way out. Crews received warnings to tuck their chins close to their chest and to arch their backs into a boomerang shape before deploying the chute to minimize the incidences of whiplash, hyper-extended spines, dislodged teeth, cuts to the face, tearing of the ears and heavy welts on the neck caused by the whipping of the parachute harness. Researchers also recommended escape procedures be revisited as the inside of a bomber became more cluttered with new technology.

Other changes to escape procedures had marginal effects on injury or survival rates. The suggestion to give crews jump training from a high altitude was abandoned as the thought of preparing a man for the eventual destruction of his aircraft created more apprehension that it was worth. Rear gunners received instructions to bail from their aircraft by rotating their turret 180 degrees and falling backward into the night sky instead of attempting an escape from the side door in the fuselage. Analysis of the use of the turret as an exit point produced inconclusive results. Slipstream protectors placed in front of escape hatches did not reduce the number or severity of injuries incurred during evacuation from an aircraft. To reduce injuries and to give men a better chance to evade capture on the ground, the RAF issued a new type of boot that remained on the foot when the parachute opened.

The problem of anoxia at altitudes from 18, 0000 to 25, 000 feet remained a problem. Men who removed oxygen masks too quickly or found their exits delayed often passed out before jumping. An unconscious man might survive if another crewman pushed him out with the chute already deployed.

Researchers continued to investigate methods to reduce the time needed to evacuate the aircraft and to increase the time between the initial attack and the disintegration of the aircraft. Modifications to existing bombers were impractical with the end of the war in sight. Suggestions for improved safety and design and better exit procedures were incorporated in new aircraft and prototypes.

Survival Training Following the Ditching of an Aircraft

Bomber Command invested considerable resources to prepare aircrews for ditching their aircraft. It ordered all crews to undergo extensive dry land and waterborne dinghy training in the early stages of their training. A sound working knowledge of all survival equipment aboard an aircraft, including life rafts, personal flotation devices (Mae West life vests), cylinders of compressed carbon dioxide, and escape ropes could improve chances of survival. Bomber Command encouraged all aviators to learn to swim. Five training films were produced: "Prepare for Ditching," "Ditching Without Hedging," "Lindholme Dinghy Gear," "Airborne Lifeboat," and "Swimming and Wet Dinghy Instruction." After completion of all aspects of training, Bomber Command advised crews to receive survival-training specific to their assigned aircraft. A major purpose of training was to teach men to react *quickly* as survival in frigid water is limited to just a few minutes. Men rehearsed extrication from a parachute harness, inflation of dinghies, righting an overturned dinghy, climbing aboard, paddling, swimming and floating as team members, helping injured comrades, keeping warm and exercising specifically to avoid muscle cramps.

The RAF equipped their squadrons with five types of dinghies: the "H", "J", "K", "L", and "Q". The J Dinghy was round, and crews found it impossible to row in a specific direction. The Q Dinghy held up to eight men; its oblong shape allowed paddlers limited success to paddle it in a desired direction. The K Dinghy, built for a single occupant, came equipped with a mast and sail. Bomber Command ordered ground crews to check onboard equipment every eight weeks.

New Defensive Technology Incorporated into Aircraft

Losses from fighter attacks outnumbered losses from flak by a two-to-one margin. The RAF continued to develop technology to protect bombers from incoming enemy aircraft, including IFF, "Monica", AGLT , Q Box and "Fishpond."

IFF (Identification Friend or Foe) monitored all incoming aircraft through a simple coding system. Incoming friendly aircraft transmitted a radio signal with the "letter of the day." Those airplanes that did not emit the proper signal were considered enemy aircraft. A limitation of IFF was its inability to identify the direction of the incoming aircraft.

Bombers were especially vulnerable to attacks from Me110 fighters equipped with upward firing 20mm cannons. Pilots of Me110s could approach unseen from astern and unleash a volley of cannon fire from below without detection. The RAF responded by developing Monica, a radar system mounted in the tail. However, the rear gunner was often unable to locate an incoming aircraft in darkness or the cover of fog. Consequently, technicians developed the AGLT

(Automatic Gun Laying Turret, code-named Village Inn), a radar-guided firing system that fired automatically at incoming aircraft. The Q Box was a technological improvement over the AGLT. The rear gunner listened to the blip of radar signals to differentiate between friend or foe. When the radar warned of an incoming enemy aircraft the gunner flipped a switch under his seat that activated his machine guns automatically when it came within range.

The best "ears" aboard a Lancaster bomber was the device called Fishpond. It warned crews of enemy aircraft from up to fifty kilometers away. A major limitation to Fishpond was the need for constant monitoring by the wireless operator. If he temporarily switched over to another frequency, he risked missing the radio impulse representing an incoming plane.

Armaments Were Perilously Light

The light .303 calibre Browning machine guns paled in comparison to the 20mm cannons outfitted in German aircraft. Rounds fired from the twin .303 machine guns in RAF bombers followed an accurate trajectory for 600 yards before petering out. The 20mm shells of German aircraft had five times the effective range. RAF air gunners likened the capabilities of their guns to "throwing popcorn at the enemy!" An ex-air gunner from Edmonton knows of senior RAF/RCAF officers who contended that the RAF erred in not providing the bombers with .50 calibre machine guns like the Americans had.

After the D-Day invasions of June 1944 Bomber Command had the wisdom to replace the light machine guns aboard its aircraft with .50 calibre machine guns. For air gunners who survived the war, the modifications came far too late as Bomber Command contributed to unnecessary casualties by giving low regard to the protection of bombers.

The RAF lost 8,570 bombers over Europe during the Second World War. Some consider this list unrepresentative of actual losses because Bomber Command classified 1082 others as "crashed" in England, instead of "lost" after incurring damage during operations. Bomber Harris understood the value of winning the propaganda battle by reclassifying how aircraft were lost. Lists excluded aircraft written off after an operation. Sometimes combat losses fell into the classification of "training accidents." Bomber Command also excluded the 120 bombers of Operational Training Units and 13 bombers of Heavy Conversion Units lost during active service, many over northern France on nickel runs (Middlebrook and Everitt 1985, 782–6). It is impossible to estimate the total number of bombers lost over the skies of Europe, but it is reasonable to assume that it exceeded 10,000.

Americans Did It Better

The United States Army Air Force attempted to protect their bombers by maximizing firepower in the skies. They equipped them with sideways-firing machine guns on both sides of the fuselage and every gunner fired the heavier .50 calibre Browning machine guns from the onset of the American entry in the war. The extra guns offered protection from more positions and extended the effective fields of fire by hundreds of yards, successfully challenging German planes with 20mm cannons from greater distances.

Flying in Bomber Streams Reduced Bomber Losses

Originally British bomber pilots flew alone to targets. Later the British changed their tactics and bombers flew in gaggles during daylight raids. The Germans recognized them on approach because the gaggles looked like a disorganized cloud. German fighter pilots disliked running at the gaggles, even though the British were less effective at warding off attacks than their American counterparts who flew in tight formations. When the RAF switched to night operations, ground crews painted the bottoms of the bombers in a flat black to make them harder for anti-aircraft batteries to spot. When the United States introduced to the European theater long-range fighters capable of escorting bombers to the intended targets, Bomber Command losses declined. German fighter losses mounted when tacticians permitted fighter escorts to break off from streams of bombers to pursue German aircraft.

Conclusion

Losses compel militaries to dedicate resources to research and development and to revise tactics in order to reduce injuries and casualties. Unfortunately the pressures of sustaining a war often take precedence over investment in new technology or modification of existing equipment.

Bibliography

Books and Articles

Allison, Lee, and Harry Hayward. *They Shall Grow Not Old: A Book of Remembrance*. Brandon, Manitoba: British Commonwealth Air Training Plan, 1996.

Anderson, R and D. Westmacott. *Handle with Care: A Book of Prison Camp Sketches Drawn and Written in Prison Camps in Germany*. Cookham, England: n.p., 1946.

Andrew, Allen. *Exemplary Justice*. London: George G. Harrap, 1976.

Barker, Ralph. *The Thousand Plan*. London: Cox and Wyman, 1965.

Brown, Kingsley. *Bonds of Wire*. Toronto: Collins, 1989.

Chorley, W. R. *To See the Dawn Breaking, 76 Squadron Operations*. Ottery St. Mary, Devon: n.p., 1981.

Churchill, Winston S. *The Second World War*. vol II. New York: Time, 1959.

Clark, Harold P. *Wirebound World: Stalag Luft III*. London: Alfred H. Cooper and Sons, 1946.

Cousens, Bryce (ed). *The Log: Stalag Luft III, Belaria/Sagan*. Cheltenham: Burr's Press, 1947.

Crawley, Aidan. *Escape From Germany: The Methods of Escape Used by RAF Airmen During the Second World War*. London: HMSO, 1985

Crighton, Arthur B. "The Organ Loft." *Anglican Messenger* (December 1991).

Fidelman, Charlie. "Prisoners of War Escapees Reunited With 'Helpers.'" *Montreal Gazette* (12 October 1989).

James, B.A. "Jimmy." *Moonless Night*. New York: Ivy Books, Ballantine Books, 1983.

Madsen, C.M.V. and R.J. Henderson. *German Prisoners of War in Canada and Their Artifacts 1940–1948*. Regina, Saskatchewan: R.J. Henderson, 1993.

Marshall, Bruce. *The White Rabbit*. London: Evans Brothers, 1952.

Martin, Gwyn. *Up and Under*. Slough, Bucks: Hollen Street Press, 1989.

Matheson, Shirlee Smith. *Flying the Frontiers*, Vol 3, *Aviation Adventures Around the World*. Calgary: Detselig Enterprises, 1999.

Middlebrook, Martin. *Berlin Raid: RAF Bomber Command, Winter of 1943–44*. London: Penguin Books, 1988.

———. *The Nuremberg Raid: The Worst Night of the War, March 30–31, 1944*. New York: William Morrow, 1974.

Middlebrook, Martin, and Chris Everitt. *The Bomber Command War Diaries: An*

Operational Reference Book: 1939–1945. London: Penguin Books, 1985.

Moyle, Harry. *The Hampden File.* Tonbridge, Kent: Air Britain (Historians), 1989.

Neave, Airey. *Saturday at MI9: A History of the Underground Escape Lines in Northwest Europe in 1940–1945, by a Leading Organizer.* London: Hodder and Stoughton, 1969.

RCAF Ex-Prisoner of War Association. *The Camp.* North York, Ontario, July 1989.

Waiser, Bill. *Park Prisoners: The Untold Story of Western Canada's National Parks, 1915–1946.* Calgary, Alberta: Fifth House Publishing, n.d.

Williams, Eric. *The Wooden Horse.* Montreal: Reprint Society of Canada, 1951.

Wilson, D.E.L. "The March from Luft III, with Air and Exercise." Camp Newsletter (June 1988).

Documents

An Examination of the Emergency Escape Arrangements From Bomber Command Operational Aircraft. AVM, Bomber Command HQ, RAF BC/S 32614/Air AS&R. 5 June 1945. DHist Ref. 90/435.

Bastable, Harold D. Evasion and Capture Report. MI9/S/P/G/LIB./24.15 May 1945. DHist File 79/507.

Campbell, T.A. Report of the Chief War Claims Commissioner on Reference Under P.C. 1953– 857. War Claims Commission. DHist.

Davidson, Barry. Attestation to the RCAF, December 1945. DHist 181.009(D624).

Dinghies Type "K": Periodicity of Servicing. 22 June 1944. Bomber Command Headquarters. DHist Ref: 76/71.

Directorate of Prisoners of War. Information Relating to Movement of Prisoners of War Camp. February 1945. DHist RCAF File 0103/6753 (P.W.2).

Evader Flying Officer D.E. Rutherford RCAF #J26725. 1 May 1945. File T.S. 45-19-15A. DHist Ref. 181.002(D68).

German Methods and Experiences of Prisoner Interrogation, 24 September 1945. A.D.I (K) Report 388/1945. DHist Ref 181.009(D624).

German Treatment of Allied Ps/W. Report by W/C G.H. Doble, RCAF Liason Officer, MI9 War Office, 15 June 1945. DHist Ref. 181.009(618).

Gilson, J.C. et al. Report on the Hazards of Escaping from Aircraft in Combat. Flying Personnel Research Committee, RAF Institute of Aviation Medicine. March 1946. P.R.C. 658 DHist Ref. 90/435.

Howatson, D.C. and Peter A. Thomson. Report of a Forced March by Occupants of Stalag Luft 7, Germany, to Swiss Commission Acting as Protecting Power, 15 February 1945.

Information to Establish Prima Facie Case Required by SHAEF Court of Inquiry, 7 Apr 1945. DHist Ref. 181.009 (D618).

Interrogation of RCAF Prisoners of War Repatriated from Germany, Jan 1945. DHist Ref. 181.009 (D624), File S.45-19-15(DofI).

Loss of Aircraft Report, May 1945, RAF. King, Gordon. DHist 73/844.

Loss of Bomber Aircraft: Questionnaires for Returned Aircraft, 405 Sqn, Aircraft P. Date of Loss 16/17 August 1944. DHist Ref. 181.009(D5966). Two accounts.

MI5. Germany and Occupied Territories Imperial Prisoners of War: Alphabetical List, Section 8, Air Forces. 30 March 1945. London.

MI9. Evasion Report by Sgt Alfred Charles Dennis Budd, RCAF #215226. 9 September 1944. DHist Ref. 79/507. MI9 /S/P/G (-) 2392.

MI9. Evasion Report, Chaster, James Barry, FSgt R92063 RCAF. March 1943. DHist Ref: 79/507. MI9 /S/P.G. (-) 1125.

MI9. Evasion Report by W/O Ralph Henry Rafter, RCAF #84923. 3 September 1944. DHist Ref:79/507. MI9/S/Pg(-)2257.

MI9. Germany and German-Occupied Territories Imperial Prisoners of War: Alphabetical List, Section 8, Air Forces, RAF, RAAF, RCAF, RNZAF, SAAF.

Regulations on the Safeguarding of Air Force P/Ws, Captured Documents and Equipment Enemy Countries excluding USSR). 31 October 1944. Berlin D.(Luft) 2709. Captured Luftwaffe Document DHist Ref 181.009(D624).

Report on RCAF Prisoners of War Organization. 7 May 1945 DHist Ref. 181.009(D624).

Royal Canadian Air Force. Operations Log Book of 408 Squadron. Linton-on-Ouse, 24 December 1944.

Special ex-Prisoner of War Report. R.61024 W/O1 M.F. Sikal. DHist Ref: 181.009[D618] File No. TS45-19-15(D of I).

Statement by Flying Officer Donald Alexander Lennie, MI9/S/PG/MISC/INT/655. DHist Ref. 79/507.

Statement by Flying Officer Martin Johann Platz (Can. J96046), No. 5 Release Centre, Winnipeg, Manitoba. 15 February 1946. DHist Ref. 181.009(D624).

Statement by Warrant Officer Richard A. Greene, of Conditions in Stalag Luft VII, Bankau, Germany, 29 May 1945. DHist Ref. 181.009(D618)

Stevenson, F/O Joel Matthew. Escape Report From Train Near Chateau Thierry (France) En Route For Germany. IS9 Interview. 2 September 1944. MI9/S/P.G. (F)2812, Dept of History and Heritage, DND File 79/507.

Summary of Information on German Personalities Relevant to the Shooting of Officer PoW Involved in Mass Escape, March 1944, Addendum 6. Dated 26 Aug 44. M.I.9/TS/BM/127.

"Swimming and Wet Dinghy Instruction: A Handbook for Instructors," 1st Edition. August 1944. Public Records Office. Ref. Air10/3505.

Wilson, D.E.L. Report on the Forced Evacuation of Allied Officer and Other Rank Prisoners of War from Stalag Luft III, Sagan, Germany, January/February 1945. 20 February 1945.

Personal Interviews and Other Sources

Bastable, Harold. Personal interviews. 8–9 July 2005. Winnipeg, Manitoba.

Bertrand, Henry. Personal interviews. July 2001–August 2004.

Budd, Denis A. Tell Them About Us. Silkworm Group [online]

Chaster, Barry. Personal memoirs. 1988, 23 April 2000, 27 March 2003.

Collard, R.C.M. Report of Stalag 3A Luckenwalde, Germany 11/4/45 to 20/5/45.

Crighton, Arthur B. Personal interviews. June 2001–August 2003.

Dunn, Frank. Notes from personal recollections.

Dunwoodie, William. Personal interviews. May 2001, November 2001, January 2004.

Dutka, Richard. Personal notes and interviews, 2002–2003.

High, David. Personal interviews. July 2001, November 2001, March 2002.

King, Gordon. Personal interviews. April 1999–March 2004.

MacNeill, J.D. Illustrations taken from "The Log" (Personal Diary) 1943–45.

Military Intelligence Service, War Department. American Prisoners of War in Germany, 1 November 1945

Museum at Lamsdorf. [online]

Nelson, R. Ernest. Personal interview. June 2002.

Rayment, A.F. Personal interviews. July 2002–March 2004.

Studnik, William. Personal interviews. July 2002, December 2002, June 2003

Taylor, Kenneth G. Personal Operations Logbook, 102 Sqn, 78 Sqn and 635 Pathfinders Sqn, 1944.

Taylor, Kenneth G. Personal Interviews. June 2001–July 2004. Edmonton.

Wanless, Wilkie. Learning by Experience. [online]
http://www.rafbombercommand.com/personals_2_dangersofwar.html

Wanless, Wilkie. Personal interviews. July 2001–August 2004.

Wiens, Ross. Personal interviews and memoirs. 2000–2001. Edmonton.

Index